NORTHAMPTON
1835-1985

Shoe Town, New Town

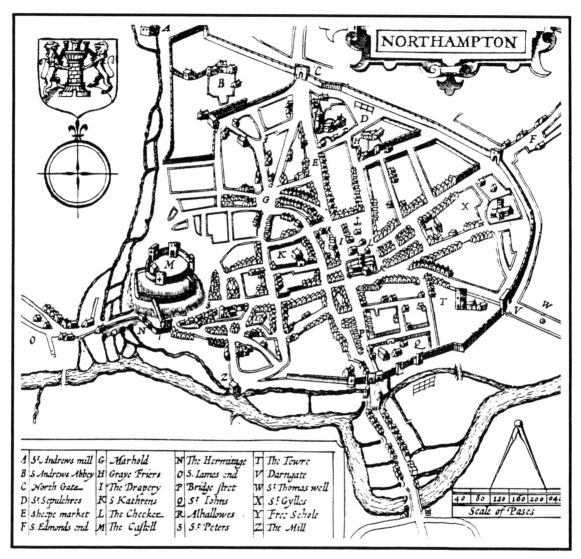

NORTHAMPTON

A	St Andrews mill	G	Marhold	N	The Hermitage	T	The Towre
B	S Andrews Abbey	H	Graye Friers	O	S. Iames end	V	Darngate
C	North Gate	I	The Drapery	P	Bridge strct	W	St Thomas well
D	St Sepulchres	K	S Kathrens	Q	St Iohns	X	St Gylles
E	sherpe market	L	The Checker	R	Alhallowes	Y	Free Schole
F	S Edmonds end	M	The Castell	S	St Peters	Z	The Mill

Scale of Paces

Speed's map of Northampton, 1610.

NORTHAMPTON
1835~1985

Shoe Town, New Town

Cynthia Brown

Phillimore

1990

Published by
PHILLIMORE & CO. LTD.
Shopwyke Hall, Chichester, Sussex

ISBN 0 85033 767 4

Printed and bound in Great Britain by
STAPLES PRINTERS ROCHESTER

Contents

List of Illustrations

Illustration Acknowledgements

The author wishes to thank the following for permission to publish illustrations: Alan Burman Photographic Collection, 11; National Union of Footwear, Leather and Allied trades, 28; Northampton Borough Council, 1, 3, 5, 9, 12, 22, 24, 27, 37, 39-44, 46-50; *Northampton Independent*, 45; Northamptonshire Libraries and Information Service, 2, 4, 6-8, 10, 13-16, 18-21, 23, 25, 26, 29-36, 38.

Acknowledgements

I am grateful to Northampton Borough Council for commissioning this book, and for providing me with much help and encouragement in the course of its writing. Particular thanks are due to Mr. Roger Morris, Chief Executive and Town Clerk, for his practical help and advice, and for his continuing encouragement; to his secretary Dawn Grant-Innes; and to Rod Prior and Val Denton of the Public Relations Department. I am especially grateful to the latter for assistance with illustrations. My thanks also go to Mr. John Dunkley and Mr. John Franklin, Town Hall Keepers, and Mr. Brian Alce, Assistant Town Hall Keeper, for their help and interest during my visits to the Guildhall archive; and to the Freemen's Trustees for providing additional information. Among the many others to whom I am indebted are Marion Arnold, Local Studies Librarian, and the staff of the Northamptonshire Record Office for help and advice with sources; Mr. Leslie Austin-Crowe for giving me an insight into the work of the Development Corporation; and Ron Greenall of the University of Leicester Adult Education Department for the loan of books and notes, and for reading and commenting on the text. All opinions expressed therein are my own, as are any errors and omissions.

Foreword

For many Northampton people, the 1989 celebrations of the 800th anniversary of the granting of the Borough's first Charter by King Richard I were an opportunity to learn more about the fascinating and varied history of this town, which across the ages has often played a prominent part in the affairs and development of England.

At an early stage, however, the 800th Anniversary Charter Sub-Committee which was planning for the celebrations realised that, despite an increasing flow recently of publications about aspects of town and country life, there was no adequate history of the development of the Borough covering the last 150 years, during which it has changed so substantially.

At the instigation of Councillors Alwyn J. Hargrave, Leader of the Council, and Stanley T. James, Chairman of the 800th Anniversary Charter Sub-Committee, therefore, the Council commissioned Mrs. Cynthia Brown B.A. of Leicester to research and write this book.

Mrs. Brown's task was to explore the period which is encapsulated by the phrase 'shoe town — new town': that appropriately rounded 150-year period from the passing of the Municipal Corporations Act 1835, when what might be termed the modern era of local government began, to 1985 when the Northampton Development Corporation, which had been responsible for the new town growth since 1965, was dissolved. This choice does not under-value the first 650 years and more of Northampton's development: far from it. Mrs. Brown's book begins with a portrait of the town as it existed in 1835. It is, however, the period most likely to jog the memories, and answer the questions, of those who worked in the shoe and leather trades or have ever wondered how the town came to be as it is.

Northampton Borough Council is pleased to join with the publishers in putting the fruits of Mrs. Brown's research before the public. It will be a lasting memorial to the 800th anniversary year and, we believe, a notable contribution to the growing literature of local history which should appeal to both serious and more casual readers. It is not a history of the Borough Council as such but of the town, and of the parts that those involved have played in it.

On the Borough Council's behalf, I commend Mrs. Brown's enthusiasm and diligence in carrying out a difficult task on schedule in only eighteen months, and hope that her work will stimulate further interest and research by others.

R. J. B. MORRIS
CHIEF EXECUTIVE & TOWN CLERK
Guildhall
Northampton.
April 1990

Preface

It was the Borough Council's intention that the celebrations of its 800th anniversary of the granting of the town's first charter by Richard I on 18 November 1189 should be as widely enjoyed as possible, and that some at least of the activities of this special year — during which I have been privileged to be Mayor — should endure. One example of this has been my successful appeal for the planting of 800 oak trees at Delapre paid for by individual sponsors: my hope is that generations to come will enjoy the mature Charter Wood, as it is to be called, and recall this memorable anniversary year of 1989/90.

This book provides another example. The Borough Council commissioned it to fill a significant gap in the written history of the town, and I congratulate Mrs. Cynthia Brown and Messrs. Phillimore, the publishers, who have combined to produce a book that is at once both handsome and authoritative. I commend to everyone interested in Northampton this lasting record of the progress of our town from 1835 to the winding-up of the Northampton Development Corporation in 1985 — in short, from 'shoe town' to 'new town'.

COUNCILLOR MALCOLM F. LLOYD
MAYOR OF NORTHAMPTON
May 1990

High Antiquity, Distinguished History

Although it is an old saying with respect to Northampton, that you may know when you are within a mile of it by the noise of the lap-stones, it would be wrong to consider the town solely as a place for the manufacture of boots and shoes . . .

Morning Chronicle, quoted *Northampton Mercury*, 1 February 1851

'Wonderfully placed at the crossroads of England' was the slogan with which the Borough Council pointed out Northampton's geographical advantages to potential new industries in the 1930s. Sixty miles from London and with ready access to the M1 motorway and other main transport routes, it could equally apply to the Northampton of today, and it would not have been out of place in 1830, when 'the great thoroughfare road between London, Liverpool, Manchester etc. for many stage coaches, gives it an air of busy gaiety and affords ample compensation to the innkeepers'.[1] Within ten years, however, much of this traffic was by-passing Northampton along with the London to Birmingham railway, proving once again that a town can be, so to speak, in the right place at one time and the wrong place at another, for now 'the town which has not a railway in its vicinity is an exception — isolated — shut out from the rest of the world'.[2]

In the early Medieval period Northampton's location on the main routes to the North and North-West was very much in its favour. Of great strategic value, reflected in the building of the Castle and the extension of the Saxon town walls, it was also a convenient meeting place for itinerant royal councils and other assemblies. Parliament met there on several occasions, the last of them in 1380 when it sanctioned the Poll Tax of Richard II. Thomas à Becket was tried there in 1164, and King John, particularly fond of the sport to be found in the royal forests nearby, spent much of his reign in residence. The General Chapter of the Benedictine Order, too, met many times at the Priory of St Andrew beyond the north gate, and for a brief period in the mid-13th century Northampton was also the site of a university, founded by students expelled from Oxford.

Royal and noble patronage of this order was a great stimulus to local trade, and by the late 12th century Northampton had become a major commercial centre ranking among the five foremost towns of the kingdom, both in terms of wealth and the privileges of self-government it could purchase from the Crown. Its first charter, acquired from Richard I in 1189 in exchange for a substantial contribution to the costs of the Third Crusade, was one of the earliest to be granted to a provincial town, and the mayoralty was also of early origin, first recorded in 1215 in the person of one William Tilly when the office was otherwise confined to those other pre-eminent towns of the early 13th century, London, York and King's Lynn.[3] Past its peak of prosperity by 1300, Northampton shared the fate of many urban centres as heavy taxation and pressure of population took their toll of trade even before the Black Death plunged the country into a prolonged economic depression — and of others as the Tudors turned their attention to maritime trade and the centre of the staple woollen cloth industry shifted to Norfolk. Its inland position was now a distinct disadvantage, and its lack of easy access to navigable water did nothing to ease it.

Few towns were still so 'inland' in this sense as Northampton by the early 18th century, some 40 miles distant from the nearest navigable point on the River Nene near Peterborough. The extension of the Nene Navigation to Thrapston in 1737 still left it 20 miles adrift, and it was not until 1761 that the navigation finally reached Northampton itself. Duly celebrated

1.   Church of the Holy Sepulchre. One of only four remaining 'round churches' in England, built
*c.*1100 by Simon de Senlis, Earl of Northampton, it was modelled on the church of the same name
in Jerusalem. The original building was extended in the 12th and 13th centuries, and restored in the
19th by George Gilbert Scott.

with a procession of 'no less than *thirty-eight* barges . . . adorned with flags and streamers'
and the firing of cannon on their arrival at the South Bridge wharf, the promise of an
'extensively-useful' facility was amply fulfilled in one respect at least. With no collieries
within 30 miles and despite the tortuous journey from the east coast, the retail price of sea-
coal brought in by this route was still much lower than that of pit-head coal carried from
Warwickshire by road,[4] but it was as a domestic rather than an industrial fuel that coal
was crucial, and the Nene Navigation did little to stimulate manufacturing industry in the
town.

'It is the richer and more populous by being a thoroughfare both in the north and west
roads', the *Universal British Directory* observed in 1791, 'but being some eighty miles from
the sea, can have no commerce by a navigation'. After 1796 the Grand Junction Canal
offered a more direct route to London and other major urban centres, but even then it came
only as close as Blisworth, four miles distant. Here, the lowest point on the uplands to the
west, its builders encountered the same obstacle which later dictated the route of the London
to Birmingham railway: a 120-foot drop into Northampton posing problems of construction
and traction which were not solved until 1815 with a four-mile link from Gayton Wharf

through a flight of 17 locks. When the Blisworth tunnel was completed in 1805 the iron railroad bridging the gap to Stoke Bruerne was relaid into Northampton, but this, as the Borough Corporation complained in 1809, was 'inadequate for the purposes intended . . . the commission is much more difficult and expensive than it would have been by water, and nearly all perishable articles of merchandise are prevented from passing along it'.[5]

Within the town itself the Early Saxon search for good land in a defensible position had other challenges in store. Northampton, noted one 17th-century visitor, 'stands on an eminence, which rising gradually, renders the scite, in some degree, hilly'; 'you come within the South-gate', said another, 'and thence keeping the Northern-road, you went out at the North-gate, overcoming three Ascents'.[6] The 'somewhat steep' ascent through Bridge Street,

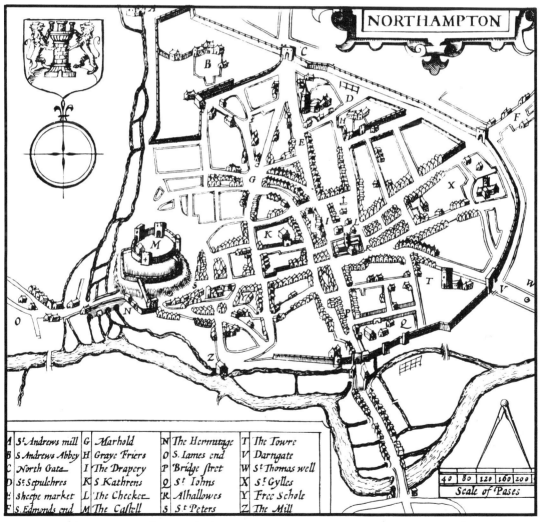

A	S.ᵗ Andrews mill	G	Marhold	N	The Hermitage	T	The Towre
B	S Andrews Abbey	H	Graye Friers	O	S. Iames end	V	Darngate
C	North Gate	I	The Drapery	P	Bridge ſtret	W	S.ᵗ Thomas well
D	S.ᵗ Sepulchres	K	S Kathrens	Q	S.ᵗ Iohns	X	S.ᵗ Gylles
E	sheepe market	L	The Checker	R	Alhallowes	Y	Free Schole
F	S. Edmonds end	M	The Caſtell	S	S.ᵗ Peters	Z	The Mill

2. John Speed's map of Northampton, 1610. The castle and town walls were slighted by order of Charles II in 1662.

though 'made easie by the diverting sight of good Buildings on either hand', was still steep enough in the early 20th century to deny the southern suburb of Far Cotton the blessings of electric tramways; and the River Nene was still so apt to overflow its banks that when the Borough Council was criticised for the 'indiscriminate erection of telegraph poles' in the 1920s, there was an element of truth in the jest of one resident, who pleaded for their retention as 'useful landmarks' in the event of a flood.[7]

Simply because it was so prone to flood the lower-lying ground to the south and west, the river did much to dictate the direction in which the town expanded. The medieval town walls were built to the north and east of the old, shifting its centre eastwards from the Horsemarket-Marefair area to All Saints' church, and so extensive were they that most of the town was still within their line when the Great Fire of 1675 all but destroyed it in a matter of hours.[8] One of the 'best-built' as well as the 'handsomest' of English towns after its reconstruction, the 'fine and profitable Gardens and Orchards' which failed to check the fire were the first resort of the builders catering for the housing needs of an expanding town in the early 19th century. Virtually exhausted by 1835, a plot near College Street was advertised soon after as 'the last estate of its kind, in the centre of Northampton, that can ever be subjected to public competition'.[9] Unlike Nottingham, however, where burgess rights in the unenclosed fields around the town so confined it that by 1845 conditions were 'so very bad as hardly to be surpassed in misery by anything to be found within the entire range of our manufacturing cities',[10] there was still ample space for future growth in the former lands of St Andrew's priory to the north and east.

Northampton itself was the administrative centre for the surrounding Shire, a function first recorded in the *Anglo-Saxon Chronicle* of 921 when the town was reclaimed from its late ninth-century Danish conquerors.[11] Relations between the two were not always cordial. The 'encroachment' of the County Justices on the liberties of the borough was an enduring source of friction, and the Borough Council's petition for separate County Borough status on the creation of County Councils in 1888 was similarly laden with talk of 'interference'; but socially, culturally and economically there were no such rigid boundaries between them. As the *Royal Commission on Municipal Corporations* noted in 1835, Northampton's now 'evidently flourishing condition' still owed much to its role as a market centre, with four annual Cattle Fairs, the Horse Fair, Ram Fair and Mop and Pleasure Fair — the annual hiring fair — in addition to thrice-weekly livestock markets.[12]

By mid-century the Saturday market also dealt in agricultural machinery, much to the distress of nearby residents subjected from dawn till dusk to the 'bewildering noise like the monotonous drone of a monster bagpipe' which it emitted,[13] but the patronage of the shire was important in other respects, and particularly so when it had one of the largest concentrations of aristocracy and gentry in the country. The records of the Great Subsidy of 1524-5 reveal something of the extent to which its economy was even then geared to the needs of its 'squirearchical' hinterland. Almost unique in listing the occupations of the taxpayers, around 70 trades were represented in all, some of them recalled in the surviving names of Gold Street, Woolmonger Street and Tanner Street. Fewer than London and other large towns could claim, they were still more numerous and more varied than in most provincial market towns of some 3,000 inhabitants at this time and included a small but wealthy group of shopkeepers dealing in such then luxury goods as spices and linen cloth.[14]

In the 17th century there were other newer tradesmen in evidence, among them clock and cabinet-makers, peruke makers and stucco artists. Although they omit a large proportion of working males and the entire female workforce of the town, which was probably sizeable, the Militia Lists of the late 18th century present a very similar picture, with masons, victuallers and tailors still prominent among the less numerous apothecaries and attorneys and Mulliner's carriage-making enterprise, established in Bridge Street in 1760 and enjoying not only noble but royal patronage.[15] Clerical work, a male occupation at this time, was one of the few obvious areas of expansion, stressing Northampton's role as an administrative and commercial, rather than as yet an industrial, centre but not surprisingly, given its position on the main road network, innkeepers were much in evidence in all three periods.

3. All Saints' church, Northampton's civic church. 'A Greatness and Beauty, both within and without, surpassing any I have seen on this side of London', wrote John Morton of it in 1712. The church was rebuilt after the Great Fire with the aid of a gift of 1,000 tons of timber from Charles II.

In the mid-18th century the town had some 60 inns with stabling for around 3,500 horses, foremost among them the *Peacock* in Market Square, the *Angel* in Bridge Street, and the *George* near All Saints' church, rebuilt on a palatial scale after the Great Fire. The numbers dropped dramatically when the railway opened soon after, but in 1830 there were still 11 coaches running daily between Northampton and London, five to Manchester and six each week to Liverpool, in addition to short-distance services and innumerable carrier services to and from country villages.[16] For other reasons too the inns were central to the life of the 18th-century and early 19th-century town, hosting a great variety of events from the annual Race Balls to trials of skill fought with 'Quarter-Staff, Sword and Buckler, Sword and Dagger, Backsword',[17] to horticultural shows and travelling theatrical performances such as Mr. Dillon's production of *Theodosius: or the Force of Love* at the *White Lion* in Abington Street, with 'curious transparent scene . . . illuminated with upwards of *One Hundred* Wax Lights'.[18] The Whigs met at the *Peacock*, the Tories at the *Goat* in Gold Street, the public at large at the *George*, and those dealing in leather, horses or agricultural seed at one of several inns where such transactions were the speciality of the house.

However, if there was one feature of Northampton on which visitors never failed to remark by 1835 it was its burgeoning footwear industry. Already of some substance in the 16th century, leather-workers were much the largest single occupational group in the Great Subsidy records, and *corvisers*, or shoemakers, were numerous among them. Here again there were clear links with the agricultural shire, with livestock farming providing a ready source of hides, and supplies of oak bark for tanning similarly plentiful. In the 17th and 18th centuries military contracts gave the trade an important if intermittent boost, and by the late 17th century Northampton was also exporting footwear to the plantations of the West Indies. The 'principle manufacture is shoes, of which great numbers are sent beyond sea', noted the *Universal British Directory* in 1791, but despite the stockings and lace it also produced, the 18th century was generally one of economic stagnation rather than expansion, confirmed by the slow growth of the town's population. Around 5,000 in 1725, it had risen to some 7,000 by 1770, but as national rates of growth began to accelerate and the population of areas of expanding industry was further boosted by immigration, it was barely any greater at the first census in 1801.

By 1831 it had more than doubled, for as the *Municipal Corporations Commission* noted in 1835, the footwear industry had 'thriven and increased' during the previous 30 years. More precisely, perhaps, its rapid expansion can be dated to the period after 1812, when the Peninsula War brought a large contract for army boots, and a strike among the shoemakers of the capital led London manufacturers to seek an alternative, less organised and cheaper source of labour, already in abundant supply in rural areas of Northamptonshire where the fall-off in demand and the agricultural depression which followed the peace in 1815 only swelled the surplus created by natural population growth. The Grand Junction link was no doubt the decisive factor, but footwear production was still very much a domestic handicraft industry. Entry into the business entailed no heavy capital outlay on machinery or premises, and Northampton quickly produced more manufacturers and factors of its own. The 12 listed in a directory of 1812 increased to 41 by 1830, 25 of them wholesalers, while the number of curriers and leather-sellers rose from 10 in 1826 to 15 in 1830. By 1831 adult male shoemakers accounted for over a third of all males aged 20 or over in the town, and to these must be added a similar proportion of women, youths and children.

The footwear industry will of course be much more fully considered elsewhere, but if it was much the largest industry in Northampton by 1835 it was not the only one. There were also two breweries, three ironfoundries and a flour mill, and though it declined quite quickly afterwards, the local lace-making industry was still turning out a product considered by some as 'infinitely superior, in texture and durability' to that of Nottingham in 1840.[19] The town-country link is also evident in these other industries, but the Assistant Commissioner despatched to report to Parliament on the condition of the municipal corporation in 1835 was more interested in something else which the ironfounders, if less often the brewers, had in common with the shoe-manufacturers of Northampton: for 'scarcely any of the master-manufacturers engaged in the staple trade of the town are members of the Established Church'.[20]

They were of course Dissenters in a town where 'Dissenters are very numerous', heirs to a local tradition of Puritanism which had its origins in the prophesyings in town and county in the later 16th century and was so deeply entrenched by the Civil War that the town's allegiance was a foregone conclusion. 'No man boweth at the pronouncing of the name of

Jesus . . . it is the greatest matter they stick upon', Archbishop Laud's commissioner informed him in 1635; 'a nest of Puritans', wrote Humphrey Ramsden of it three years later, 'malignant refractory spirits who disturb the peace of the Church'.[21] Retribution followed the Restoration, swift and thorough. In 1662 the castle was slighted along with the walls, the town was forced to pay £200 for the renewal of its charter, and despite Charles II's promise in the Declaration of Breda that 'no man shall be disquieted or called into question for Differences of Opinion in Matters of Religion', the Mayor-elect, bailiff-elect, 14 ex-bailiffs, eight aldermen and 32 of the 48 common councillors were turned off the Corporation.

· Puritans all, they were the victims not of a selective act of royal vengeance but of the Corporation Act of 1661, which reserved municipal office and the magistracy to communicant members of the Church of England and required them to swear oaths acknowledging the supreme authority of the Church 'one and indivisible' with the State. Only one of several restrictive statutes passed after the Restoration, Protestant dissenters and Roman Catholics were also barred from other civil offices, from military commissions, from the universities, and thence from the professions for which a university education was essential.[22] Commerce and industry were among the few areas where their religion was no bar, and the preponderance of Dissenters which the Royal Commission noted among the master-manufacturers of Northampton was not at all unusual. If the virtues of the godly life — industry, sobriety, thrift — were also conducive to financial success, and worldly wealth was one mark of the Elect, Dissenters were often better equipped through their own Academies with scientific, technological and other knowledge more 'useful' in these areas than a classical education.

Their worship came gradually to be tolerated, but until they organised themselves into an effective political force these isolated congregations had little hope of lifting their legal disabilities, and in uniting them into the 'Dissenting Interest' Dr. Philip Doddridge, minister to the Castle Hill Independent Church in Northampton between 1729-51, played a central role. At first reluctant to leave his ministry in Leicestershire — 'I cannot believe that I was ever born to shine in so polite and learned a county as Northamptonshire'[23] — he brought with him to Northampton the Academy which was the cause of his prosecution in an ecclesiastical court in 1733 for teaching without a licence from an Anglican bishop. Dropped in the face of national protests, the case effectively freed all Dissenting education from the control of the Church of England, but Doddridge also did much to advance the cause of Dissent in less

4. Dr. Philip Doddridge (1702-51), Congregationalist leader and Minister of Castle Hill Meeting, Northampton, 1729-51.

obvious ways, through an enormous circle of friends and correspondents of every religious and political persuasion, who — as even a brief glance at the large volume of his surviving correspondence will show — greatly valued his opinion and advice.

Locally they included Dr. John Stonhouse, co-founder with Doddridge in 1744 of the Northampton Infirmary, the Earl of Halifax, from whom he rented his Academy premises, and the Spencers of Althorp; further afield, the Anglican Bishop of London, the Methodist preacher George Whitefield, the Moravian leader Count Zinzendorf, and the ministers of dissenting churches in Europe and America, to cite but a few. Doddridge's ministry in Northampton also did much to strengthen Dissent within the town and county. Invited to move to a ministry in Nottingham in 1736, he was urged to refuse, for 'it is a matter of great importance to preserve the flourishing state of the dissenting interest in Northamptonshire (the glory of our cause in England)'.[24] His own church, Doddridge wrote to the First Church of Connecticut in 1741, was also 'in a very flourishing state', having 'about 230 members, of which 130 have been admitted since I became their pastor . . .'.[25]

Nor was Castle Hill the only Dissenting congregation in Northampton in the mid-18th century. The Quakers had their own burial ground by 1750, and a large body of Baptists their chapel in College Lane, built soon after that of Castle Hill in 1695. By 1830 there were chapels in Northampton 'for almost all denominations of dissenters', including that of the Wesleyan Methodist representatives of 'New Dissent' in Gold Street, but Dissent was often numerically stronger than its chapels suggested. The congregation often preceded the purpose-built place of worship by some years, meeting in the meantime in the homes of its members, and this was also true of Northampton's small community of Roman Catholics, holding Divine Service in a house opposite the *Saracen's Head* in Abington Street until it was granted a licence to build a chapel in 1825.[26]

The religious life of the town was not confined to worship, of course. Both churches and chapels were the focus of many social activities, from choirs to bible classes, suppers, philanthropic ventures like the clothing societies for the poor operating in the earlier 19th century — the Anglican Society for Clothing the Poor, founded in 1817, and the Nonconformist Dorcas Society established in 1829 in response to its 'enlarged success'[27] — and, above all, of the voluntary educational work which endowed Northampton with a succession of Sunday schools and day schools from the later 18th century onwards. Originally inspired by the Evangelical Revival, which placed great stress on the study of the Scriptures and thus on the teaching of reading, the momentum was sustained well into the 19th century by the determination of one denomination to outmatch the efforts of the other.

The town already had a range of private boarding and day schools for the not-so-poor, most offering a more limited curriculum than that of Thomas Crass in St Giles Street in 1762 'where Youth are taught writing, Arithmetic both Vulgar and Decimal, Geometry, Surveying . . . and other Sciences Mathematical', and where 'Artificers and others unable to attend during the day could be taught in the evenings'.[28] New charity schools had also been established to supplement the Free Grammar School founded by the grocer Thomas Chipsey in 1541: the Orange School in 1710, supported by endowments from John Dryden and Zachariah Herbert; the Blue Coat School, established in 1753 with a gift of £1,000 from James, Earl of Northampton; and the Beckett and Sargeant School for Girls, which opened in 1735 and taught not only the the 'three Rs' but the domestic accomplishments — cookery, needlework, knitting, and the arts of laundry — more highly valued by those seeking 'perfect wives'.[29]

Between them the charity schools catered for around 100 children. However, Sunday Schools were established at St Giles and All Saints in 1786 and followed soon after by one operated by the combined Dissenting churches, with pupils taught at different chapels in rotation. The Dissenters in turn took the lead in the day school movement in 1810 when William Hickson, an ex-London shoe mercer and member of College Street Baptist Chapel, proposed to establish a school run on the principles of the Quaker educationalist Joseph Lancaster. Very similar in practice to those of his Anglican counterpart, Andrew Bell, it was initially supported by leading Churchmen in town and county, but after the intervention of county clergy and the Bishop of Peterborough, plans were drawn up for a separate school 'for the education of the poor . . . in conformity with the views of the National Society', the body responsible for the educational work of the Established Church, and it was duly opened a mere two months after the Lancasterian School in 1812.

As an Anglican, said Lord Althorp, one of several county gentry who now found themselves in a delicate position, he 'must prefer the system which educated the poor in his own principles'; as a Whig he would of course 'do everything in his power to support the Lancasterian School'; for as a Christian and a prominent educationalist himself, 'he thought it his duty to extend the blessings of education as far as possible'.[30] Literacy and numeracy were marketable skills, valued above all as a route to occupational advancement. In county towns like Northampton there was a sufficiently wide range of employment to provide a genuine incentive to learn, and the gradual rise in local literacy rates, perceptible from the 1820s onwards among both males and females, is some measure of the success of these earlier voluntary schools in teaching these valuable skills. Based on the ability to sign one's name in an Anglican marriage register — a reasonable measure, since only competent readers would be taught to write and Nonconformists were obliged to marry in an Anglican church until 1836 — the rate of literacy among males rose from 68% in the decade between 1811-20 to 75% between 1831-40, among females, from 46% to 54%.[31]

Civil registers from the latter decade may suggest that the Dissenting schools were either more effective in reaching potential pupils, or more efficient in teaching them: measured from this source, literacy rates among Nonconformists were as high as 95% and 82% respectively. The Nonconformist Sunday schools, noted the *Northampton Mercury*, did turn out 'a rather greater number' of children than the Anglicans at the Coronation celebrations in 1838 — but it required a journey from one side of the town to the other to compare them. The latter were assembled in the yard of the Barracks to the north, the former at the brewery of the Liberal Borough Councillor Thomas Hagger to the south, where — one hastens to add — they too were 'liberally regaled with plum-cake and tea'. For the *Mercury*, this 'most interesting spectacle' was rivalled only by a portrait of the Queen elsewhere in the town bearing the inappropriate legend 'Victoria Rex'; but with local Tories and Whigs also celebrating this occasion of national unity in strict segregation, there could hardly be more striking proof that, in Northampton, religion was inseparable from politics.[32]

This was inevitably so while Dissent carried with it exclusion from so many civil offices and secular activities, and as Philip Doddridge well understood when he involved himself in the cause of Lord Halifax and other local Whigs, the only remedy was a political one. The legal disabilities of Northampton's Dissenters were of course shared by its Roman Catholics, and in 1827 the two made common cause and petitioned Parliament for their removal. The counter-petition organised by the Anglican Archdeacon of Northampton was ostensibly 'against the Catholic cause', but the Dissenters found their own little advanced when the Test and Corporation Acts were repealed in the following year — not, at least, so far as the municipal corporation was concerned. Given the option of admitting them to its body, the exclusively Tory/Anglican corporation remained as exclusive as ever.

As the *Royal Commission on Municipal Corporations* testified in 1835, it was far from alone. The rights of self-government vested in the municipal corporations were acquired piecemeal through charters, letters patent and other grants direct from the Crown over many centuries, some had been more energetic than others in acquiring them, and in no two cases were they exactly the same. The complaints levelled against them to the Commission nevertheless had a certain uniformity, reflecting those common privileges which they were allegedly abusing. Incorporation itself, granted in Northampton under a charter of Henry VI in 1459, gave them the legal status of *persona ficta*, a fictitious person with the same ability to acquire and dispose of property as a private individual. Thus 'we may do what we will with our own' was their standard defence when accused of misuse of corporate or charitable funds in the earlier 19th century; or as the Mayor of Northampton put it more elegantly when justifying the £1,000 voted to the Tory Sir Robert Gunning as an inducement to contest a borough seat in the general election of 1826, the funds of the corporations were 'equally at their disposal with their own individual property'.[33]

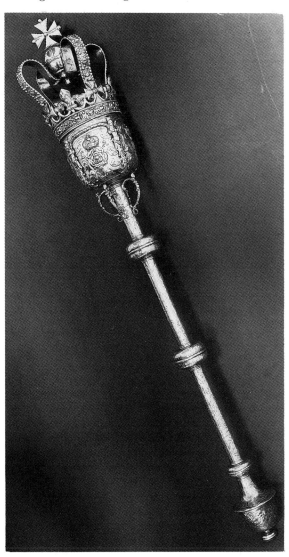

5. The Great Mace of Northampton. The symbol of municipal authority, the present mace dates from the 17th century.

By 1835 the Corporation also enjoyed the exclusive right to provide the borough justices in the person of the Mayor, ex-Mayor and three Aldermen, one which the Whig *Northampton Mercury* found 'not the least objectionable part of the present system', for when 'the administrators of justice in our borough towns are almost unavoidably active members of a party . . . their decisions upon every question upon which party feelings can be supposed to bear, are in consequence regarded with suspicion'.[34] This was particularly so when the magistracy was constituted, like the Corporation itself, exclusively from one party. Like most such bodies it elected itself, under the authority of an Act of Henry VII in 1489 which abolished the town assemblies of Northampton and Leicester on the grounds that the behaviour of these 'multitudes . . . of little substance' was 'oft times to the great breach of the King's Peace', and replaced them with 48 'representatives', Common Councillors appointed in the first instance by the Crown but with subsequent vacancies filled by co-option. The 'Forty Eight' in turn elected 24 Aldermen, and the whole body of the 'Seventy Two', with Bailiffs, ex-Bailiffs and ex-Mayors, elected the town officials.

The Corporation was now rendered as 'wholly independent, both as to its appointment and proceedings, of any control on the part of the burgesses or the inhabitants at large' as it remained in 1835.[35] Even so, as the Civil War amply demonstrated, its exclusive nature was no guarantee of loyalty to the Crown, and it was not inevitably unrepresentative of the body of inhabitants excluded from it. It was not until the earlier 18th century, in line with hardening divisions in the national political arena, that it began to assume its exclusive Tory and Anglican nature, but the complaints recorded against it in 1835 had already been aired by a Committee of Inhabitants in 1795, when — finding themselves 'deprived of legal means of continuing their corporate existence with safety' due to the persistent non-attendance of a majority of the 'Forty Eight' at mayoral elections — the Corporation had been forced to petition the Crown for a new charter.[36]

Were there 'none of it that did not feel vexed from legal Disqualification . . .', declared one handbill, 'I could give that Committee Credit for their Proceedings, and thank them to expose all corrupt Acts of the Corporation (if any exist), either in their Magisterial Capacity, or as Public Trustees of the Charities'.[37] In 1828, in fact, the borough justices were sued on these grounds in the Court of King's Bench, where they were in turn sueing a local attorney for allegedly 'composing, publishing and printing certain scandalous libels' against them in a letter to *The Times* accusing them of political bias. Two cases were cited in which, it was said, a 'friend' of Sir Robert Gunning had been fined a mere one shilling for a violent assault, while two opponents of the Corporation who had rescued a gentleman from 'a mob of vile, base and notoriously bad characters' were fined £50 and imprisoned for a month — their gallant action being construed for party political purposes as releasing him from the custody of a constable.[38]

Declaring itself 'anxious that neither party should obtain the triumph', the Court dismissed both complaints without costs; but, one of its own aldermen stated 'positively' during the same hearing, the charitable funds controlled by the Corporation were distributed 'according to the manner in which they voted at the last election . . . the poll books are referred to at the time'. Since 1826, the Royal Commission confirmed, 'the charities have been granted exclusively to voters in the Corporation interest, or their relatives'.[39] In the 18th century the expenses of electoral 'influence' fell largely on the aristocratic county families who maintained an 'interest' in the borough seats: the Montagus of Horton, the Comptons of Castle Ashby and, later in the century, the Spencers of Althorp. Their funds were often lavishly dispensed, as in the notorious 'Three Earls Election' of 1768,[40] as indeed they had to be, for until 1832 the franchise in Northampton was an uncommonly wide one, extending to all adult males not receiving poor relief.

With the final collapse of the Compton interest in 1820, however, the Corporation was left to its own devices. The electorate was in fact reduced by the parliamentary reform of 1832, but freemen of the borough retained their vote, and as the Commission rightly said, its customary mode of distributing the charities enabled it 'to exercise a very considerable influence over the poorer voters'.[41] As it also noted in passing, at least some of them took the Tory charity and voted Whig; but to the Whig government returned under the new franchise these closed and predominantly Tory bodies were not only an affront to the principle of popular representation enshrined in the Reform Act but an obvious danger to its basic purpose, that of ensuring the middling commercial, industrial and often Dissenting classes a degree of political influence in line with the influence they now exercised against landed wealth in the economic sphere.

As the *Mercury* suggested, they had still more incentive to 'interfere' in elections after the parliamentary reform of 1832 than before, for the 'very increase of the numbers, the wealth, and the intelligence of the middle classes . . . has tended rather to call forth rather than to correct the abuses of our corporations . . . for the purpose of strengthening the waning Parliamentary influence of the Corporation against the daily increasing weight of the Non-corporators'.[42] Thus the Municipal Reform Act of 1835 was, as Joseph Parkes, Secretary to the Royal Commission, described it, a necessary 'postscript' to the parliamentary Reform

Act which opened the corporations in turn to popular election and robbed them of their powers to pervert the due political process. It was the 'steam engine for the Mill built by Parliamentary Reform'; or, in the words of the Tory *Northampton Herald*, 'a mere thimble-rig juggle by which a certain party wishes to transfer into its own hands the political influence at present possessed by others . . . The cant about the abuses of corporations is a miserable pretext . . .'.[43]

The *Herald* was never one to understate its case. Founded during the reform agitation of 1831, backed by the Tory gentry of the county and informed for many years by vitriolic pen of the Rev. Francis Litchfield, curate of Farthinghoe, in 1838 it attributed the higher circulation figures claimed by the much older *Mercury* to the device of buying large quantities of the newspaper tax 'stamps' and burning them. The *Herald*, the *Mercury* retorted with customary tartness, was nothing but a 'cuttlefish': it 'possesses the singular facility of discharging a black liquid, and shrouding itself from observation amidst the discoloured water . . .'.[44] On this occasion, however, it was simply expressing a view common to many Tories, more formally stated by the Tory Corporation of Leicester in a petition to the House of Lords in 1835 claiming that its own abolition was effected by 'an illegal Commission . . . most *partial* and *unjust* . . . their rights are to be destroyed and a new system adopted at variance with all the principles of the Constitution'.[45]

The Royal Commission, it is true, was a very 'partial' body. It was packed with Whigs, and its clear function was to justify a reform which the Whig government was determined to effect. It is also true that, in Northampton, Assistant Commissioner Cockburn had some evident difficulty in carrying out his appointed task. Indeed, he found the Corporation in some respects worthy of rare praise. Its accounts had been kept with 'commendable regularity', and it was an 'honourable exception' in publishing them 'even occasionally'. The corporate and trust estates too had been managed 'on the whole . . . in a manner creditable to the Corporation', and a large body of citizens, 'among whom are to be included many persons of great respectability', had expressed complete satisfaction with the corporate government.

Nonetheless, he concluded, 'It seems impossible to justify a system which alienates from the municipal government the affections and respect of one half of the community, and which gives rise to complaints of so serious a character — complaints which, whether correct or not, it seems impossible, upon reviewing the evidence . . . to pronounce unreasonable'.[46] As a justification for reforming it even this prevaricating verdict was good enough, and the Corporation of Northampton was among the 178 of the 285 investigated to be abolished in a reform which was, in a different sense of the word, also very partial. Unable to convict them of illegality — after all, if their activities had not been for the most part quite lawful it would not have taken an Act of Parliament to put an end to them — the Royal Commission found them guilty instead of immorality.

The 'corruption' of the old corporations has now become something of an unassailable historical 'fact', but it rests rather precariously on the unhistorical device, perfected by the Whig school of historians, of judging them against the standards raised up by the Commission and the Act itelf rather than the standards of conduct prevailing in their own lifetime. Even so, there can be no question that the moral outrage felt by the Dissenting Whigs of Northampton was absolutely genuine and, from their own viewpoint, more than justified. As the Commission pointed out, they were in every way but one the equal of their Tory opponents. They were 'one-half at least of the respectable and influential inhabitants of the town', their social and economic influence as employers and wealth-producers was at least as great, and on the local Board of Improvement Commissioners, to which no religious test applied, they governed with them on equal terms. In 1828 Parliament had granted them equal rights of citizenship, and if they were 'vexed' by their exclusion before then, they were infinitely more bitter about it afterwards. They were no less so after 1835, but their own outrage was now matched by that of their Anglican opponents.

'The best form of government, to my mind', said the Rev. J. de Putron, vicar of the northern suburb of Kingsthorpe, 'is an aristocratic oligarchy . . . putting power into the hands of democracy is like giving a child of five a loaded double-barrelled gun.[47] This was in 1930, and the *Northampton Independent* had no hesitation in dismissing it as the latest of many eccentric utterances from the same source; but, prior to the constitutional reforms of 1828-35, government *was* founded on an aristocratic oligarchy, and by the tenets of the Anglican faith, it was not simply the best but the *only* legitimate form of it. The 'nation and the church are one', wrote one 'Tory of the Old School' in 1828: 'the total and unqualified repeal, therefore, of all tests of Christianity in the office-holders of the state does imply, and does effect, the separation of church and state . . . and thereby inculcates the notion that kingly government is a matter of human contrivance . . . the false opinion that the people, and not God, are the legitimate source of power . . .'.[48]

Whereas, he continued, 'the true foundation of this, and every Christian monarchy rests upon the principle that "the powers that be are ordained by God"'; and in this view immorality and illegality were plainly all on the other side. The authority exercised by the reformed Parliament was illegitimate, the Royal Commission was 'illegal', and the reform of the corporations themselves was as much 'against all the principles of the Constitution' as the Corporation of Leicester claimed. In this view too, the exclusion of Dissenters, the use of corporate funds for party political purposes, and the outright obstruction with which the Royal Commission met in some boroughs, was in the nature of a sacred duty. Kingly government under the ordinance of God was, and must be, unrepresentative government.

In practical terms, of course, lacking the power in Parliament to reverse this 'thimble-rig juggle' of constitutional principles, the old ruling classes now had to take their electoral chances with the new, and the Duke of Wellington for one did not rate them highly. 'The Revolution is made . . .', he wrote gloomily in 1833, 'power is transferred from one class of society, gentlemen of England professing the faith of the Church of England, to another class of society, the shopkeepers, being Dissenters from the Church'.[49] The sense of a fundamental shift in the bases of political and economic power was a very real one at the time, but the 'gentlemen' were far from finished as a political force, and in Northampton it took them only so long as the first elections to the new municipal corporation to prove it. Indeed, bitter as the contest might have been before 1835, it was in truth only just beginning. If Tories and Whigs, Anglicans and Dissenters had anything in common at all it was the conviction, utter and complete on both sides, that theirs was the just and lawful case, the high moral ground — and in their consuming need to prove it, again and again and again, there was virtually no aspect of life in the town which could not be turned into a political battleground.

Notes

1. *Pigot's Commercial Directory* (1830).
2. *Northampton Mercury* (hereafter *N.M.*), 7 June 1845.
3. For a fuller discussion of this earlier period, see Williams J.H., *Saxon and Mediaeval Northampton* (1982).
4. *N.M.*, 10 August 1761, which also carried an advertisement for coal at 14d. a bushel against around 20d. in the 1750s.
5. 'Two Old Railways', *Northamptonshire County Magazine*, Vol.1 (1928).
6. *Travels of Cosmo the Third, Grand Duke of Tuscany . . . Through England*, quoted in *Northamptonshire Notes and Queries* (hereafter *N.N.&Q.*), Vol.2 (1888), p.107; *The State of Northampton from the Beginning of the Fire . . . by a Country Gentleman* (1675), p.4.
7. *Northampton Independent* (hereafter *N.I.*), 6 Jan. 1923.
8. For an account of the Great Fire see *The State of Northampton from the Beginning of the Fire . . .*, op. cit.

9. *N.M.*, 11 Feb. 1837.
10. *Royal Commission on the Health of Large Towns* (1845), quoted in Hoskins, W. G., *The Making of the English Landscape* (1985 edn.), p.281.
11. Garmonsway, G. N., (trans.), *Parker Chronicle 921* (1972).
12. *Royal Commission on Municipal Corporations*, PPXXV (1935) Report on the Proposed Municipal Boundary and Division into Wards of the Borough of Northampton; mid-19th century handbill, otherwise undated, Northamptonshire Libraries and Information Service (hereafter N.L.I.S.).
13. *N.M.*, 15 Oct. 1853.
14. For a fuller analysis of these records see Dyer, A., 'Northampton in 1524', *Northamptonshire Past and Present* (hereafter *N.P.&P.*), Vol.6 (1978-83).
15. Militia lists for the years 1771, 1774, 1777, 1781 and 1786 are available at the Northamptonshire Record Office (herafter N.R.O.).
16. *Pigot's Commercial Directory* (1840). See also Kennett, D. H., 'The Geography of Coaching in Early Nineteenth Century Northamptonshire', *N.P.&P.*, Vol.5, 2 (1974).
17. 'Glimpses of Old Northampton', *N.N.&Q.*, Vol.3 (1890), p.171.
18. 18th century poster, *s.d.*, *N.N.&Q.*, Vol.4 (1892), p.136.
19. *Pigot's Commercial Directory* (1840).
20. PPXXV, op. cit., Northampton, p.14.
21. Cater, F. Ives, *Northamptonshire Nonconformity* (1912); Victoria County History of Northamptonshire (hereafter V.C.H.), Vol.3, p.36.
22. Primarily, the Act of Uniformity 1662, Conventicle Act 1664, Five Mile Act 1665, and the Test Acts of 1673 and 1678.
23. Nuttall, G. F. (ed.), *A Calendar of the Correspondence of Philip Doddridge* (1979), 316. See also Greenall, R. L. (ed.), *Philip Doddridge, Nonconformity and Northampton* (1981); Deacon, M., *Philip Doddridge of Northampton* (1980).
24. Nuttall G. H., op. cit., 442.
25. Ibid.,663.
26. *N.M.* cutting 1825, otherwise undated.
27. *Rules of the Northampton Society for Clothing the Poor* (1821); *First Annual Report of the Northampton Dorcas Society* (1830), (N.L.I.S. 198-756).
28. *N.M.*, 22 March 1762.
29. *Northampton Chronicle and Echo* (hereafter *C.&E.*), Charter Anniversary supplement (1989), p.54.
30. Lawes, J., 'Voluntary Schools and Basic Education in Northampton, 1800-71', *N.P.&P.*, Vol.6, 2, (1979), p.87.
31. Hatley, V. A., 'Literacy at Northampton, 1761-1900: Third Interim Report', *N.P.&P.*, Vol.5 (1976).
32. *N.M.*, 30 June 1838.
33. House of Commons debate, 21 Feb. 1827 (N.L.I.S. 198-781).
34. *N.M.*, 11 April 1835.
35. PPXXV, op. cit., p.14.
36. Handbill 1795 (N.L.I.S. 198-780).
37. Ibid.
38. The King v. The Mayor and Corporation of Northampton, K.B.D., 1828 (N.L.I.S. 198-781).
39. PPXXV, op. cit., p.16.
40. See also Hatley, V. A., *The Northampton Election of 1774*, Northampton Historical Series No.5 (1958-9).
41. PPXXV, op. cit., p.17.
42. *N.M.*, 6 June 1835.
43. *Northampton Herald* (hereafter *N.H.*), 8 Aug. 1835.
44. *N.H.*, 16 June 1838; *N.M.*, 23 June 1838.
45. Chinnery, D. (ed.), *Records of the Borough of Leicester*, Vol.5 (1964), 1624, 23 July 1835.
46. PPXXV, op. cit., pp.19-20.
47. *N.I.*, 25 Jan. 1930.
48. Quoted in Clark, J., *English Society* (1986), p.351.
49. Ibid., p.413.

Chapter One

More than a Shoe Town: Early and Mid-Victorian Northampton

... machinery must and will be employed ... to struggle against it is to fight with science, and to attempt to put a stop to the progress of the human mind ...

Northampton Mercury, 29 May 1859: Appeal of Isaac, Campbell & Co. to the Boot and Shoemakers of Northampton

The plan of the Society is simple, and the amount of Subscription so low, as to place its advantages within the reach of most WORKING MEN. To those who love the Independence which the Landowner, however small his possession, enjoys — to those who are desirous of a safe Investment for their Earnings — and to those who are seeking to change the habits, and elevate the tastes of the people, the promoters of this Society address themselves in confident expectation of their support and encouragement.

Handbill, Northampton Town and County Freehold Land Association (1848)

'The world has given up discussing the question of whether railways in the abstract are a blessing or an evil', wrote the *Mercury* in 1845, 'They have become "a great fact" . . . a necessity which it is sheer idleness to oppose'.[1] Northampton now had a railway, linking it by way of a station in Bridge Street to Peterborough on the one hand and to the London to Birmingham line at Blisworth on the other. Opened in May 1845, 'every station along the line was crowded with gazers . . . looking with wondering eyes upon the imposing novelty';[2] but had Northampton not been 'rather more furious than other places in opposition to railways', then the main London to Birmingham line could have been routed through the town years before. And the Kilsby Tunnel, that 'stupendous memorial to human ingenuity' which involved the London and Birmingham Company in costs of a similar order, need never have been built at all.

Or so Robert Stephenson, engineer to the company, claimed in 1857,[3] adding his own weight to a legend which survived even the carefully documented 'vindication' produced by Miss Joan Wake in 1935.[4] County landowners, fearing the ruin of their fox-hunting as well as the invasion of their estates, were certainly opposed to the route of the line when it was first proposed in 1830. Placating them accounted for some £500,000 of the company's expenses, and the Kilsby Tunnel for almost £300,000 more against a contract price of less than a third that amount. One-and-a-half miles long, its building was beset by problems. Massive flooding followed the unexpected discovery of quicksand, and the contractor went bankrupt and died, leaving the company to complete the work itself. A 70-yard stretch of brickwork collapsed, the Northampton Infirmary declared itself unable to accept 'any more cases of simple fracture . . . compound fractures and such cases only as are attended with danger can be admitted', and a riot by navvies in 1837 had to be quelled by the Militia.[5]

One of the many obstacles presented by the Northamptonshire uplands, the Kilsby ridge was nevertheless a part of the route which Stephenson himself recommended to the company in 1831, 'keeping in mind economy in the execution [and] favourable levels for the operation of locomotives'.[6] It was not a 'deviation' forced on him by opposition from the town, which was largely limited in reality to the innkeepers who feared that the railway would rob them of their trade. To a great extent it did, although some, like Thomas Shaw of the *Angel*, recouped a part of their losses by operating coaching services to and from the railway station at Roade, five miles distant, charging 1s. 6d. for an outside seat and 2s. 6d. inside.[7] The Borough Corporation, it is true, did oppose the railway at first. It had its own estate at

Bugbrooke; but it soon joined forces with a Committee of Inhabitants 'to have the railway as near to the town of Northampton as possible' — and as Stephenson himself admitted, Blisworth was really as close as it could yet reasonably come.

He 'could easily take his trains to the town', Stephenson is reported as saying of the gradient between Northampton and Blisworth, but 'it would be another matter to get them out again';[8] and having committed the 'atrocious blunder of choosing the Kilsby Tunnel', wrote one correspondent to the *Mercury* in 1859, the Company was 'not at liberty to lay the blame on the people of Northampton'.[9] Both the Company and Stephenson, it may be thought, had more than a little interest in preserving their own reputations at the expense of that of the town, and so successful were they that this myth-disguised-as-fact was still appearing in railway histories long after Miss Wake believed she had disposed of it. 'The refusal of Northampton to permit the London and Birmingham to pass through it . . . [is] well known', declared one publication in 1959; 'the opposition of Northampton, which the town afterwards whole-heartedly repented', wrote another in the same year, 'was the cause of much industrial difficulty and expenditure, for it involved the construction of . . . the Kilsby Tunnel'.[10]

In 1838 the Corporation felt obliged to appoint additional constables due to the 'disgraceful conduct' of some of the railway workers, which included ringing the bells during Divine Service at All Saints while the worse for drink,[11] but the damage inflicted on the town by the London and Birmingham line, it will be suggested, was otherwise minimal. The Blisworth-Northampton-Peterborough line, it is true, was much prone to flooding and the 44 miles of single track between Northampton and Peterborough limited the number of services which could be operated. 'We are not only situated on a branch, but on a bad branch', as the *Mercury* complained in 1859;[12] but once the line opened in 1845 passengers could travel from Northampton to London in a matter of $2\frac{1}{2}$-3 hours for a third class fare of 5s., or 14s. in the relative comfort of a first-class carriage, and passengers, machinery and livestock alike were conveyed in large quantities when Northampton played host to the Royal Agricultural Show in 1847.[13]

The Kilsby Tunnel claimed another victim when a prize bull was roasted in its van after a cinder set light to the straw, but Mrs. Armstrong, 'the largest woman in Europe', fortunately survived her own journey in an adapted horse-van to display her 445 pounds and 85-inch hips to the town soon afterwards.[14] Nevertheless, important as the railways were in terms of passenger traffic, they were of greatest value in transporting perishable or bulky goods at a greater speed and a lower cost than by road or canal: in the case of Northampton, coal into the town, and agricultural produce and footwear out of it. Indeed, in the face of the continued expansion of the footwear trade from the 1830s onwards, the notion that the delayed arrival of the railway or the lengthy absence of main-line facilities caused Northampton any serious 'industrial difficulty' can hardly be supported.

Around 1,300 in number in 1831, the 1,821 adult shoemakers recorded at the census ten years later accounted for almost a third of all males aged 20 or more in the town. By 1851 they numbered almost 3,000, 39% of the total, with a further 1,200 under 20 and a similar number of females, against the 3-400 of each in 1841.[15] The 37 manufacturers recorded in 1837 had grown to 103 by 1851, while between 1831-51 the population of the town increased from around 15,000 to over 26,000. A 'positive mania has set in for embarking in the trade', wrote the *Herald* in 1853 as gold discoveries in California and Australia boosted demand still further: 'It not only engages the money of large and small capitalists, but drains the town and neighbourhood for employees, both male and female.'[16] Almost three-quarters of the town's population in 1851 had been born elsewhere, most of them coming from rural areas of the county itself, and the same pattern of migration applied to Kettering, Wellingborough and other centres which, like Northampton itself, also 'put out' work to surrounding villages. 'Pushed' by population growth and under-employment or 'pulled' by the prospect of higher wages, many more were yet to come.

Small master-manufacturers dominated the trade, but even in 1836 there were some substantial concerns: those of William Parker, for instance, employing some 800 people and producing around 80,000 pairs of footwear in that year, and of John Groom on a similar scale.[17] At least 12 firms were employing over 100 workers each in 1851,[18] and some had established retail outlets in major urban centres — Hallam and Edens in Liverpool, Manchester and other northern cities, and George Moore as far afield as Glasgow and Belfast.[19] A large proportion of footwear was exported, much of it to the United States, but British colonial markets were of more importance from the 1860s after the Civil War stimulated the growth of an indigenous American industry. Military contracts were always an important source of work in Northampton, but much of its produce went to the domestic 'sale' market, satisfying a growing demand for ready-made boots from those of the working classes who were now enjoying a rising standard of living.

In the urban 'bespoke' trade it was still common for one shoemaker to carry out all the processes involved in footwear manufacture, but in the 'ready made' trade there was already an extensive division of labour by process and by sex. 'Clicking' (cutting the sections of leather for the uppers) was an exclusively male occupation, 'closing' (stitching them together) was carried out mainly by women and children, while 'making' (the remainder of the operation) was increasingly sub-divided into its own component processes: lasting, welt-stitching, sole-stitching or rivetting, and the trimming, scouring and polishing with which the footwear was 'finished'. Well beyond mid-century, however, the great majority of shoemakers still worked in their homes or in the small workshops which were commonly incorporated in private houses. Only the clickers and 'rough-stuff cutters', around 10% of the total workforce, were as a rule employed on the manufacturers' own premises, the latter cutting the leather for soles and heels. Like the clickers they were paid by the day rather than at the piece rates applied to most other processes, but at a level in line with a status 'lower than that of any other employee in the manufacture of boots'.[20]

The clickers, by contrast, were the acknowledged 'aristocrats' of the trade, commanding its highest wages after a lengthy apprenticeship: leather accounted for some 50% of the total costs of production, and skill in matching it and economy in cutting it were crucial to an employer's profits. Clickers often became manufacturers in their own turn, but close contact with their masters tended to encourage the same 'union of feeling and interest' as existed in their own exclusive ranks, making them as much a focus of other shoemakers' grievances as the manufacturers themselves. 'We are persuaded', wrote the Northampton Society of Operative Cordwainers in 1838, 'that the large manufacturers are not aware of the unjust system on which their business is at present conducted by their clickers . . . or we feel assured that such a destructive and oppressive system of manufacturing would cease to be pursued . . .'.[21]

The clickers also supervised the distribution of work to outdoor employees, 'such work being given out', claimed the Society, 'chiefly to a CHOSEN FEW — consisting of clickers wives and acquaintances . . . while the MANY, consisting of the wives and families of the makers, have so little that it is insufficient to enable parents to train up their children in knowledge and respectability . . . want of regular work and fair wages compelling parents to let out their little ones for a few pence towards their maintenance'. How else was it possible for 'an honest industrious workman . . . to procure a sufficiency of plain food, decent common clothing, etc.' on 12 15s. a week? 'They cannot; and consequently hunger and wretchedness must prevail unless a permanent change for the better is effected.' Higher wage rates, a more equal distribution of work, the abolition of workshops employing children and of the truck shops operated by many employers, and 'an entire change in the Competition

6. 'Going to shop' to fetch or return work in the mid-19th century.

system' were the Society's remedies, for 'when one reduces [wages], the others reduce, and are thus enabled to compete with the original reduction . . . hence the present depressed state of our trade'.[22]

These were, it is true, times of general depression in trade, but many of the conditions which the Society complained of existed to a greater or lesser degree at the best of times. Few shoemakers enjoyed regular employment or a regular income. The wholesale trade in particular was a seasonal affair, with the Spring and Autumn 'boom' characteristically followed by a 'bust' and a rapid fall-off in demand for labour, but in outdoor trades work could fluctuate from week to week. Wage rates were continually depressed by the pool of surplus labour in town and countryside, while the highest-paid female could rarely earn as much as the lowest-paid male. Even so, their own contribution to the family budget was as much a necessity as the average 1s.-1s. 6d. per week earnings of children, after a wageless 'apprenticeship' of six months in a closing room where they were so tightly packed together that they were not unusually stabbed in the eye by their neighbour's awl. Their education naturally suffered too. 'There is no locality in which the children are retained for so short a time under instruction as in this town', wrote one Inspector of Schools in 1851,[23] and an attempt by the St Giles Church School to combine paid 'shoe work' with ordinary classes quickly foundered on the hostility of the trade itself.[24] .

In some respects, as the *Royal Commission on the Employment of Children* noted in 1864, shoemaking was an unpleasant and often unhealthy occupation. Finishers constantly inhaled fumes from the gas used to heat their tools; seated for hours in a bent position, 'hand-sewn' workers were said to be prone to heart and lung disease, and 'several young men . . . told me that their health had improved since they abandoned it for rivetting'; but in rivetting workshops the 'very great' noise led to 'nervous afflictions' among employees, and 'has in some cases driven the employers to cease to employ them on the premises'.[25] However, as the Borough Medical Officer of Health was still arguing later in the century, conditions in the homes where much outwork was done were often no better than in the workshops. 'Instead of your being obliged to work in the close, confined rooms of your cottages, you will labour in healthy, commodious and well-ventilated apartments', ran an appeal from the firm of Isaac, Campbell and Co. for employees at the Campbell Square premises it opened in 1859: 'Your houses, instead of being ill-regulated workshops in which domestic duties interfere with labour, will become homes in which comfort will be possible. You will be enabled to eat, sleep, and sit at your firesides free from the smell of the materials of manufacture . . .'[26]

This is an adequate summary of the drawbacks of domestic manufacture, and combined with an offer of regular employment, two half-holidays a week and overseers of the employees' choice, the company had every hope that its 'mutually beneficial' offer would be accepted, and 'that we shall have been privileged to conduce in no slight degree, towards the social, moral, physical and economic advancement of the honest and industrious artisans of the borough of Northampton'.[27] 'Will you walk into my parlour . . .?', retorted the Northamptonshire Boot and Shoe-makers' Mutual Protection Society: 'SHOPMATES! Once within the infernal walls, once the damnable system is established . . . your social degradation is secured for another generation; and you will leave your poor offspring a legacy for which they will curse your memory'.[28] The system as it was might be the source of much 'degradation, want and wretchedness', but the shoemakers of Northampton cared still less for the alternative — the 'darling system of factory-working'.

Opposition to the factory was closely tied to the resistance to closing machines which culminated in a strike early in 1859. The first machinery to be applied to footwear manufacture, the treadle-driven sewing machine developed in the United States by Elias Howe was adapted for stitching leather in the 1850s and first used in Northampton in 1857. The Mutual Protection Society, also embracing shoemakers in Wellingborough, Kettering and other county centres, was formed in the following year, with the object of raising funds 'to prevent the introduction of Machinery . . . and also to endeavour to protect, raise and equalise our wages': for 'it is high time that the employed should have a fair share of the benefits arising from the productive industry of the country . . . and not to be obliged, in his old age, to finish a life of labour in a Poor-law Bastille and a Pauper's grave'.[29]

SEWING MACHINES.

At a MEETING of the undersigned BOOT and SHOE MANUFACTURERS of NORTHAMPTON, held at the PEACOCK HOTEL, on MONDAY, February 7th, 1859,

RESOLVED:

"That in consequence of Sewing Machines being extensively used in the Cities and principal Towns of the United Kingdom, so as seriously to affect the demand upon the Wholesale Houses, any further delay in the introduction of them, by the Manufacturers of Northampton, would be permanently injurious to the interest of the trade generally."

And, in accordance with this conviction, it was decided to

Introduce the Machine-Sewn Tops

Simultaneously, into their respective Trades,

On the 14th February;

and to inform their Men by this Hand-bill of the proposed change; and that the same be duly advertised in the Times, the Local Papers, and Staffordshire Advertiser.

Fredk. Bostock	Wm. Jones
S. Isaac, Campbell & Co.	J. Wetherell & Co.
Wm. Parker & Sons	William Bunting & Son
Hollis & Son	Henry Marshall
Jeffery & Hard	Richard Turner
Henry Harday	James Trench
M. P. Manfield	S. G. Edwards
Poole & Co.	Jonathan Robinson
George Parsons	Ager & Milne
G. & C. Turner	Robert Derby.

7. 'Sewing machines': 1859 poster announcing the intention to adopt closing machines in Northampton.

Reduced demand for labour, wage reductions and the displacement of males by females were the immediate fears, shared by the shoemakers of Stafford where the machines were also opposed; but they were introduced elsewhere with little resistance, and 'in consequence of Sewing Machines being extensively used in the Cities and principal towns of the United Kingdom, so as to seriously affect the demand upon the Wholesale Houses', concluded the principal manufacturers of Northampton in February 1859, 'any further delay . . . would be permanently injurious'.[30] It was this declaration of their intent to adopt the machines which provoked the strike, but it was broken by mid-May and the immense hardship suffered by many families was to no avail. By 1865 around 1,500 closing machines were in use in the town, and the process soon became almost exclusively a female preserve, having 'a directly appreciable effect on education by enabling a large number of boys . . . to stay longer at school',[31] and wholesale manufacturers of uppers, 'closers to the trade', also began to appear.

Many of the machines were in fact rented out to employees in their own homes, but this did nothing to dispel the longer term fears of the shoemakers: closing today, another process tomorrow — and then the factory. The 'monster warehouse' built in Campbell Square for Moses Philip Manfield in the late 1850s would 'ride rough-shod over them', it was said at a public meeting in 1858. It was 'the general opinion that the warehouse in question was to be used as a factory . . . and that the operatives were to be confined within its walls . . . The owner denied it [but] the proof of the pudding was in the eating, and they would see'.[32] A warehouse it was, but Isaac, Campbell & Co. denied in turn that they planned to adopt the factory system in their own 'extensive premises'. Married women could have work at home, parents could bring their children as apprentices, men and women would work in separate rooms: what they were proposing was nothing more than 'a carefully considered system of constant, orderly, regulated work'.[33]

Constant, orderly, regulated — everything that the working life of most shoemakers was not, to the eternal frustration of the manufacturers. 'They begin in the morning when they like, but if any mortal thing happens they are up from their stools and after it', complained one London master in the 18th century.[34] 'Your . . . rivetter and finisher must keep 'St Monday sacred', ran one later complaint, 'he must attend the local race-meetings, rabbit-coursings, trotting, bicycling and foot-racing handicaps' and, in Northampton, election meetings, or the Militia training which coincided with the Spring 'great rush' or, until the 1870s, the annual harvest.[35] In the workshops, as much a place of social exchange as of work itself, the men bet on horses, pigeons and dogs and the results of municipal elections. In the workshops, in the popular view, they also plotted sedition, and there and elsewhere they practised the 'religion' ascribed to them by the author of an article in *Good Words* in 1869: 'Beer . . . decided members of the Alcoholic persuasion.'[36]

'Shoemakers have always been addicted to drink', claimed one maker-turned-master in 1915, 'Mondays were always off days, when no shoemaker, on principle, would work';[37] but Mondays were also the day when outwork was commonly collected from the manufacturer, shoemakers in turn complained of the time consumed by 'going to shop', and no matter when it was done, long hours of work were always necessary to earn a living wage. 'There is many an intelligent, temperate, industrious, frugal, generally moral Northampton shoemaker', the *Good Words* correspondent admitted — but drunk or sober, profligate or thrifty, they had one thing in common. Machinery and factory discipline had not yet changed their customary way of life or robbed them of their independence. They set their own hours and they regulated their own output — and, as they told their own trade union of its attempts to abolish outwork in the 1890s, 'they did not want their liberty meddled with'.[38]

Until the development of new or more sophisticated machinery from the 1870s onwards it was not reduced on any significant scale. Machinery was applied for cutting soles, and the American Blake Sole-Sewing machine was introduced on a limited scale in the 1860s. Producing a more flexible boot than hand-rivetting, its product was still much inferior to a hand-welted boot, while early machinery for rivetting was so crude that a hand-rivetter could easily outstrip it in both quality and speed until the 1890s. George Turner of Turner, Hyde and Co. claimed to produce over 100,000 pairs of footwear a week in 1866 against the 10,000-15,000 of the late 1850s,[39] but like M. P. Manfield and other leading manufacturers, this increased output was achieved largely by employing more labour and more sub-division of hand processes, and even in 1870 only around a fifth of their workers — clickers, closers and rough-stuff cutters — worked on their employers' premises.

There were other industries and sources of employment in the town, of course. Next to shoemaking domestic service was the largest source of work for women, but brewing continued to be important, with several smaller breweries alongside the Phillips Bros. Phoenix Brewery in Bridge Street, established in 1854, and the older firm of Phipps and Co., founded in Towcester in 1801 and also based in Bridge Street since its move to Northampton in 1817. Directed during this period by Richard and Thomas, and later, Pickering Phipps, their 'New Brewery' was built on the site of the old in 1866-7. Always a substantial employer, the construction industry was boosted not only by industrial and commercial projects such as this but by expanding demand for housing, while the iron-founders in turn found markets here for products beyond the nails, wagon fittings and hurdles they supplied to the agricultural sector, and the portable steam engines and other farm machinery produced by William Butlin and William Allchin and Son. Transport too was an expanding area of employment, most particularly on the railways, with the town's facilities enlarged in this area in 1859 by a line running from the new Castle Station to Market Harborough, and a line to Wellingborough in 1866.

Many of the town's employers were also involved in local parliamentary and municipal politics, making them a ready target for accusations of intimidation until the introduction of the secret ballot in 1872. 'Pray don't talk about shoemakers here being independent', wrote one to the *Herald* in 1853:

> We are all of us slaves, as much as if we had been born in Africa and worked in America. At five elections I have voted for the Liberal candidates, and every time against my conscience. I love the Church, yet I must join with those that want to put it down . . . Is this not slavery? I think so. I know so. But I cannot bear to see my wife starve and my children beg.[40]

Like the curriers William Williams and Edward Cotton, and the ironfounders Thomas Grundy and Edward Harrison Barwell — who allegedly discharged 18 of his Eagle Foundry workforce for 'insisting on voting as they pleased' in the 1841 general election[41] — many of the shoe manufacturers were prominent and active Liberals. They included, to name but a few, William Marshall, John Groom, Thomas Hallam, Joel Edens and Moses Philip Manfield.

Thomas Hagger excepted, the town's brewers were more often to be found on the Conservative side, which was not immune from the same such accusations. However, between 1832 and the extension of the suffrage in 1867 shoemakers accounted for around a third of the town's parliamentary electorate, and working-class males as a whole for almost half, more than sufficient to have a decisive influence on the outcome. From 1837 until 1874 the Liberals had a monopoly of the borough's two parliamentary seats: Raikes Currie until 1857, Robert Vernon Smith until 1859, and then Charles Gilpin and Lord Henley. So was it intimidation on the part of employers which ensured that Northampton remained 'subservient to the Whig ascendancy' for so long; or was this simply a reflection of the true wishes of the electorate?

Intimidation was certainly a possibility, and an electorate of less than 3,000 was perhaps small enough to make it practical; but until 1855 at least municipal politics followed the

8. Moses Philip Manfield (1819-99). Leading shoe manufacturer and Liberal politician. Mayor of Northampton in 1883 and M.P. for the Borough 1891-95, he was knighted in 1894.

same course on a different electoral base, and when the Conservatives took control of the Corporation in that year, it was very much a matter of them stepping into a Liberal breach. The same was true of their capture of both the borough parliamentary seats in secret ballots in 1874, but the Liberal in-fighting which culminated in this 'degradation' was by no means unique to Northampton. Here, as elsewhere, it was rooted in a mid-century challenge to mainstream Liberalism or 'Whiggery' from a relatively small group of independent artisans and shopkeepers whose own Liberalism was more radical, less deferential, and often combined with Freethought rather than Nonconformity. Led in Northampton by Joseph Gurney, a master tailor, and John Bates, a basket-maker and retailer of radical publications, the twin pillars on which their policies rested, the extension of the suffrage and the secret ballot, were the means to the end of wider working-class representation.

It was they who later brought Charles Bradlaugh onto the local political scene, but until the late 1860s, they called themselves not Radicals but 'Ultra-Liberals': they were simply a little more 'advanced' than their party colleagues. Indeed, despite the proverbial association of both with shoemaking, the working classes of Northampton were no more conspicuous for their political radicalism in the earlier 19th century than for the 'infidelity' with which the town itself was later tagged, and Bradlaugh's decision to contest one of the borough's parliamentary seats in 1868 was not quite as 'natural' as is often assumed. Chartism did not go unsupported — both Gurney and Bates were active in the local movement — and in Northampton as elsewhere it was fuelled by economic distress and popular resentment over the Poor Law reform of 1834 which, in theory at least, denied relief to the able-bodied poor except on the harsh conditions of the workhouse. 'Had not the Whigs', asked one local Chartist in 1840, 'backed by the bloody Priests of the country, given them a new Poor Law to throw them on their own resources, after they had been deprived of every resource left to them?'.[42]

Even so, it never commanded the same level of support in Northampton as it did, for instance, in Manchester, Leeds and Leicester. The Chartist candidate in the 1841 general election polled only 176 votes, and the six who contested the 1843 municipal elections 36 between them. Electoral support is only a part of the measure, of course, and from the viewpoint of the authorities mass meetings and demonstrations were much more threatening. In April 1848 they felt compelled to swear in hundreds of special constables and to hold the military in readiness at the Barracks for a demonstration coinciding with the Chartist National Convention in London. Attended by around 2,500 people in heavy rain, it was punctuated by 'murmurs of dissent from the moral force doctrine', and the local leader James Pebody was shouted down when he spoke against the 'physical force' faction at a meeting soon afterwards. Nevertheless, the attitude of the town was perhaps best summarised by another local leader, Thomas Phillips, at the same meeting. 'For men to assert that the working classes of Northampton were willing to die for the Charter . . .', he said, 'was a gross falsehood'.[43]

In the view of the *Mercury*, local support for Chartism was limited by 'the good sense which is characteristic of Englishmen . . . a thorough conviction that 'Universal Suffrage' is not the specific by which all the ailments of our body politic are likely to be cured'.[44] A more accurate answer may lie in the country areas from whence came the majority of still vote-less migrants into the town and into the footwear trade in particular. There were notable exceptions like the Bouveries of Delapre and the Wakes of Courteenhall, who shared the Whiggery of the Spencers and other greater gentry, but many rural areas and the county magistracy in particular were dominated by a closely-knit group of lesser gentry and clergy, often related by marriage and Tory and Anglican to a man.[45] It was this alliance between such as the Knightleys, the Gunnings and Cartwrights and the Rev. Litchfield which financed and directed the *Northampton Herald*; and it was their 'consistent and enduring toryism' which reinforced a long tradition of rural anticlericalism, expressed in the countryside itself in opposition to enclosures, tithes and church rates.

Translated to the town, it had more than a little in common with the anti-Church, anti-Toryism of Liberal Nonconformist employers and political leaders — sufficient, perhaps, not only to swell the ranks of Nonconformity itself, but to mute the Chartist appeal to class conflict and to delay the emergence of a self-conscious labour movement until later in the century. The Religious Census of 1851 suggests something of the weight of Nonconformity in mid-century Northampton: of those attending evening services on Census Sunday, more likely to attract working-class worshippers after a week's toil than the morning, the Church of England claimed 31%, the Baptists 25%, the Wesleyans 20%, and the Independents 12%. Even so, allowing for those who attended more than one service on that day, it seems likely that some 50% of the town's inhabitants attended no place of worship at all, falling into that group described by Horace Mann, compiler of the Census, as 'unconscious secularists'.[46]

For some, however, as yet small in numbers, secularism was a conscious choice, expressed through formal freethinking organisations like the local branch of the Owenite Universal Community of Rational Religionists. Formed in 1839, Gurney was its secretary from 1840-42, but it was one of the latest branches to be formed and one of the smallest, and the movement as a whole·declined after the failure of Robert Owen's Land Scheme in 1846. It was followed in 1847 by a branch of the Society of Theological Utilitarians, founded by G. J. Holyoake, who lectured in Northampton on several occasions; and in 1854 by the Northampton Secular Society in which Gurney and Bates once again played a prominent role. In 1859, when they first invited Bradlaugh to lecture in the town, it had around 70 members — although in the opinion of one correspondent to the *Herald* soon after, 'there are nearly 1,000 persons in this town professing more or less infidel opinions'.[47] Secularism was now enjoying something of a national revival, led by Bradlaugh himself, who was also promoting the radical cause through the pages of his *National Reformer*, but neither Free-thought nor political radicalism had to be numerically strong to be influential.

As the Tory municipal victory of 1855 demonstrated, if the 'Ultras' could not win elections on their own account, they could split the vote sufficiently to ensure that the Liberals lost them. Until 1868 municipal politics were the main arena of contest between them, with consequences which are more fully discussed elsewhere, but Freethought and Nonconformity were never mutually exclusive. When Chartism spent its force in 1848 Nonconformist radicals like Pickering Phipps Perry and the Rev. Thomas Phillips joined forces with Gurney and Bates and Pebody to contest local elections, and in 1857 this same radical alliance secured the election to Parliament of the Quaker Charles Gilpin as an 'extreme' Liberal, and of Gurney to the municipal corporation. Nonconformists also worked alongside Free-thinkers in the Northampton Town and County Freehold Land Society — of which more will be said later — and the local branch of the National Reform League. Established in July 1866, it claimed over 500 members by October of that year, and at a demonstration in November Bradlaugh and Gurney shared the platform with moderate Liberals such as John Middleton Vernon and M. P. Manfield.

The Reform Bill, said Bradlaugh, was 'intended to attack the sham of class distinction ... every man in the State should have a voice in the making of the laws he was compelled to obey ...'.[48] By extending the vote to the male urban working classes it increased the parliamentary electorate of Northampton from under 3,000 to over 6,000, embracing many of those whose rural background was likely to incline them towards Liberalism; and that done, said the local Reform League committee in February 1868, it would see 'how the new Bill works before taking any new political action'.[49] In June, however, at a meeting in Market Square chaired by John Bates, Bradlaugh forced the pace by announcing his intention to contest a Northampton seat at the forthcoming general election. He ended fifth of six in the poll, ahead of the rival candidate promoted by the Nonconformist wing of the League, F. R. Lees, but in little doubt as to the nature of the task ahead. Freethought alone did not have the numbers to elect him: he needed the support of Nonconformist Liberals, and it would not be readily forthcoming.

'NONCONFORMISTS OF NORTHAMPTON. You are earnestly requested to support Charles Bradlaugh, and are told he correctly represents your views', as one handbill put it, 'You are now asked to show that in your minds the man who in ribald and offensive language has blasphemed God, and held up to ridicule all that you profess to hold sacred, is a man on whom you are prepared to confer honour — in whom you are ready to place trust'.[50] Would they do so? Not in sufficient numbers to elect him until 1880, and only then as an act of self-preservation, for as P. P. Perry declared in 1874, much as he 'deprecated personal infidelity ... there was one thing he feared far more than what was called freethinking ... THAT WAS SACERDOTALISM'.[51] The compromise induced by this fear of 'priestly rule' and Bradlaugh's subsequent battle to take his seat in Parliament belong elsewhere in this volume; but contrary to the impression which parliamentary politics alone may give, the Anglican/Conservative alliance remained alive and active in Northampton, and in other areas of town life it was still very much a force to be reckoned with. In the parish vestries, for instance, and many a battle was fought there over the issue of compulsory church rates until they were abolished in 1868. The 'English Church Robbery Bill', wrote the *Herald* of a measure to abolish them in 1835, which was defeated by only five votes, a part of the 'slow but stealthy and deleterious progress by which the Test Acts, the Emancipation Bill, and the Reform Bill, made their way in Parliament till the enemies of the state were ultimately victorious ...'.[52] The 'principle which now recognises a Church in connection with the State would be abandoned', wrote the Rev. Litchfield, 'and Protestan-tism would soon cease to be the great law of England'.[53] Like many Anglicans, he feared Catholicism or 'Popery' still more than Nonconformity, but the views of the latter were amply conveyed in a petition to Parliament from the Corporation in 1840, claiming that 'all persecution for conscience sake including forced contributions levied by one dominant sect in aid of their own exclusive tenets upon other classes of professing Christians [is] contrary to the doctrines and example of Jesus Christ, calculated to impede the progress of religion, destructive of humane and neighbourly feelings, opposed to common justice, and dangerous to all good Government'.[54]

On several occasions, usually by forcing a poll of the parish, they succeeded in preventing the rate from being levied: in St Sepulchre and All Saints in 1837, for instance, and in St Giles in 1854; but in All Saints in 1849 James Pebody and a number of other radicals went to prison rather than pay it.[55] Freethinkers were as much opposed to church rates as Nonconformists, but if they won the eventual victory here, the Church drew well ahead in the educational race. Under the Althorp Act of 1833 both denominations had the advantage of government grants in aid of school buildings, and in 1839, largely through the efforts of the vicar, the Rev. William Wales, a new parochial school with 150 places was opened in All Saints, the most populous of the town's parishes. This was followed in 1844 by an infant school in the adjacent parish of St Katharine, and in 1845 by mixed schools in the northern parish of St Sepulchre, where an influx of 'poor working people, the chief part shoemakers, the rest labourers and mechanics' continued to swell its own population.[56]

The Nonconformists opened a new 600-place British School on The Mounts in 1846, and in 1851, according to a survey by the London *Morning Chronicle*, a total of 3,552 children were attending Northampton's denominational day schools and Sunday schools, with the Nonconformists claiming 1,296 of them, the Catholics 150, and the Anglicans 2,186.[57] Around two-thirds of all children under 10 were still lacking provision, but almost 2,000 more places were provided between 1851-71, and by the Anglicans alone: in St Peter's in 1855; in St Andrew's and St Edmund's, where much new residential building was taking place, in 1858; and in St Giles', where a new parochial school was supplemented by the 'Mission Schools' established in an old warehouse in Dychurch Lane by the vicar, the Rev. W. H. F. Robson, in an endeavour to alter the 'unenviable character' of some of his parishioners.[58] A new parochial school was also opened in 1866 just beyond the borough boundaries in the rapidly growing suburb of St James's End.

In the borough itself almost 80% of elementary education was provided in Church schools in 1870, and their pupils included many children of Nonconformists, the question of religious education amicably resolved by the Anglican practice of offering instruction 'without forcing it on any children that did not belong to them'.[59] However, providing school places was one thing, and securing attendance something else altogether. Fees were often waived in the case of the very needy, but 'trifling' as they might be, many parents could scarcely afford to lose the wages their children could otherwise earn. The following extracts from the Log Book of the British School are also typical of the experience of the voluntary schools: 'Small attendance . . . military review'; 'St George's Fair . . . thin attendance'; Soldier's funeral . . . thin in consequence'; and 'Attendance this week is only 66, that is, 211 less than last week in consequence of the Races'.[60]

The sons and daughters of the shoemakers shared the culture of their fathers; but government grants were based in part on average attendance, and 'the loss of grant . . . will be more than the school fees for the week'. This was ever a cause of concern, but when they did attend some pupils were difficult to instruct. 'The boys who attend this School', wrote an Inspector of the St James's Church School in 1866, 'are so unruly that the Master must exercise the utmost firmness and good temper to bring them into proper habits of discipline'.[61] At the British School girls and boys alike were regularly caned for such misdemeanours as 'sliding in the infants' playground and coming in late in consequence', for playing truant, and for 'careless work'.[62] Nevertheless, despite all the difficulties, literacy rates for both males and females continued to move upwards. Based on Anglican marriage registers, and assuming a lapse of 10 years between leaving school and marriage, they moved in line with the expansion in provision: from 81% and 69% respectively in the decade between 1851-60, to 85% and 78% between 1861-70, and 89% and 84% in 1871-80 — while on the basis of civil registers, literacy rates for Nonconformists in the latter decade were as high as 95% and 92%.[63]

There was still room for improvement, and there was still a shortfall in places, but when the Northampton School Board was formed in 1871 it found its task much easier than many. Like the Board schools, however, the voluntary schools aimed to teach more than the subjects on the formal curriculum. 'The political economist, the philanthropist, and the Christian, have powerful reasons to impart knowledge to the ignorant', wrote the Committee of the British School in 1851, which was supported by subscriptions from prominent citizens of both political persuasions: Thomas Grundy and Thomas Hagger, for instance, and Conservative advocates of unsectarian religious education like Dr. Archibald Robertson of the Infirmary and the solicitor and future Town Clerk John Jeffery. Many were also active in the Borough Council, the Improvement Commission or on the Poor Law Board, and they were honest enough about their aims. 'The stability of government, economy in the administration of laws, security of property . . .', they declared, 'all these depend on the intelligence and moral character of the mass of the people; indeed, there is no mode conceivable or possible by which a community can be rendered free, prosperous, and happy, except by knowledge and virtue'.[64]

Knowledge and virtue — the knowledge, that is, of one's proper place in society, and the virtue of accepting it; and the governing middle classes did have 'powerful reasons' for seeking to impart it. They were governing from a position of insecurity, and they were well aware of it. Pressed on the one side by a still-powerful aristocracy, they were faced on the other by the labouring classes, 'now brought into large masses, and possibly increasing facilities for mischief' in the towns.[65] Between 1831 and 1871 the population of Northampton grew from around 15,000 to over 40,000, the latter figure representing a six-fold increase since 1801. 'Physical strength lies in the governed', as the political philosopher William Paley observed in 1785, it 'wants only to be felt and roused, to lay prostrate the most ancient and confirmed kingdom';[66] but if the sheer numbers of the urban masses were frightening in themselves, their evident addiction to debauchery, depravity and vice of all kinds was more alarming still.

These were generalised complaints, but in artisanal towns like Northampton, where workers had yet to be confined to factories and regular working hours and their leisure was taken at will, much of it was spent not only in the public houses — said to be haunts of all kinds of vice beyond that of drinking itself — but also in the streets, where their 'degenerate' behaviour was exposed to full public view. Here, young and old alike, they gambled, fought each other, committed unspecified 'gross amoralities', and invaded the peace and privacy of private homes with 'oaths, curses and indecencies'.[67] In 'the lowest parts of London', wrote the *Good Words* correspondent in 1869, 'I never heard such a general superfluity of obscene naughtiness issuing from youthful lips as I heard during my stay in Northampton'. After nightfall, he continued, 'its noble Market Square is disgraced by scenes of juvenile depravity quite as shameless as those which ever and anon, when police supervision has grown slack, may be witnessed after church-time on Sunday evenings in the Westminster Road'.[68]

After nightfall, too, complained one resident of the town in 1847, the public streets descended into a 'very disgraceful state . . . Dissolute women and groups, nay swarms of young people, obstruct or sweep the pavements'.[69] After nightfall, it may be added, these dreadful goings-on were illuminated in a 'flood of radiance' from the street lighting paid for by the Improvement Commission and provided by the Gas-Light Company;[70] but that did not make them any more reassuring. What the masses did out of sight was perhaps more worrying still, but unless it involved encounters with the opposite sex — even no closer than the mutual inspection conducted during their parading of the streets — the way in which females passed their free time was of less concern than the activities of their menfolk. Their patterns of work, and thus of leisure, were often quite different, and what little of it married women enjoyed was often spent on their own doorsteps, with the social life of church or chapel and the customary high days and holidays of town life offering wider diversions. However, women were still so firmly excluded from the world of organised politics that the notion that they might be plotting revolution was barely conceivable.

Some of the masses were no doubt as intemperate, shiftless and depraved as they were said to be. The working classes themselves distinguished between the 'respectable' and the 'rough', just as the shoemakers had their own distinct hierarchy with rivetters, lasters and finishers ranking only a little above rough-stuff cutters; but middle-class concern with their morals was perhaps a better measure of their own feelings of insecurity than of reality. 'Civil authority', as Paley also noted, 'is founded in opinion'; that is, in values shared by both governed and governors to an extent that the 'many' would submit to the rule of the 'few' of their own free will. They could not all be coerced, but in an industrial and urban setting the bonds of paternalism and patronage and personal contact which had tied society together were strained if not altogether broken, and the new governing classes had in effect to create an 'opinion' of their own, by raising up new values and standards and persuading the masses to accept them. If they did so, they were in effect conceding the right of their governors to impose them, their legitimate right to govern — and thus demonstrating their 'knowledge and virtue'. A failure to do so, an unshakeable attachment to their own standards of conduct, implied that the few were not beyond challenge and might yet be dislodged — and therein lay their 'ignorance and vice'.

The less secure the middle classes felt, the more ignorant and depraved the masses were found to be, and the greater the effort to 'civilise' them. They felt safer with the decline of Chartism, but they were never complacent, and in Northampton as elsewhere an enormous amount of time and money was invested in efforts to 'improve' or 'rescue' the working classes and to otherwise instill in them those Victorian virtues which their masters preached without always practising: self-help, industry, thrift and sobriety. 'Respectability' in short; but many such efforts were inspired as much by genuine humanitarianism and a sense of the duty of wealth to poverty as an 'urge to control', and it would be quite wrong to ignore this. Sobriety and thrift and education could improve the quality of life, but if many of the working classes could work this out unaided, the poor could not easily finance their own 'improving' institutions. And if some forms of 'vice' were the result of financial rather than moral destitution — as the 'respectable and benevolent gentlemen' of the Northampton Society for the Suppression of Prostitution recognised — then the destitute could not easily rescue themselves.

Formed in 1838 with the aim of 'restoring to virtue and comfort such of the numerous unfortunate girls haunting our streets, as may be anxious to abandon their present mode of life', the 'penitentiary' proposed to this end may account for the Society's apparently brief existence .[71] There was something of the double standard in it too, but the Northampton Mechanics' Institute, opened in 1833 with the object of instructing working men in 'the principles of the arts they practice, and in the various branches of science and useful knowledge', was a more successful venture.[72] 'It is for us to erect institutions for the education of the people . . . so that useful knowledge, and virtuous conduct, may take the place of ignorance and vice', wrote one of the town and county gentlemen who gave it their support — for Northampton 'stands alone, content with the degraded condition of its working classes. The patrons of that town . . . seem to deem the cultivation of a cauliflower, the magnitude of a melon, or the varieties of a violet, objects alone worthy of the public'.[73]

The Institute's patrons included its first President the Marquis of Northampton, the editor of the *Mercury* G. J. de Wilde, and Lord Althorp and Sir William Wake. The bulk of its income came from donations or subscriptions from the wealthier sections of the community, but for 1s. 6d. a quarter working men could have the use of a reading room and a library with some 9,000 volumes by 1850, and at 6d. a time, access to lectures on philosophy and the arts as well as scientific subjects. With 300 members within three months it soon had to abandon its rented schoolroom in Horsemarket for larger premises in King Street, moving thence to George Row in 1844 and to its final resting place in the Corn Exchange in 1852. In fact, so much was it flourishing by 1839, and now so much of a Liberal Nonconformist affair, that the Rev. Wales founded a rival Conservative and Anglican organisation, the Northampton Society for the Diffusion of Religious and Useful Knowledge, and by undercutting the Institute's subscriptions by 6d. a quarter he succeeded in relieving it of a significant number of members.

Even so, the 300 claimed by the Society in 1849 was still only half the number of the Institute, and although it outlived the latter, it was never really equal to the challenge. Like its counterparts elsewhere, however, the Mechanics' Institute went far to defeat its own objectives. At 6d. a month membership was largely limited to the already industrious, sober and thrifty. The 'sinners' could not afford to be reformed, but when subscriptions were reduced in 1852 to 1s. a quarter to make it more accessible, the influx of new working-class members was matched by an exodus of the middle-class members who were the Institute's financial bedrock. Those who paid the piper expected to call the tune, and as one speaker declared to a meeting of Wellingborough shoemakers in 1859, Mechanics' Institutes were 'a kind of middle class affair altogether . . . their lecturers seldom lecture on those subjects which concern your bread and cheese'.[74]

If middle-class efforts such as this did not provide what the working classes wanted, they could always abandon them — or they could take them over instead. By 1876 the Mechanics' Institute was offering bagatelle, billiards and draughts instead of lectures, but its members were still leaving. In 1869, on the other hand, faced with the alternative of closing it or allowing it to be 'reconstructed on popular principles', the gentlemen patrons of the Northampton Working Men's Club in St Giles Street chose the second option, and working men began to flock to it.[75] The Club originated in a reading room and evening class established in 1863 by the Rev. Robson, vicar of St Giles, who secured a donation of £500 — the proceeds of his latest novel — from Major Whyte-Melville of Wootton Hall, towards the building of the W.M.C. proper in 1865. The bulk of the running costs were initially provided by 'honorary members' — undivided here by politics or religion, they included M. P. Manfield and the Conservative alderman and carriage-maker Francis Mulliner — and ordinary members paid a subscription of only ½d. a week.

9. Northampton Working Men's Club, St Giles Street/Fish Street. Built in 1865 with a donation of £500 from Major Whyte-Melville of Wootton Hall.

However, the Club failed to flourish. Like other such bodies, it was intended as a diversion from the public house, and alcohol was barred from the premises — until 1869, that is, when the Committee decided to provide it at cost price, and to place the management of the Club in the hands of its ordinary members. Their numbers quickly increased, and in due course it was boasting musical and sports societies, a debating club and other evidence that the working classes had aspirations and organisational skills of their own. Middle-class patronage continued, but on working class terms and increasingly on political lines. M. P. Manfield, elected as a borough M.P. in 1891, served as President of the W.M.C. for 25 years, and by 1893 it too was regarded as such a hot-bed of Liberalism that the Conservatives founded one of their own.

More effort and infinitely more faith was invested in providing 'diversionary' leisure facilities than in outright attempts to suppress popular amusements, if only because this was likely to provoke outrage from beyond the town itself. Large public gatherings were always a source of anxiety, but the Races, for instance, were highlights of the county social calendar as well as an occasion for much lower-class drinking, gambling and general merriment. The annual fairs and regular markets, too, drew in large numbers from the county, and they were no more willing to have their own amusements restricted than the townspeople themselves. Here, of course, they could always count on the support of local publicans. Under new Licensing Laws in 1872, for instance, the justices reduced the opening hours of the town's pubs by $44\frac{1}{2}$ hours a week, requiring them *inter alia* to close at 11p.m.; this, it was claimed in a petition from the Licensed Victuallers Association, was simply too early for the convenience of market day visitors.[76]

Bound by ties of Conservatism as well as profit, they were naturally backed by the brewers, but the temperance lobby in the town was always a force to be reckoned with. The Northampton Total Abstinence Society claimed over 200 members in 1844, and an attendance of more than 400 at a lecture on the 'physical, intellectual and moral advantages arising from abstinence from all alcoholic liquors'.[77] The Northamptonshire Temperance Union, which counted the former Chartist J. H. Hollowell amongst its most active members, operated on a larger scale later in the century, but the town clergy could always find common ground on this issue. The counter-petition to the L.V.A. in 1872 was signed by the Rev. Robson and the Rev. H. S. Gedge, curate of All Saints, as well as the ministers of Doddridge Chapel, Prince's Street Baptist, and the Unitarian congregation which counted the Manfield family among its members — and on this occasion at least they had their way.

There was little competition to the pubs as yet from commercial leisure ventures, though these were not quite so sparse as the claim of Thomas's Music Hall in 1867 to be 'the Only Place of Entertainment Open in the Town' might suggest.[78] The Theatre Royal, for instance, opened in Marefair in 1806, was popular not only for its on-stage dramas but for the opportunities it afforded to drop orange peel, lighted paper and other objects onto higher-paying patrons in the pit.[79] However, the Mechanics' Institute, the Useful Knowledge Society and the W.M.C. were far from the only means by which the town's governing classes attempted to re-create the bonds of patronage and paternalism. There were, for instance, the Rifle Volunteer Corps, formed originally in county areas in as a means of promoting 'good feelings' between the gentry and their tenants, and finding little favour at first in urban centres of Nonconformity. Both Northampton and Kettering were castigated for unpatriotic 'apathy', but in 1860 Isaac Campbell and Co. formed their own corps, and E. H. Barwell, Captain of the 5th Northamptonshire, also recruited from his Eagle Foundry workforce.[80]

The Rifle Corps in turn stimulated the growth of brass bands, a means in themselves of encouraging feelings of loyalty to their patrons or to the community — and altogether too successfully on occasion. In the first brass band contest held in Northampton in 1861 the band of the town-based 4th Northamptonshire Rifles was attacked by the crowd at the end of the proceedings, having subjected it to the humiliation of coming second to the Thrapston Nene Side Foundry Band. Complaints of the ungentlemanly practice of using professional players were also rife in this area, and the Northampton United Band, which won a contest 'as expected' in Leicester in 1859, was deprived of its victory at Peterborough soon afterwards for allegedly having two within its ranks. However, the bands flourished, and ten of them turned out to accompany the Christmas Waits 1862, amid many complaints of 'pandemonium' and, of course, 'riotous debauchery'.[81]

Athletics, another activity promoted in the cause of healthy minds as well as bodies, also drew complaints from some quarters — of 'naked' young men training on Sundays[82] — but in general it was very popular with participants and spectators alike. The Northampton and County Amateur Athletic Club was founded in 1863 under the patronage of such leading citizens as the Liberal shoe manufacturer Richard Turner, William Rice, who took over the Eagle Foundry in the 1870s, and Thomas Phipps and his son-in-law, the Conservative councillor and stationer Mark Dorman. One of the oldest athletic clubs in the country, it held an annual August Bank Holiday Monday fete, with prizes for 'Gentlemen Amateur' competitors donated by its patrons, and additional entertainment provided by bicycle races and the ubiquitous brass bands.[83] Mark Dorman was also President of the Northampton Gymnastic Club, founded a few years later with M. P. Manfield as Vice-President. At 1gn. a year subscription it was rather an exclusive affair, but the public could still admire its performances of the 'various exercises' taught by a professional gymnast.[84]

Cricket, another import to the town from the estates of the county gentry, was also popular, with the Northampton Town XI, successor to a club formed in the 1820s, taking pride of place among a plethora of local clubs formed by tradesmen, churches, chapels and Sunday schools and the like. By the 1870s the more wealthy of them were renting prepared pitches from the Town XI, which leased a portion of the Racecourse, a part of the town's common lands, from the Corporation — an arrangement which later embroiled it in a lengthy dispute with the Freemen who still held rights of pasture here. At 12s. 6d. a game, complained 'One of the Working Class' in 1872, this was a 'very bad way to encourage cricket', but spectators were not yet charged for admission, and working class players could always resort to the 'rough', where grazing cattle often added to the excitement. 'I cannot send my children there to play, or take my wife for a walk', one resident complained in 1867, 'The parish bull is still at large. Freeman's Common will not be properly and decently conducted until a Trustee is gored'.[85]

The commons also included Cow Meadow and Midsummer Meadow to the south and the New Commons on the Bedford Road, and despite such hazards they were much used for recreation. For those who wished for land to cultivate, however, there was the Artisans' and Labourers' Friend Society, founded in 1842 at the instigation of Henry Billington Whitworth, banker and first Treasurer to the reformed Corporation, with the aim of fostering habits of 'industry, prudence, and economy'. Here too its patrons were drawn from both sides of the political and religious divide. John Becke, Liberal Churchman, solicitor and long-time Borough Coroner was among the most active, but its early Committee also included the Rev. Wales, Dr. Robertson, E. H. Barwell, Samuel Percival and the former Liberal mayor and engineer to the Gas-Light Company, Thomas Sharp, joined in 1848 by James Pebody and another leading Chartist, George Bass. The Society rented out land to working men as allotments, and on the strictest of terms. It was to be cultivated 'to the satisfaction of the Committee', but never on a Sunday and on the understanding that members convicted of poaching, theft or drunkenness would be promptly expelled.[86]

By 1850 the Society had 248 allotments covering some 50 acres, and was controlled by a Committee of 'gentlemen' and working men in equal numbers. Most ordinary members were shoemakers, their physical health now much improved by fresh air, exercise and a cheap supply of fresh vegetables, and their morals similarly elevated, it was said, by 'diverting them from the public house and the beer shop'.[87] It is quite possible, of course, that the Society attracted those who were already industrious, prudent and economical, but there were certainly genuine benefits to be had from it. It also operated a Coal Fund during the summer, and a year-round Provident Fund with contributions of 1d. a week repaid at interest of 4% on reaching the age of 60, when many would otherwise face the prospect of the Workhouse and a pauper's funeral. Indeed, so successful was this aspect of its work that in the 1880s it began to advance money to members on the security of freehold houses or land, enabling many to realise the dream of becoming their own landlords.

Others achieved this through the different route of the Northampton Town and County Freehold Land Society, but here the objective of changing the habits and elevating the tastes of the masses was underpinned by another which was openly political: 'a stake in the Country, and a voice in the Election of Members of Parliament'. Founded in 1848, the Northampton Society followed the model of the Birmingham Freehold Land Society, a Chartist-inspired body formed in the 1830s with the aim of extending the vote to some of the still-excluded urban working classes by enabling them to qualify as freeholders of property to the value of at least 40s. a year. Subscriptions of 1s. 6d. a week were allowed to accumulate until there were funds enough to purchase a sizeable plot of freehold land. This was then divided into allotments of equal size, and offered to 'members good upon the books, according to seniority of membership' at a charge of around $2\frac{1}{2}$d. — or as Joseph Gurney put it, a pint of beer — a foot — with the option of paying on a mortgage executed by the Society's Trustees.[88]

The actual plots were allocated by ballot, but once in possession the holder could do with it what he would: 'he may erect a Cottage, cultivate a Garden, etc., etc. — either occupy it himself or let it to others'.[89] And vote, of course; and the Northampton Freehold Land Society was very much a Liberal affair. Thomas Sharp served as President until 1864, to be succeeded in turn by Charles Gilpin, Henry Labouchere, Joseph Gurney, and M. P. Manfield. Its early Committee included Gurney, Bates and Pebody, and its Trustees the Liberal grocer and Improvement Commissioner Gray Hester and the shoe manufacturer George Moore. Thomas Grundy was also involved with it, as was the hatter and Borough Councillor Peter Derby, who struck republican horror into the hearts of the Whigs by refusing to wear his ceremonial gown during the visit of Queen Victoria to Northampton in 1844 — although he was simply protesting, he said, at the amount of money the Corporation had spent on the occasion.[90] John Dyer, Master of the British School, was its Secretary, William Shoosmith, future Liberal Town Clerk, its solicitor, and the Northamptonshire Union Bank of the Percival brothers its Treasurer.

It was no doubt true, as Grundy claimed, that there were many of the other party's voters among its members; but in 1851 the Conservatives responded by forming the Northamptonshire Permanent Benefit Building Society, which enjoyed powers common to such bodies of buying and selling land. Commonly known as 'Pierce's Society' after its long-time manager, the Conservative councillor W. J. Pierce, it had its successes — but they were modest by comparison with the progress of the F.L.S. The Society took possession of its first two estates either side of the Kingthorpe Road at Primrose Hill in January 1851, with a procession from the town centre 'headed by an excellent band. A considerable crowd followed . . . some of the 'mauvais sujets' of which behaved very disgracefully, pelting the members with matters more tangible than their foul language'.[91] It had 152 members at this time, 390 and a branch society at Kettering by February 1852, and close to 500 in the following year when it purchased more sites on the Billing Road, opposite the General Lunatic Asylum, and at Far Cotton. The Holt's Field estate to the south of Primrose Hill

NORTHAMPTON
TOWN AND COUNTY
FREEHOLD LAND SOCIETY

PRESIDENT---RAIKES CURRIE, ESQ., M.P.

AT THE

MEETING

OF THE ABOVE SOCIETY,

To be held on Monday, January 13th, 1851, in the Hall, Newland, Northampton,

JAMES TAYLOR, ESQ.,

Of Birmingham (the Originator of the Freehold Land Movement), will attend.

Thos. Grundy, Esq. Vice President,

Will preside.---Chair to be taken at half-past SIX o'Clock.

PROCESSION
AT THREE O'CLOCK.

TEA, ONE SHILLING EACH, AT HALF-PAST 4.

ADMISSION TO THE MEETING, THREEPENCE EACH.

FOR FURTHER PARTICULARS, SEE OTHER BILLS.

10. Northampton Town and County Freehold Land Society poster, 1851.

was added in 1860, but by then the Society had already advanced hundreds of pounds to members to enable them to build houses on their allotments.

Its original objective was overtaken by the extension of the suffrage in 1867 but, with over 1,000 more voters registered between 1852 and the Reform Act, this activity became more and more important. Nevertheless, even in mid-century the people of Northampton were already better housed than many, both in terms of the quality and quantity of dwellings. 'There are several of the back courts and alleys . . . which call for the interference of the sanitary reformer', noted the *Morning Chronicle* in 1851,[92] but the town was 'generally speaking, well built and clean', and new housing had kept pace with population growth to the extent that the average of 5.4 persons to each inhabited dwelling was only a fraction higher than in 1800. Even by 1835 there had been a 'vast increase' in working-class dwellings, most built within the line of the old town walls, but already spilling onto vacant land in the parishes of St Sepulchre and St Giles to the north and east.[93]

Small speculative builders provided most of them, but some operated on a more ambitious scale — like the versatile Mr. Grundy, who bought his own brickyard in the 1830s and developed his 'Newtown' estate on the Wellingborough Road in the 1850s, naming one of its six streets after the Liberal Prime Minister Lord Melbourne, and another for his local party colleague Edward Bouverie. Around 7% of adult males in Northampton were employed in the construction industry in 1851, and by then there were also some 500 houses on the town's extra-parochial land, catering mainly for middle-class occupiers who enjoyed immunity from the Poor Rate until 1857 as well as seclusion from the poor themselves. Even so, the residential segregation of the classes which was so advanced in London that the inhabitants of different districts were said to regard each other with 'much the same curiosity and astonishment as would nowadays be exhibited . . . at the appearance of an Esquimaux in Hyde Park',[94] was as yet much less marked in Northampton than in many other large towns.

By 1850 there were stretches of superior housing on the eastern fringes of the town — Victoria Place, Spencer Parade and the southern part of Cheyne Walk — and a little beyond them, on Billing Road, the Cliftonville estate, built in the 1840s on land sold by the Corporation with the proviso that only high-class dwellings should be erected. However, there was none of the mass exodus of the middle classes by which Leeds, for instance, was said to be deprived of the 'civilising influences and mutually respectful feelings' which might head off the development of self-conscious working class movements to reform or replace the capitalist system.[95] On the contrary, the governing classes of Northampton remained highly visible and busily 'civilising', and if not for this reason alone, open conflict between the classes remained as yet muted. And besides, complained one correspondent to the *Mercury* in 1846, there was such a 'peculiar want of suburban residences' in Northampton that those who would have liked to detach themselves from the masses really had nowhere to go.

No sooner did a suitable site for 'neat and genteel buildings' come onto the market than 'lo! up start square lath and plaster-looking deformities as near to the old "Northampton Rookery" pattern as possible'.[96] Of 'uniform appearance', it was said more politely in 1835, such housing was 'almost entirely occupied by journeyman shoemakers',[97] and here as elsewhere it was the staple trade which very largely dictated the built landscape of the town, dominated in Northampton not by the factory chimneys of northern industrial centres, but by the straight rows of five-or six-roomed houses which accommodated the domestic workshops of their occupants, interspersed with the warehouses and 'shops' which they served. Those who 'do not require shops or centrally-situated residences' might well hanker for suburban seclusion, and they might have the means to afford the higher rents and costs of transport; but shoemakers needed to live close to the source of their work, they needed functional housing at rents they could afford, and it was to their needs rather than the middle-class desire for 'country-looking dwellings' that the housing market was still responding.

Middle-class desires were gradually satisfied, but in 1915 Northampton was still notable for its 'row upon row of modern brick dwellings', to which the Freehold Land Society had made no few additions; but if these new dwellings were a little lacking in beauty, they had the advantage of newness and of the minimum building standards laid down by the Improvement Commission from the 1840s, and later improved upon in turn by those of the Borough Council. In matters of housing and the health of its occupants, prevention was better than cure and, given the limitations of 19th-century medical knowledge, it was certainly more pleasant. Among the standard treatments for cholera, for instance, were doses of castor oil, strychnine, carbolic acid, and injections of beef tea, 'as various as they were ineffective', noted Dr. Clifton, Medical Officer to the Northampton Homeopathic Dispensary in Abington Street, in 1866. On the principle of 'like cures like', the homeopathic remedies included camphor, copper and arsenic, claimed to be at least twice as effective as those of the conventional medical practitioners, the 'allopaths', with whom Dr. Clifton enjoyed a relationship of mutual contempt.

So 'illiberal' were they, he said, that the *Lancet* refused to publish letters from his colleagues elsewhere, and despite the difficulties of caring for the poor in their own homes, the Northampton Infirmary 'resolutely shuts its doors' against his patients unless they agreed to abandon all homeopathic treatment.[98] In fact, despite its charitable intentions, the Infirmary was not easily accessible to the town's working classes. Originally sited in George Row, its 40 beds were increased to 60 by an extension to the building in 1750, and in 1793 it was replaced by a new 70-bed hospital on the Billing Road. Costing over £12,000, 'nearly all the contractors became bankrupts through loss in the undertaking', but additions to the building had brought its total beds to 100 by 1850. However, patients were normally admitted only on the 'tickets' dispensed by subscribers to the hospital, and this was a form of patronage which many were unable or unwilling to use. This did not apply to casualties, but the Infirmary served the county as well as the town, and in common with most such institutions it also excluded certain categories of patients: children under seven, 'incurables', most midwifery cases, and those with infectious diseases.[99] Its beds were still tied up for lengthy periods while patients recovered from surgery, with the benefit of anaesthesia from 1847, or until medicine or rest and a proper diet effected a cure.

The mentally ill were in some ways more fortunate. Until 1876, when they were moved to the new County Asylum at Berry Wood, pauper lunatics were treated at the Northampton General Lunatic Asylum, opened on the Billing Road in 1838 and also much reliant on subscriptions from town and county. The hospital was also open to 'lunatics in the middling classes of society, and also to patients of the higher classes, paying liberally of course for their accommodation'; but pauper or not, said the *Morning Chronicle* in 1851, all were treated with 'great attention and kindness'. Here the hospital's first medical superintendent, Dr. Thomas Pritchard, pioneered a policy of total non-restraint, abandoning strait-jackets and ankle chains for a library, musical evenings and other amusements, and encouraging the inmates to teach each other reading, writing, Latin and German.[100] The Northamptonshire poet John Clare spent several years as an inmate, but so little confined that he became a familiar figure seated for hours at a time beneath the portico of All Saints' church.

Medical services provided through the Poor Laws after 1834 were otherwise tainted with the same stigma of improvidence as able-bodied pauperism. Those who could pay much preferred to do so, if not a private physician then on the 'provident principle' on which the Homeopathic Dispensary and its larger conventional medical rival, the Royal Victoria Provident Dispensary, were operated. Founded at the suggestion of John Becke to mark the

11. Northampton Royal Victoria Provident Dispensary, Albion Street. Built to mark the visit of Queen Victoria to Northampton in 1844, the funds devoted to the purpose were originally intended to provide a roast beef and plum pudding dinner for the poor of the town.

royal visit to the town in 1844, the £1,300 costs of building the Victoria Dispensary were raised by public subscriptions from 'gentry and tradesmen', and its governing body included Earl Spencer, E. H. Barwell, Mr. Becke himself and the Rev. Gedge. Middle-class 'honorary members' continued to support it, but in 1869 their subscriptions accounted for less than a tenth of its total income, with an unusually high proportion of the rest coming from the 2d. per week subscriptions of ordinary working-class members — over 5,500 of them by 1871.[101]

In exchange they could call on the services of three medical officers and of midwives, and in their own homes if need be: over 26,000 home visits were made in 1869. 'The poor set the greatest value upon the institution, as they feel a degree of independence in connection with it, which they would not were it conducted upon a merely charitable principle', it was noted in 1850;[102] and indeed they did, for charity implied an obligation to the giver which deterred many from accepting it. Opposing a move to exclude those capable of paying for private care, Mr. Becke thought it 'better to err on the side of too great liberality to those you desire to help',[103] but for its middle class sponsors the great virtue of the 'provident principle' lay in helping the poor to help themselves. 'To clothe the naked and feed the hungry is good', as the legend heading the rules of the Artisans' and Labourers' put it: 'but to teach the poor to clothe and feed themselves is better'.[104]

In the town's Friendly Societies, however, some of the working classes had long been practising the virtues now pressed on them from above. Drinking was an integral part of their meetings, normally held in a private room of a public house, but drunkenness was tolerated by none of them. If 'any member . . . shall enter the club room disguised in liquor, he shall forfeit 2d.', ran the rules of a Society based at the Shakespeare in Gold Street, and this was only one aspect of the 'respectable' behaviour they insisted upon. 'In order to preserve good decorum', declared the rules of the 'Friend in Deed' Society,

> no member shall be allowed to call a brother member any ill name . . . or cast any reflection on his birth, religion or circumstances . . . or use any provoking, insulting or obscene language, offer to lay wagers, promote gaming, talk of state affairs, or challenge anyone to work at his trade during meetings.[105]

Offenders were fined or expelled if they persisted, losing not only the society of their fellows but also their entitlement to the sickness and death benefits which were the basis of the Societies' activities.

For a monthly contribution of 1s. 3d. in 1819 the Shakespeare Society paid sickness benefits of 9s. a week for up to six months with lower rates afterwards, and a death benefit of £4 for a member and £2 for 'one wife only' — sufficient to avoid not only the immediate destitution into which illness or bereavement could plunge a family, but the ultimate social disgrace of a pauper funeral.[106] Benefits were usually refused in the case of illness or injury attributable to fighting, drink or venereal disease, and to stretch limited funds as far as possible none who were already ill, engaged in hazardous trades, or over the age of 30-35, were normally admitted. Many Societies also insisted on a minimum wage of 15-20s. a week, insuring their own income so far as possible but effectively excluding all but a fairly small group of artisans enjoying the luxury of regular and relatively well-paid work. In the earlier 19th century, of course, Friendly Societies were often craft societies in all but name, a cloak for trade union activities outlawed until the repeal of the Combination Acts in 1824, but others of later origin were less exclusive.

In Northampton they included Lodges of the Ancient Order of Foresters, the Manchester Unity of Oddfellows and the Wesleyan General Provident in addition to several purely local societies. Like the Northampton Progressivists Industrial Society, formed in 1861 by a merger of three small local co-operatives, they were largely formed and directed by working men themselves, and here they practised thrift and sobriety and other virtues for the same reasons that they took advantage of what the middle classes offered them — financial security and independence, an insurance against the exigencies of life, and a greater share of its comforts. However, the self-help which co-operatives and the Friendly Societies practised owed little to the narrow individualist gospel which gave the victory to the strong and let the weak go to the wall. 'To bear each other's Burthen's, to provide for each other's Necessities, and to sympathise with each other in Affliction', as the rules of the 'Friend in Deed' put it, 'be it our mutual concern — to maintain Unity, Peace and Concord, and to continue in Brotherly love, be it our constant aim — and may Heaven bless and prosper us'.[107]

Some did prosper, but many working-class organisations were defeated by limited finances, limited free time, and the same limited success in enlisting the 'rough' as the middle classes. With all our boasted improvements', wrote one of the latter in the 1860s, 'the mind, taste and feelings of vast masses of the people are as yet scarcely touched . . . habits the most grovelling continue to flourish. In the midst of civilisation [there is] a kind of barbarism — not abject or poverty-struck, but vigourous and self-willed'.[108] 'Too fond of displaying a spirit of independence', complained one shoe manufacturer of his workers in 1886, still much given to drink and 'debauchery', still taking 'fresh air' at their own will, and most importantly of all, still depriving him of control over his own output. Frustrating as this was, it did not yet pose a serious threat to his ability to compete. Indeed, by 1870 the local footwear industry was booming as never before, and as it prospered so did the town as a whole.

In the 1871 census adult male shoemakers accounted for around 43% of all adult males in the town, against 38% in 1861, while many others were employed in supplying the industry's needs, direct or indirect: curriers, mercers, clerical workers, transport workers, the construction workers who provided its warehouses and housed its workers, the gas-workers who illuminated their homes and workshops and their street life, and the breweries which refreshed them. Construction in particular provided the ironfounders with new markets beyond a thriving agricultural sector which continued to make its own substantial contribution to the prosperity of the town, selling at its markets and fairs, buying its goods and its services, and sharing in its social and cultural life.

For all the growth of its industry, Northampton still retained the role, and the atmosphere, of a market town. Before too long, however, both town and county would feel the effects of foreign competition and of the falling prices which marked the period of the 'Great Depression' for some 20 years after 1873; and as the shoe manufacturers were forced to compete on new terms, the shoemakers would have cause to remember the warning delivered by Isaac, Campbell and Co. in 1859. Machinery 'will and must be used', and the shoemakers must and would be gradually deprived of their cherished independence. Even in the confines of the factory they would not surrender it lightly; but the factories would in due course do more to change their habits than all the 'civilising' efforts of their masters. And when paternalism was confronted by fraternal self-help in the unwelcome form of trade unionism and socialism, the governing classes of Northampton would have to find new ways of promoting unity and maintaining the bonds of society.

Notes

1. *N.M.*, 7 June 1845.
2. Ibid.
3. Letter to Samuel Smiles, quoted in Hatley, V. A., 'Northampton Re-vindicated', *N.P.&P.*, Vol.2, 6 (1959).
4. Wake, J., *Northampton Vindicated, or Why the Main Line Missed the Town* (1935). Miss Wake was for many years Hon. Secretary of the Northamptonshire Record Society.
5. Leleux, R., *Regional History of the Railways of Great Britain*, Vol.9, The East Midlands (1976); *V.C.H.*, Vol.3, p.39.
6. 'Northampton Re-vindicated', op. cit.
7. *N.H.*, 7 April 1838.
8. *Northampton Vindicated*, op. cit.
9. 'Northampton Re-vindicated', op. cit.
10. Ibid.
11. Northampton Corporation (hereafter N.C.), Minutes, 8 Sept. 1838.
12. *N.M.*, 20 Aug. 1859.
13. For an account of this event, see Hold, T., 'The Royal Agricultural Show at Northampton', *N.P.& P.*, Vol.7 (1988-9).
14. Rhodes, J., *The Nene Valley Railway* (1983).
15. Published Census returns.
16. *N.H.*, 2 July 1853.
17. Hatley, V. A., 'Some Aspects of Northampton's History, 1815-50', *N.P.&P.*, Vol.3 (1965-6), p.246.
18. Published Census returns.
19. Hatley, V. A., 'Some Aspects of Northampton's History', op. cit., p.247.
20. *Boot and Shoe Record*, 11 Oct. 1890.
21. *An Appeal from the Northampton Society of Operative Cordwainers* (1838), (N.L.I.S. Footwear Collection).
22. Ibid.
23. PPXL (1852), p.289.
24. See Hatley, V. A., *The St Giles Shoe School*, Northampton Historical Series No.4 (1966).
25. PPXXII (1864), pp.122-6.
26. *N.M.*, 29 May 1859.
27. Ibid.

28. Manifesto of the Northampton Boot and Shoemakers' Mutual Protection Society (1859), reprinted in *Northampton Daily Echo*, 30 October 1929.
29. *Rules of the Northamptonshire Boot and Shoemakers' Mutual Protection Society* (1859), (N.L.I.S. Footwear Collection). For a counter-argument see Plummer, J., *Strikes and their Causes* (1859), (N.L.I.S. Footwear Collection).
30. Handbill, 1859, (N.L.I.S.).
31. PPXXII, op. cit., p.126.
32. *N.M.*, 12 Feb. 1859.
33. *N.M.*, 29 May 1859.
34. Quoted in George, D., *London Life in the Eighteenth Century* (1930), p.199.
35. *Shoe and Leather Record*, 22 Nov. 1890.
36. 'Snobopolis', reprinted with commentary by V. A. Hatley, Northampton Historical Series, No.1 (1966).
37. Arnold, W., *Recollections of William Arnold: A Northamptonshire Shoe Manufacturer's Autobiography* (1915).
38. *Boot and Shoe Trades Journal*, 10 Dec. 1892.
39. *N.M.*, 1 Dec. 1866.
40. *N.H.*, 12 Nov. 1853.
41. *N.M.*, 10 July 1841.
42. Ibid., 12 Dec. 1840.
43. *N.H.*, 6 April 1848.
44. *N.M.*, 29 Sept. 1838.
45. See Shorthouse, R. W., 'J.P.s in Northamptonshire, 1830-45, Part 1', *N.P.&P.*, Vol.5, 2 (1974).
46. PPLXXXIX (1852-53), cclvx.
47. *N.H.*, 1 Sept. 1860. See also Royle, E., 'Charles Bradlaugh, Freethought and Northampton', *N.P.& P.*, Vol.4, 3 (1980).
48. *N.M.*, 27 Oct. 1866.
49. Ibid., 22 Feb. 1868.
50. Undated handbill (N.L.I.S.).
51. *Northampton Radical*, 11 November 1874.
52. *N.H.*, 1 April 1837.
53. Ibid., 1837 cutting, otherwise undated.
54. N.C. Minutes, 7 Feb. 1840.
55. Handbill 1849 (N.L.I.S. 198-700).
56. Lawes, J., 'Voluntary Schools . . .', op. cit., p.89.
57. Quoted in *N.M.*, 1 Feb. 1851.
58. *N.H.*, 23 Jan. 1869.
59. *N.M.*, 21 Jan. 1871.
60. Speed, P. F., *Learning and Teaching in Victorian Times* (1964). (N.R.O., R.O.P. 557).
61. St James's Voluntary Provided Schools: Nineteenth Century Notes, (N.L.I.S. 1-75).
62. Speed, op. cit.
63. Hatley, V. A., 'Literacy at Northampton . . .', op. cit.
64. Report of the Committee of the Northampton British School (1851).
65. Quoted in Storch, R. D., 'The Problem of Working Class Leisure: Some Roots of Middle Class Moral Reform', McCann, P.(ed.), *Popular Education and Socialisation in the Nineteenth Century*.
66. Paley, W., *Principles of Moral and Political Philosophy* (1875), Book VI, Ch.2.
67. *N.M.*, 18 Sept. 1847.
68. 'Snobopolis', op. cit.
69. *N.M.*, 18 Sept. 1847.
70. Established 1823 by Thomas Sharp, civil engineer, and Richard Dennis, auctioneer. Several share-holders were also Improvement Commissioners. For a history of the Company, see Roberts, D. E., & Frisby, J. H., *The Northampton Gas Undertaking, 1823-1945*.
71. *N.M.*, 9 June 1838.
72. *Rules of the Northampton Mechanics Institute* (1833).
73. *N.M.*, 11 Aug. 1832.
74. Ibid., 12 March 1859.

75. Ibid., 25 Dec. 1869.
76. Ibid., 31 Aug. 1872.
77. Ibid., 29 June 1844.
78. Ibid., 23 Feb. 1867.
79. *Northampton Albion*, cited in Warwick, L., & Burman, A., *Northampton in Old Picture Postcards* (1988).
80. The first Rifle Volunteer Corps were formed in Devon in 1852, following the *coup d'etat* of Napoleon III.
81. *N.M.* 1 June 1861; 10 Sept. 1859; 27 Dec. 1862.
82. *N.H.*, 27 Sept. & 4 Oct. 1862.
83. Northampton Amateur Athletic Club poster (1873), (N.L.I.S. 1-571).
84. Northampton Gymnastic Club handbill (1868), (N.L.I.S. 1-571).
85. Sibley, G., *Northampton Club Cricket: A Centenary History* (1986).
86. *Rules of the Northampton Artisans' and Labourers' Friend Society* (1844).
87. Quoted in *N.M.*, 1 Feb. 1851.
88. Handbill, Northampton Town and County Freehold Land Society (1848) (N.L.I.S.).
89. Ibid.
90. Manuscript Diary of Municipal Politics, 1835-97 (N.L.I.S. 198-781).
91. *N.M.*, 18 Jan. 1851.
92. *Morning Chronicle*, quoted in *N.M.* 1 Feb. 1851.
93. PPXXV, Report on the Proposed Municipal Boundary . . ., op. cit.
94. Quoted in Perkin, H., *The Origins of Modern English Society, 1780-1880* (1974 edn.), p.174.
95. Ibid., p.173.
96. *N.M.*, 15 Aug. 1846.
97. PPXXV, Report on the Proposed Boundary . . ., op. cit.
98. Northampton Homeopathic Dispensary Annual Report (1865-6).
99. Northampton General Infirmary Annual Report (1853). See also Waddy, F. F., *A History of Northampton General Hospital, 1743-1948* (1974).
100. Quoted in *N.M.*, 1 Feb. 1851.
101. *N.H.*, 6 March 1869.
102. Unidentified newspaper cutting 1850, otherwise undated.
103. *N.H.*, 6 March 1869.
104. Rules of the Northampton Artisans' and Labourers' Friend Society (1844).
105. Rules and Orders of a Friendly Society held at the Shakespeare, Gold Street (1819).
106. Rules of the 'Friend in Deed' Friendly Society of Tradesmen (1828).
107. Shakespeare Society, op. cit.
108. 'Friend in Deed', op. cit.
109. William Chambers, quoted in Storch, R. D., op. cit.
110. *Shoe and Leather Record*, 5 June 1886.

Chapter Two

Separate Tables: Local Government and Municipal Reform

We wish we could state that persons of various politics, forgetting for the day the animosities of party, met at the same board; but as we were prepared to expect, while the Corporation and a party of Liberals, with the Mayor in the chair, dined at the George Hotel, the Conservatives held their festival at the Angel . . .

> *Northampton Mercury*, 30 June 1838, on the occasion of the Coronation of Queen Victoria

There is a growing disposition on the part of the Liberals who were dominant in the town, towards a close corporation and a self-elected body. (Cheers) A glimpse at the political horizon was sufficient to show that Radicals must figure greatly in the future of the nation.

> *Northampton Mercury*, 30 October 1869: Report of a Radical meeting

The first elections to the new Corporation in December 1835 'excited great interest in the town, but nothing like disorder occurred'.[1] Bolstered by a Tory victory in the North Northamptonshire constituency only days before, the *Herald* exhorted 'every true friend to the institutions of this country to rescue the town from the possibility of being placed under the domination of Radical tyranny . . .'. The *Mercury* welcomed the appearance of 'Gentlemen, in station far above those who have usually filled our municipal offices' among the Tories contesting the East ward, while the Tory candidates in the West assured the voters that 'we have not obtruded ourselves upon you from motives of personal ambition; we have only offered ourselves as candidates from the fear that you might (in our absence) be represented by a band of destructives whose greatest delight would be to see your sacred edifices levelled to the dust'.[2]

This so-called 'band of destructives' included Thomas Sharp, Thomas Grundy and the auctioneer Richard Dennis, part of an impressive array of Whig candidates also embracing Samuel Percival, William Parker, E. H. Barwell, and George Peach and Joseph Adnett, merchants in wool and corn respectively. On the Tory side, no less impressive, were Thomas and Richard Phipps, the solicitor Charles Markham, member of one of Northampton's oldest-established families, Hugh Higgins, Chamberlain of the old Corporation, Drs. Kerr, Robertson and Terry of the Northampton Infirmary, and the chemist George Barry, a leading figure in the Anglican Sunday School and Day School movement. 'Gentlemen' all, they were the economic and social elite of the town, testimony to the value of the prize.

This was not measured in terms of what the Corporation might do but in those of what it represented: antiquity, tradition, the pre-eminence enshrined in the chief citizenship held by the mayor, and the high moral ground over which the political and religious battles of the past decades had been fought. As a symbol of legitimate authority, of legitimate leadership in other spheres, it was almost beyond price, and political power in its body did not have to be used to be valued: it had only to be *possessed*. The Municipal Reform Act itself only served to encourage this view. Overly concerned with how the new bodies should be constituted and what they should not now do, it barely insisted on them doing anything at all. Control of charitable funds was transferred to boards of trustees, and although Northampton retained a separate Commission of the Peace, corporate influence was now largely restricted to the *ex officio* appointments filled by the Mayor and ex-Mayor, with other magistrates appointed direct by the Crown. At the same time it left other reponsibilities in the hands of local bodies untouched by the reform — in Northampton, the Improvement

Commission and the new Poor Law Board — and the corporations themselves with no direct powers to extend their activities by their own choice.

Unable to levy a rate or raise a loan for any purpose not specifically sanctioned by law, they had to acquire them through a Local Act or await the permissive powers conferred through a general Act. The municipal reform, in short, produced nothing akin to the instant 'revolution' often attributed to it. Even the franchise was carefully limited to a mainly middle class group of male ratepayers fulfilling a residential and property qualification, and the property qualifications attached to municipal office itself limited the pool of available candidates still further.[3] Even so, it could not be a mere device for handing political control of the boroughs from Tories to Whigs — or as they were now coming to call themselves, from Conservatives to Liberals. Both had to take their chances with an electorate, and in some towns it did produce an instant and quite dramatic transfer of power. In Leeds, for instance, the Whigs claimed 51 of 64 seats on the new corporation, and in Leicester 48 of 52. 'A Tory corporation will henceforth be as great a rarity in any of our large towns as a Whig one was a year ago', the *Mercury* declared with almost unmitigated delight, 'the exception in this instance only more clearly proves the rule . . .'.[4]

The exception 'in this instance' was Northampton itself. The Liberals took all six seats in the West Ward, but the Conservatives claimed four in the East and five in the South, splitting the 18 seats at stake evenly between them and ensuring that the first meeting of the new Council would be marked by a bitter struggle for its control. This rested in the first instance on the election of the six aldermen required to complete its numbers. A concession to the Tory-dominated House of Lords, the retention of indirectly-elected aldermen was something of a blot on the 'democratic' nature of the Municipal Reform Act for, as some members of the Corporation complained in 1842, it 'permits of Parties rejected by the Burgesses as Unfit and unworthy to represent them . . . to be elected by the Council . . . such Clause being . . . contrary to every principle of popular election . . . and subversive of common sense'.[5]

In practical terms it meant that a party deadlocked or defeated at the polls could still hold a majority in the Council, and when it convened for the first time at midnight on 31 December 1835, both were willing enough to use it. Equally determined to concede no ground to the other, however, the preliminary question of which should hold the chair was still unsettled some five hours later: with one 'chairman' on each side, 'question upon question was put, and decided by each party in its own favour . . . while the other party voted the contrary'. The aldermanic election proceeded in similar fashion, both proposing to elect all six from their own party until Town Clerk Theophilus Jeyes spelt out the alternatives: a compromise or the Court of King's Bench, with no certainty of the outcome save that the losing party would pay the costs of both. The aldermen too were divided equally between them. Control of the Council now turned on the mayoralty alone, and in the person of Alderman Charles Freeman, last mayor of the old Corporation, the Liberals conceded it to the Tories.[6]

With it they gained a moral victory of infinitely more importance than the casting vote on a hung council, and the Liberal councillors were throughly rebuked by the party rank-and-file for allowing them such an 'easy' triumph. It was a brief one, nonetheless. Councillors were elected for three years, but one in three had to retire annually — 'just enough', said the Manchester reformer Richard Cobden, 'to remind the other two, if they don't behave themselves, that their turn is coming'[7] — and in the 1836 municipal elections Thomas Hagger took a Tory seat in the South ward and gave the majority and the mayoralty to the Liberals. The new mayor marked his election by displaying the mace from a window at his home — 'Is it not true', asked the *Herald*, 'that Mr. George Peach had the mace placed beside him in bed, on the night of his being appointed?'[8] — and from thereon until it was de-politicised in the 1930s, the office was not negotiable. No matter how it deplored the practice when in opposition, the party in power claimed an absolute right to fill it.

The Liberal majority rose to eight in 1837, and in 1839 the Tories allowed them to return all six candidates unopposed. In the following year only the East ward was contested, the Tory abandonment of the West to the more radical element of the Liberal party excused by the *Herald* as a strategic retreat from a contest made unwinnable by the weapons of 'Old Corruption': intimidation and bribery. The Reform Act had gone to some lengths to remove them, of course, but the practice of submitting the names of proposed magistrates to the Corporation for comment and their right of representation on the two local boards of trustees, the Municipal General and Municipal Church Charities, still left them open to the suspicion of political bias and 'jobbery'. In the case of the magistracy this was largely dispelled by an 'honourable agreement' to endorse an equal number of candidates from each party, and so rigidly was it honoured that the Lord Chancellor himself was later accused of the 'very peculiar' practice of constituting it 'almost exclusively of one particular party'.[9]

The charities, however, remained a fertile source of dispute. 'The radicals are now in power', declared the Herald in 1837, 'and last Wednesday Sir Thomas White's loans . . . were given by our *immaculate* town-council to forty burgesses. Of whom *thirty-eight* were Whig-radicals, and 'save the mark', only two Conservatives!';[10] while on the Conservative side, the painter and plumber Charles Mobbs was prosecuted for employing less subtle means of influencing results. 'I have no doubt he gave the man the money', one juror allegedly declared after he was aquitted, 'but I was not going to find anybody guilty of bribery!'.[11] In the West Ward in 1840, the *Herald* claimed, not only were the Liberal agents 'in and out of the Whig public houses with their voters like dogs in a fair', but the electorate 'consists of poor operative shoemakers who dare not have a will of their own'.[12] Nevertheless, the poor were usually too poor as yet to have a vote in municipal elections, and the Tory failure to contest even their former South Ward stronghold in that year, followed by the formation of the Northampton Oak Club in 1841, suggests rather that they were demoralised, disorganised, and well aware of the fact.

12. Joseph Gurney (1814-93). Chartist, freethinker and Radical leader. Mayor of Northampton in 1879, he also served on the Northampton School Board and was a leading figure in the Town and County Freehold Land Society.

Headed by Charles Markham and Richard Phipps, the Oak Club's object was to break the Liberal hold on the Borough Corporation, the first priority to ensure the more efficient registration of potential supporters on the electoral roll. Some ground was regained in the early 1840s, but the task was still beyond it. Indeed, by 1851 the Corporation was scarcely less of a one-party affair than the body it had replaced. The Conservatives held only three of its 24 seats, and it was as yet small consolation to know that Gurney, Bates and their 'Ultra-Liberal' colleagues were now complaining bitterly of their own exclusion from municipal office. With the Chartist challenge dissipating, the working classes apparently — if only apparently in many cases — enjoying a rising standard of living, and British supremacy in world markets as yet to be seriously challenged, mainstream Liberalism was entering a conservative phase born in no small part of complacency. Demands for the extension of the suffrage and the secret ballot were too 'advanced' and off the agenda, and for the foreseeable future they could be — or so it appeared — safely ignored.

'It has long been well known', wrote a Tory correspondent to the *Herald* in 1853,

> that individual freedom is not allowed to those who enter the Council on Liberal principles. Before the honour of a seat at that board can be obtained by the aspiring Whig, his individual freedom must be sacrificed at the shrine of the political Moloch, that holds his orgies at the Peacock. When that sacrifice has been made, the poor degraded thing becomes a Liberal Town Councillor — a puppet, to speak and act as his master may pull the string or find him breath . . . some spirits have fretted under the sense of degradation until they have been tempted to rebel against their taskmasters. But where are they? . . . consigned to the limbo prepared for refractory Whigs — a limbo said to be guarded by tide-waiters, custom-house clerks, and other placemen . . . [13]

This is an accurate if unkind summary of the Ultras' dilemma; but they had a powerful power to divide, and in the 1855 municipal elections mainstream complacency was rudely shattered. Asked to choose between competing Liberal claims, the voters handed control of the Corporation back to the Conservatives.

There would not be another Liberal mayor for 14 years; but there were perhaps other reasons why the mid-century Council was inclined towards 'tide-waiting' conservatism. In occupational terms the first elected body was very similar to the old, with merchants and the professional classes in the majority. Its manufacturing element was enlarged by the admission of Dissenters, but as much by the ironfounders at first as the shoe manufacturers who dominated the town's economy. The latter accounted for only three of the 36 candidates in the first elections, the Liberals William Parker and Thomas Hallam, who were elected, and the Conservative exception to the general rule, Thomas Marshall, who had to await election until 1841. By then shoe manufacturers accounted for over a third of the elected councillors, among them Hallam's partner Joel Edens, John Stimpson, Henry Marshall, and John Groom. Like William Parker, they were large-scale producers and themselves exceptions in an industry still dominated by small master-manufacturers. Most of the latter were effectively excluded from municipal office, if not by a failure to fulfil the property qualification, then by a shortage of the time and money which had to be sacrificed to it.

Meetings of the full Council were held out of business hours in the evenings, but to these must be added those of its various Committees, and the ceremonial or social occasions which required their attendance. With few paid officers as yet to assist them, much time was also devoted by, for instance, members of the Estates Committee to the personal inspection of corporate properties, by the Watch Committee to the condition of the Borough Gaol, and by the Finance Committee to the state of corporate funds.[14] The obligations of the mayoralty were particularly heavy, and the office had been most strenuously avoided in the days of the old Corporation. Year after year a succession of 'mayors' were elected and paid a £10 fine to be excused, while in 1666 Richard Rands marked his own reluctant election by refusing to provide the customary feast for the Corporation. 'He had more wit', it was observed, 'than to spend his money like others before him',[15] but the expenses of the office were as 'considerably beyond' the allowance from corporate funds after 1835 as before, and the ability to spend one's own money without suffering the same fate as George Peach was still as essential. Mayor for the two years between 1836-8, he was declared bankrupt in 1839 and automatically disqualified from further municipal office.

Municipal office could serve to confirm individual claims to leadership in other spheres, and this was often a part of its attraction within the framework of party politics. For this reason it was not unusual for the occupational composition of the corporations to reflect changes in the structure of the local economy, or as seems to have been so in the case of the shoe manufacturers, in the scale of production in the staple industry. By mid-century, however, small tradesmen — the so-called 'shopocracy' — were also gaining seats at the expense of professionals and merchants. Few citizens paid their rates cheerfully and willingly, but businessmen tended to bear the greater burden of them, and small business-men felt it most acutely. The most useful public office in this respect was in fact that of Poor Law Guardian, for it was the poor law authorities who determined the property assessements on which the level of the Borough and Improvement Rates as well as the Poor Rate itself hinged. By mid-century the 'shopocracy' had captured the borough representation on the Northampton Union Board; but no matter the office, once the resentful ratepayer gained it, he became, more often than not, an 'Economiser'.

It is difficult, it must be said, to find any period in the Corporation's history when the ratepayers were *not* complaining of their grevious burden, and it may also be that the old political guard was giving way to the new simply because the former no longer had the energy or the taste for battle. 'I am saying no before being asked', wrote Edward Cotton, one of the new Corporation's first aldermen, in 1844; but 'as each year revolves I feel less inclination for political and other turmoils'.[16] It must also be said that, with the possible exception of the new Borough Gaol opened on The Mounts in 1846, the Corporation had not hitherto been notably extravagant. Indeed, such was its reputation for 'economy' that, so the *Mercury* reported, Thomas Phipps' proposal at a public meeting in 1838 that it subscribe to a fund for the relief of poverty was 'greeted with roars of laughter; which were renewed upon the Mayor stating that . . . he for one would vote for subscribing every shilling left by the Old Corporation'.[17]

A corporate contribution would now have been illegal and as individuals its members gave generously, but the old Corporation had left debts of some £800, and if these were not large by comparison with those inherited elsewhere, the first concern was to discharge them. This was done by selling part of the corporate estates rather than laying the whole burden on the rates, and in selling part of the meadow beyond the South Bridge known as the Bailiff's Hook to the newly-formed Northampton Waterworks Company, the Corporation achieved a double economy. Its rents had formerly gone directly to the Town Bailiffs, but along with several other officials these were now judged sufficiently redundant to be paid only 'by the task'.[18] However, while rents and tolls brought in some £1,400 in 1835-6 against less than £1,000 from a 1s. rate, the rates were a more elastic source of income, and they inevitably came to bear the greater part of corporate expenditure.

Unlike the Poor Law Board, the Corporation could levy a rate on the extra-parochial land of the town where most new residential building was now taking place, and once its finances had been restored to reasonable health the usual level before mid-century was no more than 6d. in the pound. For many years after 1835, despite a part of the cost of pay and clothing being paid by central government, much the single largest part of it was consumed by one of the few obligations the Municipal Reform Act did impose: the policing of the boroughs. From 1856 these central grants were contingent on an annual certificate of efficiency which the borough force acquired with regular ease, having been thoroughly re-organised in 1848 after a rather half-hearted reform in 1836 which consisted mainly of reducing the daily pay of the existing Constables and conferring the title of Superintendent on the former Head Constable, Joseph 'Old Joe' Ball. By then the population of the town was some 40% greater than in 1831 and its built-up area much expanded, but Chartist activity in the town and revolution in Europe, one suspects, may also have convinced the Corporation that a part-time force of 24 Constables was now quite inadequate.

Largely the creation of Alderman Barwell, past Chairman of the Watch Committee, the new full-time force consisted of a Superintendent, two Sergeants and sixteen Constables, with a maximum joining age of 30 and a minimum height of 5ft. 9ins. — the latter requiring the dismissal of seven of the old force. In 1851 Joseph Ball was also replaced by Henry Keenan, formerly of the Manchester City Police and now designated Chief Constable. An impressive figure at 6ft. 4ins., his suitability was questioned on the grounds that he was a Roman Catholic; but the religious affiliations of its officers, the Council concluded to its credit, were really none of its business. The town was now to be patrolled 'every hour of the day and night', for as the regulations based on those of the Metropolitan Police made clear: 'the principal object to be obtained is the PREVENTION OF CRIME . . . The security of property and person, and the preservation of public tranquility and good order in the Borough . . . will thus be better effected than by the detection and punishment of the offenders after they have succeeded in violating the laws . . . The absence of crime will be considered the best proof of the efficiency of the Police'.[19]

Crime was never as absent as the Chief Constable wished, and criminal statistics can be notoriously misleading — the number of crimes recorded, it need hardly be said, may bear little relation to the number actually committed — but Northampton generally compared well with other industrial towns, both in the level of recorded crimes and their nature. Larceny was much the most common, drunkenness not uncommon, but serious offences against property or the person were relatively rare, and there seems some reason to doubt that Northampton was criminal enough to justify the sizeable debt incurred in building the new Borough Gaol. Indeed, far from being over-crowded, the old Borough Gaol in Fish Street had been so little used that by 1843 both the building and its staff were in a state of decrepitude, the Governor of the gaol being removed from post 'in consequence of his great age', and his wife similarly 'become incapable' of exercising the duties of Matron. The borough prisoners had in the meantime been consigned to the care of the County Gaol in George Row at a cost of 1s. per head per day.[20]

The Mounts prison was part of a plan for a new civic complex also embracing a new town hall and police station, a modified version of plans drawn up in 1838 for the town hall, Market Hall and Square, and cattle market. Corporate finances would not then 'admit' of their execution, and both the town hall and police station were eventually sited elsewhere; but there were perhaps two reasons for the priority accorded to the gaol over these other schemes 'of so much importance to the Inhabitants of the Town and neighbourhood, and conducive to the convenience of all persons', neither of them directly related to the level of crime in the town.[21] A separate borough gaol 'in a fit state for the confinement of prisoners' was a condition of the separate Court of Quarter Sessions for which the Corporation had petitioned as early as 1836. Without this the County Justices retained some jurisdiction in the Borough, and immunity from their 'interference' was as much desired as ever.[22]

Perhaps this was sufficient in itself to justify an unprecedented departure from a regime of 'economy', but the new prisons springing up around the nation in the first half of the 19th century also had a symbolic value which made them, so to speak, worth their weight in gold. If 'jails and treadmills and dungeons have now become the most striking edifices in every county in the country', as William Cobbett noted in the course of his *Rural Rides*,[23] they were not so much proof of growing criminality among the labouring classes — this remains unproven even now — but a symptom of the insecurity which drove the middle classes to 'civilise' the masses and rescue them from their 'degeneracy'. In their monumental turreted and embrasured imitations of the castles of feudal barons they were an assertion of ruling class authority and the confidence which the ruling classes truly did not feel; and Chartism and the economic distress of the 1840s did nothing at all to bolster it.

At a total cost of some £16,500, it should be said, the governing classes of Northampton stamped their own authority in stone with more economy than was often the case, but the Corporation also had powers of coercion in the form of by-laws, the first of them published in 1838. Many 'nuisances' were already subject to by-laws passed by the Improvement Commission, and in their final form those of the Corporation were mainly concerned with protecting the populace from open coal vault covers, runaway wagons and 'ferocious' dogs, and from the 'wilful' and 'wanton' knocking of doors or ringing of doorbells, punishable by a fine of 10s. if perpetrated after 10 p.m.[24] Prostitution, 'indecency' and the publication or distribution of 'obscene' or 'profane' literature carried a 20s. fine. Very much matters of general concern at this time, they were a standard target, but in those boroughs where it was strongly represented Liberal Nonconformity could leave its own moral mark on the municipal government and insist — or try to insist — that the inhabitants lived by its own stern standards of conduct.

By, for instance, forbidding them to 'bowl or bundle any hoop or fly any kite or fling any stone or play at bandy or football or any other game to the annoyance of passengers in the public streets' or 'to the number of three or more . . . stand idly upon the pavement'. In the light of 'every person who shall drown any dog or cat or other animal or cast any flesh or noisome matter into the River Nene . . .', the prohibition against bathing in it less than 100 yards from a dwelling or public highway was perhaps unnecessary, but these were among the thirty or more draft bye-laws on which the Home Secretary wielded his own Liberal axe.[25] Although Mr. Hagger 'thought it should be pointed out to Lord John Russell . . . that similar laws had been allowed at Coventry', only nine survived it. The rest were dismissed as 'objectionable; some relating to offences of too minute and trifling a nature'[26] — and when they regained control of the Council in 1855 the Conservatives applied much the same adjectives to the Council's past expenditure. Economy had its place, but 'parsimony . . . kept them behind'.[27]

The Council would 'see at once' said Christopher Markham, first mayor of this new Tory regime, in 1859, 'how great a control the ratepayers really exercised over the gentlemen sent there to take care of their pockets . . . otherwise they would long ago have had a new town hall'.[28] Dating at least from the 15th century, the old Guildhall on the corner of Wood Hill and Abington Street was not only 'a disgrace to the town' and 'perfectly inadequate' for its purpose, but a positive danger to the health of its occupants, 'suffocated as they were by the foetid breaths and foul stenches arising from breathing the same atmosphere over and over again'.[29] Nevertheless, in an arrangement which went some way to mute Liberal cries of extravagance, the ratepayers' burden was limited to the maximum one penny rate permitted for the funding of municipal libraries and museums under the Public Libraries Act of 1855. The remainder of the anticipated cost of £12,000 was raised by the sale of corporate property, £1,200 of it from the old Guildhall itself. Sold to a local wine merchant, it was demolished soon afterwards in the course of a road-widening scheme.

A public library, said one early Liberal convert, would be a 'first step towards redeeming the character of their town', too much given to 'dissipation and vice'.[30] Only the museum was provided at first, but the building of a new town hall was no simple question of providing adequate accommodation for the conduct of municipal business. 'It may seem a small matter to those who have not studied these matters of local politics', wrote one commentator of the controversy the same issue aroused in Leeds, 'whether a Town Hall in a provincial city shall be of one style of architecture or another, whether it shall be small or large, handsome or the reverse. As a matter of fact, a great deal may depend upon the decision . . .'.[31] Civic pride depended on it, and if there was anything capable of closing the local political ranks, this was it.

How would posterity judge it? Would it be, asked the Liberal William Shoosmith, a monument 'of their taste and of their efficiency', or the reverse? Would it be 'pointed at with pride, or . . . regarded with shame'?[32] What would it say of the municipal government, and of the town to the country at large? 'If I mistake not, the erection of this town hall will in many ways exert a favourable influence on the future prospects of the town . . .', said the Mayor, Pickering Phipps, on the laying of its foundation stone in 1861, 'The municipal institutions of the country have a great influence on society, and produce a feeling of self-reliance which would be lost if government were more centralised'.[33] 'In a certain sense', wrote the *Herald* in 1892, when an unanticipated increase in the scale of municipal business demanded that it now be extended, 'the Municipal institutions may be regarded as the pulses of the boroughs of England. If the pulse throbs healthfully it is a sure indication that the life of a town is possessed of vigour and vitality'.[34]

Should it be in the Classical style favoured by many northern industrial cities, or the Gothic of the building it was replacing? The advertisement inviting designs to be submitted to open competition did not specify, much to the annoyance of the eventual runner-up who 'could have designed a Gothic building had I known that style would be preferred', but local opinion favoured the latter as more in keeping with the antiquity of the town and its corporate government. 'New towns and new municipalities', wrote the *Mercury*, 'may reasonably enough adopt a classic design if they prefer it, because they are not restricted by early associations. But Northampton has a history going far back into the past . . . the building and the history should be linked together instead of standing aloof from each other'.[35]

The new Guildhall did so almost to perfection. Built to the design of the 27-year-old Bristol architect Edward Godwin, the completely symmetrical building topped by a 110ft.-high clock tower was faced with limestone and sandstone, with the elaborate exterior and interior stonework executed by Godwin's own 'carving man', R. L. Boulton of Gloucester. Figures with historical links with Northampton were represented in a series of statues above the first floor windows, among them Thomas à Becket, Eleanor, Queen of Edward I,[36] and the Northamptonshire-born poet John Dryden. Below the ground floor windows were shields representing the trades of the town, and above them, scenes of historic events in town and county. Along with the carved tableaux in the vestibule, and the Mayors' Names Gallery at the head of the staircase displaying shields recording the name of every Mayor since 1377, the building 'almost answers the purpose of a guide book to Northampton'.[37]

In the course of building the Town Clerk had to do much 'conferring, advising and mollifying', some of the accounts were paid only 'under protest', but the Corporation was justly proud of the finished result. 'You must agree with me', said Mayor Mark Dorman at the opening ceremony in May 1864, 'that the architect of such a building as our new town hall must be a remarkably clever man — but what I want to say is this: what is the use of having a clever architect, or a clever design, unless you have a clever corporation to pick it out?!'.[38] Northampton had, 'at last, a public building worthy of a town so celebrated', wrote *Building News*, and the townspeople who clambered onto 'dizzy and perilous perches' to view the laying of its foundation stone and greeted its opening with flags and bunting and 'loud hearty cheering' clearly agreed.[39] Civic pride was satisfied, and in the process of satisfying it relations between the parties acquired a cordiality which did much to widen the rift within the optimistically named United Liberal Association itself.

In 1862 Liberals and Tories abandoned their customary separate tables and dined together for the first time since the municipal reform. In that year's elections the Liberals left the South Ward uncontested and fielded only one candidate in the East, where — in the view of their radical wing, now represented in the Council by the solitary figure of Joseph Gurney — they had every chance of winning both seats. John Bates contested it as a 'Democratic Liberal', and in 1863, the Ultras opposed the official Liberal candidates in

13. The Guildhall, St Giles Street. Engraving issued by the *Northampton Mercury* to mark its opening on 21 May 1864.

both East and West, testifying to 'a real split in Liberalism in the town'. Unity was briefly restored during the reform agitation of 1866 and the Tories deprived of their majority, but it was completely shattered by the decisive Liberal victory in the 1868 municipal elections, which gave them both Tory seats in the South ward and a majority of ten in the Council. The Radicals, as they were now calling themselves, were once again surplus to Liberal requirements.

The Radicals, said one of their number, 'wanted to see men on the Town Council who would look after the interests of the working classes and not men to look after the interests of the middle classes' — a warning directed in particular towards shoe manufacturer councillors like Moses Phillip Manfield who were now employing machinery in the trade, and one made, of course, against the background of the extended parliamentary franchise.[40] In fact, Bradlaugh's appearance as a candidate in the 1868 election only served to reinforce the 'growing disposition on the part of the Liberals . . . towards a close corporation and a self-electing body', but when an electoral agreement in 1871 handed both South Ward seats back to the Tories, the *Mercury* itself was moved to protest.

The 'just claims of the Radicals to some say in both municipal and parliamentary electoral affairs' ought now to be met, it declared, and not for the sake of justice alone, for while 'neither in the Wards or the Borough, are the Radicals strong enough to carry a candidate of their own . . . they are strong enough if they insist on dividing the party to facilitate the return of a Conservative'.[41] And so they were. In 1872 both Radicals and Liberals fielded a full compliment of candidates in East and West, the Liberal vote was hopelessly split, and the Tories took five of the six seats. An electoral pact recouped some of the losses in the following year, but it took the shock of the Conservative parliamentary victories in 1874 to produce a more permanent power-sharing agreement. In the meantime, however, the Council had been assailed from another direction by a body whose own view of it was amply conveyed by its title: the Ratepayers' Defence Association.

In 1869 it had revived long dormant plans to build a new cattle market. A 'nuisance and a disgrace to a civilised town', the existing Market Square site was inconvenient and inadequate, and local farmers and London butchers alike were now diverting their trade to Rugby and Leicester.[42] Various alternatives were considered, including the Corn Exchange opened on the Parade at the north of Market Square in 1851. Used not only for the sale of corn but for public meetings, balls and concerts, 'its resonance is intolerable', complained the *Mercury* on one such occasion, and its 'miserable lighting' could only be likened to 'a congregation of gossiping new moons in a fog'.[43] On the grounds of health as well as easy access the Council rejected it in favour of Cow Meadow, part of the town commons to the south, provoking opposition from two quarters — hence the ponderous title of 'People's Commons and Ratepayers' Defence Association' under which battle was first joined, and the unlikely alliance of leading Liberals like Gurney and J. M. Vernon with Conservative publicans and solicitors.

'Almost to a man . . . owners, and occupiers of property in the streets and places where the Market is now held', the latter would, in their own view, pay for the cattle market twice over: once through the inevitable addition to their rates, and again through the loss of their market day profits.[44] From its own offices on the Parade, the *Mercury* weighed in to support them. 'Nothing under Conservative rule was ever so absolute as this', it cried when the Mayor refused to convene yet another public meeting to discuss the matter: 'This is old obsolete Toryism, the Toryism of the days anterior to the Municipal Reform'. So 'Liberalism is come to this! We must die to save our characters', retorted one councillor; but when the scheme had been passed four times by the Council and sanctioned by Parliament, should 'a few hundred people at a public meeting over-rule the opinion of those elected by thousands'?[45] Certainly not, in the view of one 'Disinterested Ratepayer', for 'the public interest ought to prevail above private inconvenience'.[46]

PEOPLE'S COMMONS

AND

RATE-PAYERS' DEFENCE
ASSOCIATION.

President—Mr. COUNCILLOR VERNON, Ex-Mayor.
Vice-President—Mr. ALDERMAN GATES.
Treasurer—Mr. THOMAS OSBORN.
Secretary—Mr. HENRY BECKE.

The object of this Association is to preserve the Common Lands within the limits of the Borough of Northampton, viz. The Race Course, Cow Meadow, **Midsummer Meadow, and Baulmsholme,** and the rights and privileges connected therewith.

Also to watch, in the interest of the Rate-Payers, the large increase of local taxation with which the Borough is threatened, by the Markets and Fairs Bill proposed by the present Corporation.

Within the last few years Part of Midsummer Meadow, and Baulmsholme to the extent of about FOUR ACRES, have been absorbed, and now SIXTEEN ACRES of the Cow Meadow are attacked by the proposed Markets and Fairs Bill.

Any Persons willing to become Members, or in any way to assist this Association, are requested to communicate with the undermentioned Gentlemen, or with

HENRY BECKE,
Honorary Secretary.

Mr. COUNCILLOR HIGGINS	Mr. FRANCIS, Drapery	Messrs. HENSMAN & EARL, Abington Street
„ COUNCILLOR GURNEY	„ W. SANDALL, „	Mr. R. COSFORD, Abington Street
„ COUNCILLOR COLLIER	Messrs. MOBBS, SNOW & WOOD, Market Square	„ NORMAN, Ram Inn, Sheep Street
„ COUNCILLOR JEFFERY		„ NORTON, Bull Inn
„ JEYES, Drapery	Mr. FRANKLIN, Market Square	„ MULLIS, Hope's Place
„ TUFFLEY, „	„ PERKINS, „	„ CHR. GIBSON, Primrose Hill
„ BAND, „	„ MOORE, „	„ MATTHEWS, Lady's Lane
„ SONNTAG, „	„ LIVERMORE, „	„ AMBIDGE, Grafton Square
„ OSBORN, „	„ POOLER, Waterloo House	„ HOMAN, Green Dragon
„ BATES, „	„ HAYNES, "The Lord Palmerston"	
„ PRESSLAND, Jun. „	„ SMITH, Corn Exchange	
„ MARSH, „	„ DAVIES, Abington Street	

All Subscribers are considered Members.

A Member of the above Association will call and solicit your name and support.

14. People's Commons and Ratepayers' Defence Association poster, *c.*1870. A transitory alliance of leading Liberals with Conservative publicans and solicitors in opposition to plans to build a new cattle market on Cow Meadow.

On this occasion it did. The new cattle market was duly opened in 1873, but the 'incessant controversy' it provoked raised questions which would be asked again and again of local government in the 19th century and beyond. What was its proper role? Should it be providing cattle markets, public water supplies, parks, tramways and houses — or was this the proper sphere of private enterprise? How far should the public interest be served at the cost of the private individual? Having paid once, for a private water supply for instance, should the ratepayer be forced to pay again so that '*what they may call poor* should have water for nothing'; and how much 'private inconvenience', how much 'interference' in his individual freedom should he be expected to tolerate? In the area of the public health at least some of these questions had already been answered.

In Northampton, until the Borough Corporation became an Urban Sanitary Authority in 1872, this was largely the preserve of the Board of Improvement Commissioners, first constituted under a Local Act of 1778 with responsibility for street paving, lighting and scavenging, the provision of a night watch, and the control of such 'nuisances' as wandering cattle, pigs and poultry. As the town grew in size its powers were found 'in many respects defective and insufficient for the purposes thereby intended' and extended by further Acts, notably that of 1816, which not only provided for the 'better' execution of its existing duties, but for the rebuilding of the South Bridge, then 'in a very decayed state and dangerous to travellers passing over the same'.[47] The Commission was not subject to election until 1843, but eligibility for office rested entirely on property qualifications and Dissenters were always much in evidence. Party politics had their place — subscriptions to major projects like the South Bridge were almost obligatory on the part of the Borough M.P.s and the 'interested' county gentry — but to a great extent, both before and after 1835, they were submerged in the common self-interest of the business community which provided its members.

Better paving and lighting, security of property and the person and the free passage of traffic could pay dividends in terms of trade and investment, and if the Commissioners were the first to enjoy them, the general interest did not go unserved — nor, by virtue of that fact, un-rated. Around 2s. in the pound early in the century, the differential rates levied in the 1830s were closer to the level of the Borough rate: 9d. in the pound on property sited in smooth-paved streets, with a 50% discount in those still lacking this convenience. Membership of the Improvement Commission and the Borough Corporation over-lapped, but so did their responsibilities and powers, and relations between them were sometimes strained. In the view of the Commission in 1779, for instance, Sheep Street was 'a very improper place for holding the Sheep Fairs, the Highroad passing through the same which is thereby rendered very incommodious and a great nuisance to Travellers'. This was undoubtedly true, and well within the Commission's legitimate sphere of concern; but responsibility for the town's fairs and markets was vested by charter in the Corporation, and in presuming to tell it where to locate them the Commission was judged guilty, at the very least, of gross impertinence.[48]

The Commissioners of the Nene Navigation, who included representatives of the Corporation, responded in similar vein in 1851 when the Improvement Commission served them with a notice to clean up the river, said to be 'in a filthy and unwholesome condition, being a continuation throughout of mud . . . in which are embedded numerous carcases of animals in a putrid state'. They refused to do so on the grounds that it was 'sufficiently open for the purposes of Navigation — but they would give permission so far as they could for the Commissioners of the town, at their own expense, to cleanse out those parts of the river complained of'. 'So far as they could' referred to the fact that parts of the river banks were owned by the Corporation, in which case that body itself was responsible for the adjacent stretch of river — or, as the Town Clerk explained to a rather bewildered Council when a similar question arose in 1929, only so far as its mid-stream if it owned only one side of its banks.[49]

The Corporation itself opposed the Improvement Bill promoted by the Commission in 1843, requesting that its powers be transferred jointly to itself and the Poor Law Board. Failing this, principle as well as common sense demanded that the Commission too be constituted by popular election : for not only would it be 'absolutely impossible' to transact any business in a body composed of the more than 400 males who fulfilled the proposed property qualifications, the Corporation 'cannot omit to express their sense of the injustice of a measure by which it is proposed to lay heavy taxes upon their fellow Townsmen without giving the Rate payers a voice in the election of those who are to impose them'.[50] Both points were taken, 48 Commissioners were appointed under the Act and the one quarter obliged to retire each year were then replaced by elected representatives. 'Words imputing the masculine Gender only shall include Females', the Act also declared, but contemporary perceptions of 'femininity' were as effective a barrier here as the law excluding women from the municipal corporations, and it would be some decades yet before any local body in Northampton acquired its first 'lady member'.

However, along with authority to borrow up to £20,000, the Commission now acquired powers to manufacture gas — although the Gas-Light Company had been doing so quite adequately since 1823 — to operate a fire engine, and to lay down minimum standards for the construction of new housing, both of the latter potentially saving of money on insurance premiums as well as lives. Most importantly, it now assumed broader responsibility in the field of the public health. Here it was much-influenced by Edwin Chadwick's *Report on the Sanitary Condition of the Labouring Population* in the previous year, which likened the mortality of the earlier 19th century to the ravages of war and concluded that much of it was in fact preventable.[51] Urban mortality rates throughout Britain showed a marked upward trend from the early 19th century, and although Northampton was below the national average of 23:1,000 in 1848, it was no exception to the general rule.

Tuberculosis, or 'consumption', was usually the most common cause of death recorded in local Bills of Mortality, but it was often displaced by epidemics of cholera or smallpox, the latter so frequent in the 18th century that the customary dirge attached to the Bill in 1755 was devoted to the question: 'What art thou, so foul, so bloated black, So loathsome to each Sense, the Sight or Smell, VARIOLA, what art thou?'.[52] Many deaths were accounted for by the 'fevers' and 'fits' of infectious diseases yet to be separately identified, such as typhoid, typhus, dysentery, measles, diptheria and scarlet fever, always endemic, often epidemic. And while some lived long enough to die 'aged' — 11 of the 83 recorded in the Bill of 1849 were over the age of 70 — a high proportion died very prematurely indeed. Children under two were almost invariably the single largest group, and the majority of them died in the first few weeks or months of life. The Bills gave details for the parish of All Saints only, but this was much the largest of the four town parishes at this time, and this pattern of death and disease is wholly characteristic of the Victorian urban scene.

Chadwick identified the sources of contagion as noxious gases emitted by 'decomposing animal and vegetable substances, by damp and filth, and close over-crowded dwellings'.[53] Bacteria rather than bad smells were the real culprit — but removing the one often served to remove the other — and thus the Commission now acquired powers to provide public sewers and cesspools, and to regulate such 'nuisances' as dunghills, defective drains, and the slaughter-houses, pig-styes and soap- and tripe-boiling premises liberally scattered among the residential areas of the town. However, while it would investigate complaints the initiative lay largely with the townspeople themselves, and they, it seems clear, were not always sure what fell within the terms of the Act. His neighbour in the central thoroughfare of Abington Street, wrote one complainant in 1844, 'keeps and slaughters pigs on average three or four times a week. The noise arising from the killing is a great nuisance, and the burnt straw flying over into my premises on such occasions, covers my garden with sooty particles, making it impossible to use it during the operation, and it is impossible to open my back windows as it would fly into my rooms, as it has on several occasions'.[54]

But was this a *nuisance*, he asked the Commission? It was, and the offender was duly served with an abatement order. Complaints in 1872 about the state of the footway by the river were dismissed with the retort that 'it is quite good enough for Boat Horses, and if the inhabitants desire to use it as a Footway they may mend it if they please to do so',[55] but an epidemic of cholera in 1849 brought a spate of letters about dwellings in the Bridge Street area, said to be in a 'filthy, unwholesome condition . . . foul and offensive'.[56] Forty-three deaths were recorded in this area alone, but cholera was no respecter of wealth or class, and if 'one life were saved . . .', said one Commissioner of plans to culvert the ditch in Cow Meadow to remove a likely source of infection, 'it would be cheaply made even at the cost of £1,050'.[57] Money was ever an obstacle to effective sanitary reform, but if some things could clearly no longer be left to 'take care of themselves', and departures from the non-interventionist doctrine of *laissez faire* justified on the utilitarian grounds of 'the greatest good of the greatest number', even the most limited of public health measures might be regarded as an invasion of individual liberty.

Only 'the beginning of an attempt, under the pretence of providing for the public health, to regulate by legislation, by boards and commissioners, every business in every town of the Empire . . .', declared *The Economist* of the Public Health Act of 1848, which set up a central Board of Health and provided for local Boards with powers to undertake sanitary reforms.[58] Only those towns with death rates above the national average were compelled rather than permitted to adopt it; but the property-owning members of local authorities often had vested interests of their own. Would they order themselves to put their own insanitary properties into good order, or enforce the regulations against prominent and powerful members of the local community? The Improvement Commission showed no such inhibitions in 1872 when it ordered the owners of the 'villas' on part of the Cliftonville estate to pave, drain and sewer the street. Among them were the former Town Clerk John Hensman, the shoe manufacturer Richard Turner, and Pickering Phipps, now managing the family brewing firm and twice Mayor of the Borough — and in default of their compliance the Commission carried out the work itself and sent them the bill.[59]

Nevertheless, sanitary reform proceeded to a great extent by trial and error, and not unusually measures designed to remove one hazard to health only succeeded in creating another. The 'want of space for burial' in the parish of All Saints, said the prospectus of the Northampton General Cemetery Company in 1846, 'is so great, that in many instances corpse is piled upon corpse until scarcely the depth of eighteen inches divides the living from the dead'. In return for their investment in a new cemetery on the Billing Road, shareholders were offered not only the prospect of a longer life , but 'a profitable return' and an eventual burial service conducted by the Company's own chaplain 'or any minister according to the desired ritual', for 'no liberal Dissenter will object to other parties enjoying the same privileges as they seek for themselves'.[60] By 1874, however, it could 'safely be said that Northampton has placed its dead where the living ought to be, and the living where the dead ought to be buried'. The cemetery was now virtually enclosed by residential building, while for want of this site of 'adequate dimensions for the Interment of many generations', houses were being built in southern areas of the town where proper drainage was 'almost impracticable'.[61]

In common with other such bodies, the Improvement Commission's own efforts were hindered by an 'imperfect knowledge of science'. Its by-laws regulating drainage, said the Borough Medical Officer of Health in 1887, were 'only to be recommended for the object of instructing people how drains ought not to be laid':[62] that is, with 90 degree joins in the pipes, which easily became blocked and flooded the streets with dirty water and sewage.

15. Billing Road cemetery, opened in 1847 by the Northampton General Cemetery Company. 'Monuments and Grave Stones are furnished by the Company on the Lowest Terms'.

Still more seriously, after being treated at the Houghton Road sewage works, themselves blamed by the committee of the nearby General Lunatic Asylum for an outbreak of dysentery among the inmates in 1874,[63] the effluent was discharged directly into the River Nene at Abington Mill; and in 1869-70 the Commissioners were served with a series of injunctions from owners of adjacent land to abate this nuisance of their own making. Faced with a sequestration order from the Court of Chancery and a claim for damages of £10,000, they had to acquire additional powers and finance under a further Improvement Act in 1871 to provide the alternative which more advanced scientific knowledge now favoured — an irrigation farm.

Sited beyond the borough boundaries at Ecton on the 'fairest piece of land for a Sewage Farm in all England', the Commissioners took such pride in it that when their powers and responsibilities were transferred to the Borough Corporation in 1875 the formal handing-over ceremony took place at the sewage farm itself. However, such were the capital costs of many sanitary projects that local authorities were rarely able to take immediate advantage of each and every technical improvement or scientific discovery. The ratepayers might bear the initial costs of a scheme without too much complaint, but assured as they usually were that it would meets local needs 'for many years to come', they expected it to do so. And they might well object even to this: 'Shall the town obtain money by a tax upon a few and appropriate it for the benefit of the many . . . without those few who find the money having any direct control over its expenditure or any possible means of having it repaid'.[64]

There were no easy answers, and although the Sanitation Act of 1866 marked an important departure from *permission* to *compulsion* in the field of public health legislation, not only extending the powers of local authorities but insisting that 'these powers be exercised in good faith and with reasonable vigour', it was far from resolving the ideological arguments once and for all.[65] Nevertheless, if there was one thing more persuasive than a cholera epidemic in convincing the ratepayer that the greater good coincided with his own, it was an appeal to his pocket; and as Alfred Haviland, first Medical Officer to the Sanitary Authority of Northampton suggested in 1874, the few who were taxed for the benefit of the many did have a real prospect of having their investment repaid —·for sanitary reforms 'have saved many hundreds of lives, and consequently much pauper money'.[66] Some 75% of poor relief in the mid-19th century went to the victims of illness, including those left destitute by the death of a breadwinner, and 'the amount of burthens thus produced', Edwin Chadwick noted as Secretary to the Poor Law Commission in the late 1830s, 'is frequently so great as to render it good economy . . . to incur the charges for preventing the evils . . .'.[67]

The reform of the Poor Laws themselves in 1834 was also undertaken with the saving of money in mind, but here the cost of relief to the able-bodied rather than the 'impotent' sick, bereaved or aged pauper was the main concern. Until 1834 poor relief was administered on the basis of the Poor Law Act of 1601, the 43rd of Elizabeth, which left individual parishes with a high degree of freedom to devise their own systems of relief. Informed on the one hand by perpetual fears of social disorder, on the other by the precepts of Christian charity, the result — so the argument for reform ran from the late 18th century onwards — was not only a total lack of uniformity in the treatment of the poor, but levels of relief so generous as to be a positive encouragement to idleness, improvidence and vice. 'What encouragement have the poor to be industrious and frugal when they know for certain that should they increase their store it will be devoured by drones', asked one would-be reformer in 1786, 'or what cause have they to fear when they are assured, that if by their indolence and extravagance, by their drunkenness and vices, they should be reduced to want, they shall be abundantly supplied?'.[68]

The parish workhouse of All Saints in Northampton was, in the view of the *Royal Commission on the Poor Laws* in 1834, a prime example of the faults of the old system, being 'very comfortable, so much so that the inmates, old and young, were allowed bread and meat five days in a week, and the only work done was sweeping in the streets, which was done in the usual idle style . . . The notion of making the workhouse a place of discipline never seemed to have occurred to anyone . . .'.[69] The notion that poverty was the self-inflicted result of defective moral character rather than misfortune, a matter for punishment rather than paternalistic concern, was not one which occurred naturally to many people at the time, but it was on this principle that the reform proceeded. By offering relief only on conditions of stern workhouse discipline   and disenfranchising those who accepted it — the able-bodied pauper would find his position 'less eligible' than that of the labourer who supported himself, and would make the parish 'his last and not his first resort'. Forced onto their own resources, the argument continued, the able-bodied poor would be free to realise their full potential, to become masters and mistresses of their own fate — and this was really a *more* humane approach than that of making them 'comfortable'.

Individual parishes were now combined into unions, managed by elected Boards of Guardians whose activities were overseen by a three-member central body, the Poor Law Commission. However, although the reform had cross-party support in Parliament, poor-relief was an important source of local patronage, and despite these precautionary measures it was not to be lightly surrendered. Indeed, as the county gentry around Northampton quickly proved, it did not have to be surrendered at all. In their 'most convenient' form, the Poor Law Commission directed, the new unions would be 'of a circle, taking a market town as a centre, and comprehending those surrounding parishes whose inhabitants are accustomed to resort to the same market'.[70] The Northampton Union formed an oblong running from the adjacent parish of Hardingstone to the south to a point some miles to the north-east, and the Brixworth Union to the north-west was in turn such a deviation from the norm that the Guardians succeeded in having their registry office located in Northampton itself on the grounds that none of their 33 parishes was either 'a post town, a market town, or a place of general resort'.[71]

They comprised the estates of Lord Spencer and lesser Whig gentry, influential enough to have the boundaries drawn to their own rather than the Commission's order — while to the south-west those of Lord Northampton and a number of co-Tory squires, were married to that of the Whig Edward Bouverie in the small Hardingstone Union. 'Apt to object to anything which will break in upon the exclusiveness of Hardingstone', Bouverie had first to be assured by Assistant Commissioner Richard Earle that 'out of 26 Guardians . . . he would command 3, Sir Robert Gunning 3, Ld. Northampton 4 . . . and so on and in short, there was no one except those with whom he is in the greatest intimacy, that would have any material influence'.[72] So much for uniformity and an end to local patronage, but within the borough itself, said Mr. Earle, there was 'a very prevalent notion that it would be inexpedient and injurious to unite Town and Country parishes'. Here the Liberals had done their own political arithmetic, and they did not care for the answers, for the majority of Guardians returned by the country parishes would certainly not be Liberals.

Almost always farmers, most were as Tory and Anglican as the two rural clergymen appointed as *ex officio* Guardians in their capacity of county justices — a privilege which the Act denied to the justices of the boroughs. Even without them, the 13 rural parishes eventually combined with the four of the town had an inbuilt majority on the Board.[73] Despite a combined population less than half that of the borough they were allocated 17 of its 33 seats — although much depended on how conscientiously the Guardians attended its weekly meetings, and with the advantage of convenience the town often had the actual majority. However, the Liberals were often in a minority here too. Most country Guardians were returned unopposed, but town elections were usually contested on party lines, and initially at least the victory went to the Liberals. They claimed 14 of the 16 borough seats at the first elections in 1836, but they took only six in the following year and thereafter they were largely reduced to conducting the guerrilla warfare which, in Mr. Earle's view, went regrettably far to divert the Board from its proper task.

'Party and sectarian feelings', he noted in 1838, 'prejudice the proceedings'.[74] Many a battle was fought in the Northampton Board over the appointment of officials, another form of patronage which the reform did not dispose of. In 1838, taking advantage of a temporary majority, the Liberals elected one of their own Guardians, Henry Jacob, as a rate collector. His appointment was quickly overturned on the dubious grounds that his handwriting was illegible, but a much more serious conflict arose in the previous year when the Guardians proposed to appoint an Anglican Chaplain to the Union Workhouse, at a salary of £50 p.a., 'which they can at any time increase to £100 or more as has been done with their Tory Clerk. The effect . . . will be to prevent any Paupers ever leaving the Workhouse to attend a place of worship, the Commissioners ever refusing them this right when a Chaplain is appointed . . .'.[75] A petition to the Commissioners themselves predicted still more dire consequences: 'if the appointment is confirmed by you . . . from the known feeling of hostility of a large portion of the Ratepayers and inhabitants to any Church encroachment, this town will be plunged into Riot and Disorder'.[76]

Nothing so serious ensued, but a little discretion here would no doubt have avoided a deal of ill-feeling. The town clergy offered to compromise by providing unpaid ministers for all denominations, but the county Guardians outweighed them, and in confirming the

16. Handbill protesting against the new Poor Laws, 1841. The reform was undertaken by a Whig government, but commanded wide cross-party support.

TO THE
WORKING CLASSES.

Working Men in Health.

The election is in your own hands. Pity those that are suffering within the Workhouse prison from want or sickness, age or sorrow. Think of *them,* and do not, for money or drink, oh ! do not vote for any member, or any supporter of a *cruel Workhouse Government.* To vote either for Smith or for Currie would be to vote your poorer neighbours into the Bastile first, and youselves into it afterwards !

If any person desires you to vote for *a Workhouse Candidate,* refuse at once. If you do not at once refuse, at all events take a little time to consider of it. During that time ask your *WIVES* what they, who may one day become widows, would wish. Can they wish to end their days in the Bastile ? Ask your *Children* what they, who may one day become orphans, would wish. *Can* they wish to live---if living it can be called--in a Bastile ?

One word more. Ask *YOURSELVES* what you, as well as they, are likely to wish, should you live to become aged, sick or poor.

Think of all this before you give a vote to a poor man's enemy, *against the Poor Man's Friend.* Think of all this now that your poor countrymen everywhere have their eyes upon your votes, hoping that you will *elect the poor man's friend.*

May you come to a humane and Christian conclusion. Thus may the working man's election prove the working man's blessing. Thus may Sir Henry Willoughby be rewarded for all his past resistance to the workhouse system by the confidence of the Poor. And thus may Sir Henry Willoughby be enabled in Parliament *again* to prove himself *the poor man's friend.*

Electors ! Forget not the Poor ! as advised by

A NON ELECTOR.

17. Northampton Union Workhouse, Wellingborough Road. Now St Edmund's Hospital. The central part of the building is the original workhouse, designed by George Gilbert Scott and built in 1836.

appointment the Commission chose to ignore local circumstances in its pursuit of uniformity. Not for the last time; but over the issue of temporary unemployment among the able-bodied it felt the full and united wrath of the Board itself. The labouring classes knew from bitter experience that even the most virtuous and industrious would find themselves out of work at some point, hence the enduring popular resentment of the stigma of idleness and vice attached to a resort to the parish, and the preference for almost any alternative to the workhouse. In 1840, a year typical enough of the proportions of each, the 121 inmates of the Northampton Union Workhouse consisted of 42 'old and infirm', 11 'temporarily disabled', 61 children under 16 years of age, and seven 'able-bodied' females, mostly widows and deserted wives with dependent children.[77] Whatever the year, the able-bodied were always in a small minority.

In any event, the new system was directed largely towards the elimination of *rural* pauperism, and it was simply not equipped to deal with mass urban unemployment rising from depression in trade or the seasonal vagaries of different industries. Charity was always a more substantial source of relief, but its limits were quickly reached amid general distress, and if many of those thrown out of work were sooner or later faced with the last resort, there was never a workhouse large enough to take them. The Northampton Union built a new one, at a cost of around £7,000, as early as 1836. Designed by George Gilbert Scott, better remembered for his contribution to Victorian church architecture, it was sited on the Wellingborough Road beyond the borough boundary, and intended to accommodate some 300 inmates. More than once, however, it was barely able to house even the 'impotent' poor in need of institutional care. Indeed, so desperate were the Guardians for space in the winter of 1842 that they invited some of the less infirm elderly paupers to discharge themselves with an offer of outdoor relief; but 'none were desirous of going out and expressed their satisfaction at their present treatment'.[78]

In February 1842, faced with renewed Chartist activity on the one hand and the impossibility of their task on the other, the Guardians poured their pent-up frustrations and fears into a petition to the House of Commons, worth quoting at some length. It was of 'the entire witholding of discretionary power from the Boards of Guardians to able-bodied men in judging cases which come before them' that they complained:

> the principle of the bill being to deal with pauperism by a penal process in contradiction to the broad basis of Christian principles which enjoins sympathy for our poor fellow sufferers that we should administer to their necessities and not oppress them — which principles are repugnant and condemnatory of separating man and wife, parent and child and that the effect of the 'Workhouse Test' to able-bodied persons in poverty arising from inclemency of weather or depression in Trade is calculated to pauperise and demoralise many who would by a different treatment become honourable and respectable members of society, but who by the want of discretionary power in the Boards of Guardians are one and all, deserving and undeserving, thrust into the Union workhouses, compelled to leave their cottages and are thereby breaking asunder the Bonds of Relationship which marks an inroad into domestic life no divine law and which no Christians ought to sanction.[79]

This is as thorough a condemnation of the system as may be found from any contemporary source, and if it bears all the hallmarks of Tory paternalism, the Liberal minority on the Board found some of its effects equally disturbing. A Liberal motion to apply for discretion to grant outdoor relief in 1840 pointed to categories of paupers who were quite clearly not the masters or mistresses of their own fate: not only the able-bodied victims of economic cycles but widows, women 'of good character' whose husbands were in prison and, of course, their children.[80] The separation of man and wife in the workhouse might reduce the birth rate and head off a Malthusian crisis, but the 'sundering' of those joined by God in matrimony, the destruction of the family life so exalted by the Victorian middle classes, could lay as uneasily on the conscience of a Nonconformist as an Anglican. And if the 'deserving destitute', the innocent victims of misfortune, were to be thrust into the company of the 'undeserving' architects of their own downfall, was this not more of an encouragement to vice and immorality than the out-relief which kept them from the workhouse?

The prostitutes who used it as 'an asylum when in a state of disease . . . subject to no particular discipline on account of the cause of their admission', were a case in point, and 'a Husband or Father who cherished for his wife or daughter a proper feeling of affection and respect would submit *with* them to any Extremity of want and woe rather than expose them . . . to the Debasement of such companionship'.[81] Nevertheless, the Guardians did have some discretion, if they wished to use it. In 1837, for instance, they voted to partition off one room 'for the convenience of such old married couples as the Guardians may permit to sleep together'. The Poor Law Commission sanctioned this, but the new Board elected in that year was accused of failing to honour the agreement and of 'CHARGING THIS ABOMINABLE CRUELTY ON THE LAW', for the law 'does not require the separation of Man and Wife, but leaves it entirely to the pleasure of the Guardians'.[82] This was essentially true. The Poor Law Commission's regulations required it, but except where matters of finance were concerned these had no legal force. The Northampton Board could be, and was, obliged to repay the £5 1s. 10½d. spent in 1841 on extra Christmas provisions for the inmates, against the Commission's orders;[83] but the Guardians of the Leeds Union could, and did, delay building a new workhouse until it suited *them* — which was not for 15 years.

Regarded by many as the thin end of an undemocratic centralising wedge, an attack on the historic freedoms of the localities, the Poor Law Commission's ability to frame uniform regulations was not matched by an ability to enforce them. In the words of Richard Earle, it had 'no power to drive and must be content to lead'. The same was true of the Poor Law Board, and the Northampton Guardians were quite prepared to stand their ground, for instance, over the Workhouse dietary. They were 'quite satisfied' with the diet currently provided for the children, they informed the Board in response to new guidelines in 1856. Not only was it 'more generous' than that recommended, but the children were 'not very fond of pudding', much preferring the soup served as an alternative.[84] Their diet remained unchanged; but the sheer volume of regulations ensured that at least some would simply go by default. Ordered to dismiss one of their Medical Officers in 1856 for not having the requisite double professional qualification, the Guardians pointed out with some pleasure that this deficiency had passed unnoticed for a full 20 years.[85]

The paupers did not often get just what they wanted, but the Guardians were determined that they should have what they were entitled to. When they complained to the Poor Law Board in 1854 of the problems posed by the extra-parochial areas of the town, they rested their case not only on the fact that property-owners there 'do not in any way contribute towards the expenses of the Poor', but on the denial of the last-resort rights of the poor themselves, 'there being no Fund from which they can receive Relief while residing in extra-parochial property'.[86] This 'peculiar situation' was resolved by an Act of Parliament in 1857 which allowed for the incorporation of such areas in existing Unions, but in 1841 the Relieving Officer was 'severely censured' for his negligence in failing to attend to a case of sickness and destitution. In the opinion of the Guardians, 'he ought to be discharged, but inasmuch as he hath admitted the facts and expressed his regret for the offence . . . for the next offence he will certainly be discharged'. Found guilty later in the year of a further 'gross error', he was.[87]

Two porters were dismissed for taking 'indecent liberties' with female inmates, but low pay or the strict conditions of their work were responsible for a high turnover of staff. The annual salary of the Workhouse Master in 1841 was £50, the same as that of the Chaplain and half that of the Clerk to the Board, both of them employed only part-time. The married couple appointed as Schoolmaster and Mistress in 1842 received £40 p.a. plus rations between them and were required to live in the Workhouse. Escaping from it in the evening, the Schoolmaster returned several times 'intoxicated' and both were dismissed. At £20 a year, porters were particularly difficult to keep, and even at £140 the Relieving Officer sometimes found his duties 'more than he could properly manage'.[88] From their own salaries of £25-50 p.a., with additional payments for midwifery cases, the Union Medical Officers also had to provide their own medicines, leeches and other requirements.

The value of the Poor Law in providing medical services can easily be overlooked, and here the Medical Officers themselves were often instrumental in improving their quality. A separate Infirmary was built at the Northampton Workhouse in 1842 at a cost of £1,000 and largely on the insistence of the same Mr. Woods whose qualifications were later found to be incomplete. Here the occupants enjoyed, on medical grounds, a bed to themselves, a privilege extended only to adult males, on moral grounds, in the main workhouse,[89] but most relief of this kind was administered on an outdoor basis, often in the form of additions to the diet which were perhaps more effective and certainly more palatable than many of the medical treatments employed at the time. However, the Guardians did not encourage the poor to regard this aspect of the system as anything but a last resort. Proposals to provide medical care virtually on demand were 'unanimously opposed' by them in 1860 on the grounds that this would 'render less provident the Poor themselves, who, if they find they are entitled to Medical Orders so easily, and that the relief is not to be deemed parochial relief . . . will no longer enter into sick and benefit clubs, or dispensaries'.[90]

The Guardians were also the agency through which since 1841 central government had provided free vaccination against smallpox, which became compulsory for infants in 1853. Less than a tenth of the babies born within the Northampton Union area in 1859 were actually vaccinated, but the Board was unwilling to pursue the matter beyond persuasion. 'No comment' was its usual response to the many complaints of 'serious neglect' from the centre, and in the light of the popular opposition roused by the more stringent terms of a further Act in 1871, discretion here was much the better part of valour. Medical opinion itself was divided about the effectiveness of vaccination and its risks,[91] but popular opposition rested more on a view of compulsion as an attack on individual liberty. 'We don't believe in it' was the flat response which successive Medical Officers of Health were still receiving well into the 20th century, and prosecuting people for standing on their principles was not calculated to enhance the popularity of a body which was never of the most popular.

Indeed, if central authority had little else to recommend it to the localities, it did have the virtue of providing someone else to blame for measures which rarely pleased either the rate-paying electorate or the voteless poor themselves. Even so, despite the thankless and time-consuming nature of the work, there was rarely any shortage of willing candidates in Northampton. There could be personal compensations of course, not least the satisfaction of a sense of duty to the less fortunate. Control over expenditure and thus the level of the poor rate was an obvious attraction, and although the Poor Law Board ranked some way below the Corporation in terms of collective and individual prestige, the Guardians could also enjoy a certain status in the community and command a degree of respect and loyalty from the labouring classes, if only because the latter might find themselves pleading their case for relief before them at some future point.

The political value of the office is never to be forgotten, of course, and in the war on all fronts conducted between the parties after 1835 the contesting of elections on party political lines was much to be expected. Even before the extension of the franchise in 1867 the labouring classes of the town had a significant stake in parliamentary elections as freemen of the borough or 40s. freeholders, and these were often decided in the light of local as much as national concerns. Paupers lost their vote *pro tem*, but past and potential clients of the Board could well be influenced by their own treatment or the reputation of its component politicians. Elections to local bodies too could be decided on issues of the moment which were beyond their own immediate sphere of activity; and if John Bates had no real hope of election when he contested a seat on the Board in All Saints in 1860 — he ended bottom of the poll — one platform was as good as another for keeping a politician and his cause before the public eye.

Membership of the Poor Law Board, the Improvement Commission and the Borough Council often overlapped, and, politics apart, this too was much to be expected when property qualifications as yet limited all three offices to a fairly narrow social group. Women were not otherwise excluded as Guardians, but the distinction of gaining the first 'lady member' of a local body in Northampton went in due course to the Northampton School Board, set up under the Forster Act of 1870 to supplement the already considerable achievements of the voluntary schools. Like the Poor Law Board, the School Board could provide a useful training in the arts of political debate and the procedures of local decision-making for those who aspired to higher municipal office, and it too was a natural arena for political and religious contest. Its own work will be considered later; but the addition of another autonomous body to the variegated list of existing English and Welsh local authorities did nothing to introduce order into a 'system' which so little dignified the word that one Cabinet minister described it in 1871 simply as 'a chaos'.

In this respect as in others the 'revolution' heralded by the municipal reform of 1835 still had some way to go. It was in motion, nevertheless, and it had some surprises in store for those accustomed to holding the reins of local government in their own hands. Women would in due course invade the male bastion of the Poor Law Board, if not as yet the Borough Council, and as both became more accessible to working-class members, Liberals and Conservatives would find themselves in the company of Socialists. In some respects, however, the direction of local government over the next few decades was already clear. On the one hand local authorities would continue to make the revolution for themselves, acquiring new powers on their own initiative and engaging in new areas of activity by their own choice. In Northampton these would include leisure facilities, water and tramways and, a little before the First World War, municipal housing.

On the other hand, central government would provide the localities with more and more permissive powers, and as they proved unequal to the needs of the time or simply went unused, it would substitute permission for compulsion. This was particularly so in the field of public health, where the Sanitation Act was followed by a new Public Health Act in 1872 and by a succession of statutes conferring new powers or adding to duties which, said the Borough Medical Officer of Health in the early 1890s, were already 'multifarious and onerous': 'we have on the one hand to see in administering these statutes that the health of the community is zealously protected, and on the other that private interests are not heedlessly interfered with, or personal freedom needlessly infringed'.[92] This was always a difficult line to tread, but the M.O.H. was still much in favour of this sort of central direction of local affairs. Others resented it as a curtailment of local autonomy; but if this was enough in itself to place some strain on central-local relations, in Northampton at least the main source of stress lay in the failure of government to match its 'interference' with its money. As the obligations laid on the localities increased, the proportion of the costs borne by the Exchequer diminished — and thus, whatever form the 'revolution' took in the future, the hapless ratepayers would have to dig deeper and deeper into their own pockets to finance it.

Notes
 1. *N.M.*, 2 Jan. 1836.
 2. *N.H.*, 31 Dec. 1835; *N.M.*, 2 Jan. 1836 & 26 Dec. 1835.
 3. That is, to occupiers of rateable property in the borough with an annual rateable value of over £30, or with personal property to the value of at least £1,000, who had paid rates for the previous 30 months. Candidates were also required to live within seven miles of the borough.
 4. *N.M.*, 2 Jan. 1836.
 5. Northampton Corporation (hereafter N.C.) Minutes, 6 June 1842.
 6. *Northampton Chronicle*, 2 Jan. 1836. See also Hatley, V. A., 'Battle for the Mace', *N.P.&P.*, 3, 4, (1969-70).
 7. Quoted in Fraser, D., *Urban Politics in Victorian Britain* (1976), Ch.3.
 8. 'Battle for the Mace', op.cit.
 9. Northampton County Borough Council (hereafter N.C.B.C.) Minutes, 3 June 1891.
10. *N.H.*, 2 Sept. 1837.
11. *Manuscript Diary of Municipal Politics, 1835-97*, 1858. (N.L.I.S. 198-781).
12. *N.H.* cutting 1840, otherwise undated.
13. Ibid., 12 Nov. 1853. The Liberals had been meeting at the Peacock in Market Square since the 18th century. Rebuilt after the Great Fire, the balcony of the inn overlooked the Square and provided a convenient 'platform' from which to address public meetings.
14. The development of the Committee system was largely a matter of administrative convenience. At this time only the Watch Committee was a legal requirement.
15. Cox, J. C. (ed.), *Records of the Borough of Northampton* (1898), Vol.2, p.35.
16. Letter to the Mayor, 2 Nov. 1844 (N.L.I.S. 198-780).
17. *N.M.*, 24 Feb. 1838.
18. N.C. Minutes, 13 March 1837; 14 June 1836; 4 Dec. 1837.
19. Northampton Borough Police, *Rules, Regulations and Orders* (1849). See also Williamson, J., *A History of Northampton Borough Police, 1850-1950* (1950), and Cowley, R., *Policing Northamptonshire, 1836-1986* (1986).
20. N.C. Minutes 9 Jan. 1843; 3 Oct. 1836.
21. Ibid., 9 Nov. 1838.
22. Ibid., 28 Jan. 1836.
23. Quoted in Ellis, C., *History in Leicester* (1948), p.121.
24. N.C. Minutes, 20 Nov. 1837.
25. Ibid.
26. *N.M.*, 12 May 1838.
27. Ibid., 5 Jan. 1860.
28. Ibid.
29. N.M., 11 Feb. 1860.
30. Northampton Borough Council, *Northampton Remembers the Guildhall* (1989), p.20.
31. Briggs, A., *Victorian Cities* (1968 edn.), p.159.
32. *N.H.*, 23 Feb. 1861.
33. *N.M.*, 26 Oct. 1861.
34. *N.H.*, 15 Jan. 1892.
35. *N.M.*, 20 April 1861.
36. The Eleanor Cross on the London Road near Delapre Park is one of the three surviving memorials erected by Edward I marking the route of her cortege to London in 1290. The others are at Geddington, Northants., and Waltham.
37. *N.M.*, 15 Dec. 1887, letter from Isaac Tarry, 'ratepayer and amateur architect'.
38. Ibid., 21 May 1864.
39. *Building News*, Vol.7 (1864); *N.M.* 26 Oct. 1861 & 21 May 1864.
40. *N.M.*, 30 Oct. 1869.
41. Ibid., 4 Nov. 1871.
42. *N.H.*, 27 Nov. 1869.
43. *N.M.*, 21 May 1864.
44. Handbill signed 'One of the Seventeen', 1870 (N.L.I.S. 198-842).

45. Handbill signed 'A Town Councillor', 29 March 1870 (N.L.I.S. 198-842).
46. Handbill signed 'A Disinterested Ratepayer', 8 Dec. 1870 (N.L.I.S. 198-842).
47. Northampton Improvement Commission (hereafter N.I.C.) Minutes, 22 Sept. 1813 (N.R.O.).
48. Ibid., 10 Aug. 1779.
49. Ibid., 3 March 1850; Northampton County Borough Council (hereafter N.C.B.C.) Minutes, 3 June 1929.
50. *N.C.* Minutes, 15 May 1843.
51. P.P. Lords, Vol.26 (1842), Report on the Sanitary Condition of the Labouring Population.
52. Northampton Bills of Mortality (N.L.I.S. 198-752).
53. P.P. Lords, Vol.26 (1842), op.cit.
54. N.I.C., Minutes of Survey and Buildings Committee, 26 Nov. 1844.
55. N.I.C. Minutes, 7 Feb. 1872.
56. Ibid., 19 Sept. 1849.
57. *N.M.*, 10 Aug. 1850.
58. *The Economist*, 20 May 1848.
59. N.I.C. Minutes, 7 Feb. 1872.
60. Prospectus of the Northampton General Cemetery Co. (1846). Joseph Adnitt, Thomas Grundy and Charles Mobbs were among its promoters.
61. Report to the Sanitary Authorities of the Counties of Northampton, Leicestershire, Rutland and Buckinghamshire (1874).
62. N.C., Health Report (1887).
63. N.I.C. Minutes, 6 Jan. & 3 Feb. 1875. The Commissioners concluded that there were 'within the Asylum itself causes sufficient to produce fever, diarrhoea and dysentery'.
64. *Leeds Intelligencer*, 29 Oct. 1836.
65. Quoted in Fraser, D., The Evolution of the British Welfare State (1980 edn.), p.61.
66. 'Report to the Sanitary Authorities . . . of Northampton', op.cit.
67. Quoted in Fraser, D., op. cit., p.57.
68. Ibid., p.35.
69. *Royal Commission on the Poor Laws* (1834), App.A, Pt.1, p.104.
70. First Annual Report of the Poor Law Commissioners (1835).
71. Brixworth Union Minute Book, 13 Oct. 1836 (N.R.O.).
72. Brundage, A., 'The Landed Interest and the New Poor Law', *English Historical Review* (Jan. 1972), p.39. See also Brundage, A., *The Landed Interest and the Establishment of the New Poor Law in Northamptonshire* (1970), unpublished Ph.D. thesis U.C.L.A.
73. The rural parishes of the Northampton Union were Abington, Great and Little Billing, Nether and Upper Heyford, Kingsthorpe, Weston Favell, Bugbrooke, Dallington, Duston, Harpole, Kislingbury and Upton.
74. Earle to Poor Law Commission, 1 June 1838, P.R.O., M.H. 12/8737.
75. Handbill, 18 July 1837 (N.L.I.S.).
76. Petition to Poor Law Commission, July 1837, P.R.O., M.H. 12/8080.
77. Brundage, A., unpublished thesis, op. cit.
78. Northampton Poor Law Union (hereafter N.P.L.U.) Minutes, 1 Feb. 1842 (N.L.I.S.).
79. Ibid.
80. Northampton Union Guardians' Motion Book, 1836-1930, 14 Jan. 1840 (N.R.O.).
81. N.P.L.U. Minutes, 23 May 1843 (N.L.I.S.).
82. Handbill, 18 July 1838, op.cit.
83. N.P.L.U. Minutes, 12 April 1842 (N.L.I.S.).
84. Ibid., 6 May 1856 (N.R.O.).
85. Ibid., 3 June 1856 (N.R.O.).
86. Ibid., 21 Feb. 1855 (N.R.O.).
87. Ibid., 13 July & 12 Oct. 1841 (N.L.I.S.).
88. Ibid., 7 March 1843; 27 June 1843; 25 Jan. 1842 (N.L.I.S.).
89. Ibid., 29 March 1842.
90. Ibid., 24 April 1860.
91. See, for instance, the report of a meeting on this issue at the Corn Exchange in *N.H.*, 2 June 1860.
92. N.C.B.C., Health Report (1893).

Chapter Three

Radical Northampton: From Bradlaugh to the Great War

... the trade has now developed into one of large concerns ... Who shall say this state of affairs is
for the good either of the town, the trade, the employers, or the employed? Yet we must take it as
we find it, for the great are becoming greater, and the small are gradually going to the wall.

Shoe and Leather Record, 26 June 1908

Bradlaugh taught men that Atheism was not wrong. Ministers of the Gospel were compelled to
preach that it was ... in Northampton there are more religious men and women, and more professed
Atheists and Agnostics, than, size for size, there are in any town or city in England.

Northamptonshire Nonconformist, March 1891

Atheism was wrong, said Pickering Perry in November 1874, but he 'would not quarrel
with any of those who were Secularists'.[1] Nonconformity, in his view, could no longer afford
to quarrel with Free-thought, for in the space of a few months 'and with a majority in the
Borough of 1,500 Liberal voters', Liberal Northampton had become, at parliamentary level
at least, Conservative Northampton. In the February general election Pickering Phipps
pushed Gilpin into second place and Charles Merewether relegated Lord Henley to fourth,
while Merewether himself was elected in the October bye-election which followed Gilpin's
death. On both occasions the man who split the Liberal vote and allowed the Tories to
'steal into the representation' ended at the foot of the poll, but each time Charles Bradlaugh's
share of the vote increased as that of the Liberals fell.

The moral of these events was painfully clear, and within a short time an agreement
negotiated by Joseph Gurney and John Middleton Vernon had given the Radicals equal
rights with the Liberals to nominate future parliamentary and municipal candidates. 'We
would endeavour to knit together the two great sections of the Liberal party ...', declared
a handbill from the local elections of 1874, 'We ask no sacrifice of principle. All that has
been sought or conceded is a mutual recognition by two equal divisions of the party, that
they do possess, and ought to possess between them, united if practicable, at all events
without opposing each other, the right to regulate the Parliamentary and Municipal
Representation of the Borough'.[2]

There was 'no alternative but political extinction'; but others were not so sure. No friend
of Bradlaugh before the event, an attack on its offices by his supporters in the post-election
rioting in October 1874 did nothing to soften the *Mercury*'s hostile line, while John Bates
was one of several Radicals to resign rather than accept a compromise with the Liberals.
In 1876 the United Liberal Association also split, with the Rev. Thomas Arnold of Castle
Hill and the Primitive Methodist minister Joseph Ashford prominent among the anti-
Bradlaugh element which now founded the New Liberal Association. The U.L.A. became
in turn the Old Liberal Association, headed by Vernon, Perry and M. P. Manfield, but it
would not yet accept that the Radical candidate it was pledged to support would have to
be Bradlaugh himself. On the contrary, said the *Mercury* in 1877, when he appeared as a
defendant in one of the most celebrated obscenity trials of the century, it would certainly
not be Bradlaugh, and 'all can now cordially co-operate in selecting men worthy to
represent this important constituency in the interest of our common cause'.[3]

Along with Mrs. Annie Besant, also a leading secularist, Bradlaugh had re-published
The Fruits of Philosophy, a pamphlet of birth-control advice written in 1830 by the American

18. Charles Bradlaugh (1835-91). Radical leader and freethinker, M.P. for Northampton 1880-91. 'A sincere friend of the people, his life was devoted to freedom, liberty and justice'.

19. The Great Northamptonshire Stakes. Handbill from the October 1874 by-election. Bradlaugh ended in third place, behind the Conservative Charles Merewether and the official Liberal candidate William Fowler.

Dr. Charles Knowlton. At 6d. a copy it was, in the view of some, a laudable attempt to make such advice more accessible to the working classes; nothing but an incitement to moral depravity in that of others. A 'filthy, dirty book', said the Solicitor General of it at the Bradlaugh-Besant trial, and was the man who published it fit to be a Member of Parliament, asked one local minister in a lengthy 'Expostulation' to the voters of the borough? Along with many Nonconformists whose votes were crucial to Bradlaugh's election, he did not think so, but when the Liberal nominee A. S. Ayrton was thrown from his horse three weeks before the general election of 1880 and forced to withdraw, he would get their support nonetheless. Invited to replace Ayrton, Henry Labouchere agreed on condition that Bradlaugh received the second nomination. After all, he argued, 'whatever the religious opinions of a candidate might be, they were sending him to Parliament to perform certain political duties, and if his political views were in accordance with their own, religion had nothing to do with it'.[4]

Faced with a repeat of 1874, the Liberals surrendered. Labouchere himself topped the poll, but 'they've swallowed Bradlaugh after all', as he commented when the results were declared. Rural anticlericalism, radical free-thought and religious nonconformity had finally come together to present a united Liberal front, confirmed soon afterwards by the formation of the Northampton Liberal and Radical Union. Northampton, as the Birmingham Nonconformist minister Robert Dale concluded, 'is not a conspicuously irreligious town . . . among those who sent Mr. Bradlaugh to the House there must be a considerable number who regard Mr. Bradlaugh's religious position with strong hostility . . . [but] they preferred to be represented by a Liberal, even though he was an avowed Atheist, to being represented by a Tory . . .'.[5] Bradlaugh's problems were not yet over, for when it came to swearing the parliamentary oath of office, religion had everything to do with it. Not for six years was he allowed to take his seat in the Commons, but on this issue of constitutional liberties, Nonconformity was behind him every step of the way. Capable too of inspiring great personal loyalty, he was 'the Greatest most fearless of Democrats that I ever knew', wrote one working man of him: 'I never left that man — Politically — till Death parted us. I was in all his Struggles. When they kicked him out of Parliament I helped to put him back'.[6]

Five times Northampton sent him back, in bye-elections in 1881, 1882 and 1884, and in the general elections of 1885 and 1886, before Parliament finally conceded its right to be represented by its chosen representative. The N.L.R.U., however, soon found itself facing a new challenge. He 'disliked anything in the shape of class distinction', said Gurney in 1874, when the Radical choice of two employers as municipal candidates was criticised: 'He did not like the idea of any working man setting up as a class in opposition to another class because one was the employer and the other the employed'.[7] Put into practice in 1886 through a local branch of the Marxist Social Democratic Federation, he liked it still less; but few as they were at first, and 'for the most part contemptuously ignored . . . or reviled as advocates of bloodshed and plunder', the Socialists soon found a chance to press their case in the trade dispute in the footwear industry in 1887. Originating in a dispute over wage rates in July of that year at the firm of Cove and West, it ended in January 1888 in a compromise which left not only the S.D.F. but the footwear trade union itself 'unquestionably . . . more numerous and better combined'.[8]

Founded in Stafford in 1873 after a split in the footwear craft union, the Amalgamated Cordwainers Association, the National Union of Operative Rivetters and Finishers had as yet made limited progress in Northampton. A weekly subscription of 6d. entitled members to sickness, funeral and other benefits as well as financial support during official trade disputes : but 'the majority of our men here would rather spend their money at the public house than pay towards the improvement of their social position', wrote the local branch secretary in 1878.[9] Sixpence was no small sum even to the most sober, but the 1859 strike was still close enough in memory to account in part for apathy on the one side and hostility to the union from employers on the other. 'If a man gets work in a shop', the secretary noted in the following year, 'he is obliged to be very careful not to mention that he belongs to a Trade Society, for if he does, it means the sack, and this in a town that boasts of its liberties'.[10] 'No man had the right to step in between himself and his men', said one employer in 1882, 'who if not satisfied with such terms as he chose to offer, were at liberty to seek employment elsewhere'.[11]

So they were, but wage-cutting was the first resort of employers in the face of the falling profits of the 'Great Depression'. The shoe and leather trades were less severely affected than others, but trade was still 'far from brisk', the *Mercury* noted in 1878, and the export trade 'the one redeeming feature'.[12] It was still buoyant enough to attract more migrants to the town, and between 1871-91 the population grew by almost 20,000 to a little over 61,000. However, hiring labour by the day or week instead of at piece rates, sub-dividing lasting and finishing processes to use unskilled labour, putting out 'basket work' to cheaper rural workers, and re-classifying work to reduce piece rates were all employed to cut production costs. As the agricultural depression of the 1870s swelled the pool of surplus labour and reduced its bargaining power still further, few workers were in a position to dictate their own terms. With only 600 members among the 15,000 or more local shoemakers in the mid-1880s, the footwear union was in a poor position to negotiate them on their behalf. Local wages were so low by comparison with those of the strongly unionised London trade that its manufacturers were once again shifting production to Northamptonshire, and by the mid-1880s the Union Executive was under pressure from its London Metropolitan branch to deal with the Northampton 'blackspot', to narrow the differential in wages and protect the position of shoemakers elsewhere.

Cove and West had been 'long an eyesore re wages', it was said in 1887, and when the firm rejected a new wage statement proposed by the Union, its workers came out on strike. The dispute was referred to the local Arbitration Board, revived in 1885 after a short-lived experiment earlier in the decade, but it was still unsettled in November when the Northampton Manufacturers' Association drew up a uniform statement — applicable to all its member firms — which left the classification of work, and thus the determination of piece rates, in their own hands.[13] Close classification of work, they said, would simply drive custom elsewhere; but the union was now determined to establish its position in Northampton, and after a five-week lock-out ending in January 1888 it could claim not a little success. Under the final settlement all questions of classification were to be referred to the Arbitration Board and judged against a specially-commissioned case of standard samples from bests to sevenths. While some piece rates were reduced, others were brought closer to the London level, and if the results were 'not all that we could have desired', the union concluded, 'still . . . we have awakened the men of Northampton to the necessity of combining for the protection of their own wages, as well as the wages of our members in other branches'.[14]

The Northampton branch gained 250 members in the course of the dispute, and the Union as a whole emerged with a more confident and aggressive attitude which employers found not a little disturbing. It also began to organise new groups of workers: rough-stuff cutters, female closers on a limited scale, and the clickers who formed the Northampton No.2 branch, their 'aristocratic' status eroded by the use of clicking presses and cheaper youth labour. In 1890, when it adopted the more appropriate name of the National Union of Boot and Shoe Operatives, manufacturers responded by forming a National Federation of local employers' associations, 'a body which we shall have to watch very closely', said Fred Inwood, President of the Northampton No.1 branch, 'so as to prevent ourselves from being caught napping'.[15] Labour and leather accounted for some 80% of the costs of finished footwear, and as union pressure on the one hand and price-fixing by American cartels on the other pushed up the cost of both, manufacturers were in fact looking more and more to machinery to cut production costs. Welt-stitching, heel-building, paring and buffing machines were all available by the late 1880s, and most significantly — since it had long been thought too delicate an operation to be mechanised — lasting machines.

Costly in itself, most of this machinery also required a large investment in suitable premises, but beyond the economies of scale achieved by concentrating all processes in one place, factory production promised to deprive the shoemakers of the control they retained over their hours of work and their output. 'There seems to be no control over rivetters and finishers', one employer complained in 1885, 'they appear to have every licence to do as they like, while . . . the clickers and other indoor hands must expect summary dismissal if they are not at their work regularly and turn out so much work'.[16] For reasons of its own N.U.B.S.O. was also anxious to see an end to outdoor work. 'Basket work' in particular depressed the wages of other operatives, and indoor workers were easier to organise. Indoor working was largely achieved in Northampton by 1894, but on this and other matters the Union leadership was out of step with some of its own rank-and-file.

Many 'protest against Union interference with their liberty . . . the bulk of Northampton men would rather let matters remain as they are', it was noted in 1892.[17] 'There is an idea amongst a few of our members here that Arbitration is not so good as the old system of strikes', the Northampton branches reported in the same year.[18] Pressed to abandon the one for the other, in 1894 five local officials resigned within a matter of months, but here as elsewhere the leadership was coming under challenge from Socialist unionists who found its approach to the employers altogether too moderate. It had its successes, even so, and in an agreement which narrowly averted a general lock-out in 1892, the Union secured higher wages for clickers and rough-stuff cutters, a 54-hour week, a uniform meal break and restrictions on the number of youths employed in clicking, lasting and finishing departments. More than generous concessions in the employers' view, their own patience was tried by the Union's failure to fulfil its agreement to enforce discipline in the workplace.

First and foremost this was a matter of keeping the workers inside it. 'Business operations have this week been partially suspended owing to the Spring race meeting which is looked upon as an historic institution', it was said in 1892, 'Neither depression in trade nor disputes offset the success of this annual holiday, for the shoemaker will have it'.[19] Like the annual Militia training, this was the occasion for a general exodus, but production was constantly disrupted in pursuit of the many day-to-day diversions which constituted 'fresh air'. Outdoor workers were still accustomed to coming and going as they pleased, and when employers took to locking them in the workshop during 'working hours', they simply went on strike. Unofficial strikes, however, were only a part of the rearguard action fought by the shoemakers against machinery and factory discipline, and everything it implied in terms of their status, their customary working practices, and indeed their whole lifestyle.

Factory production might curtail their liberty, but it did not prevent them from restricting their output. If they 'run a machine for five minutes at full speed', wrote the editor of the *Shoe and Leather Record* in 1892,

> they seem to think it necessary to stop it and see that no breakage has occurred. Then they walk about the shop and borrow an oil can or spanners wherewith to do some totally unnecessary thing . . . if the operator is questioned he says 'machines are no good; I could do the work quicker and better by hand'. And so he could, for he takes care not to let a machine beat a shop mate working by hand on the same job . . . does all he can to induce manufacturers to abandon mechanised devices and go back to hand labour.[20]

Faced with a twelve-fold increase in American footwear imports in the previous year, and convinced that N.U.B.S.O. was in the grip of the 'anti-commercial spirit of the new socialist religion, which . . . does not fit in with the more rapid production of goods', in 1895 manufacturers in Federated centres made a concerted effort to break its power and capture control of production once and for all.

Following strikes in Leicester and Northampton in March that year, they locked out their workers and waited until hardship and exhausted union finances forced them back on their own terms. The 'Great Lock-Out' lasted for almost six weeks, the union emerged £56,000 the poorer, and the employers with 'a charter of rights . . . under which three-fourths of the disputes which affected the industry would be impossible'.[21] They included the option of imposing day work or piece work, and the right to make 'reasonable regulations for time-keeping and the preservation of order'. New factory rules were quickly imposed in Northampton, providing for the locking of doors during working hours and prohibiting amongst other things 'swearing, using obscene language, singing, shouting or unnecessary noise; sending out for beer or other intoxicating drink, throwing leather or other articles at each other, and writing or drawing upon the walls or doors'.[22]

Most disputes were in future settled by arbitration, and relations within the industry entered a more harmonious phase. Nevertheless, unofficial stoppages remained common. Often provoked by complaints of rudeness from supervisors, rigid enforcement of the factory rules or the speeding up of machinery, they were testimony in part to the stresses of exchanging one way of working, one way of life, for another. In Northampton, however, in a campaign orchestrated by its S.D.F. members — among them James Gribble, who as N.U.B.S.O. national organiser led the march of the Raunds shoemakers to London in 1905 — the Union itself opposed the introduction of Quantity Statements in the early 20th century and went some way to defeat their object. Providing for a minimum wage in exchange for an agreed weekly output, work done over and above this was paid for at piece rates. This 'supplementary wage' system was accepted with some enthusiasm elsewhere, but the Northampton trade held to the principle of 'sharing out the work', keeping as many employed as possible by producing enough to earn the minimum wage, and no more.

They had 'an altruistic attitude towards each other', wrote one trade journal in 1903, 'one man fearing to do too much lest he should rob his fellow-workman of employment or set him an inconvenient pace'.[23] Not that it approved; for how could employers compete effectively when their output was restricted in this way? Many managed quite well despite it, but for different reasons others did fall by the wayside. The number of firms in the town fell from 505 in 1893 to around 180 in 1914. Between 1885-1913 a total of 269 businesses went into liquidation, among them that of Robert Derby, former Mayor, Alderman and J.P., and one-time possessor of 'a considerable fortune'. There was 'something almost pathetic' in the downfall of this, 'one of the oldest and most respected' firms in the trade, wrote the *Boot and Shoe Trades Journal* of its collapse in 1900 — but the machinery sold at auction was outdated, there were no lasting or finishing machines among it, and it 'illustrates once more the folly of men continuing in business beyond their times, in vain hope of making old notions square with new.[24]

A. E. Marlow's St James's Works were described in 1909 as 'simply an unrivalled economic machine, in which the machine proper and the human agent are component parts', but as he pointed out, the capital to finance new premises and machinery were not the only requirements of the new times. 'The modern manufacturer must combine wide knowledge with technical skill', he said, 'He must be a judge of men and a judge of machinery. He must be fertile in original ideas, and have the power of initiative. He must join with unfailing foresight and breadth of vision a faculty for detail. And he must be a born traveller, and have a first-hand acquaintance with the markets of the world'.[25] The leasing of machinery enabled some small manufacturers to stay in business and others to enter it, but 'the tendency of the times is for the great to become greater, and the less to be crushed out of existence'.[26] In the early 20th century the average number of employees per firm rose to around 200, but in 1908 1,000 workers were employed at the single-storey, 400-foot frontage Manfield factory, opened on the Wellingborough Road in 1892 and now managed by M. P. Manfield's sons James and Harry.[27]

In that year it produced some 400,000 pairs of footwear, sold like those of other leading manufacturers through a chain of retail shops in Britain and abroad. By 1914 Crockett and Jones and the 'True-form' works of Sears and Co. were also employing over 1,000 workers, and Charles and Edward Lewis had closer to 1,500 at their St James's End Works. The Barratt brothers, William and David, were more recent entrants to the trade, beginning in 1903 with mail order sales designed to tap the dispersed rural market. Customers sent a traced outline of their feet with their order — hence the name of the 'Footshape' Boot Works on the Kingsthorpe Road to which the business moved in 1913 — but David Barratt also held shares in a rather different operation, the Pioneer Co-operative Boot Society. Founded in 1905 by James Gribble with the aim of supplying boots to members of the S.D.F. and devoting the profits to its work, it was more successful than some similar ventures. One co-operative set up after the 1887 strike folded within five years, but the Pioneer was reconstituted after the S.D.F. split in 1917 and continued to trade until 1924.

However, said William Barratt, whose own socialism did not endear him to his co-manufacturers, 'he who has goods to sell should holler, and not whisper down a well'. Like other leading firms, the Barratts did their 'hollering' through advertisements in national newspapers and periodicals, through catalogues and commercial travellers, and by adopting their own distinctive brand names. Among those used by Church and Co. of Duke Street, for instance, was the 1884 Crystal Palace Exhibition medal-winning 'Adapted', made in six widths and 'every conceivable style and material'; or from the 'Waukerz' factory of G. T. Hawkins, the 'Demon Ventilated Tennis Shoe' with air chamber between sole and insole.[28] Regional specialisation within the trade was also well-advanced by the turn of the century. Children's and women's fashion footwear was largely the preserve of Leicester, and high-quality women's shoes of Norwich, while Northampton specialised in the male mass market and, along with Street, high-quality men's footwear. Most manufacturers still employed some 'hand-sewn' workers for this market, and to some extent this slowed down the rate at which labour was displaced by machinery.

Even so, half the applicants to the Northampton Distress Committee in 1910-11 were shoemakers, 80% of them lasters and finishers, and a third of the total cited machinery and other labour-saving changes in work practices as the cause of their unemployment.[29] Adult male labour was also 'diluted' by the use of cheaper female or youth labour for some processes, and although the numbers employed in the Northampton trade rose from 16,276 to 16,961 between 1901-11, the increase was very largely accounted for by female operatives, with the number of adult males showing a significant if as yet small decline. The 'displaced workers live and must live', as one trade journal wrote in 1888 — but what were they to do for work? The very changes which had brought the industry to this point had of course created new openings in other areas. The firm of Horton and Arlidge, for instance, supplied it with cardboard boxes, moving in 1913 from Derngate to the old Isaac, Campbell & Co. factory in Campbell Square. Local firms printed its labels and catalogues, others made its lasts, and the company of William Wren supplied not only dyes but the boot polishes produced in 1909 at the rate of 16,000 tins an hour.[30]

Leather tanning and dressing were also important, with new processes and new materials catering for more varied tastes — chrome tanning, for instance, to produce glace leather, and the imported Indian goat skins also supplied by the British Chrome Tanning Co. in

.20. International Goodyear Shoe Machinery Co. central depot, Abington Street/Lower Mounts, *c*.1891. 'One of the·most chaste architectural features of the town', it was built to the design of the local architect Edmund Law close to the site of the medieval East Gate.

Grafton Street. So too was the marketing or manufacture of footwear machinery. Founded in 1888 by seven major manufacturers, the Northampton Shoe Machinery Co. first marketed American lasting machines and then manufactured them under licence. The International Goodyear Shoe Machinery Co. had its national depot in a handsome building on the corner of Abington Street and Lower Mounts, while the Northampton Machinery Co. was established in the late 19th century by John Veasey Collier, son of the shoe manufacturer Simon Collier who had abandoned Liberalism for Conservatism during the Bradlaugh controversy. In 1906 it was amalgamated with the machine-making business of his fellow-Conservative C. W. Phipps, one of several local firms who also acted as wholesale mercers to the trade.[31]

These new areas of employment served in turn to increase the town's dependence on its staple trade, but engineering and metal-working received a new stimulus from agriculture, also,employing more machinery during this period, and from the re-location of the London lift-making company of Smith, Major and Stevens at St James's End in 1910. Demand was boosted too by the manufacture of bicycles and, in due course, motor vehicles. A keen cyclist himself, Joseph Grose founded his cycle-making business in 1888, and graduated to building automobile bodies by way of the profits from his patent leather adjustable chain guard and Northampton's first prosecution for speeding. In 1898, driving a three-wheel Coventry Motette along the Wellingborough Road, 'the defendant sounded neither gong, bell or whistle, and was going at such a furious rate that he ran over a dog . . . he was going, witness should think, at the rate of 15 or 16 m.p.h.'.[32] Mr. Grose was fined £1, but by 1912 he was distributing Rovers and Renaults, fitting his own bodies to imported Benz chassis and engines, and running taxi-cabs at the more sedate speed of 10-12m.p.h.

From the Advance Motor Co. in Louise Road came aero engines and the power units for the motorised sledges used in Scott's first Antarctic expedition. In 1907 Mulliner's also turned its works to the manufacture of automobile bodies under the seventh-generation direction of Arthur Mulliner, a founder member of the Royal Automobile Club. 'Be your chassis how good soever', ran one of its advertisements, 'unless the body of your carriage is Mulliner's you have yet much to learn'.[33] One such body, produced for the stage illusionist Lafayette in the early 20th century, was finished in dove grey and mauve with blue, grey and violet stripes, cushions which could be converted into a bed, and images of his dog Beauty on the radiator and headlights. Such was the demand for the company's services in this area that it had to abandon its experimental work in aircraft manufacture for want of mechanics and space.

'Some of the most beautiful models ever put on the market' were produced at the Kingswell Street works of W. J. Bassett-Lowke, pioneer manufacturer of working miniature models, sold throughout the world by mail order. Amongst those offered in 1904-5 were a printing press at 12s. 6d., the L.N.W.R. express locomotive 'Lady of the Lake' at 34s., and for 4s. 6d.-8s. 6d., the authentic 'Railway Smash', two sets of passenger cars with engine 'so constructed that when a collision occurs they fly to pieces'.[34] The new workshops added in 1904 were one of the many building projects which boosted the construction industry, and since 1890 industrialists had also been assured of a 'constant supply of Electricity, day and night' and a 'most perfect and steady form of lighting' by courtesy of the Northampton Electric Light and Power Company's works in Angel Street.

The Gas-Light Company was still flourishing, with some 60% of its output in 1885 consumed by lighting, and much of the rest by the domestic cooking stoves which it rented out. Its own works were extended in 1887, and until the turn of the century the Electric Light Co. provided no real competition. Persuaded in 1892 to install two 1,000-candle-power lights in Market Square as an experiment, the Corporation was no more impressed by their cost — £70 a year — than the inhabitants by their irridescent glow, far too bright for some tastes. As domestic lighting electricity also had its drawbacks, beyond a price of 8d. a unit for the first hour and 4d. thereafter. 'If a customer wishes on any special occasion (not more than once a month) to use all the lights in a private house', declared the company's tariff in 1897, 'he can obtain this privilege by giving 48 hours' notice to the Engineer'.[35] However, as the mains were gradually extended and electric cooking and heating appliances became more available, the number of consumers gradually rose, the price came down, and in 1915 the company moved to a larger site at Nunn Mills.

Among the investors in the Electric Light Co. were Pickering Phipps, and Samuel Seckham, former Oxford architect and chairman of his main local business rival, the Northampton Brewery Co. In brewing too during this period there was a tendency for the great to grow greater at the expense of the small, but through takeovers and mergers rather than bankruptcies. Large-scale integrated production offered economies of scale, but the later 19th-century scramble to 'tie' licensed premises to breweries also increased the capital needs of the brewers and encouraged them to limit their legal liability. Founded around 1874 with a takeover of the Phoenix Brewery, the Northampton Brewery Co. was producing around 100,000 barrels a year when it was converted into a limited company in 1887, and

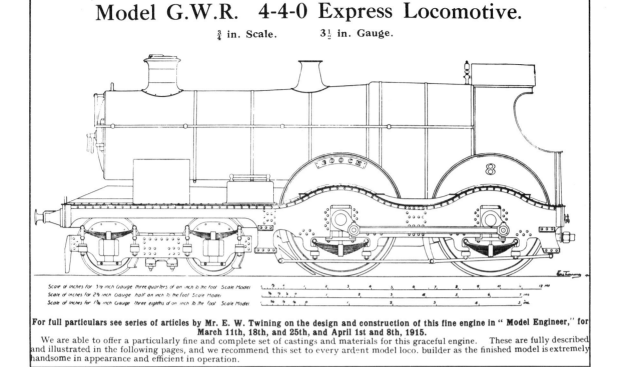

Model G.W.R.   4-4-0 Express Locomotive.

$\frac{3}{4}$ in. Scale. $3\frac{1}{2}$ in. Gauge.

Scale of inches for 3½ inch Gauge three quarters of an inch to the foot Scale Model
Scale of inches for 2½ inch Gauge half an inch to the foot Scale Model
Scale of inches for 1¾ inch Gauge three eighths of an inch to the foot Scale Model

For full particulars see series of articles by Mr. E. W. Twining on the design and construction of this fine engine in " Model Engineer," for March 11th, 18th, and 25th, and April 1st and 8th, 1915.

We are able to offer a particularly fine and complete set of castings and materials for this graceful engine.   These are fully described and illustrated in the following pages, and we recommend this set to every ardent model loco. builder as the finished model is extremely handsome in appearance and efficient in operation.

21.   W. J. Bassett-Lowke & Co. catalogue advertisement, 1915. The company was founded in 1899 by Wenman Joseph Bassett-Lowke, who later served as a Labour councillor and alderman.

22.   Phipps Brewery, Bridge Street, 1905. The company was founded in Towcester in 1801 and moved to Northampton in 1817.

in 1890 it also took over the Lion Brewery of Allen and Burnett. The company was renowned for its N.B.C. Stout and pale ales 'which are esteemed by many in preference to Burton ales', but its full range included milds, bitters and a double-strength brew with the cautionary title of Imperial Stingo.

Like Phipps and Co. it also did a large trade in imported wines and spirits, and owned a string of hotels and pubs in Northampton and beyond: 86 in all in 1887 in five Midland counties.[36] Phipps and Co. took over the local firm of Ratcliffe and Jeffery in 1899, but in the early 1890s its own Bridge Street brewery was already producing over 150,000 barrels a year. 'One of the most perfectly appointed in the country', waste heat from the fermentation process was used to heat water for the public baths opened by Pickering Phipps close by in Cattle Market Road in 1876. Mr. Phipps himself was twice Mayor of the borough, one of its two M.P.s during the Liberal eclipse of 1874-80, and M.P. for the Southern Division of the county from 1881-5. As a permanent memorial to a life undeniably well-spent but indelibly associated with the liquid downfall of many a Northampton shoemaker, his son financed the building of St Matthew's church on the Kettering Road. Built to the design of Matthew Holding and opened in 1893, it was popularly known as 'Phipps' Fire Escape'.

Domestic servants remained one of the largest female occupational groups in Northampton until the First World War, many coming from rural villages to a 'petty place' at the age of twelve or thirteen. Rising to the level of housemaid, in the later 1870s they they could earn a maximum of £26 a year plus board, more commonly £15-20. By the 1890s relative scarcity was strengthening their bargaining position and Northampton households were much troubled by the 'servant question': how to obtain them at a modest price and keep them 'in their place' when an expanding range of female occupations was offering more attractive alternatives.[37] Clerical work, shop work, teaching and nursing were foremost among these, but a growing number were also employed in printing and bookbinding, in cardboard box making, and in the manufacture of ladies clothing, with the Brook Manufacturing Co. in Clarke Road leading the way.

The Northampton Street Tramways Company was a further source of male employment. Founded in 1880, the company was promoted by the chairman of the Cambridge Street Tramways Co., J. S. Balfour M.P., with W. J. Pierce the lone local representative on its first board of directors. 'Northampton is at last being awakened from its normal state of lethargy', declared the *Herald* unkindly in 1881, 'but that principally from outside sources . . . some doubt was expressed as to whether such a thing was required in Northampton, and even whether the running of trams was practically workable in the town'.[38] It was not practical in the case of Bridge Street, but by October 1881 several miles of track had been laid from St James' End in the west to the Kettering Road in the east by way of Castle Station and the Racecourse, and from the town centre to the Catholic Cathedral on the fringe of Kingsthorpe. In the following year the tracks were extended to Kingsthorpe itself, and to Melbourne Gardens beyond St James's End.

So popular were they that the trams were often packed well beyond their 36-passenger horse-drawn capacity. 'Seated in a car sometime since', complained one resident, 'I asked the Conductor how many he was licensed to carry. The impudent answer was "as many as we like" . . . The other night I rode up with 29 inside and 26 on the top. It is time this was put a stop to'.[39] It was; but communications between Northampton and elsewhere were also improved during this period with a mainline railway link from Roade to Rugby through Castle Station. Providing direct routes to Birmingham and London, the Northampton-Rugby section was opened to passengers in December 1881 and the line to Roade in the following April. In the meantime the castle ruins were demolished and the River Nene diverted for a quarter of a mile to make way for a new goods depot and the re-building of the station. 'Northampton now becomes a suburb of London', declared the *Mercury* on its re-opening: 'A gentleman who begins business at ten and finishes at four can now run up to town by train, complete his day's work and return to the bosom of his family in time for a fashionable dinner'.[40] In terms of the carriage of freight it was more useful still, but both the railways and the tramways played a part in advancing the pace of suburban development.

'Everyone is leaving the town and going further off to live', the vicar of All Saints reported in 1910. The 'better class of the working people migrate to the improved artisan dwellings which are being erected in the suburbs', noted the vicar of St Katharine's five years earlier.[41] The lowest income groups were more likely to move within the central areas than beyond them, but census figures confirm this general outward movement. All Saints excepted, the inner town parishes continued to gain population until late in the century, their cheaper rents attracting the bulk of new migrants, but by 1901 that of St Sepulchre and the small southern parish of St Peter was also shrinking. Between 1901 and 1911 the population of the town grew by only 3,000 to just over 90,000, but the exodus continued. The highest increases were recorded by Kingsthorpe, St James's, and Far Cotton, all three embraced by the extension of the borough boundaries in 1901, and in the outer eastern ward of St Edmund; the greatest losses by the innermost wards of Castle and South.

To some extent their population was forced outwards as low rental housing made way for the business and commercial development which pushed up central land prices. The further out the cheaper the land as a rule, and the Freehold Land Society was now spreading its own net ever wider. In 1877 it acquired the 50-acre Kingsley Park site near the racecourse, followed by the East Park estate on the Kettering Road in 1884, and the Whitworth estate which joined it from the Wellingborough Road in 1891. In 1894 it also bought a large site providing over 700 plots some two miles east of the town centre, formerly a part of the Monks Park estate of the draper William Collins. The remainder of the estate was later purchased by Henry Randall, the Conservative shoe manufacturer whose well-known expectation of a knighthood made him the butt of an uncharitable local riddle: 'Why is Monks Park like Heaven? Because there's no (k)night there'.[42] It was duly conferred in 1905, but by then the Freehold Land Society was also developing its Wantage No. 1 site north of Abington Park, completing this impressive list with the adjacent Wantage No. 2 in 1914.

On the Kingsley Park estate a restrictive covenant prohibited the use of houses for the sale of intoxicating liquor. Fears of lowering the tone of the estate rather than objections to drink as such would seem to be behind this move, but until 1887 there were no licensed premises on any of the Society's estates. In that year the Society bowed to popular demand from the residents to provide one such facility, but its application for a licence was opposed by 170 members of the Licensed Victuallers Association on the grounds that it constituted unfair competition.[43] This was perhaps as much a political as a business ploy, for if most publicans were as Tory as ever, the Freehold Land Society was no less Liberal than in its earlier years. Joseph Gurney succeeded Henry Labouchere as President in 1891, while the list of directors in 1895 reads like a roll call of eminent local Liberals: Samuel Smith Campion, for instance, proprietor of the Mercury since 1885;[44] the confectioner Francis Tonsley; F. O. Adams, now running the family bakery of Gurney's Radical colleague Thomas Adams; and Stephen Clarke, former Chartist and co-operator. Richard Cleaver, Robert Derby and the draper Frederick Adnitt were joined as Trustees by one of the Society's few active Conservatives, the builder Henry Martin.[45]

A 'sort of government within a government', wrote that champion of disgruntled citizenry, *The Ratepayer*, in 1886:

a most remarkable and extraordinary influence is being developed more and more every day, in the wonderful power of the Freehold Building and Land Society in the Northampton Town Council . . . arising from the fact that many directors of the Building Society are members . . . We would be the

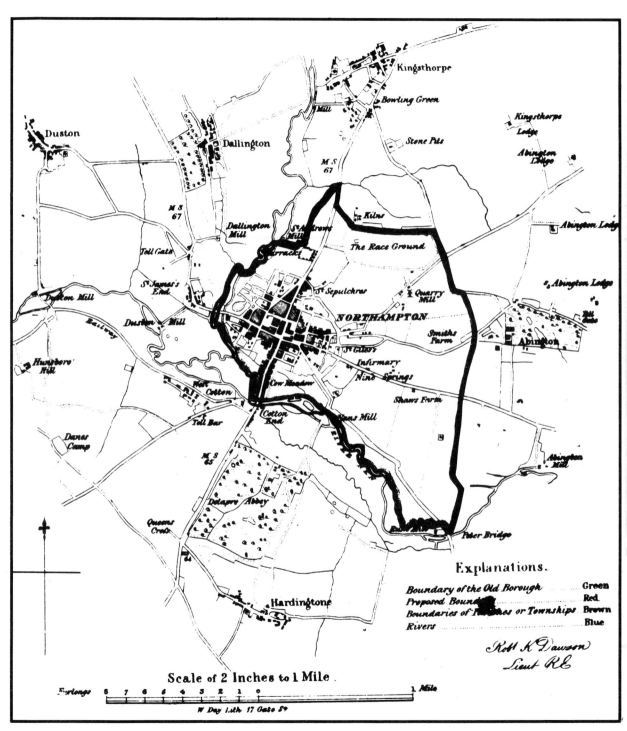

23.   Dawson's map of Northampton, 1835.

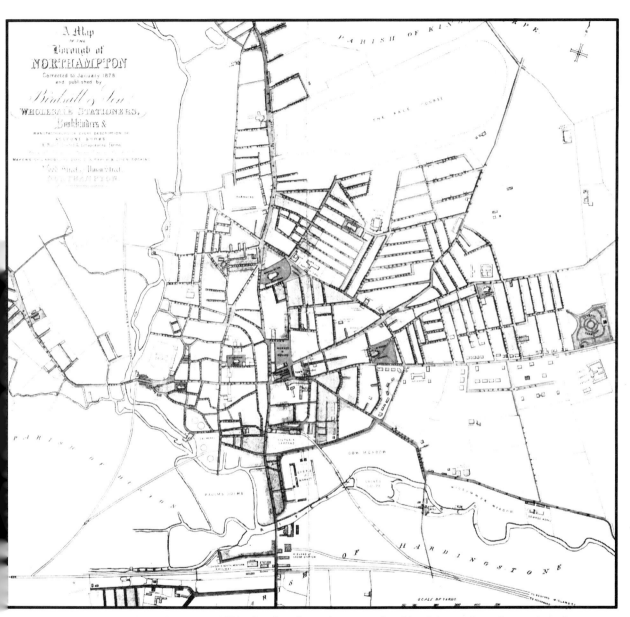

24. Birdsall's map of Northampton, 1878, showing the main areas of residential growth to the north and east.

last in the world to impute or insinuate anything wrong against any man connected with the administration of the town.[46]

Or the first; but William Shoosmith, for instance, was not only solicitor to the Society, he was also Town Clerk and thus legal adviser to the Council itself. So he was, and not only had he been combining both roles for some 20 years, in the Conservative view his probity was so far beyond question that during their lengthy period of municipal control in the 1890s they saw no reason — as they had done in 1855 — to appoint a Town Clerk of their own political persuasion.

How far the Freehold Land Society served to attach its ordinary members to the Liberal cause is impossible to say, but in the view of H. M. Hyndman, national leader of the S.D.F., home ownership itself encouraged complacency and opposition to socialism — and thanks largely to the Society's efforts, it was claimed in 1897, more working-class families owned their own homes in Northampton than in any other town in England.[47] Rising real incomes made it a genuine option for some, but recent research has suggested that the Society's claims were exaggerated. By 1893 its seven estates had provided 2,865 houses, around 25% of the total dwellings in the town, and it was this figure which it cited in evidence to a Parliamentary Select Committee in 1893-4 as representing working-class homeowners. However, it had no accurate record of the number of manual workers among its members, and if the general trend of ownership during this period is any guide, it seems likely that most were drawn from the lower middle classes, and that a proportion of houses were purchased for rental rather than occupation.

Less than 5% of housing in Northampton was owner-occupied in 1884, the majority of it by tradesmen, white-collar workers and skilled footwear or building workers. In 1925 the figure was 21.75%, but even in the municipal wards embracing the bulk of the Society's housing — Kingsley, Abington and St Michael — working-class owner-occupiers accounted for only 21-28% of the total, and over the town as a whole for less than 15%.[48] These figures alone must cast doubt on the Society's claims in the 1890s, but this is not to suggest that working-class families did not benefit from its activities, nor to deny the valuable contribution it made to meeting the housing needs of an expanding town. Other local building societies continued to operate during this period, among them the Artisans' and Labourers' Friend, the Permanent Benefit and, later in the century, the Northampton and Midlands Conservative Building Society. New housing for rent was also provided by, for instance, the shoe manufacturer James Branch around his Bective works at Kingsthorpe, and by Henry Green, builder of the Manfield factory on the Wellingborough Road, who purchased a large site close by and built dwellings for its workforce.

The slowing of the rate of population growth after 1891 was also important here, but by 1911 the average of persons per occupied house had fallen to 4.7 from 5.4 in 1881, and as a study of Northampton and three towns of similar size concluded in 1913, its inhabitants were very reasonably housed by comparison with some. Only 8.7% of Northampton's dwellings were classed as over-crowded, against 13.5% in Reading, 19.7% in Warrington and 50% in Stanley, and while the latter was 'remarkable' for its two-roomed houses, in Northampton the six-room types incorporating the now redundant domestic workshops accounted for 61.5% of the total.[49] Even in 1913 there were still few areas of the town distinctly claimed by the middle classes or abandoned to the working classes. Queen's Park, to the south of Kingsthorpe, and Abington to the east of the centre, were perhaps closest to the former; to the latter, Far Cotton and St James's End, the one with a large population of railway workers, the other with a concentration of shoemakers and engineering workers. Here as elsewhere, however, instead of the residential and industrial zoning which developed in other manufacturing towns, areas of residential building were liberally scattered with factories and warehouses.

Free from the need to fetch and carry, it may be thought, there was no longer any real need for shoemakers to live close to their work. The tramway system was admittedly limited and the cost of fares something to be considered. Cheap workmen's fares were introduced in the early 20th century, but Northampton was still compact enough to be walked with relative ease, and Manfield's, for instance, provided a mess room for employees too distant to go home for dinner. Not every manufacturer could afford to build on the Manfield scale, and many simply stayed where they were, adapting or extending their premises for machine processes; but old habits died hard, and if they must work inside a factory, the shoemakers preferred one close to home, escaping there in the dinner hour and wasting as little time in travelling as possible. From an employers' point of view, reliable, efficient and loyal workers were to be valued, and when a manufacturer also had his political base in a particular area — like the Lewis brothers in St James's, for instance — he might have other good reasons to keep his factory doorstep close to theirs.

As for living on it himself, by the end of the century the wealthier manufacturers were following the trail blazed elsewhere and migrating to country estates. George Turner, for instance, moved in 1883 to Upton Hall, complete with 665 acres of park and farmland, and James Manfield to a Jacobean-style house built for him on a 100-acre site acquired at Weston Favell in 1899. A new wave followed over the next decade: Harry Manfield to Moulton Grange, A. E. Marlow to Preston Deanery Hall, and J. G. Sears to Collingtree Grange.[50] In due course several became members of that formerly reviled species, County Justices; but none were more than five miles distant from the town, and along with their colleagues closer to home, they remained as much involved as ever in its political and social life. This was much to be expected. Never willing to leave it to the Tories, they now had to contest it with Socialists too.

There were exceptions, like G. T. Hawkins, who had 'a hatred of publicity that has unfortunately hindered him from applying his administrative abilities to civic life',[51] but more than a third of the town's leading manufacturers held public office at some time during the later 19th and early 20th centuries, foremost amongst them the Manfields, Edward and Thomas Lewis, Henry Wooding and A. E. Marlow, and on the Conservative side, Henry Randall and Simon and John Veasey Collier. More than two thirds were involved in some kind of social or cultural organisation, almost half were active members of local chapels or churches — the majority were still Nonconformists — and a smaller but still considerable number involved in philanthropic and educational ventures, Friendly Societies, building societies and sporting organisations. Many of these ventures might be seen as a substitute for the 'factory paternalism' exercised in northern manufacturing towns, through industrial welfare schemes, sports and social clubs and the like.[52] There was little scope for this in Northampton until the 1890s, and prosper as they might, few shoe manufacturers could match the wealth of the cotton barons. Over two thirds left personal estates of under £1,000 at death.[53]

However, if the governing elite was as anxious as ever to maintain the bonds of society, it would be wrong to suggest that this was the only or even the main motive behind their activities in the town. 'He had a very keen sense of the responsibility of citizenship, and when it came to him, the responsibility of wealth', it was said of James Crockett, for 'it was the duty of everyone who had the opportunity to give a certain amount of his wealth and a certain amount of his time to public service'.[54] Religion was an important influence here, but Nonconformity had no monopoly of virtue in this respect. The Liberal Anglican Crockett made substantial gifts to the Northampton Church Charities and to the Infirmary — or as it became in 1903, the General Hospital — and invested much time in the School Board, the N.S.P.C.C. and the Charity Organisation Society. Knighted in 1922, he was the son of a shoemaker who started his working life as an errand boy, one of the few manufacturers whose humble origins were a matter of fact rather than the 'rising from the seat' myth promoted as part of the self-help ethic.

Sir Henry Randall, for instance, had not 'come to Northampton with half-a-crown . . . I had nothing and no pocket'.[55] He was in fact the son of a local draper, the nephew of a shoe manufacturer, and began his manufacturing life as a partner in a well-established business; but his 'almost passionate love of his native town' was shared by many of its inhabitants, and this too inspired many an effort to improve the quality of life for all its citizens. Among the many public services which contributed to his own knighthood was the formation with Chief Constable Fred Mardlin of the Good Samaritan Society in 1893, to aid parents 'silently suffering in a struggle with adverse circumstances' by providing clothes, boots and bedding for their children.[56] This was the pioneering model for similar police-assisted societies later established in Glasgow, Birmingham and elsewhere, but in the other voluntary efforts to which civic pride contributed there was in turn much to be proud of.

The Royal Victoria Dispensary, for instance, was so thriving by 1879 that local doctors were complaining of its 'monopoly'.[57] Some 2,000 Friendly Society members and their families were in fact otherwise catered for by the Friendly Societies Medical Institute, founded in 1872 and occupying purpose-built premises in Broad Street by the early 1880s; but as its governors acknowledged, the Victoria Dispensary was now so well established that it could quite well have become self-supporting. Anxious as they were to maintain a middle class presence, it continued on its original basis. However, home nursing was now provided by the Town and County Institution for Trained Nurses, established in 1877 and later working in co-operation with district nurses from the Queen Victoria Institute for Nurses — another body in which Henry Randall played a prominent role. The Institution financed its work with the sick poor from fees paid by private patients. Charges in 1902 ranged from £1 10s. a week for 'ordinary cases', 2gn. for infectious or malignant diseases, plus 1gn. 'for disinfection of nurse' at the end, to 6gn. for a four-week period of maternity care. Surgical cases were treated at a nursing home opened in December of that year by the Institution's Patron, H.R.H. Princess Christian.[58]

For 2-3gn. a week the mentally ill could also be nursed in their own homes, but in practice most were cared for in the County Asylum at Berry Wood or at the former General Lunatic Asylum, re-named in the 1870s as St Andrew's Hospital for Mental Diseases.[59] Ambulance services were also provided on a voluntary basis from 1888 by the Northampton Ambulance Corps, using a horse-drawn ambulance supplied by Mulliners' at a cost of £54 10s. — £6 10s. of it expended for reasons of comfort on rubber tyres. This was replaced in 1912 by a £700 motor ambulance, financed jointly by the Borough Council and an appeal by the Mayor, William Harvey Reeves, who was an active member of the Corps.[60] Several extensions were also made to the Infirmary during this period, including the new wing with a 12-bed children's ward added to mark the Jubilee of Queen Victoria in 1887. The foundation stone was laid by Prince Albert Victor in October that year, in the midst of the Cove and West dispute. Although he was generally warmly welcomed, the *Mercury* reported, there were 'distinct sounds of hissing and booing' at certain points in the procession, and John Bates caused a 'great reaction' by flying the black flag of republicanism.[61]

In the 12 months to July 1887 the Infirmary treated a total of 1871 in-patients in its 144 beds, 793 of them recorded as 'cured', 368 as 'relieved', and one 'absconded'. Tuberculosis and heart disease were the most common medical conditions, and the removal of tumours, circumcision and the amputation of fingers or toes the most frequent forms of surgery. The diagnoses recorded in 1887 were much more precise than the 'fits' and 'fevers' of the Bills of Mortality, but some of the 2,677 accidents and emergencies recorded in that year suggest a rather loose definition of the words. A cut throat certainly qualified — but what of 'wart in the ear' or 'sweating feet'?[62] Perhaps low income groups tapped into the hospital's services in this way in preference to those of the Poor Law, for it was otherwise no more accessible to many than in the past. Among the grounds advanced in 1906 by the S.D.F. for its takeover by the Borough Council was the argument that this would 'abolish the necessity of going begging for letters of admission and often not being able to obtain one'.[63]

Their motion was defeated, but adult education too was still much dependent on voluntary effort. The Mechanics' Institute folded in the mid-1870s and the Useful Knowledge Society in 1884, but from 1885 a series of University Extension Lectures were delivered by academics engaged by the University of Cambridge. The first course on 'Masterpieces' drew an average audience of 500, but from the early 20th century working-class adult education was provided by a branch of the Workers' Educational Association, tailored to the demands of the consumers themselves. On offer in 1907 were lectures on economics, evolution, allotment gardening 'or any other subject . . . to suit as many as possible', delivered at no cost beyond an annual subscription of one shilling or 2s. 6d. per 50 members of affiliated organisations.[64] Although 'definitely unsectarian and unpolitical' in nature, the advent of a national educational organisation run by working men and women themselves was not welcomed in some middle class quarters. 'Knowledge is Power', as the distributors of illegal 'unstamped' radical newspapers proclaimed in the 1820s and '30s, and where the working classes controlled their own education, they would doubtless learn what others preferred them not to know.

Education was also commonly a part of the activities of co-operative societies, and if not for this reason alone they too met with a mixed reception. Were they a reassuring demonstration of the virtue of self-help, or a sign of dangerous working class independence? Producer co-operatives were often short-lived: an alternative to the capitalist system of production, they still had to compete with it. Retailing was the real way to prosperity, the loyalty of members held in the first instance by the dividend paid on purchases. This was the route taken by the Northampton West End Independent and Provident Society, which was founded in 1870 and marked its survival of three turbulent decades by changing its name to the Northampton Co-operative Society in 1900. Membership grew slowly at first, and in 1874, maybe on the part of local traders anxious for their profits, there was a 'malignant attempt to ruin the society by destroying the confidence of its members'. In 1895, having opened four stores and built its own bakery in the meantime, it came close to bankruptcy; but by 1910 it had eight stores with a quarterly turnover of some £10,000, and was also selling coal, drapery, clothing and furniture.[65]

Along with tuition in such things as book-keeping and sales techniques for employees, the Society's educational work embraced classes in the principles of co-operation and a range of social activities for all ages, including in due course a choir, orchestra and drama society, 'junior circles' and an annual children's fête. From 1893 onwards there were also two local branches of the Women's Co-operative Guild, a body which surprised many male co-operators who thought their womenfolk innocuously engaged in more conventional 'feminine' pursuits by mounting an effective national campaign to improve maternity services shortly before the First World War. In general, however, the Northampton Society was as yet little interested in the political potential of the movement, and a request from the Co-operative Union for funds to sponsor a parliamentary representative was flatly refused.[66] Nevertheless, such was the range of activities undertaken by co-operative societies and the commitment of many members to their underlying principles that co-operation could become, as indeed it was intended to be, a whole way of life.

The life of the shoemaker was irrevocably changed by factory production, and by the end of the century the distinctive artisanal culture of Northampton had very largely disappeared. No more downing tools at a whim, but regular hours of continuous work and 'fresh air' restricted to evenings, weekends and Bank Holidays. In 1901 there was still one public house in the town for every 164 inhabitants, but by 1907 Sir Henry Randall was actually complimenting his workforce on their 'temperate habits'. One drunken operative could disrupt the work and lower the wages of a whole team of factory workers — but the monotonous nature of machine work, combined with the need for 'unceasing attention' was said in turn to discourage intellectual leisure pursuits. 'Their opportunities for culture are few', concluded one observer, 'and the exacting demands of the factory leave a tired mind and body, and kill any desire to dig deeply into art, science or literature'.[67] Instead, said a local clergyman, there was 'a great yearning for excitement, for something that will relieve the monotony of a life spent at a machine', which encouraged a passive resort to commercial amusements.[68]

These were now available on the wider scale which rising real incomes demanded, and they too went some way to change the street-based patterns of leisure in the town. In 1884 the Theatre Royal was joined by the Royal Theatre and Opera House in Guildhall Road, designed by Charles John Phipps, architect of the Savoy Theatre in London, for the baker, hotelier and leisure entrepreneur John Franklin. The theatre opened with a performance of *Twelfth Night* by the touring company of Edward Compton, later one of its co-proprietors, and it later staged the first provincial production of *The Mikado*. Open air Shakespearean productions were also staged at the former Melbourne Gardens of John Collier, father of Simon, bought by Franklin in 1886 and re-opened as Franklin's Gardens in the following year. In addition to a large lake 'adorned with swans and other water fowl', they boasted a swimming tank, racecourse, cycle track, cricket ground, and the 'Champs Elysee of Northampton', a one mile promenade lined by lime and poplar trees. For 6d. all day, balloon ascents, firework displays, trapeze acts and brass bands provided additional entertainment on August Bank Holiday Monday in 1887, when there was also a choice of the Temperance Society's Horticultural Show at Delapre Abbey, the Athletic Association's sports at the Racecourse, or railway excursions to Blackpool, Llandudno and Rhyl.[69]

Twice the size of the Royal Theatre and also catering for lower-brow tastes through variety shows, the New Theatre opened in Abington Street in 1912, some years after Thomas's Music Hall at the corner of Gold Street had been converted by way of a Temperance Hall of Varieties and Grose's cycle works into the Palace of Varieties. In 1912, however, the Palace went the way of the future and was converted in turn into the Picture Palace cinema. The Royal Theatre, the Temperance Hall on Newland, and the Wesleyan School at Kingsley Park also doubled as cinemas, the content of films as strictly governed by the licensing regulations of the Council's Watch Committee as the safety of patrons of this highly inflammable form of entertainment:

> No profanity or impropriety of language, no indecency of dress, dance or gesture, nor any offensive personalities ... nor anything calculated to produce riot or breach of the peace, nor any exhibition, recitation, acting or singing which in any manner tends to bring into contempt the Christian religion, or is in any shape offensive to public decency.[70]

The Council took its role as public guardian as seriously as ever, but middle-class attitudes towards the working classes, said James Manfield in his presidential address to the Working Men's Club in 1900, had changed since his father's day when 'they thought that their amusements should be restricted'.[71] Now the factory had gone so far to restrict them, they could afford to change; but the attempt to promote 'rational' recreation had by no means been abandoned. A People's Café or 'coffee tavern' offering a temperate alternative to the pubs was opened in 1879 by the Rev. K. B. Hull, vicar of All Saints, with Gurney, M. P. Manfield and W. J. Pierce among its investors and directors.[72] The temperance lobby also turned out in force to oppose applications for a liquor licence, and the licensing justices themselves restricted the number of pubs in the town by requiring the surrender of an old licence in exchange for a new. On several occasions the Council too used its planning powers to prevent the construction of new music halls, invariably accompanied by a licence to sell drink.[73]

A 'cause of crime and ruin only second to intemperance', efforts were also made to combat gambling. In 1891 the *Northamptonshire Nonconformist* ran a campaign pointing out *inter alia* 'the utter absurdity of pinning his faith on the sporting prophets of the press'. Their record in the Alexandra Park races was admittedly not impressive. *Sporting Life* was 'right in one case, wrong in seven', and the *Licensed Victuallers' Gazette*, demonstrating 'the invariable if not necessary connection with drinking, betting and prize-fighting . . . right once, wrong six times'.[74] However, in targeting young males in particular, the *Nonconformist* was reflecting one of the major anxieties of the later 19th and earlier 20th centuries. On the youth of the nation depended not only success in the contest with the industrial might of the United States and Germany, but on its males in particular, its ability to keep its Empire and to fight the military conflict which growing tensions between the European powers made an ever more likely prospect. Much effort was thus invested in attempts to improve their physical fitness, and to promote the manly virtues of courage, discipline and 'team spirit'.

There was some local opposition to 'militaristic' youth organisations during this period, but companies of the Boys' Brigade, the Church Lads' Brigade and the Girls' Life Brigade were well-established by the end of the century, and they were followed soon afterwards by the Boy Scouts and Girl Guides.[75] The Gymnastics Club and the Athletics Association continued to flourish, but greater stress was now placed on team games, in which non-players could of course participate as spectators. Northampton had been enjoying its cricket for some time already, but this now continued on an expanding and more organised scale. New grounds were provided, and the Northampton Town Cricket League was formed in 1886, its member clubs competing for the Town Challenge Club donated in that year by the Northamptonshire County Cricket Club. Founded in 1878, from 1886 the County Club was based at the purpose-built County Ground near Abington, owned by the Northamptonshire Cricket Club and Recreation Grounds Co. and financed by a capital issue of 5,000 £1 shares.

In 1905 it was promoted to the First Class Counties League, ending an average of 10th in the pre-war years and as runners-up to Yorkshire in 1912. 'Gentlemen amateurs' as yet, C. N. Wooley and G. J. Thompson were among the players who made their mark in this period, the outstanding all-round skills of the latter earning him a cricketer-of-the-year accolade from *Wisden* in 1906 and the Club itself the popular title of 'Thompsonshire'. The County Ground also had facilities for athletics, bowls, tennis and football, and it was here that the Northampton Town Football Club later played its own home games. Like the Catholics Cricket Club, first winners of the Town Challenge Club, many adult sports teams were organised by churches or chapels, and both they and the schools ran a large number of schoolboy teams. Local schoolteachers — a lone female among them — played a prominent part in the formation of the Northampton Town F.C. in 1897, but the initiative here came from A. J. Darnell, Borough Coroner for 40 years, who became its first president.

The Town ended its first season in the Northamptonshire League in fourth place and £65 in debt. The first home game against Rushden Reserves netted less than £1 in gate money, but as it began to record some notable successes, so the number of spectators increased. In 1898-9 it gained promotion to the Midland League, and in a friendly match which cast some doubt on national military prowess the Grenadier Guards were beaten 10-1. Home games now regularly drew crowds of 2-3,000, but some 15,000 spectators paid a total of almost £400 to see the Town lose 2-0 to Sheffield United in the First Round proper of the F.A. Cup in 1901. Many women were among them, and as family entertainment, as a diversion from Saturday afternoon drinking and a unifying focus of local loyalty, football received a good deal of middle-class encouragement. However, both players and crowd often sullied the ideal of modesty in victory and dignity in defeat, the one setting the proverbial 'bad example' by assaulting each other on the field and disputing with the referee, the other impugning his mother's honour and displaying an unsporting desire for victory at all costs.

There were few such satisfactions in 1905-6. Languishing at the foot of the Southern League table, insult was added to injury by a poster advertising a match between Crystal Palace and New Brompton as 'the game to see who is nearly as bad as Northampton'.[76] In the following year the club bowed to popular displeasure, expressed in declining gates, and paid Swindon Town £200 for the services of Edwin Lloyd Davies, a defender with mutton-chop whiskers and remarkably uplifting effects. In 1908-9, before home crowds of some 5-6,000, Northampton won the league championship, and the team was duly feted by a large crowd at Castle Station on its return from the clinching match against Queen's Park Rangers. However, football's resort to buying, selling and paying players in search of results took it one step further from the middle-class ideal of sportsmanship, pushing it into the business sphere and leaving it much at the mercy of a fickle and mainly working-class public.

The Gentlemen v. Players argument also invaded the cricket field to some extent, but it was not permitted to intrude into rugby football. Among the many local clubs here was the St James's Improvement Class Rugby Section which in 1891 merged with the Unity Club to form the Northampton St James's F.C. 'There is no more improving club in the Midlands than Northampton', wrote *The Field* in 1895 as the 'Saints' carried the honour of the town onto the national scene; but local rivalries were strong, and in 1897 there was a sharp exchange of mock obituary cards between Leicester and Northampton: 'In memory of the Northampton F.C., Who Perished after a Severe Mauling by the "Leicester Tigers". . . Game to the "Last"', ran the first after the Tigers' home victory in October, but local honour was restored at Franklin's Gardens in November amid scenes of jubilation which blocked off the streets of St James's for hours afterwards. 'Death of Leicester Tigers . . . Resurrection of the Saints', declared the avenging card: 'the Saints on the pitch were a little too tough, And the funeral cards are giving them snuff. R.I.P.'[77]

'Saints' they remained, but in the following season the club became simply the North-ampton Football Club. From 1896 club members viewed home games from the seated and carpeted comfort of a special stand, but such was its popular following that five special trains were required to convey supporters to London for its first match against Harlequins in 1897-8, and home crowds regularly exceeded those drawn by Northampton Town. The opposition, too, was often of a more illustrious order, including the Racing Club of Paris in 1903-4, and the New Zealand national team two years later. Among the players who contributed to this international reputation were the brothers W. H. and H. E. Kingston, graduates of the Abington House School team, and Edgar Mobbs, Club Captain from 1907-13 and seven times capped for England, who commanded the 7th Battalion of the Northamptonshire Regiment during World War I and was killed in action at Ypres in 1917.

Cycling clubs of varying degrees of exclusivity also flourished during this period. The Northamptonshire Bicycle Club counted James Manfield, E. J. Allchin and T. P. Dorman among its riding members, paying a subscription of 15s. and wearing — on penalty of relegation to the rear of the column — a uniform of dark green Norfolk serge shooting jacket and breeches, stockings and black polo cap. The Victoria Cycling Club for gentlemen amateurs, Joseph Grose among them, sported a navy uniform with silver shield and charged a more modest 7s. 6d., while members of the College Street Club, whose Committee included the proprietor of the glass and china firm W. T. Church, paid only 1s. and dispensed with the uniform.[78] Several clubs also grew out of local pubs, formed by regular patrons or at the instigation of other working men who — like the Captain of the Rovers

25. St James's Cycling Club, pictured at Franklin's Gardens in 1898. Seated on the wooden chair in the centre is the Club President, the shoe manufacturer Edward Lewis.

Club, the temperate but inveterate poacher James Hawker — hoped to persuade them out of it.[79]

With the exception of the Socialist Clarion Clubs, cycling clubs were still largely male affairs, and when on the road they demanded military-style obedience. Safety was important, of course, and members of the Northamptonshire were advised to 'use great care in descending unknown hills'. However, the signals of the bugler — lesser clubs used a whistle — were to be instantly observed, and no matter the wealth or status of his fellows, the authority of the Captain reigned supreme. At 3gn. for admission and an annual subscription of 2gn. in the early 20th century the Northampton Golf Club had a dearth of working-class members, but it did have lady members, admitted at reduced rates and often displaying that prowess at the game which the Independent cited in 1912 as an unwelcome sign of things to come. Inspired by 'the daring feat of a local lady teacher in climbing the Vigo chimney . . . without a tremor and with a brisk breeze blowing too', it contemplated a dismal future shaped by 'The Triumph of Women'.

'Their dominance may be discerned in almost every walk of life', it declared with journalistic excess, 'at tennis, golf, hockey, yachting, mountaineering and other pursuits, women equal and surpass men . . . they will probably pursue their progress to greater lengths, and not be satisfied until women are sitting in Parliament. Once in power they will elect a Cabinet of ladies, and mirabile visu, a lady Premier!'[80] Hardly an immediate prospect, in 1912 the great majority of women were still awaiting the right to vote — less than patiently in the case of the suffragettes, and several were unceremoniously ejected from a Guildhall meeting to celebrate the Liberal landslide victory of 1906. 'Confused tangles of intertwined humanity tumbled down the steps amid the vociferous approval of the audience and the defiant shrieks of the ejected', the *Mercury* reported, 'Umbrellas were freely plied during the melee, and the sufragettes retaliliated with fists and banner poles. One produced a dog whip with which she belaboured the man who removed her'.[81]

Working class women received scant support in this matter from the Socialists. 'Said the Socialist to the Suffragist; "My cause is greater than yours! You work only for a Special Class, We for the gain of the General Mass"'', as one suffragist derided their approach to 'the Woman Question'. In the early 20th century, Margaret Bondfield — who later became Labour M.P. for Northampton — still 'deprecated votes for women as the hobby of disappointed old maids whom no one wanted to marry'.[82] By the later 19th century, however, free thought and the atheism which at least some Socialists professed had gone some way to close the gulf between Anglicans and Nonconformists, reminding them of their shared Christianity and giving an added impetus to their efforts to reach the working classes. 'St Andrew's', said its vicar in 1878, 'is Bradlaugh's stronghold. The whole parish has been covered by his atheistical principles and many more Christian helpers are needed to counteract the mischief done'.[83]

St Andrew's Church was one of three new Anglican churches to be built within the borough in the earlier 19th century,[84] but since 1874 the Northampton Church Extension Society had also been working to improve provision for a larger and more dispersed population. The first Extension Society church to be consecrated was that of St Lawrence in 1878, and in keeping with its simple Early English style and his own solid evangelicalism, its first incumbent, the Rev. L. H. Loyd, promised no 'elaborate church music . . . nor anything in which the people would not heartily unite'.[85] However, his successor, the Rev. T. Lea was one of a growing school of ritualists, cruelly parodied thus in an anonymous poem:

> . . . And there's bowings and scrapings and turnings and flexions,
> Its hard work to mind all the proper directions,
> He'll first chant a sermon, then turn round his stole,
> Then wheel to the East with a sort of a roll . . .[86]

The pomp and pageantry of such services was often very popular with the working classes, adding a little colour perhaps to a drab existence; but in their dislike of 'fancy ritual' many Anglicans also found much in common with Nonconformity, and the Rev. Lea's 'surrender' was eventually secured by Evangelical threats to cut subscriptions to the Extension Society. Even opponents of ritualism would only oppose it so far, however, and when a Liverpool clergyman was imprisoned in 1887 for ritualistic practices, a petition for his release was signed by 17 Northampton clergy and over 1,000 communicant members of the local churches.[87] The Salvation Army, on the other hand, provoked unusual hostility in a town noted for its defence of religious liberty. By 1887 it had around 300 local members, but in the same year a procession escorting its leader General Booth from Castle Station was set upon and stoned by a mob. Meetings the following day had to be abandoned through rioting, but many of those later prosecuted were otherwise law-abiding working men, and the General was not alone in wondering 'whatever is it all about? Whatever does it mean?'. Temperance campaigners commonly marched through the town, crusades against atheism were common fare in Northampton, and if the Salvation Army was admittedly 'a bit too noisy for him', said the Mayor, that was hardly a cause for riot.[88]

The Church's own 'missionary' approach under Bishop Magee of Peterborough was in fact responsible for much of its success in Northampton. Anglican sittings grew by only some 15% between 1851-81, while non-Anglican sittings almost doubled in number. Among the latter were 550 Catholic sittings provided mainly through the Cathedral of Our Lady and St Thomas, which replaced the collegiate chapel of St Felix on the same site in 1864.[89]

However, an unofficial census conducted in 1881 suggested that attendances at Anglican places of worship were some 87% higher than those recorded on Census Sunday in 1851. Non-Anglican attendances were also some 40% greater, but given the growth in the town's population in the meantime, Nonconformity was clearly losing some ground.[90] Indeed, in 1891 the *Northamptonshire Nonconformist* wrote openly of the 'decline of Dissent', laying the blame on 'the degeneracy of the middle class, in whom at one time it found its chief strength . . . the vulgar worshipper of wealth or fashion sees his Churchmanship as a passport into society . . .'.[91]

There was some truth in this. In Leicester, for instance, there was a drift to evangelical Anglicanism among the leading families of the hosiery trade, formerly pillars of local Nonconformity. No such trend is evident among the shoe manufacturers of Northampton, but their high profile in the local dissenting chapels may have served in turn to alienate working-class worshippers by suggesting that they were largely a middle-class preserve. Some turned instead to Nonconformist 'fringe' sects like the New Jerusalem and Brethren churches, but it was Primitive Methodism which gained the most ground in this period. The most democratic of the Methodist connexions, the colourful and emotional services which earned its followers the tag of 'Ranters' also had a particular appeal to the working classes — although it also counted the shoe manufacturer Joseph Gibbs among its most active local adherents.

By the later 19th century religion was fighting an increasingly unequal battle against the secularising influences of industrial society, but in Northampton at least Charles Bradlaugh's denial that atheism was wrong served to strengthen the will to fight it. Direct comparisons between the Religious Census of 1851 and the unofficial census of 1881 are difficult — Sunday School children were included in the former, for instance — but the proportion of the population attending morning services in 1881 was 17% against 28% in 1851, 25% against 27% in the case of evening services, and while these figures suggest a significant decline in formal religious óbservance, it was still less marked here than in many other industrial towns. Attendance at a place of worship is not necessarily an accurate measure of religious belief, of course — many a believer could simply be too tired to turn out after a week's work — but it may also be, as the *Northamptonshire Nonconformist* suggested, that devout atheism rather than apathy was responsible for many of Northampton's empty seats. This too is impossible to measure, but of one thing at least there can be little doubt. Even those who retained their faith found it severely tested by the mass slaughter of the First World War.

'People work or play very much as usual', the *Independent* noted in its early weeks, 'The only serious shortage is in the war news . . . the crumbs and scraps vouchsafed to us are about as satisfying as a bun to a bear'.[92] Alongside an exodus of local recruits came an influx of some 17,000 troops of the Welsh Territorial Division, billeted in Northampton until December 1914 and received 'with a zeal and kindness which deserves our most grateful thanks'. The xenophobia manifested in a campaign to remove the German-born manager of the municipal tramways, Joseph Gottschalk, was less pleasant but by no means unique to Northampton. Resident in Britain since the age of eighteen, Mr. Gottschalk had a British wife, a son serving in the British army, and had lost his German nationality 20 years before. His belated application for naturalisation was immediately granted, and the Council itself voted to retain him; but while 'deeply grateful to the members . . . who so nobly defended me from attack . . . I do not want to be a cause of conflict and bitterness'. He resigned, but in the expectation of an early end to the war the Council continued to pay him a retainer.[93]

'The war has not brought to any of the great English towns a wider range of emotions than to Northampton . . . one of the few industrial towns whose head and hand are essential to the success of the Allied cause', wrote *The Times* in January 1915, 'The boot and shoe trade has never enjoyed such a season of prosperity. There is work for all at high wages'.[94] At that time it was producing some 140,000 pairs of boots a week for the Belgian and French as well as the British forces, and over the course of the war it supplied a total of 23 million pairs of footwear including infantry boots, flying boots, ski boots and canvas shoes. A further 24 million were produced in other county centres of the trade. Town and county together accounted for over two-thirds of British footwear output between 1914-18, but the people of Northampton also contributed almost nine million pounds in war loans and savings, subscribing £1.6 million during 'Tank Week' in the Spring of 1918 alone.[95]

Mulliner's works were converted to the manufacture of munitions and military vehicles, the County Asylum and the Abington Avenue and Barry Road schools to military hospitals, and part of the Racecourse to allotments. Women replaced men in the factories and — as conductresses only — on the trams; but barely a family in town or county was not touched by the human tragedies of the war. Recruited together, the members of local regiments all too often died together, plunging whole communities into mourning at a stroke. At Ambers Ridge on 15 May 1915, 17 of the 26 officers of the 1st Northants. and 541 of its 750 other ranks were killed, injured or reported missing; at Neuve Chapelle in the same month, 12 of 22 officers and 211 of 594 other ranks of the 2nd Battalion were killed and more than 200 wounded. Over 6,000 members of the Regiment died in the conflict, 1,700 of them from Northampton itself, and in 1919 the survivors were officially welcomed home with an excess born of relief that the killing and maiming was finally over. Past a cenotaph decorated with wreaths and flowers, some 8,000 ex-servicemen and women marched to Abington Park to consume nine roast bullocks, 350 hams, 24,000 pastries, and over 20,000 pints of beer.[96] By then, however, Northampton had its eyes firmly on the future, one of confronting the industrial reality which the war had temporarily obscured, of providing homes fit for heroes and heroines, and of introducing some local light into the gloomy national picture of inter-war depression.

Notes

1. *Northampton Radical*, 11 Nov. 1874.
2. Handbill, Nov. 1874 (N.L.I.S. 198-800).
3. *N.M.*, 30 June 1877.
4. Quoted in Royle, E., 'Charles Bradlaugh, Freethought and Nonconformity', *N.P.&P.*, Vol.6, 3 (1980), p.149. Both Bradlaugh and Mrs. Besant were convicted of publishing an obscene work, fined £200 and sentenced to six months' imprisonment. The verdicts were over-turned on appeal in 1878.
5. Ibid.
6. *A Victorian Poacher: James Hawker's Journal* (1979 reprint), p.23.
7. *Dictionary of Labour Biography*, Vol.5, p.94.
8. N.U.B.S.O. Monthly Report, Dec. 1887.
9. Ibid., June 1878.
10. Ibid., Oct. 1879.
11. Ibid., Oct. 1882.
12. *N.M.*, 5 Jan. 1878.
13. For an account of this dispute, see Porter, J., 'The Northampton Arbitration Board and the Shoe Industry Dispute of 1887', *N.P.&P.*, Vol.4, 3 (1968-9); Swann, J., 'A Sequel to the Shoe Industry Dispute of 1887', *N.P.&P.*, Vol.4, 4 (1969-70).
14. N.U.B.S.O. Monthly Report, Dec. 1887.
15. Ibid., June 1891; report of a mass meeting at the Temperance Hall, Northampton.
16. *Boot & Shoe Trades Journal*, 23 May 1885.
17. Ibid., 26 Nov. 1892.
18. N.U.B.S.O. Monthly Report, March 1892.
19. *Boot & Shoe Trades Journal*, 2 April 1892.

20. *Shoe and Leather Record*, 19 Feb. 1892.
21. *The Times*, 25 April 1895.
22. Rules of the Northampton Manufacturers' Association, 21 April 1895.
23. *Shoe & Leather Record*, quoted in Cox, H. (ed.), *British Industries Under Free Trade* (1903).
24. *Boot & Shoe Trades Journal*, 21 July 1900.
25. *Footwear*, Feb. 1909.
26. *Boot & Shoe Trades Journal*, 13 Oct. 1900.
27. For a description of the Manfield factory, see *Ancient Order of Foresters Guide to Northampton* (1908).
28. *Where to Buy in Northampton* (*c*.1891), p.27 & 29.
29. N.C.B.C. Minutes, 5 Feb. 1912.
30. *Footwear*, March 1909.
31. See Garnett, R., *Phipps-Faire: A History, 1822-1988* (1988).
32. *N.H.*, 10 Oct. 1898.
33. Quoted in *Gentleman's Journal*, 3 August 1907.
34. Bassett-Lowke & Co. Catalogue, 1904-5.
35. Richards, G., 'Power in the Past: Northampton Electric Light and Power Company, 1890-1920', *Electricity News* (Jan. 1973).
36. *Where to Buy in Northampton*, p.22; *N.M.*, 19 Feb. 1887.
37. 'Upstairs, Downstairs in Victorian and Edwardian Northampton', Northampton Central Museum lecture, 2 Aug. 1989.
38. *N.H.*, 4 June 1881.
39. Ibid., 5 July 1881.
40. *N.M.* 1881, otherwise undated.
41. Episcopal Triennial Visitation Returns, All Saints, Northampton (1910); St Katherine (1905) (N.R.O. 1915).
42. Bailey, B. A., 'Monks Park, Northampton: The Story of a Town Property', *N.P.&P.*, Vol.6 (1981-2).
43. *N.M.*, 27 Aug. 1886.
44. The *Northampton Mercury* was founded by Robert Raikes and William Dicey in 1720, and remained in the ownership of the Dicey family until it was purchased by S. S. Campion in 1885. The newspaper was published throughout the General Strike of 1926 and can claim the longest continuous period of publication of any provincial newspaper. It was merged with the *Northampton Herald* in 1931. S. S. Campion was a former schoolteacher, a Deacon of Commercial Street Congregationalist Chapel, and served for a total of 47 years on the Borough Council. He was awarded the Honorary Freedom of the Borough in 1923, and died in 1938 at the age of 92.
45. Northampton Town and County Benefit Building Society, *A Century of Service* (1948).
46. *The Ratepayer*, Feb. 1886.
47. *N.M.*, 26 Feb. 1897.
48. Dickie, M., 'Northampton's Working Class Homeowners: Myth or Reality?', *N.P.&P.*, Vol.8, 1 (1989-90).
49. Bowley, A. L., & Burnett-Hurst, A. R., *Livelihood and Poverty* (1915).
50. For a full analysis of the social background of local footwear manufacturers, see Brooker, K., 'The transformation of the small master economy in the boot and shoe industry, 1887-1914' (unpublished Ph.D. thesis, University of Hull, 1986).
51. Brooker thesis, op.cit.
52. See Joyce, P., *Work, Society and Politics: The Culture of the Factory in later Victorian England* (1980).
53. Brooker thesis, op.cit.
54. Obituary, *N.M.*, 13 Feb. 1931.
55. *Shoe Trades Journal*, 12 Dec. 1919.
56. N.C.B.C., Chief Constable's Report (1894). The Society continued to operate until November 1980.
57. *N.M.*, 1 March 1879.
58. Annual Report of the Northampton Town and County Nursing Institution for Trained Nurses (1901).
59. For a history of St Andrew's Hospital, see Foss, A., & Trick, K., *St Andrew's Hospital: The First 150 Years, 1838-1988* (1989).
60. MacFarlane, T., *History of the Northamptonshire Ambulance Service* (1985).
61. *N.M.*, 22 Oct. 1887.

62. Northampton General Infirmary Annual Report (1887).
63. N.C.B.C. Minutes, 1 Oct. 1906.
64. Northampton W.E.A., poster and leaflet 1907.
65. Wright, W. B., *Northampton Co-operative Society Ltd.: 75 Years Souvenir History, 1870-1945* (1946).
66. Ibid.
67. *Shoe & Leather Record*, 1 Jan. 1915.
68. Episcopal Visitation, op.cit., St Sepulchre, Northampton.
69. *N.M.*, advertisements August 1887.
70. N.C.B.C., Conditions of Licences for Cinematograph Performances (1909).
71. Ashplant, T. G., 'Northamptonshire's Working Men's Clubs, 1880-1914', *N.P.&P.*, Vol.8, 1 (1989-90), p.63.
72. *N.M.* 27 Dec. 1879.
73. *N.I.*, Pubs Special Issue (Sept. 1978).
74. *Northamptonshire Nonconformist*, March 1891.
75. For a history of the Boys' Brigade in Northampton, see Eason, A. V., *Remember Now Thy Creator* (1982).
76. Grande, F., *The Cobblers: The Story of Northampton Town Football Club* (1985).
77. *Northampton Football Club Centenary, 1880-1980* (1980).
78. Rules of the Northamptonshire Cycling Club (*s.d.*); Northampton Victoria Cycling Club Programme (1888); College Street Cycling Club Programme (1890) (N.L.I.S. 1-571).
79. Hawker, op.cit., pp.25-6.
80. *N.I.*, 7 Sept. 1912. The chimney at the Vigo brickyard near Cow Meadow was around 250 ft. high. The brickyard was closed around 1910 and the chimney itself demolished in 1919.
81. Unidentified newspaper article, 1978 (N.L.I.S.).
82. Both quoted in Liddington, J., & Norris, J., *One Hand Tied Behind Us* (1978).
83. N.R.O. M.L.58, St Andrew's.
84. St Katharine (1839); St Andrew (1842); St Edmund (1852). A fourth church, St James's, was built just beyond the western borough boundary in 1871.
85. *N.M.*, 19 Oct. 1878.
86. 'Ritualistic Progress: the Complaints of a Parish Clerk', reprinted in *N.I.*, 1 March 1930. The Extension Society also built the churches of St Michael & All Angels (1882); St Mary Far Cotton (1885); and St Paul (1890), followed in the 20th century by Christchurch (1906) and Holy Trinity (1908).
87. *N.M.*, 28 May 1887.
88. *N.M.*, 29 Jan. 1887.
89. The Roman Catholic Diocese of Northampton was established in 1850. The Cathedral of Our Lady and St Thomas, which was consecrated in 1864, was designed by Augustus Welby Pugin, son of the architect of the Collegiate Chapel of St Felix.
90. *Nonconformist and Independent*, 2 Feb. 1882.
91. *Northamptonshire Nonconformist*, Dec. 1891.
92. *N.I.*, 22 Aug. 1914.
93. N.C.B.C. Minutes, 7 Sept., 5 Oct. & 26 Oct. 1914.
94. *The Times*, 15 Jan. 1915.
95. Holloway, W. H., *Northamptonshire and the Great War* (1923).
96. Ibid.

Chapter Four

Revolution on the Rates: The Expanding Role of Local Government

Mr. Justice Phillimore . . . took things as he found them, although he was not over-pleased with what he found . . . He still hoped to see a genius arise, who would abolish rates and merit a statue in Whitehall.

> N.C.B.C. Minutes, 24 July 1911: Report of Cllr. S. S. Campion
> on the National Conference on the Prevention of Destitution

. . . the provision of working class dwellings (unless under exceptional circumstances) is outside the province of the Corporation and can safely be left to private enterprise . . .

> N.C.B.C. Minutes, 6 May 1912: Resolution from the Northampton Ratepayers' Association

'As in other departments of human activity', wrote the Northampton Liberal and Radical Union in 1897, 'the corporate life cannot stand still; it must move. Backwards or forwards? Decadence or revival? Progress or retrogression? Which is to triumph? It is for the citizens to answer'. Out of office for seven of the last eight years, the Liberal answer to a Conservative majority of 18 in the Council and a 200-strong branch of the Social Democratic Federation was a 'progressive programme' which included the municipal takeover of the private gas, electricity and tramways companies, for 'Socialism, as some people choose to call municipalisation . . . means nothing more than partnership, comradeship, a policy of combination for general advantage'.[1] The citizens answered, and two years later the Council was back in Liberal hands.

However, the corporate life had a momentum of its own, and so much had the scope and scale of its work expanded over the past decades that there could be no doubt, said Mayor Edwin Bridgewater in 1892, of the 'great necessity' for an extension to the Guildhall. In a competition limited this time to architects born or practising in Northampton, the task of making a 'harmonious whole' with Godwin's design went to Matthew Holding. 'Nothing short of the work of a genius', wrote the *Mercury* of the finished result, 'the beauty of the old obtains fresh grace and symmetry by the addition of the new'.[2] Holding's plans for the interior were judged 'not half so good' as his exterior, however, and rejected in favour of those of Albert Jeffery, architect of the Guildhall at Winchester and son of the former Town Clerk of Northampton John Jeffery. A new police station was also built at the rear of the Guildhall in Dychurch Lane, where 'the comforts of your officers and those whose misfortune it is to require accommodation here have been well considered',[3] and where the steam fire engine purchased for the Volunteer Fire Brigade in 1878 also found a new permanent home.

The duties of the Brigade were taken over by the police in 1888, albeit under protest. Resenting the slur on their efficiency, the volunteers declined to serve under the new Fire Superintendent, and 'under the circumstances', wrote their leader Captain Peacock to the Watch Committee, 'I shall not be able to attend any fire in future . . . kindly give orders to have the telephone removed.'[4] However, responsibility for the Fire Brigade was only a part of the 'very onerous' duties outlined by Chief Constable Fred Mardlin in 1891 when appealing for an increase in his salary, which 'is only £16 13s. 4d. per annum more than my predecessor receives as a retiring allowance'.[5] A former Detective Inspector with the Leicester Borough Police, Mr. Mardlin succeeded Henry Keenan in the midst of the trade dispute in 1887, gaining immediate respect by his decisive handling of a stone-throwing crowd; but even this was an aspect of a Chief Constable's lot rather more to his liking than

26. The Guildhall following Matthew Holding's extension in 1892. Holding also designed
the Abington Park Hotel and the churches of St Matthew, St Mary, Far Cotton, and St Paul.

the 'records, statistics, etc., that I have been compelled to introduce', or the attempt to 'rightly construe the voluminous instructions issued by the Secretary of State', in which he had to enlist the aid of the Town Clerk.[6]

So far as 'the work itself' was concerned, between 1881 and 1888 alone Northampton gained 9½ miles of new streets, 852 houses, 72 shops, 46 factories and workshops and around 10,000 inhabitants. Effectively a part of the borough for policing purposes, the suburban areas beyond its boundaries also continued to grow apace. 'A Salary of £250 after 16 years of Public Service', Mr. Mardlin concluded, 'is not adequate, and I entertain a sanguine expectation that this application will command your favourable consideration'.[7] It did; and now, said the Chief Constable, he really must have the long-awaited additions to his complement of 70 officers. In recognition of his own 'incessant and cheerfully and ably performed work', the Borough Surveyor William Brown also had his salary increased in the following year — but his own staff, he complained yet again in 1893, was simply 'not large enough to cope with the increased duties arising from the growth of the town'.[8]

These included the surfacing and repair of highways and footways, street lighting and cleansing, sewers, the inspection of plans for 'ever-extending' building operations, and the maintenance of corporate properties; but in 1890 Mr. Brown also attended 96 Council or Committee meetings and spent two full days each week working out the wages of the 120 employees under his control.[9] Little wonder that two years later the Borough Auditors found his accounts 'in a very backward state . . . No accounts have been made out and rendered except those of urgent character since October 1891 . . . Summary of Horses Work is in arrear since February 12th, 1891'.[10] In 1889 the Borough Accountant himself had appealed for aid in keeping the corporate accounts, 'which he alleges are becoming so complicated and extensive, that he finds it impossible without further help to keep up the work satisfactorily'.[11] His own burden was lightened by a salary increase which enabled him to employ his son as an assistant, and that of Mr. Brown by additions to the clerical staff and the appointment of his deputy Mr. Gibbins as Borough Engineer. However, much of their work was concerned with public health matters, and here as elsewhere the growing number of compulsory duties laid on the localities by central government was as much responsible for their increasing workload as the rapid growth of the town itself.

The appointment of a Medical Officer of Health was one of the obligations imposed by the Public Health Act of 1872, which created a nationwide network of Sanitary Authorities with responsibility for roads, sewers, the containment of infectious diseases and food inspection. In the towns these duties fell on existing local Boards of Health or, as in the case of Northampton, the Borough Council. The Improvement Commission itself was wound up in 1875, but in some respects conditions in Northampton were already much more favourable than in other urban areas. Virtually free of the smoke which shrouded many northern industrial towns, it had none of their notoriously unhealthy cellar dwellings, and although many older properties in its central areas were found to be 'ill-kept and dirty' in 1870, 'even this is not so general a fault as in most large towns'.[12] In 1874, Northampton's first M.O.H. Alfred Haviland felt able to 'heartily congratulate' the Sanitary Authority on a mortality rate below the national average: but 'in doing so I trust that you will do all in your power to facilitate this downward movement, for it is not like the *facilis descendus Averno*, on the contrary it requires all our work and labour'.[13]

'Smooth the descent and easy is the way' was never the case in public health matters, but if there was still room for improvement in the town, conditions beyond its boundaries in the suburbs now virtually enclosing it on three sides were such that Northampton was a veritable paradise by comparison. In Far Cotton in 1870: 'Water standing in the ground three feet below the surface, and this water furnishing a large part of the supply for domestic use and for drinking. Wells often only four or five yards off cesspools'.[14] Kingsthorpe, said

Mr. Haviland in 1874, 'with a magnificent supply of pure spring water, is in a most loathsome condition. The water is contaminated by the filthy oozings and drainings from slaughter-houses, wells converted into cess-pools, obstructed drains, muck heaps, and surface water'.[15] Both were surpassed by St James's End, 'that most insanitary of rural districts', where the 'filth, over-flowing middens, lagoons of liquid sewage, an absence of drainage, filthy houses, poverty' were vividly described in 1879 in an article in the *Sanitary Record* baldly entitled 'Waiting for the Plague'.[16]

Here, claimed the *Mercury*, members of the Rural Sanitary Authority were also owners of the offending properties, but the suburban inhabitants themselves were opposed to incorporation with the borough on the grounds that 'expenses will be increased. And doubtless this is true. It will cost more money to form an acknowledged part of a civilised community than to maintain, under the name of independence, the present disastrous negation of decent government'.[17] The public health did not come cheaply, it is true. At 2s. 10d. in the pound in 1888 the General District Rate for sanitary purposes was double the level of the Borough Rate itself, but in the same year the M.O.H. was urging the Council not only to dispose of the 'living organisms of formidable dimensions' inhabiting the municipal water supply, and to pass new bye-laws regulating house drainage — requiring more officials to enforce them — but to replace the 'hideous hovels' constituting the smallpox hospital at Kingsthorpe with a permanent isolation hospital.[18]

Quite modest requests by comparison with those put to it in other years, they were also couched in language more polite than the M.O.H. often employed. Recalled as a man of 'intrepid temper and caustic wit', Lee Fyson Cogan was only 27 years of age when he succeeded Mr. Haviland in 1876. The son of a Wiltshire clergyman and a graduate of Guy's Hospital, he was never satisfied with either the pace of sanitary reform, the resources devoted to it, or the results. No M.O.H. worth his salary — £100 in his case — ever was, for the more the energy devoted to eradicating one 'intolerable evil', the greater the knowledge and the expertise acquired, the more it became clear that dunghills and dirty water were only the tip of an unhealthy iceberg. Even in well-housed and uncrowded Northampton, said Dr. Cogan with customary bluntness in 1889, there were such

> haunts of filthiness and unwholesomeness ... that if physical life is not subjected to actual devastation, it is irreparably damaged ... it is in these sullied regions that the all-powerful aid of the legislature should be extended for the suppression and extermination of these striking illustrations of inactive and pusillanimous sanitation, whose existence cannot be too harshly denounced as a slur on humanity and a reproach to modern civilisation.[19]

Parliament had already provided local authorities with permissive powers here through the Artisans' Dwellings Act of 1875, which allowed them to replace insanitary housing. Under the Housing of the Working Classes Act of 1890 they also had powers to order defective housing to be put into a proper sanitary condition, to demolish it if not, and to rebuild it; but, said Dr. Cogan in 1893, the Committee 'have not yet shown any disposition to respond to the appeals made to them to bring this Act of Parliament into more frequent operation than has hitherto been done in Northampton. This, no doubt, is due to the Council not feeling justified at present in incurring the expenditure of the great sum of money this would involve, and not to any want of appreciation on the part of our governing body of the necessity and value of sanitary reform in this direction'.[20] No doubt; and if sanitary reform here meant demolition without replacement and a consequent increase in over-crowding — which it usually did — then there was something to be said in the Council's favour.

The M.O.H. himself was reluctant to use the law to deal with over-crowding. 'The well-to-do working classes are amply provided with comfortable and healthy dwellings', as he noted in 1894, 'but the rent of such habitations cannot be afforded by the poorer sections of the community'. Through unemployment, sickness or bereavement, even the well-to-do could soon find themselves 'from want of means having to forsake the separate dwellings they occupy in times of prosperity',[21] but such were the imperfections of the housing market that 535 of the houses recorded in the borough at the 1881 Census remained unoccupied while in the same year one two-bedroom dwelling in Cow Lane was found to be inhabited by 13 people, 10 of them adults.[22] However, with the backing of Cllr. Frank Buszard, a local doctor and Conservative member of the Sanitary Committee, the M.O.H. had his way over the provision of a permanent hospital for infectious diseases, opened on the Harborough Road at Kingsthorpe in 1892 at a cost of £3,500.

'More or less uncontrollable' by any means but isolation, epidemic diseases such as diphtheria, scarlet fever and measles remained prevalent, and 'in working class communities such as Northampton . . . patients cannot receive adequate attention in their own homes, either in nursing, lodging or feeding. Neither the time nor the means are at the disposal of the working class which is necessary to be bestowed on the infectious sick of this most deserving portion of the community'.[23] Working class mothers received scant sympathy otherwise. Infant mortality rates remained stubbornly high as general mortality rates began to fall from the 1870s, and at 188.4 per 1,000 live births in 1878 that of Northampton was well above the national average of around 150. A similar proportion of children survived their first year of life only to die before the age of five, but in Dr. Cogan's view sanitary reforms were of only limited use here.

The highest proportion of deaths occurred from respiratory diseases in winter and from epidemic diarrhoea in summer, suggesting some sort of link with the weather; but, said the M.O.H., while the infant death rate in Northampton was certainly

> far greater than it should be . . . to those who are acquainted with the habits of the mass of the working population of our town, it will not be surprising. In fact, seeing the indiscretion, if not negligence, so commonly shown by parents in the treatment of their infants . . . it is fortunate that so many escape the injurious influences to which they are exposed, and arrive at a mature age.[24]

Early marriages, illegitimacy and poor domestic hygiene were among the factors cited as 'obviously adverse' to infant health, but by 1889 poverty, poor housing, 'sickly' parents and working mothers had been added to the list, for 'manufacturing towns in which married women are engaged in occupations involving daily absence from their homes are found to have a high infant mortality rate'.[25]

This was generally true, but in 1870, when a high proportion of female labour in Northampton was already employed outside the home, one observer concluded that 'the occupation of mothers does not appear to affect on any large scale the care of the younger children'.[26] Most were quite adequately cared for through family and neighbourhood networks, but the professional disapproval directed towards working mothers was informed by the Victorian ideal of motherhood as a career in itself, and the notion that they worked from choice rather than necessity was very persistent. Public creches, suggested James Beatty, M.O.H. from 1903-7, should be provided in towns like Northampton where 'it is unfortunately the custom for married women to work'.[27] Around 15% of married women in Northampton were in paid work at that time, not all of them with children, but the coincidence of high infant death rates with higher than average rates of female employment, it may be thought, is stronger evidence of financial need and its own adverse effects on health than of negligence.

Genuine or not, however, the latter was attributed to ignorance of proper infant care, and here, said Dr. Cogan, the Authority could usefully follow the example of Manchester, Glasgow and other authorities in appointing a Lady Sanitary Inspector and Health Visitor. Miss Alice Gough became Northampton's first such official in 1903, and like her counterparts elsewhere she was initially engaged in the inspection of workshops employing women, a part of the general statutory duties imposed on Sanitary Authorities in 1891. More fortunate than some in enjoying 'an entire absence of friction' from her male colleagues, most of her time was soon devoted to the investigative and educational role envisaged by Dr. Cogan when he first recommended the appointment in 1900: visits to the homes of all new-born infants, advice about feeding, hygiene and the treatment of infectious diseases, and enquiries into the circumstances of infant deaths, the latter requiring 'a considerable amount of tact and discretion'. Not surprisingly, 'a proportion of the mothers seemed to fear that the enquiries were being made owing to an idea that they had neglected their children'.[28]

In fact, as Miss Gough discovered, most cases of infant diarrhoea occurred in clean homes among families in 'comfortable' circumstances, suggesting the use of difficult-to-clean 'long tube' feeding bottles as the likely culprit. Breast-feeding for at least six months, during which the mother should 'live quietly . . . avoid hard work, but may do most of the ordinary housework',[29] was the suggested alternative, and if it was an unrealistic option for many, once Miss Gough had overcome the initial suspicion of her role both she and her advice were generally welcomed. Often asked 'why she comes after the infants die, and not before, when the instructions she gives would have been so much more valuable', her services were later supplemented by those of the middle-class ladies of the town, recruited on a voluntary basis by Dr. J. Doig McCrindle, Dr. Beatty's successor.[30]

Lady volunteers were often suspected of condescending 'slumming', and if those of Northampton were found 'in many instances to obtain greater sympathy and more willing approval from the mother', this must be a tribute to their own tact and discretion. By 1911 they were also helping to run two weekly 'Mothers and Babies Welcome Centres', freeing the Health Visitor for other projects like the classes for expectant mothers begun in 1913 in an attempt to reduce the number of infant deaths attributable to poor maternal health. Here, in addition to talks on ante-natal care and demonstrations of how to convert an orange box into a cot, the women were also offered cost-price material for baby clothes and the use of a sewing machine.[31] However, infant mortality rates varied considerably within different areas of the town, and the innermost mainly working-class wards regularly recorded the highest figures.

In the Castle ward, comprising most of the old West ward after the 1901 boundary extensions, the annual average of deaths per 1,000 live births between 1907-11 was 136; in the South and North wards around 124, against only 95 and 83 in the outer eastern wards of St Michael and St Edmund. Low incomes and the poor diet and sub-standard housing which went with them had more than a little bearing on this pattern, but if public health work had its limits in such circumstances there seems no reason to doubt that it made a significant contribution to reducing infant mortality in Northampton from an annual average of 157.7 between 1890-99 to 122.6 in the following decade. Indeed, so certain was he of the value of Health Visiting work elsewhere that Dr. Cogan had confidently expected the Council to act on his proposal 'forthwith'. Disappointed in this matter as so many others, in 1902 his patience gave out with an audible snap.

Accustomed as it was to sarcasm and damning-with-faint-praise, the Council was stunned by the ferocity of his attack. 'Faulty and pernicious administration which ought not to be countenanced in any well-regulated community . . .', he wrote of the evasion of new building regulations passed in 1894: 'In this direction the busy municipal reformer may utilise his unexhausted energies'. The town sewers were 'notoriously offensive', refuse collection was carried out in a 'slovenly' manner, too many streets were 'badly-made and ill-kept . . . depicting negligence, preventable filthiness and maladministration', and while he had drawn the Council's attention to these and other matters 'year after year', he had simply been 'silently ignored'. In short, and 'conceding that the death rate in Northampton is not high, this fortunate incident, I submit, affords no justification for the cultivation of a disastrous policy of inactivity in conventional sanitation, or in the initiation of administrative reforms and measures for the protection of the public health'.[32]

At 14:1,000 in 1901 the general mortality rate in Northampton was certainly not high by comparison with the 21.7 recorded in Dr Cogan's first year of office, nor with those of many other towns at the turn of the century. In every single year since 1882 it had also fallen below the national average, still hovering around 17:1,000 in 1901 despite the deflationary effect of lower rural death rates. If public health measures were by no means solely responsible for the downward trend in mortality in the later 19th century — the more varied and abundant diet made possible by cheap imported foodstuffs and rising real incomes was arguably more significant — the Council was perhaps entitled to a little credit for what was on the surface a very satisfactory situation. Dr. Cogan himself had nothing but praise for its record in acting 'without hesitation' against landlords of slum properties — but like any competent M.O.H. he looked below the surface, and the further he looked the less he cared for what he saw.

With a high proportion of young adults in its population — the 20-40 age group accounted for 35% of the total in 1901 — Northampton's lower than average death rate was to some extent 'fortunate', but mortality was no guide to the health of the living, and tuberculosis was a disease which not only killed later rather than sooner, but one to which shoemakers appeared particularly vulnerable. In 1898 mortality from TB among shoemakers was 38% above the average for occupied males in Northampton, and contrary to all expectations the incidence of pulmonary TB actually increased between 1881-1911 as more footwear manufacturing processes became factory-based. The concentration of numbers and low resistance on the part of rural in-migrants were probably most significant here, coupled with the nature of particular processes. The dust inhaled by finishers was a prime suspect, but the disease was twice as common among clickers. Relatively light work, it tended to attract 'the delicate one of the family', who quickly developed the classic deformity of the rib-cage known as 'bootmakers' chest', along with 'a thorough hatred of open windows . . . regarded by them as bringing a death-dealing draught'.[33] Both were the product of long hours bent in one position over a cutting board.

Under the National Insurance Act of 1911 the Council received a grant of 50% of the cost of treating TB patients from the Local Government Board, the body with central oversight of local authorities between 1871-1919, and by 1914 many of the recommendations made in turn by Dr. Cogan and Dr. Beatty had been put into practice. Advanced cases were first isolated in a hospital on the Welford Road, but it became so associated in the public mind with impending death that many sufferers refused to be admitted. From 1907 they were treated instead at the Harborough Road hospital, while in a joint venture with the County Council a sanatorium for those considered curable was opened soon afterwards at Creaton. Compulsory notification of the disease was introduced under the Northampton Corporation Act in 1911, and a dispensary offering treatment and advice to sufferers and undertaking general educational work was opened two years later, aided by the voluntary efforts of a local branch of the Association for the Prevention of Tuberculosis.

'How much more may be done by private, apart from municipal or state effort . . .', wrote Dr. Beatty in 1904, 'An enormous amount of good work could be done by someone who is not an official, and who is not looking for a seat on the Council, and who could therefore not be accused of having an axe to grind'.[34] Music to the ears of the Sanitary Authority, it was still accompanied by the sound of axe-grinding from Dr. Cogan himself, who had clearly discerned where the real power lay. Following his resignation in 1902, occasioned more by the Council's wish for a full-time M.O.H. following the extension of the borough rather than any irreparable breach in relations, he was elected to its body two years later and duly appointed to the Sanitary Committee. He was soon chairing it, and in the course

27. Lee Fyson Cogan, L.R.C.P., M.R.C.S. Eng.
and Fellow of the Society of Medical Officers of
Health (1848-1937). Borough Medical Officer of
Health 1876-1902, he was elected to the Council in
1904 and served as Mayor in 1911. He retired from
public life in 1929 at the age of 81, but continued
in medical practice until a few weeks before his
death in 1937.

of a distinguished political career from which he finally retired at the age of 81, he also served as an Alderman, a Justice of the Peace, as Mayor in 1911-2, and had 'many a glorious row in the Council chamber' besides.[35]

Caustic to the last, 'I should be much better off', he concluded, 'if I had left municipal affairs to look after themselves', but 'I shall, at least, have some pleasure in recalling that I have been able to render a fair share of public service. Not, however, that they have ever complimented me — nor do I suppose they will, alive or dead!'[36] That the voters of the Radical stronghold of the Castle Ward should have elected a Conservative to represent them was, one feels, a compliment in itself; but his tempestuous relationship with his own elected masters was neither unusual nor, it may be thought, unhealthy. 'Expert' officers often viewed the 'amateurs' with barely concealed contempt, but many councillors became experts in turn through service on specialist committees, and on the early 20th-century Sanitary Committee they came ready-made in the persona of Cllr. Buszard, its Chairman for many years, and Cllr. Robert Milligan, a local doctor and Chairman of that rather different body, the Northampton Football Club.

The deaf ears on which many of the M.O.H.'s pleas fell were usually those of the full Council rather than the Committee, but Members could be easily provoked in turn by a suggestion that the electors had reposed their trust and their rates in people incompetent to discharge them. In 1908, for instance, the District Auditor advised the Finance Committee that 'cutting down the estimate and reducing the amount of the call is neither good economy nor good finance'. 'It is for them to exercise their own discretion . . .', was the brusque reply, 'When they want his opinion on what is sound finance, they will ask for it'.[37] Dr. Cogan's own conduct was judged 'nothing short of insubordination' on occasion — 'persons like myself occupying servile positions should humbly submit to the direction of those in authority'[38] — but from the other side of the municipal fence he had to confront the difficulty which, more than anything else, was responsible for his frustrations as M.O.H. And by 1906, with the declaration that the 'excessive, reckless and rapidly developing expenditure of the Municipal Authority is to be regarded with serious misapprehension', he too had become an economiser.[39]

Excess and recklessness were a matter of opinion, but if a local authority did no more than the minimum required of it by law, it could still not avoid continual increases in its expenditure. 'Men of all parties', as Samuel Smith Campion noted in 1912, 'have long felt that the tendency of modern legislation has been to put additional duties on local authorities, with consequent largely increased expenditure, without making equivalent grants in aid of the same from the Treasury. The result has been a considerable addition to local burdens'.[40] The sentiments of the Ratepayers' Protection Association were as clear as those of its predecessor, but in the view of the *Northampton Daily Chronicle* it had little enough to complain of. 'Rents and rates', it declared in 1899, 'are so excessively moderate that even the most economical find it a privilege to live in this Midland Oasis. The salaries of the officials whose duty it is to look after the comfort of the Public . . . are so very meagre that they must be looked upon as Martyrs of charity . . .'.[41]

Hence the many 'respectful' requests to individual Committees for pay increases, perhaps; but over the preceding decade the rates levied by the Council — the Borough Rate and the General District Rate — increased from 4s. 3d. to 5s. 1d. By 1912 they had risen to 7s. 7d., and in the following year the Education Committee declared itself 'anxious and willing' to fulfil its legal obligations, but 'the burden on the ratepayers . . . in respect of education has reached a point of intolerable strain, and constitutes a menace to the best interests of education . . . in the absence of more adequate contributions from Imperial sources it may become impossible for the Authority to continue to fulfil such obligations'.[42] Expanding obligations and a shrinking financial base: the problem was not a new one and an attempt had been made to ease it under the Local Government Act of 1888, which created county councils and conferred the status of county boroughs on municipalities with a population of over 50,000.

Originally intended to apply only to those twice this size, Northampton was one of many smaller boroughs which successfully resisted 'interference' in its affairs by

a new and less experienced authority . . . the sacrifices made by them for the purposes of their local government, the large debts which they have incurred upon the faith of the municipal powers being extended rather than reduced, and the extent to which they may suffer by permanent union with the small urban and rural districts with widely different interests, are sufficient reason why those boroughs should be . . . unfettered by the control of the proposed County Councils.[43]

The country gentlemen of the new County Council were no doubt happy to leave a borough where 'the mildest Liberal . . . would be termed a Radical elsewhere' to its own devices.[44] However, the income from Local Taxation Licences and two-fifths of Probate Duties was now transferred by the Exchequer to the county and county boroughs — but these Assigned Revenues, as they were known, replaced existing central grants in aid of the police, pauper lunatics, and the salaries of Poor Law teachers and medical officers, and the surplus left to the Borough Fund for the part-year ending March 1890 after these payments was only a little over £500.

In 1890 the proceeds of additional duties on beer and spirits — the 'Whisky Money' — were also assigned to them,[45] but income from central sources completely failed to keep pace with increases in local expenditure, as figures issued by the Association of Municipal Corporations in 1910 demonstrated. Education apart, between 1892-1910 there was an increase of 85% in net expenditure on locally-provided 'national' services — services, that is, 'as essential to the national well-being as to the welfare of the different localities' and including public health, poor relief and main highways. Over the same period Exchequer contributions in support of them increased by only 18.7%, while the proportion raised by local rates grew by almost 125%. 'The defects of the present system, or lack of system', concluded the Finance Committee in 1910, 'are so obvious that . . . every possible step should be taken . . . to bring the matter in the most forcible way to the attention of the Government'.[46]

Well aware of it already, in 1901 the Royal Commission on Local Taxation had considered, amongst other possible solutions, a local income tax, an income-related rate on inhabited houses, and higher Exchequer contributions to the cost of 'national' services:

'getting at the Income taxpayer' instead of the ratepayer, as Mr. Justice Phillimore put it in 1912.[47] 'The ratepayers are always demanding to be relieved at the expense of the taxpayers . . .', wrote one observer in 1899, 'it is not Imperial but local taxation from which the pinch comes, or at any rate, where it is felt'.[48] All the more so, wrote another in 1912, when the services they paid for were seen as 'onerous' rather than 'beneficial' — of no direct personal value and consumed, moreover, by those who contributed nothing to their cost: for while they 'demand with menaces that their town council shall spend some more of their money on tarring the roads to keep down motor dust, because they think it will be more comfortable . . . when they spend money on the poor or on education, they do it because it is their painful duty . . .'.[49]

By the earlier 20th century some local politicians had abandoned any pretence that the fulsome promises with which the ratepayers were normally wooed could be fulfilled. 'We are told we are going to have a big reduction in the rates', said the Conservative publican and councillor John Brown during the 1905 municipal elections: 'I wish somebody would tell me where it can be done'. There was 'no liklihood of reducing the rates', said Thomas Lewis bluntly during the same campaign, 'except by reducing the standard of good living'.[50] 'Good living' in this sense embraced not only the efficient discharge of statutory duties but the broader responsibility for the well-being of the community which municipal authorities had increasingly assumed on their own initiative during the later 19th century, in the varied form of libraries and museums, cemeteries, parks and baths, water, gas and electricity supplies, tramways, and, although on a very limited scale as yet, housing.

This gradual widening of the sphere of municipal activity was often a pragmatic response to local circumstances — to the failure of private enterprise to provide essential services such as water, for instance — but the extension of municipal 'trading' to gas, tramways and the like was first and foremost an attempt to bridge the gap between local expenditure and central government funding, to increase income from other sources and relieve the burden on the rates. Civic rivalry also played a part, and so did the sort of idealism expressed through the 'civic gospel' of Joseph Chamberlain's Birmingham, where Liberal radicalism and religious nonconformity combined in the proud claim that 'we are a corporation who have undertaken the highest duty that is possible for us; we have made provision for our people — **all** our people'.[51] '[We] should find it our loftiest pride', wrote the N.L.R.U. in presenting its Progressive Programme in 1897, 'to do our best in the communal race of life . . . It is our duty, as it should be our pleasure, to develop and extend our internal resources to the uttermost, and make ourselves not only a "live" commercial centre, but a happy and pleasing residential spot'.[52]

The extension of the borough boundaries was the first step, accomplished under a Local Act of 1901 which also created nine three-member municipal wards, bringing the total strength of the Council including aldermen to 36 and redressing the imbalance between the three old wards which arose with the movement of population into eastern areas of the town. Roughly equal in 1835, by 1895 the electorate of the East ward was almost five times as great as that of South and close to triple that of West. Objections to the higher borough rates were disposed of by levying differential rates for a period of ten years, but as a comparison between Northampton and Newport (Mon.) served to illustrate, the level of the assessment rather than of the rate poundage itself was the real guide to the relative lightness or heaviness of the burden. With an almost identical population and rate Newport's higher rateable values amounted to a total call on its ratepayers of some £24,000 a year more than those of Northampton.[53] Nevertheless, a 'progressive' municipal programme would cost money. The N.L.R.U. made no secret of it, but 'the temper which looks upon the rates as a burden grievous to be borne, and regards the payment of the civic dues as so much "exaction", is the exact antithesis of the ideal civic sentiment . . . We have our duty to ourselves truly, but we also have our duty to those who come after us'.[54]

Northampton had already made some moves in this direction. The Guildhall museum was supplemented in 1875 by a free reading room, and in 1877 by a lending and reference library. Composed largely of a gift of the library of the now-defunct Mechanics' Institute, some 12,000 volumes in all, it was little used at first, but once the museum and the library moved to a new site in Guildhall Road in 1884 the popularity of both steadily increased. By 1903, despite the removal of many artefacts to a second museum opened four years earlier at Abington House, the Keeper Mr. George had become 'most emphatic in his representations in favour of greater accommodation . . . in his opinion if ever the Museum gets into a building of which the exterior is not positively degrading to the town, the use of it will be far beyond the conception of the authorities'.[55] In the event, it was the library which moved into a new building in Abington Street in 1910, financed by a gift from the benefactor of many such establishments, Andrew Carnegie. Originally set at £5,500, he was persuaded to increase it to £15,000, thus fulfilling the pleas of the long-time Chairman of the Museum and Libraries Committee, S. S. Campion, for 'an arrangement worthy of Mr. Carnegie's generosity, worthier of two great public institutions, worthier of the dignity of a great self-governing community'.[56]

Both Abington House and 20 acres of the surrounding park were also acquired by gift, in this case of Lady Wantage of Overstone and largely through the offices of Alderman Henry Randall. Enlarged by the purchase of the Lower Park in 1903, Abington Park became the scene not only of such annual events as the Northampton Municipal Flower Show, first held there in 1909, but of regular Sunday and evening band concerts, organised for many years by Joseph Rogers, choirmaster of Queen's Road Methodist Chapel and later a Liberal councillor and mayor. The 1901 programme included concerts by the Town Silver and Temperance Bands, the Northamptonshire Regiment and the Kettering Rifles, later in the decade by Black Dyke Mills, the Coldstream Guards and other leading military bands, and so popular were they that 'on frequent occasions we have not been able to seat the audience who have thronged the enclosure'.[57] Here, for 6d., they could enjoy the music from the comfort of a deckchair, but the charges made for admission to other events were widely resented, and in 1899 the Council was accused of abusing its powers by denying the townspeople free access to 'their' park.[58]

'Every citizen is a shareholder in the municipal concern', the N.L.R.U. had declared, perhaps too convincingly, but 'those who pay the piper are at full liberty to call the tune, and if the piper perhaps chance to pipe to his own delight rather than to theirs, they have the remedy — change the piper!'[59] Elect us, let us govern, or turn us out, in short; but a much more serious dispute had earlier arisen over rights of access to the town's common lands. Under the Act of 1778 enclosing its open fields, control of the Racecourse was vested in Trustees appointed by the Corporation for the use of the freemen of the town. Here and elsewhere, 'from time immemorial' the freemen had held rights of pasture and other interests in the commons, and these were clearly violated in their view by the erection of boards and fences for cricket matches on the portion of land leased by the Corporation to the Town XI club.

In 1876, seeking legal clarification of the freemen's rights rather than the derisory 4s. they claimed in damages, the Trustees sued the Alma Cricket Club for 'unlawfully and wilfully committing injury to the grass and herbage on the Racecourse'.[60] Public opinion favoured the cricket club, however, and the case was quickly dropped. In the case of the Racecourse, Counsel's opinion favoured the freemen, but elsewhere the position remained obscure and the arguments continued. Finally, in an arrangement confirmed under the Northampton Corporation Act of 1882, the freemen agreed to surrender their rights in the common lands in exchange for a perpetual annuity of £800, paid by the Corporation to a reformed body of Trustees who were in future elected by the freemen from their own ranks.[61]

The Racecourse and other former commons were now utilised as public parks, and in due course the Council also provided separate bathing places for males and females in Midsummer Meadow, the latter the subject of 'adverse comments' in the *Northampton Independent* when it opened in 1908.

Those who 'came to see if they were correct', said Mr. Arnold, the attendant, 'found that the paper was entirely in the wrong. The remark that "ladies who did not care to pay a penny for a dressing box had to disrobe in an open shed" was not true, as on no occasion did this happen ... As to boys peeping under the boards, that also was stopped by that time ... there has been absolutely no word of complaint from any of the bathers'.[62] Other parks and recreation grounds were also provided in outlying areas of the town where residential and industrial development was rapidly swallowing up open space: the Victoria Park in St. James's, part of it the gift of Earl Spencer in 1898 and the remainder purchased from him in 1911; the Kingsthorpe recreation ground, purchased from Mr. F. H. Thornton of Kingsthorpe Hall in 1912; and a ten-acre site acquired from the Bouverie estate at Far Cotton in the same year.

The moral health of the working classes remained of as much concern as the physical fitness which parks and swimming pools encouraged, and at least some of the facilities provided by the Council were intended to encourage a 'rational' use of leisure. There was no obligation to use them, of course, and as an analysis of borrowers from the public library showed, even in 1914 these were far less numerous in the inner mainly working class wards than in areas with a higher proportion of middle-class residents. Readers also continued to show a marked preference for fiction rather than the 'serious books' to which the Librarian attempted to direct them.[63] To some extent, however, the municipality could dictate the terms on which its facilities were used, and these were often all the more strict where they were informed by a tradition of Liberal Nonconformity. Literature regarded as in any way 'offensive' or 'indecent' was banned from the library, although the Committee refused a request from Nonconformist ministers to 'expunge' the betting news from papers supplied to the public Reading Room. While 'deeply sympathising with the object', they concluded that no 'material inconvenience is occasioned the general frequenters ... by the use made of the evening papers'.[64]

The formal layout of public parks, their pavilions and marked-out pitches, flower-beds and refreshment rooms in sharp contrast to the 'rough' of common land, was itself designed to encourage sedate and sober behaviour, but here the ethos was reinforced by bye-laws which insisted on certain standards. No games were permitted on Sundays, and swearing or otherwise 'inconveniencing' users were grounds for ejection. Visitors to the Abington Park museum — unaccompanied children under 12 and dogs not admitted — were also warned that 'anyone behaving in a disorderly manner will be promptly removed'.[65] Audiences at the park concerts heard 'good' music only, and such was his insistence on this that Mr. Rogers once returned the programme to the bandmaster with a request to make it 'a little more classical'. Declaring 'I'll give them classical!', it was said, the result was 'the severest classical programme' he could devise: 'but I have rarely had a more appreciative audience!'. One military band was reputedly on the verge of collapse after playing a programme it unwisely allowed Mr. Rogers to choose for himself, but a working man's description of Schubert's Unfinished Symphony as 'music that makes you feel you want to be good' may suggest that the corporate faith in it as a morally uplifting influence was not entirely misplaced.[66]

None of this is to suggest that idealism and a humanitarian desire to improve the quality of life had no role in the municipal government. In the public as in the private sphere many efforts were inspired by a strong sense of duty to the wider community, and if this was often underpinned by religious belief, it could be equally shared by those who rejected religion altogether. 'We ask the co-operation of Christians with us in our great work', wrote the Northampton Social Democratic Federation in 1897 in response to attacks on its 'irreligious' creed, for

> among the professing Christians of Northampton, there are many who . . . seem to think that Socialism is much the same thing as Atheism, and that they are serving the interests of religion by opposing it to the utmost of their strength. As a matter of fact, Socialism has nothing to do either with a belief in God or the absence of a belief in God . . . some Socialists are Atheists, but many Socialists are not Atheists, and the majority of Atheists are not Socialists . . . Similar remarks apply to members of the Radical party.[67]

As they did; but the abolition of the property qualification for municipal office in 1882 removed the legal barrier to the election of manual workers, and in 1886, albeit unsuccessfully, W. L. Roberts became the first 'labour' candidate to contest a municipal election in the town. The unpaid nature of the work and — if not in Northampton — the practice of holding Council meetings in normal working hours, still excluded many in practice, but the S.D.F. gained its first local representative in 1898 with the election of C. J. Scott to the School Board. In the meantime, due in part to the S.D.F.'s ability to split their vote, the Liberals had lost control of the Council to the Conservatives. The timing of their 'socialistic' Progressive Programme in 1897 was thus significant. Offering 'good, sturdy, bracing breezes which shall clear the air of narrow and timid policy', it was inspired in great part by the fear that the political breeze was blowing towards Socialism itself. The Conservatives, however, declared that the Liberal programme was 'very moderate, and that it might be taken as the Conservative programme'.[68] No less alarmed by the advent of a third political force, they were as eager as the Liberals to reap the financial harvests of municipalisation.

In Nottingham, for instance, the Council now owned the gas, water and electricity supplies, and 'only the other day' it had purchased the tramways company for a mere £20,000. Why should Northampton too not possess these 'rich treasuries of municipal profit and communal convenience', for 'we can take it as an absolute certainty that the handsome profits of the gas supply . . . could easily bear under municipal control the interest on loan and Sinking Fund charges, and even then leave a generous margin of net profit'.[69] In fact, the Gas-Light Company had already rejected one approach from the Council in 1888, and the process of compulsory purchase was complex and costly enough for it to be left in private hands until the industry was nationalised in 1949. The water supply had been in the Council's hands since 1884, when it purchased the Waterworks Company for £200,000. Profitable as it proved, the need to maintain an essential service was the main motive here, for the Company itself was no longer able to cope with the demands of a rapidly growing community. The costs of extending the Ravensthorpe reservoir proved its final stumbling block, and with easier access to finance at lower rates of interest, this was carried out by the Council itself.

Even then, the M.O.H. noted in 1901, the supply was 'not in any sense super-abundant' for a town of Northampton's size, and if a daily average consumption per head less than half that of London suggested a 'defective appreciation of the value of thorough household and personal cleanliness', too much zeal was not really to be encouraged.[70] Inadequate water supplies were also a barrier to industrial expansion, hence the heartfelt thanks of the Northampton Manufacturers' Association in 1910 for the provision of a service reservoir at Boughton, 'which we are satisfied is of considerable benefit to the town and business community, and has secured for us the 'A' class rebate from the Fire Insurance Companies'.[71] However, despite the sinking of a new well at Ravensthorpe in 1906 the situation was described in 1911 as 'critical', and the consequences of a third year of below average rainfall as 'almost too awful to contemplate'.[72] The eventual course was a new reservoir in the

Hollowell Valley, close enough to Ravensthorpe to operate the twó in conjunction, and far enough advanced to be spared the financial cutbacks of the First World War. Completed in 1917, it proved adequate to the needs of the town until the 1940s.

The municipal takeover of the tramway system was prompted by different considerations. The Tramways Act of 1870 gave local authorities the option of purchasing private tramways after a period of 21 years, which in the case of the Northampton company expired in 1901. In strict terms it applied only to the first lines built, with the remainder coming onto the market later. While it was keen to extend its operations, the Company was unwilling to do so unless the Council made its intentions clear. Would it therefore purchase the whole system now rather than in '21 year' stages, or agree to waive its powers of purchase until 1919? The Council chose the first course, completing the purchase in July 1902 at a cost of £37,500 and in the meantime acquiring additional powers to extend the system and convert it to electric power. Completed in 1904, its opening was greeted by a mock obituary card in 'Affectionate Remembrance of the Northampton Horse Cars . . . which succumbed to an ELECTRIC SHOCK, July 21 1904'.[73]

Far Cotton was still served by horse-bus until the problem of the Bridge Street incline was overcome some 10 years later; but with 20 larger cars against the Company's fourteen, a much faster service and a universal one penny fare, Northampton now had, in the view of the Municipal Journal, a tramway system 'which from the standpoints of efficiency and general appearance is not excelled in any town of the same size in the kingdom'. Although, it added, 'the Council does not appear to have received from the Northampton public that sympathetic assistance it deserves . . . The reactionary newspapers have printed the usual "facts" and "statistics" against tramways publicly owned and operated', and 'for some curious reason [it] has declined to purchase the electric light undertaking'.[74] The Council had in fact approached the Electric Light Company in 1902 with an offer to purchase for £100,000, but the Company refused to sell for less than £140,000 and there the ratepayers ended the matter. Instead, by siting the tramways power station next to the municipal refuse destructor in Castle Street it was able to use steam from the latter to drive the boilers in the former, and despite the gloom-laden statistics cited from elsewhere, it had every hope of handsome profits.

In 1906, in fact, the tramways made a net profit of over £6,000, £1,500 of it turned to the relief of the rates; but profits would not make themselves, warned Simon Collier, Chairman of the Tramways Committee, in the following year, and not only were they falling already, no allowance had been made for depreciation — of the tracks, for instance, which would need complete replacement within the next few years. These facts, he said, 'may come as a surprise to many who have hitherto looked upon the trams not only as a great convenience, but as a source of profit to relieve the rates', but unless 'I can feel satisfied that the Committee and Council will support me in my efforts to carry out the work on strictly business and commercial lines . . . I must decline to associate myself with an undertaking . . . which can only end in disaster and discredit'.[75]

To critics of municipal trading, this was only too likely to be the outcome. Lacking any direct financial interest in success or failure, they argued, councillors would inevitably show less enterprise and initiative than a private company. The workload of municipal authorities was now so heavy that those with experience of large-scale business were simply not standing for election, leaving public undertakings in the hands of petty traders with a notorious addiction to cheese-paring and a base desire for re-election. Sacrificing future security to present popularity, they would dissipate profits in cutting the rates, and grudge the salaries necessary to entice top-class professional managers from private companies. All these things were possible, but none were inevitable, and in Northampton they did not happen. Small traders were still numerous on the Council, but despite his own dislike of the species, even George Bernard Shaw conceded that in these matters 'he is as useful as he is noxious', 'shrewd and effective enough when he is in his depth, and his local knowledge is indispensible'.[76]

However, larger businessmen were more rather than less active in municipal government in Northampton at this time. Fewer and larger firms were now the rule in the footwear industry, but the larger the firm the more its management could be delegated, and this generation of economic and social leaders was on the whole as ready as the old to assume political leadership. Among its substantial body of past or present shoe manufacturers were Henry Wooding, James Manfield, A. E. Marlow, Edward and Thomas Lewis and Simon Collier himself; and beyond their own industry, Samuel Smith Campion and one of the barons of the rival *Herald* empire, Henry Butterfield.[77] For £300-400 p.a. the Council secured the estimable services of Joseph Gottschalk as its Tramways Manager, which included keeping it abreast of such technological developments as the trackless tramway systems pioneered in his native Germany.[78] In fact, far from ending in disaster and discredit, annual profits from the tramways ranged between £5500 and £10,000 between 1908-18, a part of them paid at Cllr. Collier's insistence into a Renewals Fund, but with enough remaining to provide some annual relief to the rates.

However, when industrial and commercial prosperity also depended to some extent on a cheap and efficient system of local transport, did the municipal government not have a duty to provide it even if the position was reversed and it had to be subsidised from the rates? After all, many municipal undertakings — libraries, museums, cemeteries among them — were 'explicitly not carried on for profit . . . and even in the case of those undertakings which are run for profit, the latter is not the sole governing consideration. The public, and to some extent, the workers employed in them are allowed to benefit by it under the form of lower charges or better wages and shorter hours'.[79] That was the Socialist view of 'municipal socialism', at any rate, and as the programme of the Northampton S.D.F. in 1898 suggested, it went very much further than the Liberal programme of the previous year, and further even than the equalisation of rates, fair wages and municipal housing policies which had already gained the London County Council a degree of fame or infamy.

An eight-hour day, a minimum weekly wage of 24s. and one week's paid holiday a year for all municipal employees; a municipal bakery, coal store and pawnshop; the takeover of the Infirmary and provident dispensaries, and of all leisure facilities and housing: 'Our comrades will, if elected, work heartily in the Council for the immediate municipalisation of everything that can possibly be taken over by the town'.[80] Their opponents mocked it, but the Socialist vote almost tripled between 1897 and 1901, and in 1902 J. G. W. Smith captured the Tory stronghold of the Kingsthorpe ward. He was followed in 1903 by James Gribble in North and his fellow N.U.B.S.O. activist William Pitts in Castle. Finding unity in adversity, Liberals and Tories now began to engage in electoral pacts and gave the Socialists as rough a ride as possible in the Council. The Conservatives, claimed one S.D.F. poster during the 1905 elections 'proposed that they should withdraw their candidate from the Far Cotton Ward as the Socialists were strong, and advise their supporters to work for the return of the Liberal . . . STRANGLE THE POLITICAL SIAMESE TWINS that have been fooling you so long. Vote Socialist!'.[81]

Taken seriously enough to be excluded from both the Watch Committee and — by virtue of their advocacy of municipal housing — the Sanitary Committee, the ridicule to which S.D.F. councillors were subjected was extended to others disloyal enough to agree with some of their policies. John Brown, who was also a Guardian, was commonly greeted by cries of 'Councillor Comrade Brown' after supporting a proposal that the Poor Law Board should be taken over by the Council.[82] However, if 'a few Socialists could, of course, carry nothing themselves', as the S.D.F. admitted, they could at least 'push the other members on' by making use of formal resolutions to force a debate, for instance. Dealt with at the end of normal business, the device of walking out and leaving the Council without a quorum was often used here. Supporting a proposal in the Poor Law Board to build a Union lunatic asylum in 1903, the Liberal Guardian and Councillor Francis Tonsley declared that 'we shall soon want one according to the way Town Council business is conducted'.[83] However, said the S.D.F. journal, the *Northampton Pioneer*, some such motions were 'so accordant with the principles of justice and humanity, and so strongly supported by the most enlightened section of the electorate', that the other parties could not possibly oppose them all.[84]

In fact, these resolutions were often designed to place Liberals and Tories in a dilemma from which they could escape only by offering an alternative of their own. 'That in order to obviate the disenfranchisement of working class citizens who seek honourable work, not charity or criminal task labour', proposed Cllr. Smith in 1903, 'this Council resolves . . . that it should find work for the unemployed, unemployment involving not only great suffering to the dependents of the unemployed . . .'.[85] Would Members deny, by negativing this motion, that unemployment was a cause of great suffering, and proclaim that poverty was a civil and criminal offence? Or would they spend £1,000 on relieving it? They would do neither, but they would appoint a Special Committee to consider the matter, with the three Socialists as its only members.[86] 'I want them to have plenty of rope', as the Mayor was apt to say when asked to silence them in debate; but their report suggested 'nothing but what the Council had carried out long before the introduction of Socialist members',[87] as James Manfield admitted, and in setting up a Special Emergency Committee under his chairmanship to provide temporary employment on municipal works the Council was only following its own precedents.

It was only in exchange for work that municipal councils could provide unemployment relief, using powers sanctioned by the Local Government Board in 1893 in response to 'exceptional circumstances arising from temporary scarcity of employment'. The Council had used them in that year and several times since, most recently in the winter of 1902, when the poor state of trade was compounded by the return of local servicemen from the Boer War. By no means as indifferent to the plight of the unemployed as the S.D.F. liked to suggest, its resistance to the same course in 1903 was in the nature of a defensive retreat from the problem of structural unemployment in the footwear trade. Long-term rather than temporary, responsibility for its relief fell squarely on the Poor Law Board, but confronted in turn with a 'terribly crowded' Workhouse and the escalating cost of out-relief, the Guardians were only too willing to shift a part of their burden elsewhere. In 1904, however, an attempt was made to co-ordinate their various efforts through a Central Committee representing the Guardians, the Council, and the Unemployment Relief Fund set up by Edward Lewis on his election as Mayor in 1903 with the money normally devoted to the mayoral banquet.

In February 1905, a month typical of the proportions of relief given by each, 413 of the 837 applicants, mainly married men with children, were allocated to Council works; 237, largely single males and those unfit for heavy work, were directed to the Guardians; 56 were relieved from the Fund; and 129 were 'not entertained'.[88] This role was taken over later that year by the Northampton Distress Committee, set up under the new Unemployed Workmen's Act. Chaired first by Francis Tonsley, and later by his fellow Liberal George Wilson Beattie, James Gribble was also among its members. Winter public works were the main means of relief, but it also made grants in aid of emigration to the colonies, and an abortive attempt to persuade local shoe manufacturers to reduce their employees' hours of work to create vacancies for others. A mere half hour a day, Edward Lewis estimated in July 1905, would absorb all those currently out of work, but if this was also the course favoured by N.U.B.S.O. it found little favour elsewhere.[89]

Councillor JAMES GRIBBLE.

THE Raunds Strike.

March on London, MAY 8th, 1905.

Presented to *E. Batchelor* who took part in the March of the Army Boot Workers, to lay their grievances before the Secretary of State for War. The Party left Raunds on May 8th, 1905, marching via Bedford, Luton, St. Albans, Watford; reaching London May 12th. Mr. Arnold Foster refused to meet the Deputation, and after an attempt on the part of their Leader to bring their grievances before the House of Commons (from which he was forcibly ejected), the Party started on their homeward journey May 15th, via Watford, Chesham, Tring, Leighton Buzzard, Newport Pagnell, Northampton; reaching Raunds on Saturday, May 20th, 1905.

NAMES OF THOSE WHO TOOK PART IN THE MARCH:

CHIEF.
James Gribble

OFFICERS.
R. Baker, *Paymaster*
F. Roughton, *Billetmaster*
E. Batchelor, *Commissariat-General*

CYCLE CORPS.
J. Bass
G. Sawford
C. Mayes

AMBULANCE.
W. Morris

BAND.
W. Robinson (40)
B. Mayes (23)
E. Cottingham (34)
L. Mayes (31)
N. Fox (31)
F. Fox (26)
C. Dean (28)
J. Wilmer (29)
J. Denton (31)
L. Hodson (17)
W. Mayes (29) *Band Master*

"A" COMPANY.
Sergt. A. Coles (43)
A. Coles, junr. (22)
O. W. Allen (27)
H. W. Allen (25)
T. Chester (25)
G. Underwood (25)
W. Willmott (95)
F. Lawrence (30)
V. Willmot (20)
M. Richards (27)
S. Warner (25)
R. Smith (29)
C. Edwards (27)
W. Robinson (29)
E. Stubbs (26)
E. Head (23)
J. Hart (29)
C. Allen (28)

"B" COMPANY.
Sergt. A Mayes (21)
C. Higgs (38)
G. Andrews (34)
T. Moody (30)
A. Bugby (36)
C. Robins (37)

F. Lawrence (22)
Jack Allen (24)
Fred Allen (50)
Joe Allen (25)
Will Allen (22)
E. Betts (32)
S. Jackson (34)
R. Rooksby (31)
T. Fensome (40)
W. Cripps (28)
F. Feary (26)
J. Burton (21)
E. Spicer (33)
W. Mayes (24)

"C" COMPANY.
Sergt. A. J. Green (30)
J. Bates (53)
G. H. Kirk (28)
H. Webb (24)
G. Webb (20)
A. Webb (22)
F. Smith (21)
J. Brandon (24)
E. Haxley (23)
W. Atkins (49)
E. Atkins (22)

F. Gates (21)
W. Allen (20)
W. Nunley (24)
F. Freeman (27)
H. C. Clayton (46)
H. Percival (21)
A. C. Evans (20)
F. Coggins (27)
P. York (23)
J. Ward (30)

"D" COMPANY.
Sergt. R. Mayes (23)
H. Phillips (29)
W. Nash (20)
W. Dilley (23)
S. Ball (33)
E. Spencer (20)
G. Mayes (56)
W. Sykes (27)
H. Phillips (27)
L. Pearson (35)
E. Bird (59)
J. Archer (25)
S. Fensome (22)
H. Major (20)
R. Sawford (27)

"E" COMPANY.
Sergt. C. Copperwaite (32)
F. Mutton (26)
H. Reynolds (26)
A. Green (23)
J. Reynolds (52)
T. Lock (32)
F. Tilley (31)
H. Ward (26)
W. Whiteman (43)
W. Barker (32)
F. Bass (26)
G. Haxley (21)
F. Whitney (24)
B. Mantel (20)
C. Marsh (30)
J. Cooper (34)
H. Bunting (34)
W. Archer (38)
J. Scrivener (29)
A. Ball (31)
D. Nickerson (22)
C. Lawrence (33)

28. James Gribble (1868-1934), Socialist councillor and Poor Law Guardian, pictured here on a certificate from the march of the Raunds shoemakers to London in 1905, which he led as National Organiser of the National Union of Boot and Shoe Operatives.

In the meantime the Poor Law Board continued to confront its own particular problems. By the early 20th century a re-distribution of seats had reduced the weight of the country parishes, while the abolition of *ex-officio* guardians, plural voting and the property qualification for office in 1894 had opened the way to a more representative political and social mix. In the mid-1890s Northampton acquired its first 'Lady Guardian', Mrs. J. H. Jackson, wife of the solicitor and councillor James Jackson, who appears to have been somewhat tried by the patronising attitude of her male colleagues. There were some 'who questioned the desirability of having lady Guardians there', Chairman Richard Cleaver recalled on her retirement in 1903: 'Now, however . . . all the Guardians were perfectly satisfied that the presence of a lady was a desirable thing, and in practice had been found to be very useful'. Mrs. Jackson herself 'had felt all the time that there was work on the Board for ladies . . . it would be very much better if there were two or three lady Guardians'.[90]

By 1913 there were 'no fewer than eight ladies who now occupy seats on the Board . . . . The feminine octet certainly adds unwonted variety . . . and forms a phalanx of sympathetic natures which should be of great value . . . the days are gone when the Guardians, often composed of choleric or crusty retired tradesmen, assembled with initial prejudice and bent brows to frown upon paupers for daring to be poor'.[91] Although eligible for election to municipal councils after 1907, women gained readier acceptance on Poor Law and School Boards because poor relief and education were more overtly 'feminine' concerns than highways, sewers and the like. However, many female Guardians already had experience of public and political life before their election, through service on similar bodies or behind-the-scenes work for other members of their families. Rose Jarvis, for instance, was an active S.D.F. member who served as a Guardian in Croydon before being elected to the Northampton Board in 1907. Mrs. George Swan followed in the footsteps of her father William Rainbow in becoming Chairman of the Board, while others were the wives of borough councillors, among them Mrs. F. C. Parker, another of its Chairmen, and Rose Scott, the wife of C. J. Scott.

Sickness and old age continued to account for the great bulk of pauperism, but in 1903 plans were made to move the Workhouse children into 'scattered homes' with something more akin to a family atmosphere. This freed some space in the workhouse itself, now 'continually receiving a class of persons who were not likely to find work in the shoe trade as the shoe trade was now managed'.[92] Mainly males in the 50-60 age group, a new men's wing was added soon after, bringing its total capacity to around 500, inclusive of the 150-bed infirmary. In 1906 the *Northampton Chronicle* was sufficiently impressed by its 'scrupulous cleanliness', the 'kindliness of the officials to the unfortunate inmates', and a diet 'of a liberal character', to conclude that 'were all the facts about workhouses known the traditional horror of the respectable poor would be greatly minimised, for the deprivation of daily liberty is the only hardship inmates are subjected to'.[93] Hardship enough even without the stigma attached to it, the workhouse remained their last resort, but in 1903 the Guardians themselves were accused by the Footwear Manufacturers' Association of adding to the problem of able-bodied pauperism by crippling 'the various enterprises of machinery users . . . their difficulties increased in meeting competition with foreign countries' through a re-assessment of rateable values.

The Guardians 'had no interest of their own in the matter', they retorted. 'What were their interests except to serve the public in general and not to serve a class? Their mandate was from the public, not from the shoe manufacturers'.[94] Nor from their displaced employees, and a deputation of the unemployed led by J. G. W. Smith in that year received equally short shrift from some members of the Board. He 'did not see', said one Conservative member, 'why the Guardians should have to sit and listen to Socialists talk because there were unemployed'.[95] They had no option when James Gribble and C. J. Scott were elected to their number in 1904. He 'didn't trouble about bad rules and precedents', Scott told the Guardians at his first meeting: 'I had been elected to revolutionise the procedure of the Board in giving relief, and I was going to try my best to do it'. By, for example, informing applicants that he had recommended a higher level of relief than the Relief Committee had granted. 'The Chairman would say: The Committee will allow you 3/6 a week; and I would add: I proposed that you should have 5/-. I am a Socialist'.

'They know there are Socialists on the Board', was how he justified this 'most irregular' behaviour, 'and if we don't tell them what we are trying to do, they'll think we agree with the wretchedly small doles you give'.[96] Gribble himself was several times ejected from Council meetings for disorderly behaviour, twice fined for breaches of the peace and sentenced to a month's imprisonment in 1904 for boxing the ears of the Liberal alderman and former N.U.B.S.O. leader E. L. Poulton 'in consequence of being called a liar'. Basically 'a modest, gentle man', it was said, he was 'enthused to vigour and rigour and strenuousness by his faith and intent. A man whom you felt resented the fate of his fellows'.[97] Keeping the peace, in the S.D.F. view, only served to keep the system intact, but its tactics lost it some support from those who sought the same ends. A local branch of the Independent Labour Party rose up to challenge it in 1908, and by 1910 the S.D.F. was losing electoral ground to its more pacific and reformist approach.

However, there was one question on which the Poor Law Board itself rarely disagreed. Between 1893-7 83% of the infants born within the Northampton Union remained unvaccinated, against a national average of around 50%. Following serious outbreaks of smallpox in London and elsewhere in 1900-01 the proportion fell to 58.7%, but by 1908 it had crept above 80% once again. Generally sharing as well as reacting to the 'strong feelings of disfavour' which compulsory vaccination aroused, the Guardians left the law in 'absolute abeyance' for so long as they were allowed, and 'heartily sympathised' with the similar policy of other Boards and with 'the men who go to prison rather than have their children vaccinated'.[98] 'The Northampton Board congratulates the Gallant 45 members of the Leicester Board of Guardians who are making such a noble stand against the iniquitous Vaccination Act of 1898', ran one motion in that year, 'and pledges itself to give them their moral and if needs be their material support'.[99]

'One of the most foolish things ever done by any Parliament', said Richard Cleaver, the Act allowed conscientious objectors to obtain a certificate of exemption from a Justice of the Peace, and 'he never sat as a Magistrate upon the Bench . . . without feeling how much indignity there was in it'.[100] As for prosecuting those who failed to do so: 'you are a servant of the Local Government Board rather than our servant', was the Guardians' directive to their Vaccinating Officers, and 'if that Board gave you orders, you must take your own course'.[101] Without engaging expensive solicitors, it added; but legal costs apart, said Francis Tonsley, he had 'not much patience with people who went cadging around and wanted other people to pay for their fads and fancies . . . Why should the poor of the town who did not believe in vaccination be compelled to pay for those who did, and could afford to pay for it?'. [102] The issue was commonly greeted by cries of 'Not again!' and 'I will resign', but it was the diversion of limited finances from the relief of poverty itself which was so much resented. Of the £11.5m. spent nationally by the Poor Law authorities in 1903, only half went directly to this end, and the vaccination service accounted for a large proportion of what the Guardians described bluntly as the 'wastage'.

Both on the Board and the Council the religious conflict of their early years had been largely submerged by the end of the century. Most of the problems facing them were purely secular in nature, and the sheer volume of work involved was in itself an effective diversion. Education, however, remained a religious minefield. 'Churchmen and Nonconformists are discussing the education of the people', said one speaker at a meeting of the Northamptonshire Educational League in 1898: 'what is it that makes them so red and angry? . . . Are

they concerned with the better teaching of the children or the better training of the teachers?
. . . Not a bit of it. They are quarrelling as to what religious denomination the children in
reformatories shall be consigned to, or about the son of a Baptist blacksmith who has been
surreptitiously taught the Church Catechism'.[103]

By the 1860s even those most opposed to state education were coming to accept that
voluntary effort was not equal to the needs of the nation. However, the political implications
of an 'ignorant' electorate — or worse still, one which educated itself in subversive theories
of economy and society — weighed heavily in the timing of the Education Act of 1870. 'I
believe it will be absolutely necessary to compel our future masters to learn their letters',
said Robert Lowe, Vice-President of the Education Department, when the franchise was
extended to urban working men in 1867.[104] Even so, the education provided under the Act
was neither free nor — unless local bye-laws made it so — compulsory, and it was not
intended to replace that offered in existing voluntary schools. These continued with increased
Exchequer grants, while the task of making good deficiencies in provision was vested in
local School Boards. In the Board Schools at least 'no religious catechism or religious
formulary distinctive of any particular denomination' was to be taught, and under the
'conscience clause' of the Act parents could withdraw their children from religious instruction altogether. However, neither went far to satisfy advocates or opponents of such teaching,
and the first elections to the Northampton School Board in January 1871 were fiercely
contested, with 18 candidates fighting for its 11 seats.

Six went to Anglicans, one to Joseph Gurney, and the remainder to Nonconformists
fighting on an unsectarian platform. Mostly active politicians, on the Conservative side
they included Pickering Phipps, the architect E. F. Law, and Francis Mulliner; for the
Liberals, P. P. Perry and William Adkins, Superintendent of the Commercial Street Chapel
Sunday Schools. The poll was headed by the 33-year old solicitor's clerk and Liberal
Churchman Thomas Wright, almost 3,000 votes ahead of Gurney in second place. 'Ready
of speech, audacious in attack, reckless in ridicule, prompt at retort, and with a mental
granary crammed with chaff and banter', he was re-elected with a still larger majority three
years later.[105] However, by contrast with others elsewhere, relations on the Northampton
Board were relatively harmonious. The main source of dispute was Clause 25 of the Act,
which allowed the Boards to pay elementary school fees for necessitous pupils, and was
widely opposed on the grounds that public money would thus be paid to sectarian schools
over which the ratepayers had no control. 'There was such a strong feeling in the town
against the clause', said one Baptist member of the Board, 'that he believed if it were
adopted and they sent a precept to the Corporation, the Corporation would refuse to pay
it'.[106]

The Church party carried the vote here, but compelling parents to send their children to
a denominational school was calculated to provoke uproar, and for this reason the enforcement of a bye-law requiring compulsory attendance for 5-13 year olds was delayed until
the planned new Board Schools provided non-sectarian alternatives. On the whole, however,
the Board's energies were devoted to its appointed task, its first step to assess the educational
needs of the town and the extent to which they were already met. A total of 9,247 children
were recorded in the borough at the 1871 census. Deducting one seventh 'as belonging to
the middle and upper classes', this left 7,922 in need of school places, 5,673 of them already
provided for through denominational and charity schools and a handful of 'dame' schools.
The shortfall was not large by comparison with some areas, but there were glaring
deficiencies in some parts of the town, notably to the west of Regent Square/Sheep Street
and in expanding residental areas to the east of Abington Square.

New schools were clearly necessary, and the first of them were opened at Spring Lane
and Vernon Terrace in 1874 by the second Board, which included a Roman Catholic, the

29. Staff and pupils of the Kettering Road Board School, c.1893. The fourth of the schools built by the Northampton School Board, it cost £12,200 and was opened in 1878.

30. Marianne Farningham Hearn, journalist, author and Sunday School teacher, elected to the Northampton School Board in 1886.

Rev. Dr. Scott. At a total cost of some £13,000 they catered for over 1,500 children, and were followed in 1878 by the Kettering Road School with space for 800 more. In 1877 the British School in Campbell Square, with some 1,000 places and urgent financial problems, was also handed over to the School Board. By the time the duties of the Board were themselves transferred to the Borough Council in 1903 it had a total of nine schools with places for 9,990 children, with an additional 7,715 provided by the voluntary schools. 'The Members of the School Board have thus largely shared during the past 30 years in providing for the education of the children of the Borough', they concluded in that year, 'and for this long period have given their constant attention to the uninviting details of administration ... The Board hand over their great responsibility to their successors in confidence that they will take no retrograde steps ...'.[107]

Enforcing attendance was one such 'uninviting detail', but among those so occupied at some point were the two 'lady members' who blazed the trail for other female local governors in Northampton: Mrs. M. P. Manfield, elected on a Liberal unsectarian platform in 1877, and Marianne Hearn, long-time Sunday School teacher and girls' club leader at College Street Baptist Chapel, who also pursued a successful career as a journalist and author under the name of Marianne Farningham. She served two terms from 1886-92 and was later co-opted onto the Education Committee of the Borough Council. From the Duston School Board just beyond the pre-1901 borough boundary, however, the Council inherited nothing but a bitter dispute. Covering part of the parishes of Duston and Dallington, it embraced the expanding suburb of St James's End where a Church school had been opened in 1866. The only school within the area, pleas to the Board to build one its own fell on unsympathetic ears. Supporters of sectarian education generally had the majority in its body — but the only justification for building was insufficient existing provision, and repeated extensions to the Church school removed it. Similar tactics were used against the Northampton Board in Kingsthorpe, with less success, but by 1894 the St James's school had some 650 pupils against the 200 of 1872, 244 places were added in that year, and when it was extended yet again only four years later, bringing its capacity to over 1,000, battle was joined in earnest.

Invoking the 'conscience clause', Nonconformist parents began a mass withdrawal of their children — some 300 of them — from religious instruction. Their campaign was directed by the St James's Education League, headed by the Rev. Neale of Doddridge chapel and the Primitive Methodist minister, the Rev. Jabez Bell. It also included members of the Lewis family, one of the largest employers in the area. However, when the children were issued with medallions declaring 'We want a Board School' early in 1899, the Managers of the Church school refused them admission, and Henry Labouchere took the dispute to Parliament. 'SAGE OF QUEEN ANNE GATE thrilled House with story from North-ampton', reported *Punch* in incredulous tones: 'The Member for Sark tells me that the locked out have regularly organised themselves, and serious trouble may ensue ... cry of the children from Northampton smothered by majority of 102'.[108] Nonconformity was not amused, the Education League opened two rival schools at Doddridge Memorial and St James's Hall, and it was left to the Borough Council to provide a non-sectarian alternative in 1904 through a temporary 'Tin School', later replaced by a permanent building at a strategic distance from the Church school itself.

The Balfour Education Act of 1902 also met with Nonconformist opposition. Responsibility for elementary education was now vested in county and county borough councils, but although they were required to pay the running costs of voluntary denominational schools — now known as Non-Provided schools — they did not exercise full control over their management. On the principle again that public funds should be fully controlled by public bodies, the Northamptonshire Baptist Union greeted the Act as 'a challenge to unceasing struggle until it shall be repealed', and the Rev. Bell was one of several local protesters to be imprisoned for refusing to pay the education rate.[109] However, under the chairmanship first of E. L. Poulton, and then of the Conservative ironmonger Rowland Hill, the Council's Education Committee also had powers to provide secondary and higher education according to local needs, and while it continued to expand the primary sector, much of its energies were now channelled into these areas.

The Council had in fact been providing technical education for some time, firstly through a School of Science and Art directed by the Museum Committee, and from the early 1890s with·the benefit of the 'Whisky Money', a 1d. rate levied under the Technical Instruction Act of 1889, and contributions from local manufacturers anxious to improve the skills of their employees. In 1894 the Science and Art School merged with the Grammar School to form the Northampton and County Modern and Technical School, offering day and evening classes for both males and females; but by 1903 the building was over-crowded and the Board of Education was issuing 'scarcely-veiled threats' to withdraw its grants unless conditions were improved. No longer veiled, in 1907 its application for continued recognition 'will be confirmed only upon condition that the Board, before the end of the session, receive an assurance . . . that accommodation will be provided for the School within a time that is reasonable . . . No grant will be paid until this condition is fulfilled.'[110]

The assurance was given and accepted, but by 1910 the Board was also pressing the Council to provide a secondary school for girls. The only such publicly-funded school in the county was at Wellingborough, and 'there is no similarly populated area of the same extent with the same need in the whole of England'.[111] A threat

31. Edward Lawrence Poulton, Liberal councillor and alderman, Northampton N.U.B.S.O. Branch Secretary and Union General Secretary 1907-30. 'A sober and responsible negotiator', he also served on the School Board and as first Chairman of the Education Committee in 1902. The first working man to become Mayor of Northampton, he later joined the Labour Party.

to withdraw recognition from the Pupil Teacher Centre was the lever used here — but had central government been more generous in its funding rather than leaving the rates to bear the brunt of such projects, much of its 'do this or lose your grants' approach would perhaps have been unnecessary. Duly opened on St George's Avenue in 1915, the school was popularly known as 'St George's Palace'. It was modelled on the Smith College for Women which had much impressed S. S. Campion on his visit to Northampton, Massachusetts in 1904 to represent the 'old mother city' at the 250th anniversary celebrations of the founding of its American 'daughter' settlement.[112] In the meantime, in a programme designed to improve secondary education 'in all its branches', the Modern and Technical School moved into new premises in Billing Road in 1911, financed in conjunction with the County Council, and a municipal Technical College and School of Art was opened in its old Abington Square buildings.

In the view of its principal John Blakeman just before the First World War, there was still a 'deplorable lack' of advanced working-class education, but this was remedied in part by the introduction of 'time off' classes for local industrial workers during the war itself. Both the School Board and the Education Committee also ran evening classes in a variety of subjects, and in 1905 the latter opened the Wellington Place Special School for mentally handicapped children, one of the earliest such schools in the country. Blind and deaf children were educated at the authority's expense in schools in other areas, but from 1908 onwards it was also required to provide a school medical service, operated in conjunction with the Public Health Department. Defective eyesight, tooth decay and below average height and weight were the most common problems detected. The former were treated through a school clinic with fees waived in the case of the needy, while in a three-month experiment in 1909, financed largely by James Manfield, 110 of the poorest pupils were also given a free daily breakfast and dinner. The results were 'far from conclusive', but selective help for under-nourished children was in future provided from a private fund supported by subscriptions from several members of the Council.[113]

In the view of the School M.O., Dr. F. Bedingfield MacDonald, the health of the nation was too important to be left either to charity or private enterprise. 'I wonder when the idea that competition is necessary in the greatest of all services, the service of the People's Health, will vanish from brains, many of which seem to hibernate in congealed tradition', he wrote in 1914: 'A fully linked up State Medical Service, covering the ground from the cradle to the then much remoter tomb, seems to be a far nobler ideal than any form of free trade in the lives of the proletariat'.[114] He was ahead of his times, but two years earlier the Council itself had concluded that private enterprise alone was not equal to the task of housing the town, and had agreed to build 50 workmen's dwellings of its own. 'Surely the most uncomfortable' Council meeting he had ever attended, the *Independent*'s correspondent could hardly bring his mind to bear on this momentous new policy, for 'the perplexed Town Hall Committee had made yet another re-arrangement of the seats in a desperate attempt to provide the necessary accommodation for the prospective dozen new arrivals'.[115]

A re-organisation of the municipal wards had provided for the election in November 1912 of an additional nine councillors and three aldermen — but where were they to sit? The aldermen, suggested the *Independent*, could be placed in the 'spacious niches' around the Council Chamber, and valuable space saved by attaching portable desks to the councillors' backs; but as a more dignified alternative the Committee had relegated press and public to a hastily-constructed wooden platform at the rear, 'like canaries suspended near the ceiling . . . did they dare to move, the boards creaked and groaned and the chairs toppled over to the floor'.[116] Barely a word could be heard, he said; but Cllr. Chown, Chairman of the Housing and Town Planning Committee, gave the scheme 'such lukewarm advocacy as to astonish its supporters . . . the Chairman's obvious opposition encouraged others who had nursed disapproval . . . and the debate which started did not stop for two hours'. 'Fountain step agitation, And Limehouse legislation', declared another councillor of it, but the Liberals 'disagreed that the scheme was purely Socialistic; it was a social question, and very different from Socialism'.

In recent years the Conservatives had once again been gaining ground on the Liberals, and the latter had been engaging in electoral pacts with the S.D.F. and I.L.P. to offset their challenge. In the Liberal need for their support lay the influence of the Socialists, and in this matter they had used it effectively. However, there was no intention on any side of subsidising the scheme from the rates. The houses could be built and let at a profit, argued

32. 'How to accommodate the Councillors', a newspaper cartoon inspired by the addition of nine councillors and three aldermen to the Council's numbers in 1912. 'But perhaps the best way of saving space would be to abolish Council meetings altogether, and present committee reports to the public by means of a gramophone.'

C. J. Scott — but 'experiments made in other parts of the country prove conclusively the impossibility of a municipality making even a small percentage on their outlay', retorted the Ratepayers' Association: 'the Council is not warranted in speculating in dubious ventures of this kind'.[117] Very often, in fact, municipal housing could only be made to pay for itself by charging rents which were beyond the means of the low income groups it was intended to aid. In 1913 the majority of private tenants in Northampton paid between 5-7s. a week in rent and rates, around 20% of an average adult male wage of 25-35s., but rents for the first 20 three-bedroom houses built on the Bective estate at Kingsthorpe ranged from 7s.-7s. 6d. a week.[118]

By July 1914 only six had been let, and work on the remainder was suspended for want of applicants. Dwellings at the higher rent were equipped with both bath and cellar, for it was 'a mistake to bring the man down to the standard of the house', said one speaker to a town planning conference in 1913, 'the standard of the house should be brought up to the man, or his requirements'.[119] In that year, however, recognising the conflict between high standards and affordable rents, the Council had also agreed to build 28 two-bedroom houses, without bath or cellar, mainly in Naseby Street at Semilong. At rents of 5s. a week demand outstripped supply, and in 1915, when the Bective account showed a deficit of £100, they returned a modest profit of eight pounds. By then, of course, the war had brought municipal house-building to a halt, and when it resumed in 1919 it would be with positive encouragement from central government in the form of grants which were — for a brief time at least — on an unprecedented scale of generosity.

To a great extent, party differences were also submerged during the war, much to the delight of the *Independent*, which had 'persistently pleaded for the suppression of party politics in civic government'.[120] The welfare of the town, it said, 'should be lifted high above the welter of mere party considerations'; but when Liberal and Conservative leaders agreed in 1912 to de-politicise the mayoralty and the aldermanic offices, and went so far as to consider re-naming themselves 'Progressives' and 'Moderates', their party rank-and-file revolted alongside the Socialists. 'As democrats we object to a Socialist becoming Mayor until the majority of the people of Northampton are Socialists . . .', said the latter, but 'under no circumstances shall we vote for anyone who is not a Socialist who is put forward for election to the Aldermanic bench'.[121] As for the Liberals, said the *Independent*, they 'feel they are entitled to the full spoils . . . [and] Conservative workers look askance at their leaders bargaining with the combined opposition of Liberals and Socialists'.[122]

In all its past circumstances, asking Northampton to abandon party politics was rather like asking Bradlaugh to pledge allegiance to the Established Church — but would the welfare of the town really have been better served by apolitical municipal government? The municipalisation of the tramways and the small but significant start made to municipal housing were in fact the product of the very conflicts which the *Independent* so deplored. Liberal 'parsimony' had in the past affronted Conservative civic pride sufficiently to produce a new Guildhall, while Liberal municipal enterprise — in the field of leisure, for instance — was in part a response to Conservative 'moderation' in other respects. Now Socialism in turn was pushing both towards 'socialistic' policies, and if these stopped well short of Socialist aspirations, both Liberals and Conservatives might well have been rather less 'progressive' without this impetus.

Of course, not everyone agreed that tramways and houses were the proper sphere of local government, but there is a case for arguing that Northampton was better served by party political conflict than it would have been in its absence. And if the alternative was an unprincipled pandering to sectional interests, then even the *Independent* baulked at the thought. 'We are trying to satisfy those who kick up the most row first', said John Veasey Collier in 1914 in frustrated response to complaints of inaction on the part of the Highways

Department. 'This naive confession confirms one's suspicions', snorted the *Independent*: 'If you want the Town Council to do anything you must make a noise . . . You must persevere almost to the point of persecution until you have made yourself such an intolerable nuisance that the Council can stand it no longer . . . If you are keen on getting anything done "kick up a row"'.[123] Making a noise was in the best of municipal traditions, but both the *Independent* and Cllr. Collier himself did the Council an injustice. Its perception of its duty to the community embraced those who suffered in silence too, and neither economic depression nor the 'now you have it, now you don't' nature of central funding between the wars would stop the attempt to fulfil it.

Notes

1. Northampton Liberal and Radical Union (hereafter N.L.R.U.), *Municipal Politics: The Progrssive Programme* (1897), (N.L.I.S. 198-800).
2. *Northampton Daily Reporter*, 12 June 1892.
3. N.C.B.C., Chief Constable's Report (1892).
4. N.C. Minutes, 19 September 1888.
5. N.C.B.C., letter to Watch Committee, 31 July 1891.
6. N.C.B.C., Chief Constable's Report (1894).
7. Letter to Watch Committee, op.cit.
8. N.C.B.C., Borough Surveyor's Report (1893).
9. Ibid. (1890).
10. N.C.B.C., Report of the Borough Auditors, 17 December 1892.
11. N.C.B.C. Minutes, 17 June 1889.
12. Dr. Buchanan's Report on the Sanitary State of Northampton (1870) (N.L.I.S.).
13. N.C., Health Report (1873-4).
14. Buchanan Report, op.cit.
15. Report to the Sanitary Authorities of the Counties of Northamptonshire, Leicestershire, Rutland and Buckinghamshire (1874).
16. Quoted in *N.M.*, 22 March 1879.
17. Buchanan Report, op. cit.
18. N.C.B.C. Health Report (1888).
19. Ibid. (1889).
20. Ibid. (1893).
21. Ibid. (1894).
22. Ibid. (1881).
23. Ibid. (1901).
24. Ibid. (1878).
25. Ibid. (1889).
26. Buchanan Report, op.cit.
27. N.C.B.C., Report of the Medical Officer of Health re Municipal Milk Depots (1904).
28. N.C.B.C., Health Report (1904).
29. Ibid. (1904).
30. Ibid. (1905; 1909).
31. Ibid. (1913).
32. Ibid. (1901); Supplementary Health Report (1901).
33. *N.I.*, 11 November 1905.
34. N.C.B.C. Health Report (1904).
35. *N.I.*, 9 November 1929.
36. Ibid.
37. N.C.B.C. Minutes, 11 July 1908
38. N.C.B.C., Supplementary Health Report (1901).
39. N.C.B.C. Minutes, 2 July 1906.
40. Ibid., 24 July 1912, Report on the National Conference for the Prevention of Destitution.
41. *Northampton Daily Chronicle*, 23 May 1899.

42. N.C.B.C. Minutes, 1 December 1913.
43. Ibid., Report of Delegation to a Meeting of the Association of Municipal Corporations, April 1888.
44. Henry Labouchere, quoted in Howarth, J., 'Politics and Society in Late Victorian Northamptonshire', *N.P.&P.*, Vol.4, 5 (1970-1).
45. These revenues were set aside primarily for police superannuation and technical education.
46. N.C.B.C. Minutes, 25 July 1910.
47. Report of Conference on the Prevention of Destitution, op.cit.
48. Hamilton, E. W., *Memorandum on Classification and Incidence of Imperial and Local Taxes* (1899).
49. Cannan, E., *History of Local Rates in England* (1912 edn.).
50. *N.I.*, 2 November 1907.
51. Rev. Robert Dale, quoted in Briggs, A., *Victorian Cities* (1968 edn.), p.197.
52. N.L.R.U., The Progressive Programme, op.cit.
53. Ibid.
54. Ibid.
55. N.C.B.C., Annual Report of the Museums Committee (1902-3).
56. N.C.B.C. Minutes, 24 July 1905.
57. Annual Report of Joseph Rogers to the Abington Park Committee (1901).
58. N.B.C., *The Parks of Northampton* (1984).
59. N.L.R.U., *The Progressive Programme*, op.cit.
60. 'Legal Folklore of Northamptonshire 9: "Political" Town Clerks', *N.I.*, Feb. 1982.
61. N.C.B.C., Memorandum as to the Freemen's Annuity, March 1909.
62. N.C.B.C. Minutes, 5 Oct. 1908.
63. N.C.B.C., Chief Librarian's Report, 31 Oct. 1914.
64. N.C.B.C. Minutes, 3 April & 24 July 1905.
65. Ibid., 15 May 1900.
66. 'The Mayor of Northampton', *Northamptonshire County Magazine*, Vol. 1 (1928).
67. *Northampton Socialist*, 18 Sept. 1897.
68. Ibid., 20 Nov. 1897.
69. N.L.R.U., *The Progressive Programme*, op.cit.
70. N.C.B.C., Health Reports (1901; 1903).
71. N.C.B.C. Minutes, 25 July 1910.
72. Ibid., 18 Dec. 1911.
73. Reproduced in *Northampton Mercury and Herald 250th Anniversary Supplement* (1970).
74. 'Northampton's Tramways', *Municipal Journal*, Vol.13, 600, 29 July 1904.
75. N.C.B.C. Minutes, 7 Dec. 1907.
76. Shaw, G. B., *The Commonsense of Municipal Trading* (1904), pp.113-4.
77. *The Herald* was purchased by James Butterfield from Sir Rainald Knightly, and owned in turn by his son Henry and Grandson Cleveland.
78. N.C.B.C. Minutes 9-12 Nov. 1909.
79. *Northampton Pioneer*, May 1903.
80. Ibid., Oct. 1898.
81. Ibid., Oct. 1905.
82. Ibid., Oct. 1903.
83. Scrapbook of Newspaper Cuttings re the Northampton Poor Law Board, 3 February 1903 (N.L.I.S. 198-755).
84. *Northampton Pioneer*, Feb. 1903.
85. N.C.B.C. Minutes, 21 Sept. 1903.
86. Ibid., 9-13 Nov. 1903.
87. *Northampton Pioneer*, Dec. 1903.
88. N.C.B.C. Minutes, 6 Feb. 1905.
89. N.C.B.C., Minutes of the Northampton Distress Committee, 27 Nov. 1905.
90. Scrapbook of Cuttings, op.cit., 3 March 1903. For a full discussion of the role of women in local government, and a summary of relevant electoral qualifications, see Hollis, P., *Ladies Elect: Women in English Local Government, 1865-1914* (1987).
91. Unidentified newspaper cutting, 26 April 1913 (N.L.I.S. 198-755).

92. Scrapbook of Cuttings, op.cit., 25 February 1902.
93. *Northampton Chronicle*, 22 Sept. 1906.
94. Scrapbook of Cuttings, op.cit., 17 March 1903.
95. Ibid., 12 May 1903.
96. *Northampton Pioneer*, May 1904.
97. *Reynolds News*, 14 May 1905.
98. N.P.L.U., Guardians' Motion Book (1836-1930) (N.R.O. PL6/11).
99. Ibid.
100. Scrapbook of Cuttings, op.cit., 23 June 1903.
101. Ibid., 18 March 1902.
102. Ibid., 21 Jan. 1902.
103. Report of the Annual Meeting of the Northamptonshire Educational League (1898) (N.L.I.S. 1-75).
104. Speech to House of Commons, 15 July 1867.
105. *N.H.*, 12 Sept. 1885.
106. *N.M.*, 14 Dec. 1872.
107. Eleventh Report of the Northampton School Board (1903).
108. *Punch*, 8 March 1899. For a full account of this controversy see Roberts, F., 'A Board School for St James's', unpublished thesis, Dip. Ed., University of Leicester (1967) (N.L.I.S.).
109. Elwyn, T. S. H., *The Northamptonshire Baptist Association: A Short History* (1964).
110. Board of Education to Northampton and County Modern and Technical School, 27 March 1907. Reproduced in Walmsley, D.(ed.), *An Ever-Rolling Stream* (1989), which gives a detailed history of technical and further education in Northampton from the 19th century to the founding of Nene College. See also Lees, T. C., *A Short History of Northampton Grammar School, 1541-1941* (1947).
111. N.C.B.C. Minutes, 4 July 1910.
112. Ibid., 6-13 June 1904. Northampton, Mass. was founded by settlers from Northampton itself. Samuel Smith Campion was diverted from business in Montreal to attend the anniversary celebrations, which he recalled as 'among the most precious memories of my life'. They coincided with the opening of the extensions to the General Hospital, which was otherwise given first priority, but four bound volumes of the Borough Records were later sent after him. Informal links between the 'mother' and 'daughter' settlements still continue.
113. N.C.B.C., School Medical Officer's Report to the Education Committee, Nov. 1909.
114. School Medical Officer's Report (1914).
115. *N.I.*, 7 & 15 Sept. 1912.
116. Ibid.
117. N.C.B.C. Minutes 6 May 1912.
118. N.C.B.C., Minutes of the Housing and Town Planning Committee, 7 July 1914.
119. N.C.B.C., Report of the Midlands Conference on Town Planning Administration, Feb. 1913.
120. *N.I.*, 27 April 1912.
121. *N.I.*, 11 May 1912.
122. *N.I.*, 4 May 1912.
123. *N.I.*, 4 July 1914.

Chapter Five

Concord is Stronger than a Castle: Northampton Between the Wars

One of the results of the war is that we must look at industrial questions from an entirely different standpoint. Although we shall be required to show initiative, enterprise and business acumen, both employers and employed must regard their position more from the point of view of servants for the welfare of the whole community.

A. E. Marlow, quoted in *Northampton Independent*, 15 July 1922

Towns, like persons, are generally taken at their own valuation. Unless we cultivate civic pride ourselves, how can we expect other places to do it for us . . . Too long has Northampton hidden its lights under a bushel.

Northampton Independent, 11 August 1923

Northampton 'has a very fine motto', remarked one visitor to the town in 1927, 'Castello fortior concordia — meaning that goodwill amongst different classes of citizens is a much greater protection to the country than a fortress. I wish . . . that all people engaged in trade, both employers and workpeople, would recollect Northampton's motto. We should then have a more prosperous country'.[1] Northampton did not escape the effects of the inter-war depression, but neither did it suffer them on the scale of many other industrial centres. Local employers claimed much of the credit for its relative prosperity, and gave some to their workers in turn, but in maintaining goodwill between its citizens, whether at work or in the wider community, they were no more willing now to leave things to chance than in the past. On the contrary, in the post-war period they found some very compelling reasons to intensify their efforts. 'We must find some basis which will satisfy our employees', said A. E. Marlow bluntly to the newly-formed Northampton Rotary Club in 1921, 'or they will take a short cut to revolution as sure as night follows day.[2]

There seemed little cause for such fears in Northampton itself. Post-war relations in the footwear industry were marked by a 'sweet spirit of reasonableness' which in February 1919 produced a national agreement guaranteeing a 48-hour week and minimum wages of 53-56s. a week for adult males and 30s. for females (minimum wage rates were subsequently reduced in line with deflation, and based after 1922 on the movement of the Cost of Living Index. In the mid-1930s they were broadly equivalent to the level of 1919). Local resistance to the 'supplementary wage' system re-surfaced in 1920 as the post-war boom came to a sudden end, but despite the combination of short-time work, wage reductions and a rising cost of living, the industry remained free from serious disputes. Nor was there any real evidence of a breakdown in relations beyond the staple trade itself. There was still little of that middle-class withdrawal to suburban enclaves which testified to hardening class divisions, nor any lessening of their involvement in the political, social and cultural life of the town. And effective as it might be in pushing Liberals and Conservatives where they would rather not go in the Council chamber, Socialism still drew only limited electoral support.

Elsewhere, however, there was sufficient unrest to fuel the fear of working-class revolution. Post-war strikes among engineering, power and transport workers were followed in the Spring of 1921 by a serious dispute in the mining industry, provoked by wage cutting on the restoration of the mines to private control. No less worrying from the ruling class point of view was the discontent manifest in the ranks of the police and the army, which cast doubts on their loyalty in the event of a confrontation. This apart, central government had

120

intervened in private industry during the war on an unprecedented scale, controlling raw material supplies, restricting the output of non-essential goods, and allocating labour. What it had done once it might do again, and in their dislike of central direction, their desire to remove any possible justification for it, lay another reason for the conciliatory approach of Northampton employers to their workers. They also had much need of their co-operation in meeting the challenge of post-war market conditions.

Some export markets were lost to the development of indigenous footwear industries during or after the war, and the tariffs applied to British goods in some colonial markets were a further obstacle here. By reducing the need for skilled labour, new or improved wartime machinery also encouraged production outside established centres of the trade. So too did the use of rubber or rubber substitutes for the manufacture of whole items of footwear — wellington boots, for instance — which was largely the preserve of the rubber companies themselves. Productivity continued to increase, but there was no corresponding increase in domestic demand, and demand for high quality footwear was further affected by the economic depression. An influx of cheap German leather in the early 1920s posed new and unexpected problems for the British leather industry, and for the shoe manufacturers in turn, for 'unless some check was placed upon German competition they would begin to dump their surplus footwear here . . . as they have done in Holland, where thousands of shoemakers had in consequence been thrown out of employment'.[3]

What was to be done? Firstly, said A. E. Marlow, employers 'would have to be satisfied with a fair share out of the industry and nothing more . . . The question must be faced on the broad basis of justice . . . Labour was entitled to say it ought not to work all its life at the whim of an employer and then be cast off'.[4] The industry was in fact still shedding labour, and male labour in particular. The 7,836 male shoemakers recorded at the 1921 Census now represented 26% of occupied males in the town, against a corresponding figure of 28% for occupied females, while the number of employees in the industry as a whole fell by 7% between 1924 and 1930. Now, however, its remaining workers were admitted to a larger share in its profits through the medium of industrial welfare schemes. These often took the form of non-contributory social and provident funds, of a rather different order from the Friendly Society-type organisations promoted by employers in the past.

Richard Turner, for instance, acted as treasurer to the Good Intent Society of Finishers formed by his workers in the 1870s, but it was supported by their own 1s. a month contributions. Post-war schemes were generally based on a lump sum investment by the employer. Sickness, funeral and other benefits were financed from the interest, and administered in the case of Manfield's at least by a committee composed largely of shop-floor workers. Several of the larger companies also provided sports and social clubs. The Harlestone Road sports ground of Frederick Bostock's Lotus company was 'a revelation alike of the possibilities of an enterprising, considerate firm and of the welcome changes that have been wrought in the past few years in the recreation of shoe workers', wrote the *Independent* in 1923. The 12-acre site had facilities for bowls, cricket, football, tennis and hockey, and ample space for practice drills by the company's fire brigade, one of several private outfits in the town. Cost price refreshments were served in the dining room of the pavilion, built by the firm's employees themselves, who had full use of all facilities on Saturdays and weekday evenings for an annual subscription dependent on age of only 3-5s. a year.

This and similar ventures, the *Independent* concluded, 'must tend to promote physical and business efficiency and to create and cement that spirit of mutual good fellowship and good will between employers and employed, upon which the success of any firm in these days must inevitably depend'.[5] Health, efficiency and goodwill were precisely the objects, but footwear manufacturers were not alone in making 'wise and generous provision' for their workers. Employees of the Gas-Light Co. had their own sports ground, those of the printing firms of John Dickens and Clarke and Sherwell their social clubs, while the 'consideration shown to employees' was among the grounds on which Grose's motor cars were recommended to potential purchasers. The Barratt factory boasted air-conditioning and piped music, but many employers also financed outings for their workforce and an annual corporate dinner. There were occasional precedents here too. Richard Turner's indoor employees were invited to a dinner to mark the coming of age of his son in 1876, and the Manfield workforce to a soiree in the same year when James and Harry became partners in the firm.[6]

On the latter occasion, presentations were made to 'loyal' employees and M. P. Manfield was presented in turn with a token of his workers' esteem. Post-war dinners usually took a similar form. They were a means of promoting a 'family' feeling and maintaining the contact which could easily be lost in a large enterprise, but many employers also stressed their accessibility at other times. Mrs. E. L. Pigott, the third generation family chairman of Manfield's, was 'emphatic' that 'every employee should have easy access to the directors on any matter which could not be, or had not been, adequately dealt with elsewhere', for 'the knowledge that there would always be fair play in the dealings between employees and the board was a key constituent in the lively morale they had for many years maintained'.[7] She might also be seen, reported one industrial welfare journal in the 1920s, on the factory floor, 'clad like all the other women and girls in a simple white overall'.[8] The Northampton Brewery Company went one step further to cement the bonds of industrial fellowship. Several of those dining to the background music of the Company-sponsored quintet in 1930 had been with the firm for 40 or 50 years, but 95% of its employees had also taken up an offer to purchase shares in the enterprise.[9]

In Northampton as elsewhere these initiatives owed something to the influence of the Industrial Welfare Society, founded in 1918 by Sir Robert Hyde, and to the 'combination and conciliation' philosophy expounded after the war by the Chairman of I.C.I., Sir Alfred Mond. In meeting the challenges posed by post-war market conditions, however, local manufacturers had a philosophy of their own. In terms of technical excellence, entre- preneurial innovation and high quality goods, Northampton simply could not be bettered — and it was with this message that they set out to sell it to the world. The Shoe Manufacturers' Association took the lead in 1919 with the formation of a research body for the local industry. Also embracing tanners and leather merchants, it was adopted soon afterwards as a national project, the British Boot, Shoe and Allied Trades Research Association. In promoting the town itself a crucial role was played by the Northampton Chamber of Commerce. Founded during the war, it was financed largely by the Manufacturers' Association until the 1930s, but its efforts went well beyond their own industry.

Trade delegations from engineering and printing as well as footwear firms were sent overseas, including one to the U.S.S.R. in the 1920s, and bookbinding, car and cycle accessories and tennis racquets were among the great variety of goods and services it promoted to the home market at the Northampton Festival Trades Exhibition in 1930. Opened by the Duke of York, President of the Industrial Society, the exhibition was combined with a carnival and pageant at Abington Park, and the £7,000 proceeds of both events donated to local charities. In 1923 the Chamber of Commerce also spearheaded an 'All British Boot' campaign, designed to attract domestic customers 'sufficiently patriotic to pay 6d. or more per pair to support home industries against the Germans'. Twenty-four pairs of footwear, made entirely of British-dressed leather and ranging from men's walking boots to chrome calf tennis shoes and ladies' crocodile skin golfing shoes, were commissioned from G. M. Tebbutt and Sons, and displayed at Harrods of London to demonstrate 'the superiority of the home-made article, alike in materials and manufacture'.[10]

'There is a great and growing need for the boot trade to bestir itself if it is to be saved from the claws of our Continental competitors . . .', wrote the *Independent* of this initiative: 'Hitherto, our manufacturers have not troubled themselves much about foreign competition because they have not met with a great deal. The last great scare was the American invasion . . . The present peril is even more serious and calls for immediate and drastic remedies'.[11] Protective tariffs were its favoured solution, but fearing retaliatory action which would hit their exports in turn, the tanners and shoe manufacturers preferred to fight with their own weapons. The former diversified into fancy leathers for belts, braces and bags as well as footwear, reproducing 'the exquisite markings of various reptiles, from lizard to python, the delicate shades of tortoiseshell, the intricate patterns of textile weaves, and a hundred and one other fancy designs . . . and the demand for these products is growing daily'.[12]

'Northampton's shoe trade', reported the *Shoe and Leather Record* in 1927, 'may claim an efficiency ranking with that of any of the other great industries of the country'. The inefficient, the out-dated and the under-capitalised were still going to the wall, but the output of the 60 or 70 survivors continued to rise, and their strategy showed every sign of success. 'They are making footwear in infinite variety', the journal continued, 'the quality of which, it is agreed by some of the best judges, is unexcelled in the world. Indeed, it is another commonplace of the trade that Northampton-made footwear normally commands more money in the open market than any other, because it is Northampton-made. Such is the value of a great reputation'. The industry had also found new outlets, it added, 'in catering for the feet of the emancipated'; that is, in satisfying a growing demand for ladies' sports shoes — and if long specialisation in male footwear might account for a 'hint of mannishness' about them, 'it is no more than the kind of influence that bids the maiden shingle her hair and adopt modern forms of dress'.[13]

The *Independent* itself expended much newsprint on the subject of the 'modern woman' but, in common with other local newspapers, it also played a central role in promoting the ideal of progress through co-operation. Its underlying message was well conveyed in an interview in 1922 with Mr. J. E. A. Wyatt, retiring manager of the Northampton branch of the National Provincial and Union Bank. The National Provincial had taken over the Northamptonshire Union Bank in the previous year, for 'the whole tendency in banking is for amalgamation. It is the same in shoe manufacturing . . . [but] it strengthens the industry to be dealing with large prosperous concerns instead of many struggling ones'. Asked to comment on the changing 'tone' of local industry, Mr. Wyatt singled out relations between employers and employed. 'Years ago there was a far better feeling existing. They came to know each other better . . . The sooner Capital and Labour realise their interdependence and become better friends, the better it will be for everybody.' By way of a leading question on the 'arduous' hours of work in the past, the article also stressed the 'comparatively easy time' now enjoyed by employees — and the fact that, nowadays, even bank managers were 'not their own masters'.[14]

The *Independent* 'presents its news and reports unbiased by party prejudice', its readers were frequently reminded. Established in 1905 by W. H. Holloway in response to the partisan reportage of the Campion and Butterfield empires, it remained under his own editorship or that of his son Bernard throughout a change of ownership in the 1920s and the wholesale takeover of the local press by Provincial Newspapers Ltd. in 1931. The latter produced a once unthinkable marriage between the *Mercury* and *Herald* and their respective stablemates, the *Echo and Chronicle*; but under the editorship of Cowper Barrons, the new *Chronicle and Echo* was remodelled on the lines of the *Independent* itself, and adopted a very similar editorial stance — citizenship before party, community before class, Northampton first and foremost.

'Shop in Northampton' was the appeal made by the Mayor, Alderman G. S. Whiting through the columns of the *Independent* in 1922, 'for I cannot help saying I think it is nothing short of a disgrace that so much money, made entirely out of Northampton people, should be spent with traders in the richest city in the world instead of with traders of the town in which the money is made . . . possibly there are some to whom it does not occur at all what a serious injustice they are inflicting on a town by withholding that patronage which every loyal and patriotic citizen should feel it both his duty and his pleasure to bestow'.[15] The 'invaders' here were large London stores marketing their goods by mail order; but local traders, 'who have to bear the burden of rates, help local charities and other good causes', were among the first to feel the effects of economic recession, and several other towns had already held 'shopping festivals' in an effort to combat outside competition. Moreover, while 'town patriotism' might occasionally express itself in a thorough hatred of all 'foreigners', it had a creative as well as a defensive face.

Beyond the workplace and the marketplace themselves the ideal of progressive and enlightened service to the whole community was given substance by the inter-war policies of the Borough Council — more fully considered elsewhere — and by some notable acts of individual and collective philanthropy. Foremost amongst the latter must be counted the Bethany Homestead on Kingsley Road, a pioneering venture in housing the elderly on the part of local Congregationalist and Baptist churches which attracted national interest and renown. Opened in 1926, nursing care was provided in the main Homestead, and those capable of a more independent existence accommodated in nearby cottages. The land for the Homestead was donated by the Baptist builder, Liberal councillor and long-time President of the Artisans' and Labourers' Friend Society, Alfred Powell Hawtin, who also built its chapel as a memorial to his wife. The £17,000 costs of the project were otherwise raised through weekly collections in the chapels, and substantial gifts from — amongst others — Edward and Thomas Lewis, and the Liberal leather merchant and councillor Alfred Rodhouse.

The Bethany Homestead went some way to remove the need for and the fear of an old age in the Workhouse, but in 1921 the leather merchant David Paton Taylor financed the building of the Taylor Memorial Hall in Castillian Street, the base of the Northampton Y.W.C.A., while Thomas Lewis and his brother Charles gave 23 acres of land at Dallington for use as a public park. The Council bought the 89-acre Kingsthorpe Hall estate for the same purpose in 1938, but through the medium of the Rotary Club the business community also launched a scheme to provide 'foster fathers' for boys whose fathers were killed in the war, offering outings and aid in finding suitable apprenticeships. Northampton also acquired two new hospitals during this period. In 1924, now living in retirement in Italy, James Manfield gave his former home, Weston Favell House, for use as a hospital for crippled children. The costs of equipping it were met from the proceeds of a pageant staged at Abington Park in the following year. An event which 'united all creeds and politics', the six performances of scenes from Northampton's past involved some 1,700 performers drawn from local schools, charities, and cultural and sports clubs. The Barratt Maternity Hospital, which 'shall be open to persons in all stations of life, and not regarded as charity', was founded in 1934 with a donation of £60,000 from William Barratt.

'All parties in Northampton seem to me to be working in their own way for the town's good', said the Mayor, Cllr. J. G. Cowling, in 1926, 'most of our Town Councillors, Guardians and inhabitants generally put party second, and citizenship and the town's welfare first'.[16] The 'millenium of quietude for which we prayed seems to be upon us . . .', sighed the *Independent* in 1929, 'the political arena is more akin to a sedate company board room'.[17] In the parliamentary arena at least there were few excitements to compare with the Bradlaugh days. Northampton became a single-member constituency in 1918, and the borough electorate was swelled by over 11,000 by the extension of the franchise to women over 30 in the same year. In 1923, after two unsuccessful earlier contests, Margaret Bondfield

33. Doddridge Row, Bethany Homestead, part of the Homestead's cottage accommodation for the elderly.

became Northampton's first female and first Labour M.P., but it was a short-lived victory, achieved largely through a breakdown in support among the other parties for the Coalition candidate, Charles McCurdy.

One of Northampton's pre-war Liberal M.P.s, he found broad acceptance among local Tories — albeit in the grudging terms of 'unless a more suitable candidate be brought forward' from the ladies of the Primrose League[18] — but he was opposed by an Independent Liberal in the 1922 general election, and left in third place by a Conservative in 1923. In the following year Miss Bondfield's seat fell to General Sir Arthur Holland, the town's first Conservative M.P. since 1895. James Manfield's place at the foot of the poll was symptomatic of the decline of Liberalism as a national political force, one which had its origins in wartime divisions and its failure to meet post-war expectations. The Labour Party was a beneficiary rather than a cause of this decline, but in Northampton at least it showed little inclination to exploit the tensions which undoubtedly did exist. On the whole its leaders subscribed to the same conciliatory philosophy as their political opponents, and in the light of their economic and social background and the values which underpinned their own politics, this should not be surprising.

There were, for instance, several large manufacturers within the Labour ranks, prominent among them Wenman Joseph Bassett-Lowke, and William Barratt, who had joined the Social Democratic Federation in the early 1900s. As President of the Shoe Manufacturers' Association in 1933, Barratt waged a vigorous campaign for a shorter working week which antagonised many of its members, but both he and Bassett-Lowke fitted perfectly the image of the enterprising and hard-working individual who had earned his wealth and status on his own merits. The latter's reputation for innovation was further enhanced by the *avant garde* house built for him on the Wellingborough Road in 1925 and appropriately named 'New Ways'. Opinion was divided as to whether the house enhanced the landscape, but Bassett-Lowke was also a leading member of the Chamber of Commerce, and an active member of several local cultural societies which also drew members from all political backgrounds.

Small tradesmen too were spread through all three parties, and several Labour leaders also shared a background of religious nonconformity. The bootmaker Albert Burrows and Will Rogers, a printer and long-time President of the Northampton Co-operative Society, were both Nonconformist lay preachers. William Barratt and C. J. Scott were regular attenders at Congregationalist chapels before turning to secularism, and like his wife Rose, who became the borough's first female councillor in 1919, the latter was an active temperance campaigner. The Socialist desire 'to see the minds and bodies of everyone cultivated to the highest possible pitch of perfection',[19] their own stress on self-improvement and industry as a route to advancement, also had much in common with the governing class ethos of helping the working classes to help themselves. In fact, the tightly-knit group which dominated the constituency party in the 1920s saw its role in terms very similar to those of middle-class 'improvers' and 'civilisers': one of providing the necessary leadership, and raising the condition of the working classes through a gradual process of education, persuasion and 'amelioration'. This was quite in line with the lower middle-class background of many Labour activists at this time and, until the early 1930s at least, they followed a path very similar to that of Liberals and Tories.

In their conviction that central government understood little and cared still less about Northampton's particular problems, all three parties found still more common ground. Foremost among their complaints was the shortage of central funding for the relief of unemployment, for 'the cost of the able-bodied unemployed ought to be undertaken by the State as a national charge, and the local rates relieved therefrom'.[20] 'It is like poulticing a malignant disease', wrote the *Independent* of the £25,000 voted by the Council to road improvements to employ 260 unemployed men in 1922; but while there was no denying the distress suffered by many local families, wrote the M.O.H. in 1926, 'I do not think the condition is nearly so bad as in many of the industrial towns further north'.[21] Indeed, in 1925 two social investigators dwelt at length on the prosperity of the town, citing it in explanation of the 'extreme kindness' of the borough officials in providing information on the one hand, and the 'extreme reluctance' of the inhabitants themselves to 'surrender the facts wanted from them'.

The former, it was suggested, were motivated by civic pride, while 'desperate conditions and squalid poverty often loosen the tongue'. Many residents simply had a healthy aversion to being accosted by perfect strangers and plied with personal questions: but 'however dismal certain aspects of its life and certain areas of its slums might seem, it compares favourably with most English manufacturing towns, and still more favourably with most larger towns'. In 1924 some 97% of Northampton families were estimated to have incomes above a 'minimum standard' of 24s. a week, against 90% in 1913 — although many were dependent on more than one wage-earner — and even for the unskilled, wage increases had outstripped increases in rents and food prices.[22] Indeed, it was one of the ironies of the inter-war period that in the midst of mass unemployment rising real wages enabled many of those *with* work to enjoy a higher standard of living than before.

Nevertheless, only 8% of adult males in Northampton were registered as wholly unemployed in that year, against a national average of 10-11%. Short-time working was arguably a more serious problem, and it did not feature in such statistics. Even so, the M.O.H. concluded in 1931, 'we must be thankful Northampton has not known the unemployment and poverty which has rested for years like a pall over the industrial areas of the north'.[23] Quite so; but the worst was yet to come, and by December 1932 over 11,000 people — around a quarter of the town's entire workforce — were registered as wholly or temporarily unemployed. Many were back in work by the summer, and there were bright spots in the general gloom, notably in the construction industry, which was much occupied — it will be seen — by new municipal housing and civic buildings. However, the image of an enterprising and progressive community was battered by these events, and distinct cracks began to appear in the surface picture of harmony and cohesion.

A branch of the National Unemployed Workers' Movement, which had close links with the Communist Party of Great Britain, was formed in Northampton in 1932. Several members were former leaders of the Northampton Unemployed Association, an earlier body which had been very critical of local efforts in this area. The responsibilities of the Poor Law Board were taken over by the Council in 1930 — but it was not doing enough to relieve unemployment, the Association claimed, and moreover, 'men with large family responsibilities were not engaged on the Road Schemes, whilst men with lesser responsibilities were so engaged'.[24] As the Council pointed out in its defence, 75% of those employed on such schemes had to be ex-servicemen, 10% were skilled 'key men', and many applicants were simply unfit for such heavy work. It was handicapped, too, by the need to prove 'exceptional unemployment' to qualify for government grants, one which made most such applications as 'futile' as the hope that Northampton would receive aid under the Special Areas scheme, introduced in 1934 and targeted again on areas of 'exceptional' distress.

Northampton did not qualify, and local initiatives like the Winter Distress Fund established by Mayor Percy Hanafy in 1932-3 were no real substitute for the lack of central funding. Despite this and other efforts, however, both the N.U.W.M. and the Independent Labour Party accused the Council and local churches of indifference to the plight of the unemployed. The I.L.P. had seceded from the Labour Party after the 'betrayal' of 1931, when the Labour government of Ramsay MacDonald sanctioned a 10% reduction in dole payments as part of a package of emergency financial measures. The parliamentary party split over the issue, and the government fell, but at local level the I.L.P. became increasingly dissatisfied with the moderate stance of the constituency Labour Party. In a May Day procession in 1933 it made its own sentiments clear by carrying an image of labour crucified on a capitalist cross of gold. Chief Constable John Williamson judged it blasphemous and ordered its removal, but his own growing preoccupation with juvenile crime was itself a symptom of mounting middle-class anxiety.

Chief Constable Mardlin's reports were much concerned with this subject in the 1890s, when the condition of the nation's youth was an issue of the moment. 'Continually receiving complaints' of vandalism and 'the great annoyance and inconvenience caused by young men and women parading the streets in disorderly groups', he was 'strongly of the opinion that quite half these cases are owing to home surroundings and the indifferent conduct of the parents'.[25] Again, during the First World War, 'this class of crime is on the increase, and it is greatly to be deplored ... the facts generally disclose that the lack of home corrective instruction and the slackening of the interest of parents is a contributory cause'.[26] This has a familiar ring, but in common with other categories of crime — public order offences, for example — the level of recorded juvenile crime tended to rise and fall in line with contemporary worries: and in the mid-1930s 'we have to deplore a disquieting interest on a national scale in juvenile crime'.[27]

More crimes may have been committed by juveniles at this time, or it may be instead that contemporary perceptions of a breakdown in social relations led to a greater interest in detecting them. There was a similar concern with the 'very serious decline' in attendance at Sunday schools, the main hope of the churches in view of the continuing decline in religious observance among adults. In the case of the latter, it was noted in 1935, the removal of the population around Castle Hill through slum clearance schemes 'has made no difference to the Church, for they were never seriously in touch with it'.[28] However, between 1933-4 relative harmony within the footwear industry itself gave way to a series of disputes as ten local firms defected from the National Federation and attempted to impose a return to day working from the 'supplementary wage' system. It was successfully resisted by N.U.B.S.O., albeit at the cost of reductions in some piece rates, but four of the ten went bankrupt within the next two years.

'Northampton is often described as one big happy family . . .', pleaded the *Chronicle and Echo* in 1934, 'Let us all be brothers and sisters together'.[29] In January 1935, however, a joint Trades Council and Labour Party rally against new regulations for unemployment relief attracted large crowds, and in that year's general election the Labour vote increased sufficiently to leave the sitting Conservative Sir Mervyn Manningham Buller only marginally in possession of the seat. The Labour candidate in this contest was Reginald Paget, son of the Conservative county barrister Guy Paget, and his attacks on the capitalist system found an audience now much more receptive to appeals to class conflict. Fascist appeals to racial prejudice fell on much more stony ground, despite the 'enthusiastic reception' accorded to the leader of the British Union of Fascists, Sir Oswald Mosley, at a meeting at the Guildhall in 1934.

His declaration that British Jews should 'either put the interests of Britain before those of Jewry, or get out of Britain', was greeted with 'a chorus of dissent'.[30] Northampton had a small but well-established Hebrew Congregation with its New Synagogue on the Overstone Road. Amongst its members was the Labour councillor Saul Doffman, and despite its championship of the small trader and its 'British First' campaigns against foreign imports, Fascism made little headway in Northampton. The sole Fascist candidate in the 1937 municipal elections polled only 27 votes — but the Liberals lost five seats, two of them to Labour. Unwilling as yet to confront the changing political reality, the *Independent* blamed this crushing defeat on the identification of local Liberalism with 'modern forms of Puritanism, "anti-mania", social "prohibitionism", Bumbledom, regulation, and general inelasticity of outlook'. The 'average Northamptonian of all parties', it declared, 'has been cherishing an ever-growing resentment of the notoriety — even national notoriety — his town is gaining as a recognised centre of "kill-joyism" . . . an increasing irritation which has led on innumerable occasions to strong expressions of intended revolt'.[31]

Deficient as they might be in terms of political analysis, there was some basis for the *Independent*'s comments. In 1929, for instance, the Libraries Committee had ordered the Betting News to be 'obliterated' from the reading room newspapers. Here it was simply following the example of some local authorities elsewhere, but in the same year it also banned the novel by the German writer Erich Maria Remarque, *All Quiet on the Western Front*, from the public libraries. In the view of all but three of the Committee, the book — based on his experiences during World War I — contained 'offensive' language and some passages which were plainly 'indecent'. Not for the first time, its actions attracted 'gratuitous national publicity', but they also provoked an interesting range of local responses. 'If this is war we will have none of it', was the message of several letters from young adult males: 'and according to those who saw war, Remarque has not told half its horrors'. They were, said the Mayor, Major A. E. Ray, 'horrors of which it is vitally important that the public should be aware'.

In his view the ban was 'utterly ridiculous'. 'Why should the poorer classes be denied *All Quiet on the Western Front* while anyone with a bit of money can read it at will? . . . If the book is objectionable, which I deny, it should be censored by the proper authority'. Moreover, he suggested, the Committee should 'read through the whole of the books in the library. If they maintain their standards of probity in literature, I am afraid they would find their shelves greatly depleted . . . I fear even Mr. Shakespeare would not emerge unscathed'. 'The acid test of all matters like this', said Chief Constable Williamson, 'is, as a man, would you like your daughter to read such a book? I have read the most offensive chapter, and I certainly would not . . . It is simply indecent . . .' Although *he* had not read it, said one local bookseller, he 'felt inclined to support the Libraries Committee mainly in the interests of juvenile readers' — but it was 'easily one of the best sellers'.[32]

As another resident observed, 'the very act of banning the book frustrates its own end', but there was a genuine issue here of the relationship between an elected public authority and the public it was elected to serve — of how far one side should impose its own will, its own perception of the 'public good', upon the other. The answer was, in the view of the elected, a simple one. They were servants not slaves of the community, representatives not puppets, and they were free to exercise their own judgement within the limits of their legal powers. And within those of public tolerance — and if they pushed it too far, they would soon find themselves out of office. Moreover, many of the Council's 'prohibitionist' policies during this period had the backing of large sections of the Northampton public itself. A resolution in 1927 to prohibit a greyhound racing track on the grounds that 'such a racecourse is against the best industrial and moral interests of the town' originated in a public meeting rather than in the Council itself. The Council was sympathetic — but the Watch Committee had no powers to prohibit the betting which went on at such events, and those of the Highways Committee did not stretch far enough to hinder the enterprise by refusing planning permission for buildings.[33]

However, the playing of games on Sundays in the municipal parks or recreation grounds remained firmly prohibited. Had the Council nothing better to do, snorted the *Independent* in 1922, than 'wasting breath and brains over the futile efforts of five Councillors to allow Sunday games'?[34] As a measure of their futility, 29 members voted against a similar motion proposed by William Barratt in 1932, and only four in favour — a margin which suggests that the flood of letters, petitions and deputations which every such attempt provoked from the churches was largely superfluous.[35] The most vociferous opposition came from the Nonconformist churches, both individually and through the medium of the Free Church Council, and many members of the Council itself were still practising Nonconformists. Most of the votes cast in favour of Sunday games came from Liberal or Socialist secularists, who might otherwise be at one with their party colleagues in opposing gambling, drinking and 'offensive' literature. However, the crushing majorities by which these proposals were invariably defeated were the product of a broad Christian alliance which cut across the lines of party or denominational allegiance.

This was no more a new departure than the long-standing prohibition against Sunday games itself, but now it was reinforced by a sense of beleaguerment, a conviction that Christianity was fighting a last-ditch battle for survival — and that the whole fabric of society could crumble if it was lost. 'In my opinion', wrote the Mayor, Alderman Whiting in 1922,

> it is nothing short of pathetic to see men who call themselves reformers ignorantly attempting to destroy the very foundations on which so many of their liberties and freedoms have been built. To destroy the Sabbath would be to undermine these very foundations . . . Why did Germany in 1914 regard a solemn treaty as a scrap of paper? There can be only one answer: because she had lost her soul, and consequently her spiritual vision . . . those people who flaunt themselves in their sports garb with their implements of pleasure in our streets on the Sabbath day, offer one of the greatest insults to English customs and national sentiment they can be guilty of.[36]

To the *Independent*, and to many Northamptonians denied activities freely enjoyed by those of other towns, this was 'kill-joyism' for its own sake. To Ald. Whiting and many other Christians, it was a matter of national life or death; and if they won a victory here, 'the Church will do well to remember this question is by no means settled, and that eternal vigilance will continue to be the price of liberty'.[37] Northampton was not nearly such a unique centre of inter-war 'prohibitionism' as the *Independent* liked to suggest, but local factors did push it further in this direction than some other towns. Liberal Nonconformity was often more willing than Anglicanism to restrict popular amusements in the name of the general good. The strength of secularism, it has been suggested, served to intensify the efforts of local religious leaders and to instill a strong sense of 'one Church' regardless of denominational differences; and visitors to the town during this period did find it in more ways than one a rather sober place.

'Our astonished eyes conveyed to our unwilling brains that Beer Halls (called public houses here) came first, closely followed by churches', wrote one 'Colonial Newcomer' to Northampton in 1929, but 'it is amazing how sober the community is . . . I have seen more drunkenness in Cape Town during a single Saturday evening than I have witnessed in Northampton in a whole year'.[38] He was exaggerating, but the pubs in Northampton closed earlier than those in the county, and the 'Ten O'Clock Rush' into the more liberal territory beyond the borough boundary was an established feature of local life. Reinforced by Chief Constable Williamson's own strong views on this matter, the licensing justices refused every appeal to bring the two in line. Coincidentally or not, summer licensing hours were extended soon after Mr. Williamson retired in 1955 but, pubs apart, Northampton was said to be 'only moderately served for places of entertainment' in 1925. Eight cinemas, two theatres, the public baths and bathing spaces, 13 Working Men's Clubs, Northampton Town F.C. and 'unless a large open market twice a week, and a charabanc service on half holidays into the surrounding country, may be accounted as such', very little else.[39]

In reality, this dismal list proves only that social investigators sometimes do not investigate far enough. The Council's efforts to educate the public 'to appreciate really good music' continued, and despite 'the purgatory of sitting on hard wooden chairs, the inconvenience of which very seriously detracts from one's enjoyment of even the most attractive programme', the Abington Park concerts regularly attracted crowds of over ten thousand. They were now combined with concerts in parks in other areas of the town, and with a series of dances. These were 'much appreciated, and the behaviour was splendid'; and as for exceeding its estimated budget, 'the Committee are of the opinion that the money is well spent in providing suitable relaxation for the inhabitants'.[40] The municipal concert programme easily survived the competition posed by B.B.C. radio from the 1920s, but this was having discernible effects on cinema audiences by 1940. In the view of some, however, both radio and cinema had much to answer for in the musical sphere. 'Today we have musical films, wireless concerts, and when musical performers are needed, most of us call for syncopating saxophones rather than blatant brass bands . . .', lamented the *Independent* in 1930: 'Possibly even the Guards will parade in the not too distant future to the disrupted rhythm of a "Frivolity Five"!'.[41]

The content of radio programmes was in fact strictly controlled by the B.B.C.'s supremo John Reith, a man of strict moral standards who unhesitatingly banned anything remotely 'indecent' from the airwaves. Amongst the popular songs to meet this fate were George Formby's 'Little Ukelele', and 'She Was Only a Postmaster's Daughter' by the Durium Dance Band.[42] However, the *Independent*'s musings were prompted by the recent demise of the Wellingborough Old Volunteers Band. One of several local bands to be dissolved in recent years, this was seen as further evidence of a growing reliance on commercial forms of entertainment. 'It was pitiful', said Mr. H. G. Lewis, Secretary to the Manfield Hospital in 1930, 'that in these days the majority were always paying for someone to entertain them

34. & 35.   Foreword to the programme of the Abington Park pageant of 1925 and (*below*) a scene from the pageant itself.

FOREWORD

FROM the wealth of historic incidents in Northampton's richly storied past it has been impossible to reproduce more than a few of the outstanding events which have made this ancient town such an important centre in our national life for two thousand years.   The eight episodes chosen are those that best lend themselves to spectacular effect and at the same time furnish a fascinating insight into Northampton's great and glorious traditions and history.   The episodes will be enacted amid the sylvan old-world setting of the lawn of Abington Abbey.   Most of the expenses of producing the episodes are being borne by the participants.   In this respect too much praise cannot be accorded to those organisations and individuals who have worked together with exemplary energy, goodwill and generosity in order to provide reproductions worthy of the town, and the good cause we have at heart.

Overture   ...   Band 2nd. Battalion The King's Royal Rifle Corps
(Conductor: Mr. W. J. Dunn, M.C.)

Massed Choirs   ...   "Land of Hope and Glory"   ...   *Elgar*

Enter the Herald (Mr. J. B. Minahan) who will deliver the following :

PRELUDE

Hail ! Northampton and her story,
Dear to fame and bright with glory ;
Let our Pageant, now unfolding
Show, to each and all beholding,
How her sons have fought and perished
For the great ideals they cherished ;
How she sent her brave Crusaders
'Gainst the Holy Land's invaders ;
How—they passed—their weapons
        sheathing—
To us their sacred shrines bequeathing ;
How our heritage embraces
Sires of many warrior races ;
Briton, Saxon, Dane and Roman,
Norman knight and Border bowman,
Blood commingled, feuds requited,
Stand as Britons firm united.

Follow now throughout the ages
Stately scenes from history's pages—
Kings and Queens our rights defenders,
Councils Royal in solemn splendours—
Mothers, too, throughout the ages
Have added lustre to our pages :
They have given to the nation
Statesmen of the highest station ;
Many a scholar, many a singer ;
Bards whose haunting measures linger,

Music-makers, greatly gifted,
Touching chords that souls uplifted ;
Great divines—great painters—writers—
Sailors, soldiers, famous fighters,
Martyrs, heroes, sturdy yeomen ;
Who, for right would yield to no men,
Taking arms against oppression,
Picture them in proud procession,
Passing thus, a noble rally,
Sprung from Midland hill and valley.

Gone the tramp of armed yeomen—
Come the days of happy omen,
Plenteous peace and thought for others,
All mankind as friends and brothers,
May our children, while recalling
Warlike tales, deeds enthralling,
Yet maintain before their vision
That the past has made provision
For the present ; then aspiring
So to make *their* lives inspiring
That a future generation
Find in our's some inspiration.

Sing we thus in joyful chorus
Down the path that lies before us—
Dearest town by Nene's old river,
May we cherish thee for ever.

Let the Pageant now proceed
May we all its lessons heed !   W.H.H.

. . . sufficient knowledge should be acquired to enjoy life without the aid of manufactured amusements'.[43] As the price of radio sets fell in line with rising demand, more and more people could of course enjoy an evening's entertainment without venturing from their own homes. Or from their attics, in the case of amateur radio enthusiasts, and to judge from the flood of entries to a newspaper limerick competition on this subject, there were rather a lot of them.

'Can you not see the young wireless experimenter', asked the paper, 'obsessed by but one desire, that to hear America on the three-valve set on which he has spent every spare penny — and hour — for months past? The embodiment of tense expectancy, he sits, still as a graven image, ear one inch from the cone of the loud-speaker . . .'.[44] However, there was still ample provision for active and less isolated leisure pursuits. The Northampton Co-operative Society, which had 20,000 members by 1940, continued to expand its range of educational and recreational activities along with its trading operations. In 1930, with the aid now of grants from the Borough Council, the Workers' Educational Association was offering courses in Musical Appreciation, English Literature, Economics and Psychology, and there was a whole host of other organisations ranging from allotment societies to sports clubs and cultural societies. Foremost among the latter were the Northampton Repertory Players, an amateur dramatical society which took over the lease of the Royal Theatre and Opera House in 1927. Among their founder members was W. J. Bassett-Lowke, who staged several plays by his close personal friend, George Bernard Shaw.

> **EASTER MONDAY, APRIL 1st, 1929, for Six Nights.**
> **TWICE NIGHTLY at 6.30 and 8.50 p.m.**
>
> Northampton **Repertory Players**, **Ltd.**,
>
> Present—
>
> # "SWEENEY TODD"
>
> " THE DEMON BARBER OF FLEET STREET,"
> OR
> " THE STRING OF PEARLS."
> A Legendary Drama in Two Acts.
> By GEORGE DIBDIN PITT.
>
> Cast in order of appearance :—
>
> Sweeney Todd (the Barber of Fleet Street)   ...   C. T. DOE
> Tobias Ragg (Sweeney Todd's Apprentice Boy) CURIGWEN LEWIS
> Mark Ingestrie (a Mariner)   ...   . T. G. SAVILLE
> Jean Parmine (a Lapidary)   ...   ...   OWEN GRIFFITH
> Johanna (Mrs. Oakley's Daughter)...   ...   ESME VERNON
> Colonel Jeffery (of the Indian Army)   ...   NOEL MORRIS
> Jasper Oakley (a Spectacle Maker)   ...   OWEN GRIFFITH
> Mrs. Oakley (Jasper's Wife)   ...   MARION PRENTICE
> Dr. Aminadab Lupin (a Wolf in Sheep's Clothing)
>   ALFRED RICHARDS
> Mrs. Lovett (Sweeney Todd's Accomplice in guilt) MOLLY FRANCIS
> Jarvis Williams (a Lad with no small appetite)   JAMES HAYTER
> Jonas Fogg (the Keeper of a Mad-house) ...   PERCY PRATT
> Two Keepers   ...   .   STAGE HANDS
> Cloe (a Black Woman)   ...   .   ESME VERNON
> Three Children   ...   . F. N. BURROWS
>   DOREEN STIMPSON
>   A PLAYGOER
> Judge Brandon   ...   .   OWEN GRIFFITH
> Spectators   ...   .   EVERYBODY AVAILABLE
>
> **THE PLAY IS PRODUCED BY HERBERT M. PRENTICE.**
>
> Flowers in the Foyer by A. HOLLOWELL, 232 Wellingborough Road
> Furniture by Messrs. F. & C. H. CAVE.
> Book of Words of the Play can be obtained in the Foyer, Price 2d.

36. Playbill from a performance by the Northampton Repertory Players of *Sweeney Todd*, Easter Monday 1929.

On its third anniversary in January 1930 the 'Rep' was offering a twice-nightly production of The *Prisoner of Zenda*, which drew large audiences despite such competition as '*Beyond the Sierras*' at the Picturedrome — 'AMAZING HORSEMANSHIP' — and the 'One Hundred Per Cent All Talker' *Bulldog Drummond* at the *Exchange*, starring 'the Voice that Thrills', Ronald Coleman.[45] Cinema prices at this time ranged from around 1s. 3d. for a pre-booked seat to 6d. or 3d. for a matinee. Standing spectators paid 1s. in the 1920s to watch Northampton Town, now elevated to the Third Division of the Football League, and narrowly missing promotion to the Second in 1928-9. In 1936-7 the Cobblers had the doubtful distinction of recording the then record defeat of a League club by a non-League team, losing 6-1 to Walthamstow. By then, however, the Club was well and truly caught on the see-saw between public demands for success and the money to satisfy them.

Its dilemma was neatly stated in 1935, for 'we realise that financial success can only be assured by a successful team. Our aim will be to still further strengthen the team, but this policy can only be pursued if we receive generous support from the public'.[46] Selling one of its star players to a wealthier outfit, in the public view, was not likely to achieve either end, but it was only by doing so that it ended the season £400 in debt rather than in more dire financial straits.

In the circumstances, the £150 contributed in that year by the Cobblers' Supporters Club was a welcome addition to its funds. The Supporters Club was founded some years earlier by the Club Chairman and former Mayor, F. C. Parker, and it was to a similar course that the Northampton Football Club looked when it too found itself in a 'parlous plight financially'. Poor results were no part of the problem here. The Saints were one of the most successful sides in the country in the mid-1930s, but club officials blamed part of the fall-off in support on the deficiencies of local bus services to Franklin's Gardens, for 'women had been crushed and had their hats knocked off' in the scramble to board the few vehicles plying the route. Still more important, they suspected, was the 'jealousy' and 'snobbishness' provoked by allowing pre-paying members to book a particular seat in the stand throughout the season. This guaranteed a certain level of income, but 'people say their money is as good as anyone else's', and matters had 'even reached the point where people not in them (the reserved seats) had been referred to as the "contemptibles" or the "untouchables"'.[47]

The Supporters' Club was duly formed, and the pre-booked elite was enjoined to show a little charity towards the common herd. The virtue most required by supporters of the County Cricket Club, the *Chronicle and Echo* suggested in the same year, was eternal patience. The 'measure of a sportsman', it wrote, 'may virtually be determined by the loyalty he shows to his side in fair days and foul . . . These thoughts are inspired by the recent playing failures of the Northamptonshire County Cricket Club. The trouncing by Lancashire at Old Trafford yesterday seems to indicate that once again the long looked for revival in the County's playing fortunes is deferred'. The Club side, it pointed out in its defence, was the youngest among the first-class counties, and no doubt the 'Babes' would soon mature to greater things. In the meantime, 'let it be said of Northamptonshire and the club's followers: "Though they get few encouragements, they do play the game!"'.[48]

If their desire for amusement could not be satisfied in Northampton itself, its residents could always go beyond it. The railways were one means of doing so, but both the United Counties and the Birmingham and Midland omnibus companies linked Northampton with a number of other Midland centres, and local coach operators also ran summer excursions in addition to their regular services. Among the seaside destinations offered by Beeden's in August 1935 were Skegness, Lowestoft, Yarmouth, Bournemouth, Margate, Portsmouth and Clacton.[49] In the same year, however, Mulliner's was offering second hand Daimlers at a cost of £75, and as mass production methods brought down prices, more people were now able to acquire their own transport. Over 16,000 Road Fund Licences were issued in Northampton in 1929, against 5,740 in 1921, a growing proportion of them for private rather than commercial motor vehicles.[50] Nevertheless, said the *Independent*, returning to one of its favourite themes in 1922, intending motorists would do well to give the female of the species a very wide berth.

'Many motorists I have consulted on this matter', wrote its editor,

aver that the average lady driver, whether intentionally or not, shows little regard for the etiquette and rules of the road, and many a time is only saved from serious accident by the care of a man motorist . . . A medical man stated that women have a much more complex nervous system than men, which is probably the cause of their undoubted inability to make quick decisions on the road . . . having entered the motoring sphere of men, it is incumbent upon them to realise their physical limitations, thus to drive with caution.[51]

The ladies were insulted but undeterred. In 1930, however, under the younger generation editorship of Bernard Holloway, the *Independent* gave the Rural Dean of Northampton, the Rev. Trevor Lewis, short shrift when he expressed his own views on the 'modern woman'. 'There is a great contempt for womankind today among men', said the latter, 'I don't think that the respect of manhood for womanhood was ever at so low a level'.[52]

'If by the term 'respect' is meant the sort of sugary relationship between man and woman which apparently our grandmothers expected and received', the paper declared,

> the modern woman has definitely shown that she does not desire it . . . the modern girl herself is the least concerned of all about the matter. She just goes on shortening her hair and skirts and lengthening her days; narrowing her figure and broadening her mind; increasing her efficiency and decreasing her dependence . . . She would be the first to laugh heartily at the assertion that she or any of her elder sisters have ceased to claim masculine respect, knowing full well that her challenge in the professional and industrial world in particular claims not only respect from men, but in very many cases their anxious personal concern as well![53]

Quite so, replied 'THIRTY FIVE AND VERY MODERN', and 'when will men cease this babbling about the 'modern woman' . . . England and the race still go on, and not so badly either, despite the alleged shortcomings of the "hands that rock the modern cradles"'.[54]

Nevertheless, it would not do to exaggerate the progress made by women towards equality with men during this period. The franchise was extended to women over 21 in 1928, but female M.P.s were still a rarity, and only a handful of women contested municipal elections in Northampton during this period. Local government was itself one area of expanding female employment, but Dr. Emily Shaw, the Child and Maternity Medical Officer, was the only woman among the higher ranks of the Council's officers, and the notion of equal pay for the same work died a sudden death when employees reached the age of eighteen. In 1936, for instance, junior clerks of both sexes earned £52 a year at the age of seventeen. Thereafter the male rate of pay rose to £78 and then by annual increments to a maximum of £156 at the age of twenty-three. The equivalent rates for females were £65, rising to a maximum of £104 at the age of twenty-one.[55]

This sort of divergence was quite typical of industry as well as professional and white-collar work, and proof enough in itself that perceptions of male and female roles had not changed a great deal. The man was still regarded as the family breadwinner, and thus in need of and entitled to higher wages than a woman. In reality, of course, many women had to support themselves, and very often a family, too. Deserted wives, for instance, but the 48,000 females recorded at the 1921 Census in Northampton also included almost 4,000 widows and a large number of unmarried adults. Some no doubt chose not to marry, but females outnumbered males even before the war tipped the balance still further, and neither in Northampton nor in the country as a whole were there men sufficient to provide every woman who might want one with a husband. Moreover, because adult males were the main casualties of structural changes in the footwear trade and of the economic depression itself, many families were arguably still more dependent on female wage-earners during this period than in the past.

In wartime, however, female labour became a valuable commodity, and the women who replaced men in the footwear factories during the Second World War were paid the full male rate. 'All Northampton is now hard at work making boots for soldiers', *The Times* reported in April 1940.[56] Standard and electrically heated flying boots, waders and rubber-soled footwear for use in munitions works were also made locally, and by the end of that year the firm of Haynes and Cann were producing box calf 'escape' boots at the rate of some 80 pairs a week. By cutting away the upper part of the boot these were easily converted into civilian shoes, now virtually unobtainable by the European resistance networks which aided stranded airmen and other escapees, and came complete with concealed knife and a hollow heel containing a compass. The company also made footwear for British secret agents, producing a 'worn look' by polishing the impression of a foot on the insole, and printing just a part of the trademark of footwear firms in occupied territory.

Nevertheless, as the N.U.B.S.O. leader Len Smith observed in August 1940, 'our Union is not so fortunately placed as many other Unions',[57] and this war did not consume the energies of the industry to anything like the extent of the last. At that time only a third of the Union's members were employed on military contracts, and overall these were on a much smaller scale than in 1914-18. Convinced that war with Germany was sooner or later inevitable, the stock-piling of essentials like footwear were among the advance preparations made by the government. Demand for civilian footwear had also fallen sharply by mid-1940. Rationing and purchase tax reduced it still further, and by 1943 sales were over 25% below the volume of 1938. In 1941 some footwear factories were closed under the government 'concentration' scheme and production transferred to others. Surplus labour was directed largely into munitions work or to the Corby iron industry, and vacated premises turned to other uses.

Components for Lancaster bombers, for instance, were produced at the Barratt works, and assembled in camouflaged hangers at Sywell aerodrome. Other local industries also turned production to wartime needs, and from 1942 onwards day nurseries were provided by the Council's Maternity and Child Welfare Department, equipped and staffed at the expense of the Ministry of Health in a national campaign to enlist all available labour. Instrument panels for Wellington bombers, shells and shell hoists, bomb aimer panels and a variety of other aircraft parts were produced by the Express Lift Co., which had taken over Smith, Major and Stevens in 1930. Along with the L.M.S. railway, the United Counties bus company and the gas and electricity works, Express Lifts also formed its own company of the Home Guard. Originally known as the Local Defence Volunteers, its initials encouraged the alternative interpretation of 'Look, Duck and Vanish'.

Bassett-Lowke and Co. now turned their own works to the manufacture of 'proving' models of military vehicles, bridges and Mulberry floating harbours, and to models of Stuka bombers with a simulated 'dive', which were used to train anti-aircraft gunners. In March 1942 the Birmingham-based firm of British Timken, manufacturers of roller bearings, also began production from a factory at Duston as part of a dispersal programme. The wisdom of this was demonstrated by the heavy bombing of its Birmingham works soon afterwards, but Northampton was more fortunate in this respect. Only 38 bombs fell on the town during the war, the most serious damage occurring in January 1941 to the central wing of St Andrew's Hospital and the nearby General Cemetery. In July of that year the town had a near-miraculous escape when a Stirling bomber crashed into Gold Street. The pilot died when his parachute failed to open, and there was extensive damage to nearby properties, but the only other casualty was a fire-watcher whose leg was broken when the blast blew him off his bike.

Emergency rescue, fire-fighting and medical services and the whole range of other civil defence services within the borough came under the overall control of Chief Constable Williamson, working in conjunction with the three-member Emergency Committee of the Borough Council. This was chaired throughout the war by Alderman A. W. Lyne, past Vice-President of the N.U.B.S.O. No. 2 branch and President of the Northampton Labour Party. He later became MP for Burton-on-Trent, and was awarded the Honorary Freedom of Northampton in 1958. Mr. Williamson himself also remained responsible for the borough police force. Onerous and often thankless work, its wartime ranks swelled by the recruitment of over 400 Special Constables and 60 Police War Reservists, and the formation of a Women's Auxiliary Police Corps. However, as a 'low risk' area Northamptonshire received a flood of evacuees, mainly from London. In the first months of the war Northampton alone took in almost 17,000, most of them children or pregnant women.

'It was not altogether the quantity of the evacuees', the M.O.H. declared, 'as the quality, which left much to be desired . . . Borough residents were practically forced to take children of a standard of cleanliness and manners quite unknown to them previously — children suffering from skin diseases, verminous, and bed-wetters by the hundred . . .'. From the host families and the Northampton public at large, however, they received a more friendly welcome. Many were surprised by their poor physical condition and the intense poverty to which it testified. This was a very widespread reaction, and one which contributed to wartime and post-war efforts to improve health and social security services; but as the M.O.H. himself noted, all those concerned spoke 'very highly of the kindness shown to the strangers by local residents'.[58] For the children themselves and their families, evacuation could be a very traumatic experience. Many preferred the shared dangers of life in the capital to the safety of separation, and by January 1940 more than half had returned home. Their numbers ebbed and flowed throughout the war. Heavy bombing in London often brought a rush of unofficial evacuees, posing great difficulties of accommodation and severely straining local resources.

An acute shortage of water in the Summer of 1944 coincided with an influx of over 5,000 unofficial evacuees within a matter of two or three weeks, and on this occasion the Emergency Committee was forced to make a 'stay away' appeal through the railway companies, backed up by a warning that only official evacuees would be provided with billets.[59] Food rationing was introduced in January 1940, and by mid-1941 over 5,000 allotments had been provided as part of a 'Grow More Food' campaign, co-ordinated by the Horticulture Committee of the Council under the chairmanship of the Labour councillor Mrs. Harriett Nicholls. The Education Committee ran a series of gardening classes, the Estates Department an advisory service, and the Council also acquired a herd of pedigree pigs, fed on waste foodstuffs and qualifying it for membership of the National Pig-Breeders Association.[60] The wartime diet dictated by shortages of certain foodstuffs was, in the opinion of the M.O.H., a great improvement on some past eating habits, and 'it is doubtful if the inhabitants of the Borough were ever in a healthier state'.[61]

Northampton also played host to large numbers of military personnel. The 'Talavera' camp on the Racecourse became the No. 1 A.T.S. Training Centre and, after the war, a major demobilisation centre. Canadian troops were billeted in the town in the Summer of 1940. Given almost exclusive use of the Midsummer Meadow open-air pool, their boundless enthusiasm for swimming was said to have so disrupted the schedule of the new indoor Mounts baths as to cause 'serious inconvenience to the public'.[62] They were restricted to Mondays only, but later in the war Northampton also became a major leave centre for American servicemen. Their own preference was for dancing, but in April 1944 guests from all 48 states were also entertained at an Anglo-American dinner at the *Grand Hotel*, and cinema devotees were granted an occasional glimpse of Clark Gable himself, who was serving with an American bomber unit at a county airfield.

Many borough residents were of course conscripted into the armed forces, or served in the A.T.S., the Women's Land Army and other para-military bodies. Of the local regiments, the Northamptonshire Yeomanry formed a part of the 20th Armoured Corps until 1943, and took part in the Normandy landings in 1944. The 1st Yeomanry was then a part of the 33rd Independent Armoured Brigade which fought through to Le Havre and on through Holland to Antwerp; the 2nd of the 11th Armoured Division, which suffered heavy losses in subsequent fighting over the River Orne. Their total losses during the war were 20 officers and 799 other ranks, all but 75 of them from the 2nd. Regiment. Of the six battalions of the Northamptonshire Regiment, two were engaged on coastal and airfield defence in Britain, while the 1st Battalion served in Burma from 1943, the 2nd and 5th in North Africa, Italy and, along with the 4th, raised in 1939 as a territorial battalion, in north-west Europe.

A total of 54 officers and 889 other ranks died during the conflict, and in June 1946, 'in recognition of the glorious record of the Northamptonshire Regiment and the very long association and cordial relations which have existed between the Corporation and the Northamptonshire Regiment', it was awarded the Honorary Freedom of the Borough.[63]

The British Timken factory at Duston was among the wartime plants allocated to peacetime production by the Board of Trade, thus keeping in Northampton a valuable source of local employment. Still more importantly, it went some way to ease its continuing heavy dependence on the footwear indus-try. In 1931 this accounted for 50% of all manufacturing employment in the town but, as demand for labour continued to contract, the Borough Council viewed the local economic structure with mounting concern. As early as 1905, in fact, it had formed a New Industries Sub-Committee in an attempt to attract alternative employment to the town. Founded at the suggestion of Alderman Sidney Adnitt, its early members included Edward Lewis and James Manfield and, on the Conservative side, the builder Henry Martin and Thomas Lantsbury Wright, also a long-serving member of the Poor Law Board. Plans of vacant land and factories were produced, and approaches made to firms in various areas of Britain and the French and German Consulates. The L.N.W.R. Company was also persuaded to display hundreds of illustrated posters on its trains.[64]

The one major success in this earlier period was the arrival of Smith, Major and Stevens at St James's End, but the effort was renewed after the First World War. Local industrialists were co-opted onto the Committee, and in the early 1930s it invested in a promotional film of Northampton, produced by the Northamptonshire Natural History Society

37. Freedom of the Borough of Northampton conferred on the Northamptonshire Regiment, 8 June 1946. The certificate also displays the battle honours of the Regiment.

under the supervision of its Photographic Secretary, W. J. Bassett-Lowke. Bassett-Lowke also claimed the cash prize offered by the Chairman of the New Industries Committee, Cllr. Butterfield, to any resident responsible for persuading a new industry to Northampton: £100 or £50 according to the number of new jobs created. The aim was to 'enlist the general interest of the inhabitants by way of suggesting on every possible occasion the advantages of Northampton as a locality for the establishment of industries from a distance'. This was second nature to Bassett-Lowke, but he was a serving councillor and thus judged to be disqualified.[65]

In selling Northampton to potential new employers, much stress was placed not only on its geographical location — 'Unrivalled as a centre for Distribution' — and the modest level of its rents and rates, but also on the quality of its labour force. 'The men and women of Northampton have more than the usual industrial intelligence of workers in industrial towns' wrote Town Clerk William Kew in 1932, 'and an adaptability engendered by their training for generations. The vital statistics also show that the workers of Northampton are physically healthy, strong and uncommonly well-read and informed'.[66] 'WORKERS of both sexes — quick in mind and deft of hand — the product of Northampton's highly organised Educational system', 'Strikes practically unknown' and 'known for their orderliness, discipline and good temper' were additional points made in the Council's Official Handbook in the same year, while a notice board advertising the merits of one site for light industries bore the legend 'NORTHAMPTON, LOW RATES AND GOOD LABOUR FOR YOUR WORKS'.[67]

Prompted by an enquiry from a Birmingham aircraft company in search of an East Midlands base, the New Industries Committee — or as it became in 1933, the Industries and Development Committee — also revived earlier plans for a municipal aerodrome. Government subsidies were available for such projects, but great difficulties were experienced in finding a suitable site. In 1937 the Committee enlisted the aid of Mr. C. M. Newton, Secretary of the Sywell Aerodrome Co., who suggested that the Council cooperate in up-grading Sywell itself. The company offered to build a traffic hall, passenger accommodation and a customs hall — the latter conferring the status of an airport and making the grant of wireless facilities more likely — and to lease them to the Council. In return, the latter sought permission from the Ministry of Health to purchase shares in the company, or alternatively, to loan it the money to extend the airfield. Here this rather enterprising plan came to an abrupt end. It had no statutory powers to do either, the Ministry replied, and there the matter had to be left.[68]

In fact, for all the considerable efforts invested by the Council in attracting new industries, it made only limited progress. The Mettoy company, makers of Corgi cars, began production in Northampton in 1934, and ten new factories were opened and four more extended in the early 1930s. Producing lifts, hosiery, fancy wear and dressed sharkskins, they employed some 550 people. In the view of the Board of Trade in 1933 this compared favourably with other towns engaged in similar campaigns, but central government itself was offering incentives to industry to relocate in areas of heavy unemployment, and this was undoubtedly a major factor in Northampton's own lack of success in attracting new employment. This was reflected in the very slow growth of population during this period. Around 91,000 in 1921, it was barely 1,000 greater ten years later. Around 5,000 more were added by the extension of the municipal boundaries in 1932, but it had still reached only 104,000 by 1951.

The main areas of expansion during this period were in the service sector, mainly in retailing and in local government, and such growth and diversification as there was in manufacturing industry came largely through firms already established in Northampton, notably in the engineering, clothing and printing trades, and in the construction industry. Linked with the latter were the firm of A. Bell and Co., former ironmongers and builders' merchants who turned to the manufacture of fireplaces and surrounds after the war, and opened a purpose-built factory at Kingsthorpe in the 1930s; less directly, the Rest Assured company, manufacturers of beds. These areas of employment continued to expand alongside the service sector after the war, but in 1951 the footwear industry was still much the single largest employer of labour in the town.

However, if the Council's concern with Northampton's unbalanced industrial structure was not of recent origin, the priority it gave to the question in the inter-war period was closely linked to the same post-war anxieties which stimulated industrial welfare schemes and philanthropic ventures in the wider community. Industrialists, philanthropists and councillors were often one and the same people, and both here and in other areas of municipal policy the Council played a central role in promoting the image of a progressive and co-operative community. In adverse economic circumstances, it has been said, it was not always easy to sustain, but as the foregoing pages have suggested, it was not an image without substance. 'The amenities of Northampton are of the best', wrote the Town Clerk in 1932 without undue exaggeration, 'conducing to a happy and contented population'.[69] These were never universal emotions, of course; but over-crowded insanitary dwellings conduced to quite the opposite, and on this matter the post-war Council was fully agreed. A progressive and enlightened community could perform no higher and no more sensible service to its members than ensuring that they were decently housed.

Notes

1. *Shoe and Leather Record Supplement*, 22 July 1927.
2. *N.I.*, 1 Oct. 1921.
3. A. E. Tebbutt, President of the Northampton Boot and Shoe Manufacturers' Assn., quoted in *N.I.*, 9 June 1923.
4. *N.I.*, 1 Oct. 1921.
5. Ibid., 30 June 1923.
6. N.M., 5 Oct. 1878; 2 Feb. 1878.
7. Interview with *Journal of Industrial Welfare and Personal Management*, quoted in *N.I.*, 5 Oct. 1929.
8. Ibid.
9. *N.I.*, 11 Jan. 1930.
10. Ibid., 9 June 1923.
11. Ibid., 22 Sept. 1923.
12. *Shoe and Leather News Supplement*, 21 Nov. 1929.
13. *Shoe and Leather Record Supplement*, 22 July 1927.
14. *N.I.*, 1 July 1922.
15. Ibid., 27 May 1922.
16. *Northampton Daily Chronicle*, 10 Nov. 1926.
17. *N.I.*, 26 Oct. 1929.
18. Primrose League, Delapre Habitation, Minute Book, 16 March 1920 (N.R.O. N.C.C.A 11).
19. *Northampton Socialist*, No.1, 17 July 1897.
20. N.C.B.C. Minutes, 6 July 1931.
21. *N.I.*, 9 Sept. 1922; N.C.B.C. Health Report (1926).
22. Bowley, A. L., and Hogg, M. H., *Has Poverty Diminished?* (1925).
23. N.C.B.C. Health Report (1931).
24. N.C.B.C. Minutes, 6 Oct. 1930.
25. N.C.B.C., Chief Constable's Reports (1894; 1897).
26. Ibid. (1917).
27. Archer, J., *Northamptonshire Congregationalism* (1935).
28. Ibid.
29. *C.&E.*, 9 Feb. 1934.
30. Ibid., 4 July 1935.
31. *N.I.*, 5 Nov. 1937.
32. Ibid., 19 Oct. 1929.
33. N.C.B.C. Minutes, 5 Dec. 1927.
34. *N.I.*, 9 Sept. 1922.
35. N.C.B.C. Minutes, 5 Sept. 1932.
36. *N.I.*, 9 Sept. 1922.
37. Ibid.
38. Ibid. 2 Nov. 1929.
39. *Has Poverty Diminished?*, op.cit.
40. *N.I.*, 12 May 1923; N.C.B.C. Minutes, Report of the Bands Sub-Commitee, 7 Feb. 1921.
41. *N.I.*, 22 March 1930.
42. Curious readers are referred to the B.B.C. record *Listen to the Banned*.

43. *N.I.*, 15 March 1930.
44. Ibid., 11 Jan. 1930.
45. Ibid., 4 Jan. 1930.
46. *C.&E.*, 12 July 1935.
47. Ibid., 6 July 1935.
48. Ibid., 5 July 1935.
49. Ibid., 12 July 1935.
50. N.C.B.C., Minutes of Special Committee re Licensing (1929).
51. *N.I.*, 19 Aug. 1922.
52. Ibid., 18 Jan. 1930.
53. Ibid.
54. Ibid., 25 Jan. 1930.
55. N.C.B.C., Minutes of Salaries and Appointments Committee, 21 Dec. 1936.
56. *The Times*, 1 April 1940.
57. Quoted in Fox, A., *A History of the National Union of Boot and Shoe Operatives* (1958), p.552.
58. N.C.B.C. Health Report (1939).
59. N.C.B.C., Minutes of Emergency Committee, 5 & 7 July 1944.
60. N.C.B.C. Minutes, 2 Dec. 1940.
61. N.C.B.C. Health Report (1942).
62. N.C.B.C. Minutes 3 June & 1 July 1940.
63. Ibid., 1 April 1946.
64. N.C.B.C., Minutes of New Industries Committee, 6 April 1908; 25 Feb. 1910.
65. Ibid., 16 Feb. & 8 April 1932.
66. Statement in *N.I.*, quoted in Barty-King, H., *Expanding Northampton* (1985), p.14.
67. N.C.B.C. Official Handbook (1932); Minutes of Industries and Development Committee, 19 Oct. 1937.
68. N.C.B.C., Minutes of Industries and Development Committee, 19 Oct. 1934-Oct. 1938.
69. Quoted in *Expanding Northampton*, op.cit., p.14.

Chapter Six

With or Without the Government Subsidy: Local Government, 1919-45

For long years before the war we bemoaned the explosions of party spirit which characterised the battle of the polls . . . The rivalry of the parties remains, it is true, but only those immediately allied to the various leaders seem at all deeply concerned about their differences . . .

Northampton Independent, 26 October 1929

This vast work of local government, in its most comprehensive aspects, intimately concerns the foundations, the solidarity, the present well-being, and the future prosperity of the nation itself.

Sir James Marchant, quoted in *Northampton Independent*, 5 November 1937

'Alderman Whiting is singularly optimistic in believing that the Council is not past praying for', wrote the *Independent* lightly of the new Mayor's proposal to open its meetings in this fashion in 1921, 'but optimism is an asset in public life, as also are high ideals'.[1] Alderman Whiting himself 'had no idea that the duties of Mayor are so multifarious . . . I am consulted by all sorts of people on subjects so far apart as a cure for Bright's Disease to getting a house or a divorce . . . I am not quite sure whether it is not easier to get a divorce than a house'.[2] Divorces were a little easier to come by after legal changes in 1923, but a parliamentary statement in March 1922 claiming that post-war demand for housing was now being satisfied received a sharp response from the Council's Housing and Town Planning Committee. 'The housing situation is as acute as it was in 1918-19, and the demand for houses is even greater than it was two or three years ago', it declared; and if Northampton needed new houses, then the Council would build them — 'with or without the Government subsidy'.[3]

The subsidies for municipal housing under the Housing Act of 1919 had been generous indeed. Local authorities were now required rather than merely permitted to build working class dwellings, but beyond the product of a penny rate the whole costs of building were borne by central government itself. This largesse was prompted on the one hand by the social and political consequences of failing to honour the promise of 'Homes Fit for Heroes', on the other by the understanding that private enterprise alone could not remedy a national post-war deficit of close to a million houses. Local rates could hardly bear the whole burden of such a massive enterprise, but in 1921 the subsidies fell victim to the so-called 'Geddes Axe', a series of economy measures dictated by the onset of the depression. When they were revived in 1923 it was on the less generous scale of £6 per house for a period of 20 years, raised to £9 for 40 years in the following year. Nothing daunted, however, by June 1926 the Council had built 1,283 new dwellings, 580 with the aid of government subsidies, and 703 without.

Its original plans were much more modest. Only 83 houses were built in Northampton between 1915-18, but in 1917 it concluded that just 500 new dwellings should be ample to meet possible post-war shortages.[4] Closer to 3,000, suggested a survey by the Socialists in the following year, and in October 1919 the Council itself reached much the same conclusion. At least 1,200 were needed to meet unsatisfied demand, and almost twice as many again to replace sub-standard housing and that to be demolished under clearance schemes: 3,310 in all.[5] The Liberals greeted this programme with barely any more enthusiasm than the Conservatives. Municipal housing was still equated in the minds of both with socialism, and the election of the S.D.F. veteran Cllr. Alfred Slinn as chairman of the Housing

Committee was in the nature of an invitation to the eight-strong Labour group to commit political suicide. By the beginning of 1920, however, the parties were showing a united front on this issue, one which remained intact throughout all the financial and other pressures to which it was subjected in the years ahead.

Initially at least, this had something to do with their post-war balance in the Council. The Conservatives claimed the largest number of seats throughout this period, but for much of it they had no overall majority. A hung council was always conducive to compromise, if only because no business could be transacted without it. Nevertheless, when they were in a position to impose their will — briefly in 1922, more firmly in 1924-8, and briefly again in 1937 — the Conservative commitment to the housing programme never wavered. The highest level of completions was recorded under their control in the later 1920s, and when the Ratepayers' Association objected to the decision to build without subsidy in 1922, it was a leading Tory who put it firmly in its place. Municipal housing, Cllr. J. V. Collier informed it, was not only a sound financial investment, but 'a great moral revolution for good'.[6] Liberals and Labour spoke in the same terms. The jewel in the crown of a progressive and caring municipality, the housing of the masses had now become an all-party crusade.

The Council had aimed to build all the planned new houses within three years. By the end of 1919 work had begun on the first of 400 dwellings on the Abington Lodge Farm site, and in the meantime fourteen families had been accommodated in redundant military huts, re-erected on the eastern portion of Abington Park and converted into two-bedroom dwellings. However, the work did not progress as rapidly as was hoped. This was no fault of its own, the Housing Committee informed its new overlords at the Ministry of Health in 1920,[7] and in common with others elsewhere, it 'strongly deprecated' suggestions that local authorities were lacking in enterprise. 'Any such delays', in their own opinion, 'have been, and are being caused, by the various regulations, requirements and restrictions of the Government'.[8] These were ever the price of central funding, but inflated land prices and post-war shortages of materials and skilled labour were the most serious obstacles.

Various efforts were made to overcome them. The Council made full use of its powers under the Housing (Additional Powers) Act of 1919 to prevent the demolition of existing houses and to prohibit building which diverted resources from house-building itself. The Cinema and Picture House at Kingsthorpe Hollow and extensions to the Co-operative Society boot factory were among the projects halted by the latter. Plaster-substitutes were used in response to a dearth of plasterers and the refusal of the Plasterers' Federation to allow its members to work overtime. Several appeals were also made to government to restrict the restrictive practices of this and other craft unions, who were exploiting their post-war strength to the full. It was 'through no lack of sympathy with ex-Servicemen that the builders did not employ more', said one local contractor in 1921, 'but the operatives in the trade insisted that only a certain number should be employed'.[9]

Steel-frames were rejected on account of their cost, although four such houses were erected in 1925 in an experiment which did not prove satisfactory enough to repeat. Concrete blocks, made on site by the builders W. Higgins, were used in the construction of 58 houses on the Harlestone Road estate at Dallington in 1922. A government inspector judged them 'the best he had seen in the country', but while they were faster and marginally cheaper to build, and 'in appearance compare most favourably with the structures of brick erection', the latter were generally considered more in keeping with Northampton's overall appearance.[10] In 1920, in a further attempt to speed up the work, the Council purchased the Hollowell Brickyard at a cost of £1,500, selling the bricks to the Housing Committee at agreed prices. However, these new houses were very different from the terraced dwellings of the later 19th and early 20th century, described by one visitor as the 'Unity is Strength' order of housing, 'so uniform in plan, elevation, alignment, in fact in every way, that one gets the impression that they have been turned out by a gargantuan sausage machine'.[11]

These were semi-detached dwellings, built on the more generous scale dictated by considerations of health, a post-war surge in the birth rate, and contemporary tastes themselves. Three-bedroom houses accounted for the majority of council housing built in Northampton between the wars. Complete with scullery, bathroom and living room, many also had the parlour for which there was a strong working-class preference despite the higher rent of such dwellings: around 10s. a week in the early 1920s against 8s. 6d. for a non-parlour house. The Dallington houses were additionally equipped with a 'Municipal Grateoven', copper, hot water geysers and a variety of fitted cupboards. These internal arrangements doubtless owed something to the Consultative Ladies' Committee, set up by the Housing Committee in 1919 and comprising representatives of the Northampton Labour Party, the Women's Co-operative Guild and the Northampton Women Citizens' Association for, in such matters, 'a woman's special knowledge and experience are of the utmost value'.[12]

Most houses also had a garden large enough to supply the annual vegetable needs of the occupants. Its cultivation was a condition of the tenancy, and tenants who failed to do so received a stern warning from the Property Inspector, who also made regular checks on the internal cleanliness of the dwellings.[13] The keeping of poultry was permitted with prior permission, pigs were outlawed, but pigeons were admitted in 1930 in response to appeals from tenants wanting to engage in this very popular pastime.[14] This sort of paternalistic supervision was often resented, but the most serious disputes arose over rents and the eviction of tenants unable to pay them. Rent rebate schemes were a thing of the future, and reluctant as it might be to take this course, the Council was in a difficult position. Any deficit on the Housing Revenue Account had to be made up by taking funds from elsewhere, confirming in the process that council housing was not, after all, a sound financial investment. On the other hand, putting up rents to cover rising costs pushed them beyond the means of many tenants, particularly those unemployed or on short-time work.

The unemployed were not automatically excluded from tenancies, but all applicants with an income below a certain level — £2 10s. a week in 1931 — were required to have their rents guaranteed by another person. Both the Unemployed Association and the Trades Council served as a channel for tenants' grievances, but by the later 1930s they had their own pressure group in the form of the Northampton Tenants' Association.[15] However, they could face other problems for which even a well-designed and affordable house could not entirely compensate. Most municipal housing estates were built on the outskirts of the town, their location dictated mainly by the availability of relatively cheap land. By June 1930, a total of 2,586 new municipal dwellings had been built or were nearing completion at Abington, Kingsley, Kingsthorpe, St James's and Far Cotton, but while the Council built shops for rent on some of them, there was little attempt at first to provide schools or recreational facilities nearby.

This was not at all unusual, but there was often a considerable time-lag between the occupation of the estate and the appearance of pubs, churches and the like, and life could be very miserable without these communal conveniences. They were generally well-served by transport services, but many tenants also had further to travel to work, and as the M.O.H. Stephen Rowland pointed out in 1932, 'these poorly-paid people who are being re-housed are just the ones least able to afford bus and tram fares'. He was personally very critical of the contemporary effort to 'get people away to the outskirts whether they wished to go or not'. Far better, in his view, to build new houses on cleared sites in the central area and leave them within walking distance of their work and the hot midday meal he considered 'most desirable' for their health and efficiency.[16] 'There is a certain amount of convenience attached to this arrangement', admitted Thomas Mawson and Sons, the town planning consultants engaged by the Council in 1925; but overall, they concluded, the 'indiscriminate mixture of factories, warehouses and dwellings' which still characterised many areas of the town was 'bad for the efficiency of the industry, the surroundings of the dwellings, and the stability of property prices'.[17]

The main object of town planning, they pointed out, was to promote 'sound economic conditions'. This could only be done by planning for the town as a whole and thus avoiding the 'wasteful results' of haphazard growth. It meant, for instance, the zoning of industrial and residential development, an efficient and integrated transport system, and road-widening schemes and new radial roads to relieve traffic congestion in the town centre. Here, they suggested, the Council could usefully begin with the level crossing at the bottom of Bridge Street, the main southern approach to the town, which 'has long been a matter of serious concern'. Passing trains, of which there were many at this time, so disrupted the flow of traffic that cyclists commonly carried their machines across the footbridge, proceeding happily with their journey while the Far Cotton trams and other heavier traffic remained 'held up and disorganised'.[18]

There was an 'obvious' need for reconstruction in the central areas, they continued, and where 'the complete demolition or removal of a group or block of bad dwellings will open up the way for a new street, or other public improvement, there is no question that its removal would be the most economical arrangement . . .'. However, partial demolition would relieve some of the congestion, and much of the housing classed as defective could then be restored to a reasonable standard. 'What we advocate in these respects', they added, 'is subject always to the condition that alternative accommodation can be made available by the erection of new dwellings for those destroyed'. Victorian developers had rarely troubled to do so, and in the process of 'improving' their own towns they had gone far to create the slums by pushing the displaced population into already over-crowded dwellings elsewhere. The lessons had been learnt, but by the same token the M.O.H. was reluctant to use his own powers to order the demolition or closure of insanitary housing — for the 'remedy he could employ would probably be worse than the disease'.[19]

If it was 'probably true to say that Northampton has no real slums', in the Castle and South wards especially much of the housing was old and dilapidated and, even in 1930, still 'wanting in the real necessities of comfortable and suitable houses'.[20] By then central government too had turned its attention to such problems, and in the same year it eased the path of the localities with a new Housing Act, simplifying the procedures for clearance and partial improvement schemes and introducing a subsidy of £2 5s. for 40 years for each person displaced by them. These grants were quickly taken up in Northampton, and by 1936 a total of 442 new dwellings had been built under this particular scheme, on the Kettering Road, Abington and Dallington estates, and the St David's estate at Kingsthorpe. An additional 118 were sanctioned by the Ministry of Health in the following year, but if the Council's diligence in this area met with much central approval, it was judged guilty of excessive enthusiasm in others.

Municipal housing in Northampton, the Ministry of Health pointed out in 1930, cost significantly more to build than that of other Midland authorities. So it did, the Housing Committee replied unrepentantly, because in Northampton it was built to higher standards which not only ensured more comfortable dwellings, but reduced the long-term costs of maintenance. By way of a list of 'suggestions', the Ministry tried again in the following year: build fewer parlour-type houses, sell off some land to private builders for housing development, and invite large contractors from outside Northampton to tender for contracts.[21] The latter found no favour at all. As the 'Colonial Newcomer' noted in his letters to the *Independent* in 1929, 'a very fair proportion of our town councillors are builders, contractors and gentlemen closely associated with housing . . . sections of the community are continually commenting adversely on the fact'. Personally, he could not see what all the fuss was about. 'We in Pretoria', he recalled, 'did not kick up a dust because the local butchers developed an inordinate interest in civic affairs when the corporation contemplated the erection of public abbatoirs'.[22]

Until 1933, directors, employees and shareholders of a company with an interest in local authority contracts were normally disqualified from membership of that authority. Under the Local Government Act 1933 they were instead required to declare a financial interest, and to refrain from speaking or voting on such questions. Prior to this, however, under an agreement with the Master Builders' Federation, housing contracts in Northampton were allocated at a fixed price on a rota system, enabling councillor builders to undertake Council contracts while also retaining their office. Not only was this arrangement perfectly

38. Inter-war municipal housing in Wellingborough Road on the Abington Estate.

legal, it also ensured that the available work went as far as possible to local workers. From 1928 the contracts also carried 'fair wages' clauses, but the municipal housing programme was a major source of employment during this period, and out-of-town contractors often brought their workers with them rather than recruiting them on the spot. The Council had no desire to add to local unemployment, and while it did employ some outside contractors later, the most it would agree to on this occasion were some minimal reductions in superficial areas and the removal of some tiling and cupboards from the internal specifications.[23]

By refusing sanction for the necessary loans the Ministry could effectively compel obedience to its 'suggestions'. It had infinite patience compared with some other government departments — Education, for instance — but by 1937 Northampton had all but exhausted it. No, the Council could not build 150 new houses for 'general needs', it was told in that year. Slum clearance schemes must have priority. Perhaps it could build some such dwellings, the Ministry conceded in response to a hastily despatched delegation of members of the Housing Committee and the town's M.P., Sir Mervyn Manningham Buller; but approval of any future schemes would depend entirely on cutting construction costs. Sir Mervyn received the same answer in response to a parliamentary question later that year: no economies, no more houses.[24] Economies were made, and with the aid of subsidies under the Housing (Financial Provisions) Act of 1937 for housing built to abate over-crowding, the Council made plans for another 900 new dwellings.

These were thwarted by the Second World War, which also brought a relaxation of the pig-keeping rule in the interests of national food supplies. By 1941, however, with the completion of 94 houses already under construction, the Council had built a total of 4,765 dwellings, 48% of the new housing built in Northampton between the wars, against a national average for local authority housing of 28%. Around 5,000 more had been provided by the private sector, some with Council aid in the form of lump sum subsidies or mortgage guarantees, and many along the lines of the 'commodious villas' constituting the Spinney Hill 'Garden Suburb', built by Collier and Sons on the Kettering Road in 1922. 'The Highest and Healthiest Part of Northampton', the estate also boasted tennis courts and on-site workshops manned by 'a fully qualified staff of intelligent workmen'.[25] Rising real incomes put such dwellings within the reach of a growing number of people during this period, just as unemployment and short-time working pushed it further beyond the grasp of others; but 'why make us pay for being thrifty and using foresight?', asked one ratepayer in 1925.

He had built his own house, for there was 'nothing finer than everyone becoming his own landlord . . . it produces better citizens, better houses, and therefore, less slums'; but having done his bit to ease the housing problem, he was 'astounded' by a rate assessment three times as high as for a comparable older property. 'One more house for the town to help the rates instead of two families in one, and it is not encouraged! When will those in authority help instead of deter?'.[26] This was a common complaint, and 'if ratepayers in Northampton really wish to give practical expression to their views', said a leader of the National Citizens' Union in 1930, they should form a branch of that body and act in concert with others elsewhere.[27] Local interests were zealously enough guarded by the Property Owners Association, the Chamber of Commerce and its small businessman's counterpart, the Chamber of Trade,[28] but the ratepayers no longer had quite the same power to strike electoral fear into the hearts of councillors.

In weighing, for instance, the response of the ratepayers to higher rates against that of the working classes kept waiting for their promised dwellings, the balance of power was now tipped towards the latter. The working classes paid rates too, of course, but generally at a lower level than middle-class occupiers or tradesmen. However, the rates did sometimes go down as well as up. Post-war inflation pushed them from 9s. 7d. in the pound in 1918 to 16s. 6d. in 1921, exclusive of the Poor Rate, but in 1923 falling prices and interest rates, healthy profits from the markets and Tramways, and belated compensation for damage done to the Racecourse during its wartime military occupation allowed them to be cut by 1s. 6d. in the pound. 'This news', declared the *Independent*, will overshadow in the public mind the daily dishes re the treasures of Tut, the Royal baby, the Duke's engagement, the Ruhr rumpus . . . all concerned are certainly entitled to our thanks and heartiest congratulations'.[29] By 1930, however, legislative changes had gone some way to simplify the rating system itself, and to bridge the gap between local needs and central funding.

The Rating and Valuation Act of 1925 provided for uniform assessment procedures and five-yearly re-assessments, and combined the different local rates into a single 'unified rate' collected by county and county borough councils. Under the Local Government Act of 1929, the Assigned Revenues were also abolished and replaced by more generous central funding in the form of General Exchequer Contributions. Designed in part to compensate for the de-rating of agricultural and industrial land, they also comprised grants for various local services, weighted according to such factors as rateable value, the number of children under the age of five, and that of persons uninsured under national sickness and unemployment insurance schemes. They were a welcome if belated attempt to target resources where they were most needed, and they remained the basis of government funding to local authorities until 1948. However, central funding came with conditions attached, and the more reliant local authorities became on it, the less autonomy they enjoyed in determining their own policies and making their own spending decisions.

This was a high price to pay in terms of local democracy, but there was no question, the Ministry of Health informed the Council's Maternity and Child Welfare Committee in 1926, of it spending public money on a matter on which public opinion was 'acutely divided'. Birth control advice, that is, and the Committee's plea to make it available through ante-natal and infant welfare clinics was firmly rejected.[30] On this issue would-be reformers faced strong opposition from the Christian churches, founded in a belief that contraception was against the natural order of God. Nevertheless, as the Committee pointed out when it made another attempt in 1930, such advice was easily accessible to those able to pay for it, for 'a demand exists among working class married women for reliable and private information . . . such married women should not be prevented by lack of means from obtaining the help they desire'.[31]

As the *Independent* noted, the Committee's campaign was a natural extension of the work for which it already had a high reputation, for if 'it may seem strange that the borough which leads the country in infant and welfare work should champion the propagation of birth control . . . it is just the knowledge that Northampton has gained in the first respect which will lead it to support the second.'[32] At the heart of the issue lay the massive variations in infant death rates between different social classes, which persisted despite the overall picture of quite dramatic progress. By 1929 infant mortality had fallen to 70:1,000 from a national average of 154 at the turn of the century; in Northampton itself from 142:1,000 to 53 over the same period. There were annual fluctuations, but these did not detract from the overall downward trend, much of the credit for which has been rightly given to advances in maternity and infant care. 'The State cannot itself save the child' as Herbert Samuel M.P. wrote on reading the shocking catalogue of peri-natal deaths, still-births and miscarriages presented by the Women's Co-operative Guild in 1915, 'but it can help the mother to save it . . . it is the duty of the community, so far as it can, to relieve motherhood of its burdens . . . to make medical aid available when it is needed, to watch over the health of the infant'.[33]

By means of Health Visitors, classes and clinics, nurseries and municipal milk depots, many municipalities were already undertaking this work. In Northampton as elsewhere it was also much reliant on voluntary effort, but it was given a new impetus by the demographic effects of the First World War. The birth-rate had been declining nationally since the later 19th century, slowly at first and mainly among the middle classes, who had earlier access to contraception. It fell more rapidly from the turn of the century, and in Northampton itself, at a rate faster than the average. The M.O.H. frequently wondered why, but found no convincing answer. However, he wrote in 1922, 'the losses in our population resulting from the late war must be made good as far as possible, if we are to keep our place among nations. The falling birth-rate renders replacement as regards numbers more difficult and delayed, hence what we fail to replace in quantity must be compensated for if possible by improvement in quality. The importance not only of conserving the lives but also the health of the oncoming generation becomes paramount'.[34]

The same line of thought led directly to the Maternity and Child Welfare Act of 1918, which increased the powers of local authorities in this area and provided for central grants of up to 50% of approved net expenditure. Still composed overwhelmingly of male members, they were also encouraged to co-opt women experienced in such work to the obligatory Maternity and Child Welfare Committee. In Northampton this comprised the Public Health Committee and seven co-optees drawn mainly from the Northampton Maternity and Infant Welfare Association, a voluntary body which had been working closely with the Council for some time. From 1919 until her untimely death in 1923 the Committee was chaired by Cllr. Rose Scott, wife of C. J. Scott. In 1920, in a move 'frequently urged, but long-delayed', Dr. Emily Shaw was also appointed as Assistant Medical Officer of Health with responsibility for maternity and child welfare. Her appointment was opposed at the time by the Conservatives; but, she said on her resignation in 1928, 'I have met with nothing but consideration and kindness from all members of the Committee, who have shown the most sympathetic consideration for any development I wished to organise'.[35]

Much attention was now directed towards improving the quality of ante-natal care, in an attempt to reduce maternal mortality as well as infant deaths and stillbirths. Maternal mortality rates fell barely at all in the first decades of the 20th century. In Northampton they hovered around the level of five per 1,000 live births, slightly above the national average in 1930. The majority of working class deaths were due to complications of pregnancy or labour, but 'the fact that large numbers of women (running into thousands) can be confined in certain maternity institutions with almost negligible loss of life', the M.O.H. wrote in 1930, 'shows that a very big reduction in the maternal death rate is possible'.[36] However, as he and Dr. Shaw and the Committee were also aware, inequalities in the rates of maternal and infant deaths were very much a reflection of inequalities of wealth. Infant mortality rates in the Midlands between 1930-32 varied from around 35:1,000 live births in Social Class I, mainly comprising aristocracy and gentry, to 76:1,000 in Social Class V, which embraced most manual workers. In some areas of the country, notably the industrial North, the span was wider still, but the overall pattern varied not at all.[37]

The lower the income, the higher the incidence of infant deaths, and the key factor in this equation was the health of the mother. An inadequate diet had obvious adverse effects here. A survey of incomes and diet approved by the Ministry of Agriculture in the early 1930s suggested that at least one third of the population of England was 'so poor that they could not purchase sufficient of the more expensive foodstuffs needed for health' — a conclusion so politically sensitive that the government attempted to suppress the subsequent report. The Minister of Health, wrote one of its authors, 'held the out-of-date opinion that that if people were not actually dying of starvation there could be no food deficiency'.[38] However, the provision of free meals for pregnant women and nursing mothers was one of the earliest steps taken by the post-war Council in Northampton. Supplied through the school canteen, where under-nourished children were similarly catered for, these were 'much appreciated', and the health of the recipients was said to be much improved.

From sheer necessity, many women had to work until the last stages of a pregnancy, increasing the risks to mother and child alike and the need for specialist medical care. Those most in need of such care were also least able to afford the fees for private maternity homes, and most likely instead to use the services of the local 'handywoman' who doubled as unqualified midwife and layer-out of those at the other extreme of life. It was private philanthropy, in the form of the Barratt Maternity Hospital, which went furthest to redress inequalities in this area, but in the meantime the Council itself paid the fees for 'necessitous' cases requiring the services of maternity homes or the General Hospital. The Workhouse Infirmary also had a maternity ward, and in the M.O.H.'s view the standard of care here was every bit as high as in a private hospital. It was still used only with the greatest reluctance even after the repeal of the Poor Laws in 1929 and the transfer of the former workhouse to the control of the Council. There was 'a stigma attached to the place, and everything connected with it', as the M.O.H. noted in 1942, one which its re-naming as St Edmund's Hospital in 1934 did very little to remove.

This service was performed in part by the evacuees whose babies were delivered there during the war, who knew nothing of its past and spoke only of the excellence of their care.[39] The Maternity and Child Welfare Committee itself directed its main energies into ante-natal clinics, operating in different areas of the town, but as the *Independent* suggested, its thwarted desire to make contraceptive advice more freely available was in no way at odds with the effort invested in ensuring healthy mothers and babies. It was simply a different approach to the very same objective, one which grew directly from an understanding of the link between poverty and maternal and infant death. Working-class families were on average larger than those of the middle classes, and each additional child reduced the standard of living of all their members. Repeated pregnancies had their own debilitating effect on maternal health, but if large families were a matter of choice, then so be it. The Committee was not engaged in a Malthusian crusade against working-class procreation. It simply wanted to extend the choices enjoyed by some to those denied them by a lack of information and the money to acquire it — and in so doing to break the vicious cycle of ill health and premature death to which poverty contributed at every turn.

Older children remained the particular responsibility of the School Medical Service. Much of its work was still concerned with defects of sight and hearing and with improving the condition of under-nourished children. As the School Medical Officer noted with customary precision in 1930, over the preceding 14 years the School Dentist had also removed a total of 90,192 teeth. The proportion of deaths among the 5-15 year age group was much lower than among younger children, accounting for only 2.5% of all deaths in the town between 1921-30. However, almost a fifth of them were due to tuberculosis, and this remained a source of more general concern. With the exception of the First World War, mortality from the disease had in fact been steadily declining for some decades. In Northampton it fell from 2.6% in 1918 to 0.6% in 1943. Given the still high proportion of shoemakers in the population, this may suggest a link with changes in the nature of footwear production — the wider use of clicking presses, for instance. The M.O.H. was not sure, but the very steadiness of the decline convinced him that 'the brightest hopes regarding the future . . . lie in prevention rather than cure'.

'We find no sudden drops marking any great social or medical epochs . . .', he noted in 1932, 'the erection of so many sanatoria apparently failed to accelerate the decline to any appreciable extent . . . [but] if we take such apparently simple measures as the isolation of advanced cases of pulmonary tuberculosis, and the prohibition of spitting in public places, few could be found who would not believe these measures have prevented the spread of the disease'.[40] The pasteurisation of milk went far to remove one source of infection, but a Ministry of Health circular in 1943 announcing a change of direction with regard to pulmonary TB was welcomed as 'an awakening from the attitude which, year after year, tolerates a high incidence of advanced cases, a lack of institutional beds to accommodate them, and the building of expensive sanatoria unwilling to accept those who have passed beyond an early stage of disease'.[41]

Mass radiography was the main innovation, although its effectiveness depended very largely on the numbers who could be persuaded to use it. Tuberculosis patients and their families were also to receive allowances to offset the costs of treatment and allay the financial anxiety which was an inevitable accompaniment to the disease in working-class families. The government scheme was considered too limited in range, and the Council introduced its own more generous system of allowances in 1944. However, here as in other aspects of wartime government policy there was evidence of a changing approach to questions of health and social security, one based on the concept of a national minimum standard of income and the conquest of what the Beveridge Report of 1942 called the 'five giants': want, disease, squalor, ignorance and enforced idleness. The post-war reforms which created the National Health Service and transferred responsibility for the relief of poverty from local to national agencies were among the eventual results. In the meantime, however, the duties of the Poor Law Guardians had been transferred to county and county borough councils on the abolition of the Poor Laws in 1929.

The Northampton Guardians, wrote the *Independent*, 'can be assured that they pass out graced with the gratitude of the whole of their fellow citizens for much exacting work well and efficiently done . . . The work of the Poor Law Administration may be more cohesively and comprehensively performed, but it is certain that it can never be discharged by any body throughout the country with a wider degree of discrimination, sympathy, consideration and humanity'. [42] The Northampton Board lacked none of these qualities, but popular dislike of a resort to the 'parish' was so deeply ingrained that this too was transferred to the body which administered the new system — the Public Assistance Committee. Like the Maternity and Child Welfare Committee, it consisted of a majority of Council representatives and a minority of co-opted members. Among the former were James Jackson, its first chairman, and C. J. Scott, and Alfred Slinn, leader of the Labour Group. The latter included several former Guardians, among them Mrs. George Swan, and another ex-chairman of the Board, the publican Herbert Starmer.

Until 1934, when this function was transferred in turn to centrally-appointed Unemployed Assistance Boards, much of the P.A.C.'s work was concerned with the relief of able-bodied unemployment. Whatever it did in this respect brought criticism from some quarter. Payments were normally made only in exchange for work, and those unfit for heavy public works were generally employed in wood-chopping, in cultivating the garden of the former workhouse, or in making or repairing footwear in its 'shoe shop'. However, under national legislation applicants for such relief could be required to prove that they were 'genuinely seeking work', and the implication that unemployment was often a matter of choice was much resented in itself. Payments were also subject to a 'Means Test', abolished by the Labour governments in 1924 and 1930, and reintroduced by their successors. This too was extremely unpopular, and in 1932 the P.A.C. was urged by the local branch of the Unemployed Workers' Movement to refuse to administer it. [43]

Labour members of the Committee favoured this course, but they were outvoted. However, they made several attempts to raise the actual levels of relief. In October 1930, for instance, the Northampton Trades Council, representing some 20,000 local trades unionists, complained in emotive terms of 'the callous manner in which the capitalist class members on the Public Assistance Committee dealt with Alderman Scott's resolution re increasing the miserable pittance given to members of the working class who find themselves in distress through no fault of their own'. [44] Scott's proposals would have given a man and wife with four children a total of £2 5s. a week in relief against the £1 9s. they received at that time. Under the higher scales introduced in 1931 the same family received a total of £1 17s. 6d., but two years later the Committee was rebuked by the Ministry of Health for paying relief at a level 'substantially higher than has been found necessary in comparable areas. Persons in relief of unemployment are often granted supplementary relief as a matter of course', with 'little regard paid to the income of other members of the the the family'. [45]

This more generous policy was undoubtedly influenced by the increase in local unemployment in the winter of 1932-33 and the social tensions which were now manifesting themselves. Although it retained some powers to grant additional winter relief, the Committee's discretion here was largely removed by the transfer of this part of its functions to the

Unemployment Assistance Board. However, it continued to depart from national guidelines for other forms of relief. These were 'for general guidance only', the Unemployed Workers' Movement was assured in 1935, 'each case to be dealt with on its merits . . . all the circumstances to be taken into consideration'.[46] 'Relief given in this Area compares very favourably with that paid in other districts', it wrote to the local branch secretary in 1936, a claim supported by the disapproval with which the District Auditor viewed its accounts for that year. 'In some cases of relief', he concluded, 'it could hardly be alleged that destitution exists'.[47]

The Public Assistance Committee was also responsible for relieving the 'impotent' poor, and after 1934 this absorbed most of its attention. From the Poor Law Board it inherited five scattered children's homes and the Workhouse itself — known baldly as the Institution until its 1934 re-naming. The occupants, the majority of them elderly, were required by law to contribute to their maintenance according to their means or that of other family members, and much time was consumed in deciding who could afford to pay what. The building also housed a 188-bed hospital, staffed by two visiting medical officers and 24 resident nurses, more than half of the latter consigned for want of space to cubicles above one of the male wards. 'Very inadequate', was the M.O.H.'s verdict here on inspecting the hospital after its takeover, and while the building itself was sound enough, its overall design and much of its equipment were simply 'antiquated'. The police station in Dychurch Lane was judged similarly inadequate by H.M. Inspector of Constabulary in 1928, and for the first and only time in its history the borough force had its annual Certificate of Efficiency withheld pending arrangements for improved accommodation.

Along with a new fire station and indoor municipal baths, the requisite new police station was built on the Mounts, on the site of the now redundant prison which had taken priority over the same plan in the 1830s. Control of local gaols was transferred to central government in 1877, and the closure of Northampton Prison was part of the 'national economy' measures effected by it in the early 1920s. On the grounds of increased transport costs and the loss of local legal business, the Council waged a vigorous campaign to keep it open, citing its larger size, recent modifications and the work of the Northampton Discharged Prisoners Society against the competing merits of Bedford.[48] Geography and the lower running costs of a smaller gaol won the day for the latter, and in 1929 the Council purchased the site and demolished the prison, after opening it for several days to public inspection. The several thousand visitors whose curiosity was thus satisfied were also invited to purchase cell doors and other souvenirs, the proceeds of which were donated to local charities.

The whole Mounts complex was built by local builders to the design of the Lancashire firm of J. C. Prestwich and Sons, winners of an open competition. The fire station was opened in 1935, housing three motor fire engines at that time, and the public baths in the following year. The latter had been planned since 1924, but delayed for want of a suitable central site. The police station was completed in 1941. Designed to cater for unanticipated future demands, it was fitted with non-structural internal partitions which could be cheaply and easily re-arranged as the need arose. In the meantime steps had been taken to ensure the efficient policing of outlying areas of the town, enlarged by the extension of the borough boundaries in 1932 to include parts of Dallington, Duston, Boughton, Moulton Park, Weston Favell and Hardingstone. The extension was prompted largely by the need for additional land for housing, and was opposed with customary vigour by the County Council.

Four branch police stations were set up in the 1920s, at St James's, Far Cotton, Semilong and Abington, and cycle patrols were introduced in 1923. In 1930 the force was also equipped with two motor cycle combinations, and in 1932 with two B.S.A. tricars which covered some 52,000 miles in their first year of service. More officers were also recruited, and they now included a small number of women. Four were appointed in 1918 in an experiment which was in Chief Constable Mardlin's view 'amply justified by the results'. Much of their work was concerned with juvenile crime and assaults against women, which they were often reluctant to report to a male officer, but policewomen were also considered to play a valuable 'preventative' role. They were 'very successful in suppressing boisterous and unruly behaviour on the part of young people in the streets', said one speaker to the Chief Constables' Association in 1918, and had the 'ability to effect many settlements in disorderly and quarrelsome neighbourhoods'.[49]

Much emphasis was also placed on police training and education after the appointment of Chief Constable John Williamson from the Huddersfield Borough Police in 1924. Recalled as a man of 'great humanity and humility', he held the office for over 30 years and was awarded the King's Police Medal and Fire Service Medal for distinguished service in 1943. Larceny remained much the largest category of recorded crime in the inter-war years, but juvenile crime, it has been said elsewhere, became of increasing concern in the 1930s. However, most minor offenders were cautioned rather than prosecuted, a policy which 'has for its primary objective the prevention of young people feeling the loss of self-respect which results from an appearance before even a Juvenile Court. It is firmly believed that . . . in a dignified way, they have been saved from slipping into loose ways and possibly into further wrong-doing'.[50]

Among the adult population, the continuing decline in prosecutions for drunkenness was 'a matter for congratulation'. In 1930 they still had 396 pubs and 28 licensed clubs at their disposal, but while there was only one drunken driver among the 90 prosecuted for reckless or careless driving in that year, the increase in this category of offence caused the Chief Constable as much concern as the manpower expended on controlling the traffic itself. The installation of two sets of automatic traffic lights at the Fish Street/Abington Street and Kingsley Road/Kettering Road junctions in 1929 went some way to ease this problem. So too did the gradual replacement of the trams by motor buses, for 'the trams and their tracks constitute a real public danger. . . the tramcars' immovability from a fixed direction is the cause of dangerous traffic 'blocks', whilst the lines and setts in which they are laid become, after only short use, akin to plough furrows and a real peril to cyclists and motorists'.[51]

Snapping overhead cables and the derailment of trams by objects on the tracks were other hazards, but initially at least the motor buses served routes inaccessible by the trams, and the latter were not phased out completely until 1934. The first 28-seater buses were introduced in 1923, and equipped at the insistence of Mr. Cameron, the Tramways Manager, with interior springing and 'super cushion tyres' to eliminate the 'body-drumming' to which passengers were subjected on the wooden seats of the trams. The 'unsightly' poles carrying the cables also gradually disappeared, but in their place came a proliferation of other symbols of improved communications: telegraph poles. 'If the practice is allowed to continue our sidewalks will become impassable' declared one resident, 'and we shall perforce have to walk in the road'.[52] This complaint was delivered by way of a regular 'Where is it?' competition, which invited readers of the Independent to identify photographs of blots upon the landscape, and to provide the paper with some copy at the expense of the Borough Council.

'"Where is it?" Competition Provokes Storm of Criticism' it reported with satisfaction after its first effort, a picture of the lower end of Kingswell Street liberally strewn with rubbish: 'A veritable torrent of critical replies have poured into the office . . . All are unanimous in their deprecation of the revolting system of refuse collection'. This was succinctly described by the 13-year-old prizewinner. 'First two or three sweepers make their way leisurely down the street, pushing their brushes before them and sweeping the rubbish into small heaps. Secondly, along comes the old-fashioned collecting cart to collect the house refuse . . . the cart is usually brimming over and its attendants endeavouring to heap

39. Northampton Corporation tramways 26-seater Thorneycroft omnibus, pictured here by All Saints' church.

more refuse on top . . . much of the litter finds its way back to the ground, to be left lying there until the sweepers' next visit'.[53] The system did leave much to be desired, the Council admitted, but it was pressure from the M.O.H. rather than this transient outburst of public spleen which in due course persuaded it to invest in motor lorries and closed containers.

Severe flooding in 1926, which left the whole of St James's End under several inches of water, served to stress another long-standing problem, and large sums were also invested during this period in flood prevention schemes. Along with the municipal house-building programme and the Mounts complex, such works were a major source of employment for the local construction industry. However, the post-war Council was a large employer in its own right, and as such it was increasingly required to put its relations with its workforce on a more formal basis. In 1912, recognising the 'utter lack of system and an absence of any recognised principle in dealing with the status, service and remuneration' of its staff, it had appointed a Special Committee to formulate a grading system for each of its various departments. Most non-manual employees worked a 44-hour week at that time, with paid sick leave and holidays, but salaries were negotiated on an individual basis with the relevant Committee. This process was not only enormously time-consuming but the source of much 'chagrin and disappointment' on the part of employees whose suits were rejected.

Staff were now allocated to one of four grades, each carrying a salary within a fixed minimum-maximum range. Thus the intending new employee 'will be able to see at a glance the maximum which he might hope to attain, and the chances of promotion that the service offered', and if 'these financial rewards were not sufficiently promising, he would be at liberty to seek other spheres for the exercise of his energies'.[54] Commencing salaries in 1912 ranged from £163 p.a. in the first grade, which included the Chief Assistant to the Borough Engineer and the Assistant Secretary to the Education Committee, to £41 12s. p.a. in the fourth, comprising junior clerks. Heads of Departments remained outside the grading system, free to negotiate their own salaries which at this time varied from around £350 to £500. However, this carefully constructed system was completely disrupted by the First World War. War bonuses paid to offset the rising cost of living and the 'progressive' salaries offered to attract key workers produced such glaring post-war anomalies that some long-serving employees were receiving less pay than those recently appointed to the same posts, while here as elsewhere real wages had also been eroded by post-war inflation.

Post-war conditions and the war itself strengthened the ranks of trades unions representing local authority workers, and it was largely under pressure from the National Association of Local Government Officers that in 1924 the Council embarked on the laborious task of drawing up new salary scales. N.A.L.G.O. was founded in 1905 at the instigation of an earlier body, the Municipal Officers' Association, with the aim of combining local and professional associations of municipal workers into an effective national pressure group. Most negotiations were still conducted at local level, but 'all matters of national importance' were taken up by the Executive Council. Post-war salaries in Northampton apparently fell into this category, for they 'do not compare at all favourably with salaries paid to officials in other towns of similar size'. This rebuke was delivered by a delegation of national N.A.L.G.O. leaders in 1924, and — no doubt stung by the suggestion that it was less than progressive in dealing with its own workforce — the new more generous scales were introduced soon afterwards.[55]

Education and training were also a part of N.A.L.G.O.'s activities, but the quality of local government recruits was a matter of more general concern during this period. In 1929 the Royal Commission on Local Government pointed to the scarcity of University graduates in the service, and to the absence of any minimum educational requirement for clerical and administrative staff. Qualifying competitive examinations were among its recommendations, repeated in 1935 by the report of the Hadow Committee on the Qualifications, Recruitment, Training and Promotion of Local Government Officers. The latter also suggested that clerical workers should study the principles of public administration, and that principal officers should be recruited less on the basis of technical or professional qualifications than for their administrative abilities. The Royal Commission had similarly suggested that councils appoint a trained administrator as chief of staff, a role normally fulfilled at this time by the Town Clerk, who by virtue of the nature of much of his work was traditionally a qualified lawyer.

This found little support, but in Northampton many of the recommendations of the Hadow Report were already being applied. Employees were encouraged to study in their own time and at their own expense for professional and other relevant qualifications, and repaid by way of 'merit awards' additional to their normal salaries or promotion to a higher grade. From 1930 salaried employees also had the option of joining a contributory superannuation scheme. In that year the Council employed a total of 165 such staff, but these were outnumbered by manual and other employees who had their own trade unions or associations. After 1924 most manual and transport workers were represented by the National Union of Municipal and General workers, formed by a merger of several smaller unions in that year. The Provincial Joint Industrial Councils set up after the First World War also provided a broader forum for the discussion of pay and conditions, and questions of training, occupational health and welfare.[56]

In general, the Council welcomed the advent of collective bargaining as less time-consuming and more conducive to uniformity than individual negotiation. Following the report of the post-war Desborough Committee, however, police pay and conditions were governed by the Police Act of 1919, which also established a Police Federation through which grievances could be aired. Local schoolteachers had their own separate associations, but in 1919 they aired their own grievances by going on strike. The dispute centred on salaries, and had eventually to be referred to arbitration. The final settlement gave them a minimum increase of £30 a year, and cost the Council a total of £19,000. A supplementary rate had to be levied to raise the bulk of it, but relations were repaired in the following year with the formation of a Joint Advisory Committee composed of representatives of the Education Committee and the teachers' unions, to encourage 'the interchange of views and opinions, and closer co-operation'.[57]

In 1921 Alfred Caine Boyde was appointed from Darlington as Director and Secretary of Education. The addition of 'Director' to the title of his predecessors, Mr. Stewart Beattie and Mr. H. C. Perrin, reflected the wider post-war responsibilities he was required to undertake. These included the provision of Intermediate schools 'for the better education of older scholars', with a more advanced curriculum than that available to them in the upper forms of the primary schools. Four were established at the Barry Road, Kettering Road, Campbell Square and St George's schools, to be followed in the 1930s by the Kingsley and Bective Senior Schools, which offered a less academic curriculum than the Girls' School and the Town and County School, the former Northampton Grammar School. Pupils progressed from primary level by way of competitive examinations, but school fees were often a barrier to able pupils from low income families. However, some 45% of all pupils above elementary level in Northampton in 1924 held 'free places', financed by the Council itself, compared with a national average of 33%.

Additional primary schools were also built during this period, at St James's, for instance, where new housing development had swelled the population, and in Weston Favell and other areas incorporated into the borough by the extended boundaries. Other projects included a Nursery School in Silver Street, and an Open-air School on Kingsley Road, designed to boost the health of less robust children and those recovering from debilitating illnesses. These too were an important source of local building work, but the Education Committee continued to plead for more generous central funding of its own activities. 'Education being a national service', it complained in 1930, 'and having regard to the additional burdens which will be imposed on local Rates ... legislation should be introduced providing for an increased proportion of the costs of Education and ancillary services being borne out of National Funds'.[58] This familiar refrain was evoked on this occasion by a proposal to raise the school-leaving age from 14 to 15, one which had been aired several times before and had much to do with high levels of juvenile unemployment in some areas of the country.

Local authorities already had discretionary powers to raise the school-leaving age, but in the Committee's view, reducing the supply of juvenile labour in this manner 'will prejudice the prosperity of communities by hindering the revival or development of trade or industry'.[59] In the opposite view, prosperity would be better assured by removing some juveniles from the labour market, and allowing it to absorb the surplus adult labour which, by virtue of their cheapness, they were displacing. In the event, the school-leaving age remained unchanged until after the Second World War. However, a lack of the requisite skills was a definite hindrance to industrial prosperity, and in Northampton much effort was also invested in improving the quality of technical education. In co-operation with the Footwear Manufacturers' Association, Day Release courses were introduced in the Technical School in 1918, and full-time two-year courses in boot and shoe manufacture soon afterwards.

Entry to the latter was by qualifying examination, with a maintenance grant payable according to parental means.

The Shoe and Allied Trades Research Association was also based here until it moved to London under the auspices of the National Federation. Classes for the unemployed were offered in the 1920s, and part-time evening courses in a variety of subjects according to demand: plumbing, for example, motor body building, and — for Post Office workers — 'Electricity and Calculations'.[60] Soon after the war the School's Abington Street premises were judged inadequate for future needs, and in 1924 the Council acquired a site on St George's Avenue for a new Technical College. Building was delayed by financial cutbacks, but the foundation stone was laid in December 1931 by the Mayor, Cllr. Lyne, and Samuel Smith Campion, the last surviving member of the 1890 Technical Instruction Act Committee and still an active promoter of its cause. The college, 'an imposing structure of no inconsiderable proportions' costing almost £80,000, was built by the local firm of Glenn and Sons, and formally opened in November 1932 by H.R.H. the Duke of York. It housed domestic science and commercial sections as well as boot and shoe, leather, building, engineering and science departments, and its equipment and furniture cost an additional £14,000. A further £10,000 worth of machinery was provided on loan by local manufacturers.

A Junior Technical School was also opened there in 1934. In due course it was hoped that the college would be granted university status, and early discussions were held with a view to affiliating it to the University College of Nottingham. These came to nothing, but its full-time, part-time and evening courses catered for a total of some 2,000 students of both sexes each year. In 1937 the School of Art also moved to a new building on St George's Avenue. Internally spacious and well-equipped, its exterior was not universally admired. 'No one could imagine for a moment that art is to be taught there', declared one of its students, 'for the building is uninspired in every way and redolent of petty provincialism'.[61] This was all a matter of taste, but if the local pride which inspired much of its efforts might be accounted by some as 'provincialism', the overall achievements of the Borough Council during this period were certainly far from petty. Indeed, wrote one commentator in 1937, 'the sacrificing and voluntary labours of local councillors may be less spectacular than those of Members of Parliament, but they are of no less — many think they are of greater — value, especially to posterity, and they should become much more attractive to our best-educated and most experienced citizens'.[62]

The latter comment was prompted by research based on a sample of 3,105 county and county borough councillors from 92 English and Welsh authorities. Only 157 were women, but small traders were much the largest occupational group, followed by accountants, solicitors and barristers. Manual and artisan trades accounted for 215 of the total, builders for 199, and railway workers — mainly clerks — for 171. Pawnbrokers, undertakers and sculptors were rather scarce, as was the younger age group.[63] Northampton did not vary too much from this overall picture. Only six women held Council office between 1919-39, and even within the Labour ranks themselves manual workers were in a minority. Tradesmen accounted for 28% of all councillors during this period, builders for 10%, and the professions for 14%. However, a higher than average proportion — 26% — were industrialists. Almost half of them were footwear manufacturers, and these figures may stress the degree to which municipal enterprise between the wars was an extension of 'conciliation and co-operation' in the private sphere.[64]

Occupation is not necessarily any guide to the quality of a councillor, but the preponderance of certain groups and the scarcity of others does tend to confirm the sacrifices of time and money which had to be made to municipal office. Education completed and status established, the older age group often had more of both to spare. Working-class men and women often had little of either, and if there were among them 'many who would worthily

40. Charles John Scott (1868-1947), elected as the first Labour Mayor of Northampton in 1931. An insurance representative and former journalist, he joined the Social Democratic Federation in 1894 and served on the School Board and the Board of Guardians before his election to the Council.

fulfil the office of Mayor', as the *Independent* wrote in 1923, the Mayor of Northampton 'possesses no privileges, not even a free tram pass. He has to give up his own business for twelve months, and spend his time and money and abilities day and night for the benefit of the public'.[65] Until 1930, for just this reason, the Labour group refused to offer candidates for the mayoralty. From that year onwards an allowance was paid from corporate funds to offset the expenses of the office, and under a seven-year agreement to allocate it between the parties in turn it was finally removed from the political arena.

The distinction of becoming the first Labour Mayor of Northampton was intended to go to Alfred Slinn, the long-time chairman of the Housing Committee, but he died shortly before he was due to take office in 1931. It was filled instead by C. J. Scott, followed in 1934 by the bootmaker and veteran of the Independent Labour Party, Albert Burrows. However, the civic funeral accorded to Alderman Slinn was not only a mark of the high personal regard in which he was held, but testimony to the acceptance of the Labour party as a legitimate force in local politics. Citizenship before party, community before class, authority based on merit: that was the test of legitimacy, and as one Conservative councillor put it rather grudgingly in 1934, 'no one can deny that many Socialist representatives have done good work for the town'. Until the 1930s at least, the electoral evidence suggests that candidates for office were judged by similar criteria, and that a high local profile and a proven record of service to the community carried more weight than an association with one particular party or class.

Electoral addresses were often couched in just such terms, and still more finely tuned to the 'localism' of individual wards. For instance, among the 'strong reasons' for election advanced by Charles Wilson in Castle in 1922 were seven years' service on the Council and the 'good work' performed on individual Committees. Moreover, 'he has been associated with the Ward all his life and knows its requirements . . . he is a staunch supporter of your member, Councillor W. Smith . . . his wife is a Guardian for the Ward . . . he is prepared to devote virtually the whole of his time to the benefit of the town and of the Castle Ward in particular'. As a landlord, he added, 'he has never taken advantage of the Increase of Rents Act, as all his properties are at pre-war rentals'. This was a reference to the Conservative government's abolition of rent controls and the local evictions which had followed it. Mr. Wilson had no wish to be tainted by association, for he was — difficult as it might be to discern from this address — the Conservative candidate.[66]

'I have had the honour to represent the Ward for the past 16 years, and trust that my services have been some value to the town', was the brief message of his party colleague F. C. Parker in St Michael's in the same year.[67] Whatever their politics, such well-established candidates were very difficult to dislodge. In 1932, for instance, two of the three seats in the Delapre ward were taken by Labour, one by William Barratt and the other — with a majority of two votes — by Mrs. Harriet Nicholls. Mrs. Nicholls was the long-time secretary of the ward party in Far Cotton, absorbed into Delapre by the re-organisation of the ward boundaries in the same year and still heavily populated by railway workers. Both her father and her husband were railway workers, which doubtless carried some weight with the voters — but the third seat remained firmly in the hands of the Liberal chemist F. C. Ashford, who had represented the area since 1905. In St James's, another predominantly working-class ward, Labour made no headway at all. This remained a Liberal fiefdom, dominated for much of this period by members of the Lewis family, still one of the area's largest employers.

A high local profile also saved a great deal of personal electioneering. Many of his established colleagues, one Conservative complained in 1938, 'took very little active part at election times'. The Conservative candidate in the Abington ward in 1922, on the other hand, had been drafted in from elsewhere and had 'not had the privilege of serving in the

Town Council . . .'. Thus 'it will be my endeavour to make myself known to as many electors as possible before Polling Day, and I trust those whom I do not see will accept my regrets and apologies'.[68] A new candidate could never expect to step safely into the shoes of a party colleague, however prominent. Until 1928 Castle was very much a Tory preserve, but when J. V. Collier was elected to the aldermanic bench in that year his seat was taken by Mrs. Agnes Adams, the ward's Labour representative on the Board of Guardians. In the North ward, represented at one time or another by Alfred Slinn, C. J. Scott and Albert Burrows, the Labour vote fell when they became aldermen in their own turn and were replaced by lesser known candidates.

This is not to say that party affiliations were irrelevant, simply to suggest that they could be, and often were, outweighed by local political values. The mass media, it is true, did go some way to 'nationalise' political debate and electioneering during this period, but personal contact with the electorate remained important, and in Northampton at least, candidates were judged first and foremost on their committment to the local community. This was, after all, the central pillar in the post-war edifice of 'conciliation and co-operation', and 'when a man has done really good work for the town', said the *Independent*, 'to whatever party he belongs, he ought not to be subjected to vexatious opposition'. The paper was referring to the Labour candidates fielded in 1922 against such long-serving councillors as F. C. Parker and William Harvey Reeves, and who 'account it an honour to fight, even where they have not a ghost of a chance of success'.[69] In the same breath it was complaining of the 'general apathy' of the electorate itself. Uncontested elections, it may be thought, would not have done much to excite their interest, but by 1929 the paper was wringing its editorial hands in despair and recanting on its previous pleas for political peace.

'The public in general appear to be wholly indifferent . . .', it cried. 'Much as we may have deplored political partisanship, a measure of healthy party spirit is assuredly better than no spirit at all'. Rivalry between the parties was certainly not dead, but such was their agreement on major policy issues at this time that they were hard-pressed to pick a real quarrel with each other. In truth, the *Independent* found the longed-for 'millennium of quietude' something of a journalistic desert, but if the electorate displayed few visible signs of emotion, it was still voting in quite respectable numbers. Between 1919-31 the turnout at municipal elections in Northampton was some 10% above the national average, which may be a measure of the citizens' own sense of commitment to their community. However, as consensus gave way to conflict in the 1930s, party labels came to assume more significance and there were some perceptible changes in voting habits.

A growing number withheld their votes altogether. Many of them, it seems likely, were working-class voters hostile to Liberal and Conservative employers but unwilling as yet to vote Labour. Even so, the Labour share of the vote did increase quite significantly after 1934, and some prominent Liberals defected to the Conservatives, seeing them as 'the only defence against socialism'.[71] The main casualties were the Liberals themselves, supplanted by Labour as the second largest party in the Council in 1937 when they lost five of their ten councillors. For the first time in almost ten years the Conservatives found themselves with a majority, only to lose it again the next year when two of their seats went to Labour. All this said, however, Labour did not gain as much ground in Northampton as might perhaps be expected amid the social stresses of the 1930s. To this extent the conciliatory policies and the co-operative culture which the party itself had helped to promote had achieved their objective, aided after 1935 by declining unemployment, which went some way to ease earlier tensions.

Nationally, however, the picture was very little different. There is no real evidence of a significant change in the political status quo in the years before the Second World War, no real hint of the fundamental shift in public opinion which would sweep the Labour party to power in 1945 with a massive majority. This came during the war itself, but it bore the indelible mark of the 1930s themselves. 'If we speak of democracy we do not mean a democracy which maintains the right to vote and forgets the right to work and the right to live . . .', as *The Times* put it in July 1940. 'If we speak of equality we do not mean a political equality nullified by social and economic privilege . . . If we speak of economic reconstruction we think less of maximum (though this job too will be required) than of equitable distribution . . . The new order cannot be based on the preservation of privilege'.[72] The post-war general election — the first for ten years — was a belated but crushing verdict not on Churchill's wartime leadership nor even on the 'guilty men' whose policy of 'appeasement' and alleged neglect of disarmament were popularly blamed for the conflict, but on the years of unemployment and depression which preceded it. In the final analysis, as one commentator concluded, 'the dole queue was more evocative than El Alamein'.[73]

The decisive victory at El Alamein in the autumn of 1942 marked a turning point in British military fortunes. The war could be and would be won, and it was into this optimistic atmosphere that William Beveridge pitched his answer to the dole queue. An economist by training, a civil servant by profession, and a Liberal by long persuasion, he was well aware that his proposals were controversial. 'Social security' was what he offered, a term 'used here to denote the securing of an income to take the place of earnings when they are interrupted by unemployment, sickness or accident, to provide for retirement through age, to provide against loss of support by the death of another person, and to meet exceptional expenditures . . .'.[74] Equally aware of their appeal to a public well experienced in the insecurities of life and now confident of eventual victory in war, his timing was as well-judged as it was deliberate. Published a bare few weeks after El Alamein, it became an immediate bestseller, the symbol of a new post-war society 'which enables a man to live his life without fear of poverty'.[75]

Overwhelmingly concerned with winning the war itself, Churchill gave it a cool reception. 'Ministers in my view should be very careful not to raise false hopes as was done last time by speeches about "Homes for Heroes", etc.', he wrote, 'It is because I do not wish to deceive the people by false hopes and airy visions of Utopia and Eldorado that I have refrained so far from making promises about the future'.[76] Nevertheless, the Beveridge Plan had broad cross-party support, and in the 'White Paper chase' of 1944 promises were made of major reforms in health services and social insurance, and of policies to secure full employment. For Churchill and the Conservatives, however, it was already too late. Rightly or wrongly, early caution was construed in the public mind as lack of commitment, and it was to Labour that the post-war electorate looked to turn vision into reality. They wanted, if not Utopia, then something a great deal better than the 1930s had given them. Reputedly as much surprised by the result of the election as Churchill, even Attlee had not grasped how much they wanted it, but to no one's surprise at all, the Labour landslide was repeated up and down the country in the municipal elections of November 1945. The 'realisation of a lifelong aim and a lifetime's endeavour' for such veteran Socialists as C. J. Scott and Albert Burrows, in Northampton Labour claimed 29 of the 48 seats in the Council, leaving them with an overall majority of ten, and a difficult road ahead of them.[77]

Notes

1. *N.I.*, 12 Nov. 1921.
2. Ibid., 11 March 1922.
3. N.C.B.C., Minutes of the Housing and Town Planning Committee (hereafter Housing Committee), 20 March 1922.
4. Ibid., 25 Sept. 1917.
5. Ibid., 23 Oct. 1919.
6. Quoted in Dickie, M., 'Town Patriotism and the Rise of Labour in Northampton, 1918-39' (unpublished PhD thesis, University of Warwick, 1987).
7. The Local Government Board was abolished in 1919 and general oversight of most local government activities transferred to a new Ministry of Health.
8. N.C.B.C., Minutes of Housing Committee, 19 Jan. 1920.
9. *N.I.*, 11 Feb. 1922.
10. Ibid., 4 Feb. 1922.
11. Ibid., letter from a 'Colonial Newcomer', 23 Nov. 1929.
12. N.C.B.C., Minutes of Housing Committee, 8 Feb. 1918.
13. Ibid., Property Inspector's Reports, 16 July and 17 Sept. 1928.
14. Ibid., 17 Feb. 1930.
15. Ibid., 7 July 1938.
16. N.C.B.C. Health Report (1932).
17. N.C.B.C., *Northampton Development Plan* (1925).
18. Ibid.
19. Ibid.
20. N.C.B.C., Public Health Dept. Report re Working Class Housing to the Ministry of Health (1930).
21. N.C.B.C., Minutes of Housing Committee, 31 Dec. 1930; 26 Aug. 1931.
22. *N.I.*, letter from a 'Colonial Newcomer', 23 Nov. 1929.
23. N.C.B.C., Minutes of Housing Committee, 26 Aug. 1931. For a brief summary of the law regarding local authority contracts, see Keith-Lucas, B., & Richards, P. G., *A History of Local Government in the Twentieth Century* (1978).
24. Ibid., 15 Feb, 4 March and 21 June 1937.
25. *N.I.*, 15 April 1922.
26. *C.&E.*, cutting Jan. 1925, otherwise undated.
27. *N.I.*, 5 April 1930.
28. The Northampton Chamber of Trade was founded in February 1914. Its founding members included the grocer Ald. Charles Earl, and W. H. Holloway, editor of the *Independent*.
29. *N.I.*, 24 Feb. 1923.
30. N.C.B.C. Minutes, 4 Jan. 1926.
31. *N.I.*, 4 Jan. 1930.
32. Ibid.
33. Llewellyn-Davies, M. (ed.), *Maternity* (1915).
34. N.C.B.C. Health Report (1922).
35. N.C.B.C. Minutes, 5 March, 1928.
36. N.C.B.C. Health Report (1930).
37. Titmuss, R. M., *Birth, Poverty and Wealth* (1943).
38. Boyd Orr, Lord, *As I Recall* (1966), p.115.
39. N.C.B.C. Health Report (1942).
40. Ibid. (1932).
41. Ibid. (1943).
42. *N.I.*, 29 March 1930.
43. N.C.B.C., Minutes of Public Assistance Committee, 25 Feb. 1932.
44. Ibid., 14 Oct. 1930.
45. Ibid., 25 April 1933.
46. Ibid., 21 Nov. 1935.
47. Ibid., 14 Jan. 1936.
48. N.C.B.C., Report of Special Committee re H.M. Prison, Northampton (1922).

49. N.C.B.C., Chief Constable's Report (1918).
50. Ibid. (1930).
51. *N.I.*, 12 May 1923.
52. Ibid., 6 Jan. 1923.
53. Ibid., 4 Nov. 1922.
54. N.C.B.C., Report of Special Committee re Salaries and Appointments, 1 April 1912.
55. N.C.B.C., Minutes of Salaries and Appointments Committee, 26 June 1924.
56. See, for instance, N.C.B.C. Minutes, 1 Dec. 1919.
57. N.C.B.C. Minutes, 9-12 Nov. 1920.
58. Ibid., 27 Jan. 1930.
59. Ibid., 2 April 1928.
60. Ibid., 9-12 Nov. 1920.
61. Quoted in Walmsley, D., *An Ever-Rolling Stream* (1989), p.82.
62. Research of Sir James Marchant, quoted in *N.I.*, 5 Nov. 1937.
63. Ibid.
64. Dickie, M., op.cit., Table 6.
65. *N.I.*, 12 May 1923.
66. Ibid., 28 Oct. 1922.
67. Ibid.
68. Minutes of Party Meetings of Conservative Members of the Council, 11 March 1938 (N.R.O., N.C.C.A. 25); *N.I.*, 28 Oct. 1922.
69. *N.I.*, 21 Oct. 1922.
70. Ibid., 26 Oct. 1929.
71. They included members of the Chown family, building contractors of Kingsthorpe. Ald. Arthur Chown later served three terms as Chairman of the Education Committee between 1952-67.
72. *The Times*, 1 July 1940.
73. Howard, A., 'We are the Masters Now', in Sissons, M., and French, P. (eds.), *The Age of Austerity* (1963), p.16.
74. Beveridge, W., *Report on Social Insurance and Allied Services*, Cmd. 6404 (1942), p.120.
75. Quoted in Fraser, D., *The Evolution of the British Welfare State* (1980 edn.), p.207.
76. Churchill, W. S., *The Second World War*, 4 (1954), p.861.
77. Northampton Labour Party, *Labour's First Budget* (1946).

Chapter Seven

Facing the Future: from Post-War Reconstruction to 'New Town' Expansion

The inhabitants of Northampton recognise the extent to which the manufacture of boots and shoes has contributed to the development of the town, and they look forward to a prosperous future for the industry. At the same time a widening of the industrial interests of the town is regarded as desirable . . .

Northampton County Borough Council, Official Handbook, 1947

I am in favour of anything if it is going to mean an improvement, but I am doubtful if an improvement can be achieved by putting more power into the hands of the central government.

Alderman Sydney Strickland, quoted in *Northampton Chronicle and Echo*, 1 June 1962

'A very large number of electors in Northampton', wrote the Liberals in the municipal elections of 1949, 'will be temporarily disappointed by the knowledge that only in the Delapre Ward will they have an opportunity to support a Liberal candidate . . . But they must be patient . . . This is by no means the first time in our history that courage, patient confidence and hard work has been required . . . neither will it be the first occasion when such exertions have been rewarded with glorious success!'.[1] As they admitted, their ward committees had crumbled during the war, and they still had no local organisation worthy of the name. The appointment of an Organising Secretary did not bring the expected improvement in their fortunes, for they were in more than temporary difficulties. The partial eclipse of the inter-war years had now become almost total, the three-party system virtually a two-horse race run increasingly along party political tracks.

Understandably in their circumstances, the Liberal appeal to the electorate was still couched in pre-war terms. Cllr. Sydney Kilsby, their sole candidate, 'has been a member of the Council since 1945' and 'has devoted himself unstintingly to the welfare of North-ampton in general and Delapre Ward in particular'. 'A St James's man, I have endeavoured to work conscientiously for all irrespective of party', wrote the Labour candidate in that particular ward, but both Labour and Conservatives now rested their case on policies rather than personalities. 'Labour's policy gives security of employment; care for the sick, aged and infirm; wise town planning and good homes for the people', wrote one candidate. 'Few towns have been as well governed as Northampton', said its Labour M.P. Reginald Paget, 'and few citizens have had such value for their rates. Our Public Works Department has cheapened and speeded our Housing programme. Our Parks are better than those of any comparable town. Our Transport is good . . .'.[2] 'Do not be misled by any promises the Socialists may make about the rates . . .', retorted the Conservatives. 'The present day condition of some of the central areas of the town is an absolute disgrace, and a good example of Socialist inefficiency . . . The electors of Northampton will not be misled by continued reference to past Tory misrule'.[3]

New legislation in 1945 extended the municipal vote to all parliamentary electors, finally abolishing the rate-paying qualification; but while Labour 'are relying mainly upon their social services record to date to hold their own', the *Independent* concluded, 'even their most sanguine supporters do not anticipate more than that'.[4] In the event, they lost four seats and their majority in the Council to the Conservatives. Continued rationing, acute shortages of fuel compounded in 1947 by one of the most severe winters on record, the whole 'Work or Want' austerity of the post-war years: these fell far short of utopian expectations of a new society, and in 1951, after surviving with a slender majority in the previous year's general election, the Labour government itself was turned out of office. Promises were not easy to keep in the 'melancholy financial position' in which Britain found itself after the war, and as Cllr. Frank Lee, first Chairman of the post-war Finance Committee, observed when he presented his first budget, 'people expect a Labour Town Council to be different'.[5]

The post-war Labour group included three women and a higher proportion of manual workers, their path to office eased after the Local Government Act of 1948 by compensation for loss of earnings and 'any additional expense to which he would not otherwise have been subject' while on Council business. Like the Council as a whole, the Labour group was otherwise still dominated by small tradesmen and white-collar workers. Cllr. Lee himself was an extra-mural lecturer for the University of Cambridge. An economist by training and an accomplished local historian, one of his legacies to Northampton was a transcription of the customary law of the town, the *Liber Custumarum*.[6] However, he said, the new Labour Council 'wishes to be judged by several years' work, not by a flashy and spectacular effort', and its financial affairs would now be governed by three-or five-year revenue plans and a ten-year plan for capital investment. The latter included a new reservoir, now regarded as a matter of some 'urgency'. Built and managed in co-operation with other nearby local authorities, in the representative form of the Mid-Northamptonshire Water Board, it was sited a few miles north of North-ampton at Pitsford and officially opened in 1956 by H.M. Queen Elizabeth the Queen Mother.

41. Mrs. Harriett M. Nicholls (1884-1965), Labour councillor and Northampton's first female alderman. A former Branch Secretary of the National Warehouse and General Workers Union, she served two terms as Mayor between 1947-9 and was awarded the Honorary Freedom of the Borough in 1965.

This sort of long-term planning was certainly different, but if an increase in the rates was 'one of the few facts in life about which it can safely be stated that it gives pleasure to no one . . . I think we shall have reason to congratulate our-selves if this upward tendency . . . is stop-ped on this side of 17s. in the pound'. New government grants, higher property assessments or a deflationary economic policy were the only alternatives, and 'I hope for the first and pray against the third'.[7] The second amounted to much the same thing as increasing the rates directly — but it was high time, said Cllr. Lee, that this vexed question was seen in its proper perspective. Over 50% of occupied dwellings in Northampton had a rateable value of £15 or less. At £15 the proposed increase of 1s. 6d. in the pound would add 5d. to the weekly rates, bring-ing them to a total of 4s. 4d. Given an increase of some 76% in the average wages of male manual workers over the war years, this was really 'not much to make a song about'. It was 'less, fre-quently much less', than the average family spent on beer, tobacco or the cinema, although 'I am not attacking the popular expenditure on these creature comforts. Every civilisation must have at least one stimulant and one narcotic'. As for the long-standing argument that 'rates are mainly paid, and disproportionately paid, by business people and shopkeepers . . . there is no truth in this conception'. Domestic properties accounted for 54% of total rate income at this time, shops for 16%, and warehouses, industrial properties and licensed premises for 3% or less each.[8]

The payers were not consoled, but the Exchequer Equalisation Grants introduced in 1948 went some way to redress the imbalance of resources between different localities. Based on a national average of rateable value, weighted according to age and other factors, those authorities falling below the average now received block grants to make up the deficiency. Moreover, local authorities were also relieved of two of their heaviest financial obligations. Responsibility for the relief of destitution was removed from them by the National Assistance Act of 1948. 'The existing poor laws shall cease to have effect', as the preamble to the Act read, 'and shall be replaced by . . . the rendering, out of moneys provided by Parliament, of assistance to persons in need'.[9] Relief was now administered by the National Assistance Board, on a means-tested basis which rendered it no more popular than the bodies which preceded it. Two years earlier, however, the National Insurance Act had also provided for seven forms of benefit payable 'as of right' in exchange for a single weekly contribution. Based broadly on the recommendations of the Beveridge Report, they included more generous maternity and widows' benefits and a death grant towards funeral expenses in addition to unemployment and sickness benefits and old age pensions.

The latter were first introduced in 1908, and contributory unemployment and sickness insurance schemes in 1911, but these were far from comprehensive. The 'cradle to the grave' cover provided under the Act was as novel as the flat-rate nature of both contributions and benefits. Unrelated to income, they stressed the universal and egalitarian nature of the scheme: 'equal benefits in exchange for equal payments'. The National Health Service, another integral part of the Beveridge Plan, was also to be available on a universal and 'free at the point of use' basis, but here 'the nation itself will have to carry the expenditure'. As Minister of Health Aneurin Bevan always intended, insurance contributions would cover only a fraction of its cost — 10% in 1954, 14% in 1966. Nonetheless, even he was staggered by the £400 million spent in its first year. 'I shudder to think', he said, 'of the ceaseless cascade of medicine which is pouring down British throats'.[10] Much of it was doubtless making up for years of prior neglect, but the N.H.S. was opposed almost to the eve of its introduction by the medical profession itself.

They 'feel they cannot give of their best to individual patients unless they continue to have a full sense of personal responsibility . . . the Act would upset the traditional relationship between doctor and patient', reported the *Independent* after a meeting of North-amptonshire doctors voted 84 3 against its proposals.[11] Fears of 'direction' and of flat-rate salaries bearing no relation to the work undertaken also account for much of this overwhelming and widespread opposition. Relations were not improved by Bevan's description of the doctors' leaders as 'poisoned people' engaged in 'a squalid political conspiracy', but a belated settlement was finally reached, and along with the National Assistance Act and other apparatus of the post-war 'Welfare State', the N.H.S. came into force on the 'appointed day' of 5 July 1948. The welfare role of charities and Friendly Societies was correspondingly diminished, but it was not supplanted altogether. There would always be some needs which the State could not fulfil. However, the N.H.S. was also intended to place health provision on a more ordered and systematic basis. A patchwork of voluntary and public effort, it had long been, as a 1944 White Paper put it, 'many people's business but no one's responsibility'.

Under the three-tier system now adopted, dental, ophthalmic and general practitioner services were administered by Executive Councils composed of an equal number of professional and lay members. Local authority hospitals and maternity homes were transferred to the control of Regional Hospital Boards — in Northampton's case, the Oxford Board. Locally these comprised the Smallpox Hospital on Mere Way, the Welford Road and Harborough Road Hospitals, St Edmund's, and the County Asylum at Berry Wood, now known as St Crispin's Hospital. St Andrew's Hospital remained under private voluntary control, but the General Hospital and the Barratt and Manfield Hospitals were also taken over by the Board. Thanks to a decline in the number of children in need of its services, linked in part to improvements in diet and maternity care, the latter was now treating orthopaedic patients of all ages. Its facilities included a specialist workshop supplying hundreds of pairs of bespoke surgical footwear, splints and leg-irons each year, which was finally closed in 1967.

County and county borough councils remained responsible for personal and preventative medical services: and thus, wrote the Borough M.O.H. Dr. Carrick Payton, 'the fight between curative and preventive medicine has now begun'. In his view, one shared by many others, the division of the two between different administrative bodies was not only 'entirely artificial' but potentially harmful.[12] Mass radiography, for instance, was useless unless newly-diagnosed sufferers could be assured of ready access to other services: institutional care 'without delay', financial and other support for their families, and effective rehabilitation schemes. Responsibility for these was spread across different agencies, 'and a bottleneck at any point reflects on the efficiency of the whole. A deluded and disappointed public will show more resentment than response in the effort to eradicate tuberculosis, and their willing co-operation is vital to success'.[13] Public response to the first mass radiography survey in Northampton in 1945 was encouraging, but the results were in some ways disturbing. Only a relatively low number of new cases were detected, but the incidence of pulmonary TB was significantly higher among shoe workers than those in other occupations: around 10:1,000 against five for males and 13:1,000 against eight for females.

Clickers, lasters and finishers over the age of 35 were in the majority among males. This suggests that the younger generation were now benefitting from a healthier working environment, thanks in part to greater automation. However, rates of infection were highest among young female shoemakers. This may be linked with the concentration of numbers in closing rooms, but the incidence of pulmonary TB among young women in general had been increasing for some time. Neither Dr. Payton nor his predecessor could find any convincing explanation for this. 'One reason advanced is that modern life throws more stress on young women than before', as Dr. Rowland wrote in 1930, but

> I see nothing to make me believe that young women in factories, workshops, etc. work any harder than they did twenty five years ago . . . it is advanced that late hours, excessive amusements etc., are the cause of this rise. It does not seem very convincing. Others assert that the increased use of tinned food is the cause . . . surely the use of tinned food is not restricted to females aged fifteen to twenty-five.[14]

Vaccination against TB became available in 1950, and in due course new drugs also improved the chances of cure. Overall, however, the health of post-war Northampton was 'well maintained, and in many respects advanced'. One cause of concern was the increase in the so-called 'diseases of civlisation' — heart disease and cancer of the lung in particular — which medical evidence would increasingly link with dietary factors and cigarette smoking. Infant mortality continued to decline, but maternity and child welfare remained a large part of the Council's work under the N.H.S. Midwifery and home nursing services were initially provided under an agreement with the Queen's Institute of District Nursing. Under a similar arrangement a free ambulance service was operated by the St John Ambulance Brigade, but this service was later provided through the Borough Fire Brigade. Plans were also made to expand existing welfare services for the blind and the mentally handicapped. Wherever possible the former were provided with paid work at home or in the workshops run in conjunction with the Northamptonshire (Town and County) Association for the Blind.[15]

Greater emphasis was also placed on the community care of the adult mentally handicapped after 1948. In part this was a matter of necessity. Most institutional care had earlier been provided by the Bromham House Colony near Bedford, opened in 1931 in co-operation with the Bedfordshire and Northamptonshire County Councils, but in 1948 this fell outside the area of the Oxford Hospital Board, and the latter was 'unable to help to any material extent' in providing alternative places. The Mental Health Sub-Committee was chaired during this period by Dr. Lee Danby Cogan, son of the former Medical Officer of Health, who was first elected to the Council in the 1930s after a career in the Royal Army Medical Corps. However, while more mentally handicapped adults had thus to be cared for by their own families until the Council itself could provide more institutional places, around half were successfully placed in simple routine jobs in local shoe and engineering factories, or as farm workers and builders' labourers.[16]

Under the Children Act of 1948 the care of children 'deprived of a normal home life' came under the unified control of a new Children Department. Housed in a small office at the rear of the Guildhall, 'its scarlet dolls-house and pile of tattered comics are contemplated unwinkingly by Roland the goldfish, who since the premature death of his little friend Olwin, swims endlessly round and round. Roland works for his ants eggs . . .'.[17] Roland's task was to divert the many children passing through the office, while that of the Children Officer herself included arranging institutional or foster-care and, under a further Act in 1950, the supervision of adoptions. Much effort was also invested in 'saving' homes and securing 'if possible, a return to the care of his own parents', which may account in part for the consistently lower proportion of children in care in Northampton than in other Midland authorities.[18] Such children had formerly been the concern of the Public Assistance Committee, or, as appropriate, the Health and Education departments.

Under the Butler Education Act of 1944, education itself continued to be one of the Council's major responsibilities. Described as the 'most important gesture towards democracy made in the twentieth century, a fitting product of the People's War', the Act provided for a full range of education from nursery schools through to part-and full-time further education. Here it was much influenced not only by the Beveridge stress on eradicating the giant of 'ignorance', but by the Hadow Report of 1926 and the Spens Report of 1938. The first recommended the separate schooling of children once they reached the age of eleven, thus establishing the principle of 'primary' and 'secondary' education. The latter went one step further by adding a third category to the grammar schools and 'modern' schools at secondary level — the technical school. The object was to cater for differing educational needs and abilities among the same age groups, with each type of school being accorded equal merit and status. These were the arrangements laid down by the Butler Act, which also provided for the abolition of all fees in local authority secondary schools, and for the raising of the school-leaving age to 15 from April 1947.

The system of primary, intermediate and secondary schools adopted in Northampton between the wars was already broadly in line with these new requirements, and this eased the path of reorganisation. Along with several existing primary schools, the intermediate schools were now converted into secondary modern schools, the St George's Avenue Girls' School and the Town and County Boys' School continued as grammar schools, and the Junior Technical School at the College of Technology became the Northampton Technical High School. Additional schools were also built in new areas of residential development, generously equipped with playing fields and large windows rather than the 'high window-sills and muffled glass' of earlier school designs. However, as the Borough's former Chief

Education Officer Mr. H. C. Perrin noted in 1955, different types of secondary school did not enjoy the anticipated 'parity of esteem' in the public eye.

The curriculum of the secondary modern schools was less academically-based than that of the grammar schools. 'Free, so far as possible, from the limitations of external examinations', it was intended to allow more flexibility in catering for a range of differing needs and abilities. In Northampton, for instance, it was 'thought unwise to impose the learning of a foreign language',[19] but more time was allocated to cultural activities — music, art and drama — and more emphasis placed on teaching practical skills such as woodwork and cookery. There was a strict masculine-feminine divide in the latter areas. 'The husbands of the future should not suffer from indigestion due to their wives' indifferent cooking', wrote the *Independent*, 'for the culinary arts are now taught comprehensively'.[20] However, the secondary modern schools offered little prospect of formal educational qualifications, and were popularly regarded as inferior to the grammar schools. The abolition of fee-paying places in the latter, Mr. Perrin recalled, 'caused a good deal of consternation amongst parents and raised to prime importance the examination for admission . . . as the only alternative for scholars who failed to pass . . . was a private grammar school involving the payment of much higher fees'.[21]

Pupils who failed the '11-plus' but later showed sufficient promise might transfer to a grammar school up to the age of thirteen. However, 'the fact that a child's future depends largely on an examination taken at 11 years of age' was a major factor in the introduction of non-selective 'comprehensive' schools under the Labour government in the 1960s. It was also intended to redress the inequalities of opportunity to which the relative dearth of working-class children in grammar schools could be attributed, and to produce a broader social 'mix'. Then, as now, these issues roused strong feelings, and while comprehensive education was not resisted in Northampton, as it was in some areas, to the verge of having central grants withdrawn, it did not have an easy passage. A Labour scheme to reorganise on the lines of the existing Leicestershire system, with separate junior and senior high schools, was scrapped when the Conservatives gained control of the Council in 1965. They proposed instead to abolish the 11-plus exam, to establish non-selective area secondary schools and to preserve the grammar schools.[22]

Particular appeals were made for the Town and County School, the original Northampton Grammar School, to be treated as a 'special case', but these were thwarted by its status since 1911 as a joint Borough and County Council venture. After lengthy consultations with the teaching unions and an extension of the deadline for submission, a three-tier scheme was eventually agreed. Existing primary schools became 'lower schools', catering for children aged five to nine, the secondary schools were converted to 'middle schools' for the nine to 13 age group, and the grammar schools and technical school became the nucleus of eight planned 'upper schools', taking older pupils up to the age of eighteen. This system was retained by the County Council after responsibility for education in the borough was transferred to it under the Local Government Act of 1972, although its own comprehensive schools were organised on 'straight-through' 11-18 year lines.

Northampton had a long tradition of technical education and a high reputation in this respect, but under the selective secondary system some parents were still reluctant to accept a place for their children at the Technical High School. A range of academic subjects and General Certificate of Education courses were also offered here, but the Victorian bias against 'trade' lingered on, and industrial occupations had yet to enjoy the same status as the professions. To some extent this is still the case, but — said Mr. Perrin — parents 'should remember that the country needs technicians of the highest quality; that the financial rewards in industry far out-strip those in the "black-coated" professions, and furthermore, it is essential that the best brains of the country should be put into industry if we are to

42. Cliftonville Secondary Modern School, opened in 1964 at a cost of £200,000. Its generous windows and large playing fields are typical of school building design at this time. In the background is the mid-19th-century Cliftonville estate which housed many of Northampton's leading citizens.

compete with our goods in the world's markets'.[23] These sentiments were much in line with those of central government, which placed much stress on improving the status of technical colleges and encouraging them to undertake more research, for 'it is more than ever important if we are to restore and enhance our industrial position and attain full employment and an improved standard of life, to ensure that scientific and technical research is carried out as widely and intensively as possible, and applied promptly to production'.[24]

The College of Technology itself continued to undertake research and offer training in the shoe and leather trades, but it also worked closely with local employers, notably British Timken, Express Lifts and Blackwood Hodge, to expand its training in engineering. These and other firms also provided the college with much equipment, either on permanent loan or as a direct gift. These developments, it will be seen, were closely associated with changes in the structure of local industry, and were followed in due course by classes in computing, accounting and business management. Extensions to the Technical College were opened in 1961, but the continual widening of its activities and increasing pressure on space led directly to the building of a new and separate College of Further Education in Booth Lane. This was opened in 1973, but in the meantime provision for teacher training and University Extension and other courses had also been expanded.

Responsibility for the latter was transferred in 1962 from Cambridge to the University of Leicester, and in 1967 a University Centre with facilities for adult education was opened on Barrack Road. It was housed in Nazareth House, a former Roman Catholic orphanage and residential home for the elderly. Built in 1878, it had been empty for some years, and while its exterior had 'a certain dignity', recalled its first Warden, Ron Greenall, 'inside it was terrible . . . black and brown paint, and wards with derelict curtain rails . . . damp and very cold'.[25] Converted, refurbished and re-painted in less gloomy colours, at a cost of some £50,000, it assumed a more cheerful aspect, and within two years or so it was offering some 60 courses a year catering for around 1,000 adult students. The premises were shared by the University's School of Education, which provided post-graduate teacher training courses and in-service training for teachers based in local schools.

Full-length teacher training courses for mature students were also available from 1967 at the Northampton Annexe of the City of Leicester College of Education, housed in the former John Clare Secondary School on Kettering Road. Soon afterwards, however, Northampton acquired its own purpose-built College of Education. The government announcement that just one more teacher training college would be built came against the background of Northampton's designation as a 'New Town' in the later 1960s. Such a college was seen as making a significant contribution to this future expansion, and Northampton's advantages for its location were vigorously pressed by the Borough Council. Built on the former Home Farm of St Andrew's Hospital at Moulton, it was intended to accommodate some 800 students, including those from the soon-to-be closed Kirkby Fields College of Education in Liverpool and City of Leicester Northampton and Corby Annexes. Formally opened in 1973 by the Secretary of State for Education, Margaret Thatcher M.P., in 1975 the College was merged with the College of Technology and School of Art to form the present Nene College.

In education, as in other areas of activity after 1945, local authorities were increasingly required to conform to national policies for locally-provided services. Given the thrust of post-war government policy, this was to some extent inevitable. An economy planned 'from the ground up', as the Labour manifesto put it in 1945, had essentially to be planned from the top downwards, and if 'the ultimate objective was the creation of a society based on social justice', then there had to be some means of ensuring equal standards of service and an equitable distribution of resources. If the taxpayers were also to relieve the ratepayers of more of their burdens, they too were entitled to have their interests safeguarded, but there were important matters of principle involved here. Were local authorities 'responsible bodies competent to discharge their own functions', or were they merely 'agents of Government Departments'?[26]

Much post-war legislation, for instance, provided for a central takeover of services where a local authority was judged to be in default, and the central right of veto over the appointment of Chief Constables was extended to certain other chief officers — Children's Officers and Chief Education Officers, for instance. These powers were only rarely used, but their mere existence undermined the principle of local autonomy. For the same reason, the Borough M.O.H. regarded the new Regional Hospital Boards with undisguised distaste. A 'fundamental departure from accepted beliefs of proper government', was his verdict, 'The members of the Board are not elected by the community but selected by the Minister'.[27] After 'due consultation', it is true, and on the basis of experience and expertise, but he was far from alone in believing that elected and accountable 'amateurs' were a better safeguard of local democracy than selected 'experts', and Regional Hospital Boards were by no means the last instruments of local government to be so constituted.

Some controls were relaxed by the Conservative government during the 1950s, and the Exchequer Equalisation Grants tied to particular services were replaced in 1958 by a general Rate Deficiency Grant. This was intended to allow more local choice in allocating resources, but the overall balance of power continued to shift in favour of central government. 'We have got very little power that matters anyway . . . ', said the Chairman of the Watch Committee, Alderman Sydney Strickland in 1962 of proposals to reduce it still further:

'If anything is working well, be it men, machines or companies, I do not agree that it should be taken to pieces to see if it can be bettered'.[28] He was also much opposed to the planned amalgamation of some borough and county police forces. In his own view, 'men bred locally understand people better than anyone coming into the locality', but in that of the Home Office, those forces numbering less than 350 officers could not provide a full range of specialist skills and equipment. The authorised establishment of the Northampton Borough force in 1965 was 212, and in the following year it was duly merged with the county force to form the Northamptonshire Police.

'The first and most important duty of a Conservative Town Council', wrote the Northampton Tories during the 1949 municipal election campaign, 'will be to regain independence of action in local affairs', for 'matters which should be of a purely local character have been prejudiced by party politics to the extinction of independence in local government, which will reduce the town council to a body of "Yes" men'.[29] They were particularly critical of the progress of the municipal housing programme, which 'can only be described as a miserable contribution to a great problem'. The 'gravest problem which confronts not only Northampton

43. John Veasey Collier (1895-1965), 'Mr. Northampton'. Managing Director of the Northampton Shoe Machinery Co., post-war leader of the Conservative party and Mayor from 1954-5, he was the fourth generation of the Collier family to serve on the Borough Council. His father, also John Veasey Collier, founded the company in the late 19th century and served as Mayor from 1937-8.

but Great Britain as a whole', wrote the M.O.H. Stephen Rowland of the housing situation in 1944. Due to a certain 'misapprehension' as to his role, he had been personally as well as professionally acquainted with it. 'Persons seeking a house in the Borough', he complained in 1940, 'come to my office asking me to find them one, as though I were a house agent. I may have to take on many duties not originally intended, but . . .'.[30] In 1938 there was still a national short-fall of around half a million dwellings, and once again building virtually ceased on the outbreak of war. By 1943 there was an 'acute shortage' of accommodation in Northampton, and that year's estimate of 2,000 new houses to meet post-war shortages proved to be over-optimistic.

However, 250 new dwellings were quickly provided in the form of pre-fabricated bungalows, erected on the St David's, Bant's Lane and Delapre estates. The butt of many a joke — 'my brother thought he had mice, but it was the people next door eating dinner' — the 'prefabs' had their faults. Their aluminium panels retained the heat in summer and the cold in winter, and they were undeniably lacking in beauty, but elderly occupants in particular found them quick and easy to clean, and 'would never go back to a house with stairs after this'.[31] New permanent building also began soon after the war. Local contractors were employed at first, but in 1946 the Labour-controlled Council set up its own Direct Labour

44.   Post-war municipal housing on the Delapre Estate.

Organisation to undertake the work. Modelled on the lines of similar D.L.O.s in Derby
and Battersea, the new Public Works Department was in effect a construction company
within the Council itself, employing its own labour and building new housing roads and
sewers as well as houses themselves. In the Council's view, the 'magnitude and extent of
the work involved provides a unique opportunity to establish first class working conditions',
and its employees were not only admitted to the Council's superannuation scheme after six
months' service, but supplied with hot midday meals from on-site canteens.[32]

The Master Builders' Federation accused it of poaching not only work but workers from
private firms, and the Conservatives cited it as a prime example of dogma before efficiency.
'The electors of Northampton are asked to rejoice that the Public Works Department created
by the Socialists has built 96 houses in 30 months',[33] they declared; but while they also
employed some private contractors, the Conservatives retained the Department when they
took control of the Council, and by 1950 they were defending their own house-building record
in terms very reminiscent of the early 1920s. 'This Council does not accept the Minister
of Health's statement relating the shortage of houses to lack of municipal drive . . .', ran

one resolution in that year, 'the building industry in Northampton can build more houses if an increased allocation is given and the supply of building materials is more efficiently organised'.[34] Post-war house-building was in fact bedevilled by shortages of the requisite raw materials, and for the same reason it was also subject to much tighter central control than in the past.

After 1947 the number of new dwellings in each area was regulated by a system of building licences, with private development initially limited to a maximum one fifth of the total allocation. New private housing 'must go and be seen to go to persons in need of homes',[35] but local authorities themselves were subject to a more rigid system of loan sanctions, and the maximum size and cost of council housing was also strictly regulated. These controls were designed to ensure an equitable distribution of limited resources, but they were the cause of much local frustration. The 275 dwellings allocated for 1955 were 'far below the number of houses the Council are able to build',[36] but despite all the difficulties and delays, almost 3,000 new council dwellings were built in the ten years after 1945. Around 1,000 more were provided by private builders, and many existing properties brought to a habitable standard with the aid of Improvement Grants, payable under an Act of 1949. There was virtually no increase in population in Northampton between 1951-61, and slum clearance schemes apart, the main task was to ease the over-crowding which had resulted from wartime conditions. In 1951 over 3,000 dwellings in the town housed more than one family, but in 1957 the Council concluded that, once the 2,000 homes in the pipeline were completed, these needs would be very largely satisfied.[37]

More resources were in future directed to improving and renovating existing properties; but as the Housing Committee had warned soon after the war, quantity was not the only consideration. The 'greatest care must be taken to avoid the mistakes of the past . . .', it wrote in 1947, for the 'present urgency for houses will be largely forgotten in ten years. Whilst at the moment we are being judged by the number of houses we are building, we shall shortly be judged by the sort of houses we have built and the environment we have created'.[38] Despite being faster to build than traditional brick dwellings, pre-fabricated steel and concrete houses were still considered out of keeping with Northampton's overall appearance, and only a relatively small number were erected.[39] However, much more attention was now paid to the design of new estates and facilities beyond the housing itself. On the Dallington Fields estate, for instance, the largest post-war development, 'care has been taken not only to provide all the amenities necessary to a community of some 5,000 persons, but also to place them in the most appropriate positions in the layout.'[40] Surrounding open spaces were preserved for recreation, and Dallington village itself was spared an onslaught of traffic from a nearby industrial estate by re-routing a proposed new road to Kingsthorpe.

An experimental 'neighbourhood unit' was also built on part of the Dallington site at Kings Heath, to the design of the Borough Architect Mr. J. Lewis Womersley. The dwellings themselves, crescents of three-storey terraced houses and small blocks of flats, were grouped around 'pedestrian piazzas', sizeable open areas producing an overall effect 'somewhat reminiscent of Georgian times'. The design, which was awarded the Bronze Medal of the Royal Institute of British Architects, also embraced 16 shops, three nursery schools, an infants', junior and secondary school, community centre, cinema, two pubs, and Anglican and Nonconformist churches.[41] Mr. Womersley and his deputy Mr. G. Hopkinson had earlier taken first place in a 'Low-Cost Housing Competition' sponsored by *The Builder*, to design a three-bedroom terraced house costing under £1,000. Space was saved by omitting the conventional 'through-passage' and the hall 'which has, through the centuries, retained such a firm place . . . despite the differences in requirements between the Manor and Mansion House of the erstwhile nobility and the present-day cottage-home of the ordinary citizen'. A second W.C. was considered 'a luxury the nation cannot afford at the present time', but the living areas fell below the minimum space requirements for public housing, and the design was utilised instead by private builders.[42]

On the Eastfields estate near the Manfield Hospital a higher than average amount of space was devoted to schools, clinics, playing fields and other amenities, intended to serve not only areas of new council housing but those of adjacent private inter-war development. By contrast with the perfect symmetry of the Kings Heath development, however, the layout of the Sunnyside estate to the north of Kingsthorpe was a model of asymmetrical ingenuity. Sunny as they were, the slopes on which it was sited presented considerable difficulties of development, but here as elsewhere there was also an attempt to substitute 'visual interest' for inter-war uniformity. In part this was a matter of varying the external appearance of similar types of housing — bay windows at St David's, porticos 'with a touch of Georgian romanticism' at Kings Heath — and breaking up the general aspect with hedges and trees. On most estates, however, there was also a mix of different types of dwellings, with blocks of two- and three-bedroom houses now liberally interspersed with maisonettes, flats and one-bed bungalows.

These reflected changing demographic trends and demand for particular types of housing. Over the country as a whole, average family size declined from 4.2 in 1930 to 3.2 in 1955, and less than half of all families in the latter year had children under the age of sixteen. More people were living into old age — around a quarter of Northampton's population in 1964 was aged 65 or over — and more married women were working outside the home. These factors translated into a need for more smaller dwellings, more labour-saving internal arrangements, and fewer gardens 'for the children to play in'. Around 80% of all applicants on the waiting list for council housing in Northampton in 1959 were seeking one or two-bed dwellings, but at the initial urging of the Public Assistance Committee, 10% of new dwellings on each post-war estate consisted of one-bed flats or bungalows for the elderly. There was also a growing need for accommodation for the infirm or less mobile elderly. Those in need of nursing were still cared for at St Edmund's Hospital, but by 1960 five residential homes had been provided for those capable of a more independent existence, untainted by past associations with the Workhouse. Many more were able to continue in their homes with the support of domiciliary welfare services — district nurses, Home Helps, 'Meals-on-Wheels' — at a fraction of the cost of residential care.

Multi-storey housing was otherwise seen as the main solution to changing future needs and pressure on land. The 10-storey St Katherine's Court, which won an award from the Civic Trust in 1961, was the first such housing to be built in Northampton, followed in 1963 by the 12-storey Claremont House and Beaumont House. St Katherine's Court was built at a cost of £90,000 on the site of the 'Boroughs', the innermost residential areas of the town where the inhabitants had been in the custom of electing their own 'Mayor' in annual imitation of the official municipal elections. 'In common with His Worship at the Guildhall, he wore the cocked hat and all the requisite appendages to his dignified station', and the two exchanged cordial telegrams of congratulation. The source of much general merriment, this tradition no doubt originated as a mocking gesture on the part of the voteless, but 'his job was no sinecure . . . the mock Mayor took some of his duties very seriously, and though he could not help his 'subjects' with his pocket, he was always ready to assist neighbours who needed the help of one better-educated and more experienced than themselves'.[43]

Poorly-housed as the residents of such areas might be, the break-up of this sort of 'community spirit' through clearance schemes was often much regretted, and where possible the Council did try to provide new dwellings on the site of the old. It also employed Housing Welfare Officers to advise on a range of problems and to liaise with other welfare agencies. Almost 4,000 domiciliary visits were made by them in 1959, to 'problem families', elderly tenants, and to those complaining of un-neighbourly behaviour on the part of their neighbours. In March that year the Council had over 8,400 dwellings under its control, but only one tenant was more than three weeks in arrears with rent, and evictions were now very rare indeed.[44] A notice to quit usually had the desired effect on persistent offenders or defaulters, and was then withdrawn, but the low level of rent arrears at this time is testimony in part to the relative affluence of the later 1950s, the era of 'You've never had it so good' based on increasing levels of production and employment and rising real wages. Along with the redistribution of wealth by way of welfare benefits, this produced a more equitable distribution of income than in the pre-war years. By now, however, lower paid council tenants in Northampton also had access to a rent rebate scheme.

This Differential Rent Scheme, as it was known, was devised in 1955 under pressure of the Housing Subsidies Act of the same year. In part, the Act aimed to encourage more multi-storey housing by means of more generous subsidies. Six-storey flats for slum clearance re-housing, for instance, were to carry a subsidy of £50 per dwelling for 60 years, against the £22 1s. previously paid for all types of housing, and the £10 subsidy now proposed for 'low-rise' housing for general needs. These were quite persuasive figures, but at the same time the rate support grants which eased the obligatory balancing of the Housing Revenue Account were abolished. Worth around £35,000 in Northampton, in the following year this feat was accomplished by relieving the General Rate Fund of over £28,000.[45] The alternative was to recoup all or part of the deficit by increasing rents, which ranged at this time from 12s. 8d. a week for a one-bedroom bungalow to 18s. 10d. for a standard three-bedroom house. However, raising them to a level sufficient to cover anuual expenditure would have more than doubled them, pushing them well above the level which many could afford.

The object of the scheme was thus to secure the maximum possible from those who could pay, without placing an intolerable burden on those who could not. Rents were increased on average by 8s. a week, and rebates offered to those with gross incomes below a certain level, initially £6 a week. Such schemes often evoked memories of the hated 'Means Test' and were reluctantly taken up, but in March 1959 over a fifth of all council tenants in Northampton were receiving rebates averaging 6s. 9d. a week.[46] Some were not 'having it so good' as others, but so well had the Council judged the circumstances of many of its tenants that in the first full year of the scheme's operation, the Housing Revenue Account showed a surplus of over £42,000. However, these financial adjustments also put a temporary stop to another manifestation of working-class affluence — the sale of council houses to sitting tenants.

This was authorised under the the Conservative Housing Act of 1952, but there was no 'Right to Buy' such as that conferred in 1980. Flats, shops and pre-fabs were excluded from the scheme, and purchasers were required to pay the full market price for their houses, with no discounts for prior occupation. In Northampton prices ranged from £495-1,000 in 1953 according to type, and the Council also offered mortgages of up to 95% of the total over a maximum period of 30 years.[47] In fact, many purchasers borrowed a lower proportion over a shorter period, using accumulated savings to pay off part of the capital at the outset. The Labour party was opposed on principle to the sale of public housing, but for three of the four years between 1952-55 the Conservatives held a majority in the Council, and they promoted the scheme quite vigorously. A total of 292 houses were sold — one was subsequently re-purchased — but the fewer the rent-payers, the higher the average level of rent which would have to be charged under the Differential Rent Scheme, and the sales were thus discontinued. They were resumed in 1959 under new legislation, but dwindled away under pressure of higher selling prices and the delicate political balance between the parties in the Council in the early 1960s.

The growing number of garages built for rent on municipal estates were a further sign of the higher standard of living which many of the working classes were now enjoying, as were the television aerials appearing on council dwellings: more than 3,000 in 1955 and over 1,000 more within little over a year.[48] The cinema — along with the art if conversation, so it was widely said — was the main casualty of this extension of home-based entertainment. Six local cinemas closed down between 1956 and '63, among them the Coliseum, the Ritz, and the Temperance Hall, reputedly the oldest surviving cinema in Britain. The New Theatre in Abington Street was also demolished in 1960 as part of a central redevelopment scheme, but in November 1963 the ABC cinema was packed to swooning and screaming capacity when it played host to the Beatles. Teenagers were now major consumers in their own right — of live entertainment and pop records, of the delights of 'milk-bars' with their juke-boxes and the 'nastiness of their modernistic knick-knacks', and of new and ever-changing fashions.

In the eyes of many, these things spoke not only of creeping 'Americanisation' but of rebellion against all things conventional, of a crumbling of traditional authority and moral values. There is no doubt that a more equitable distribution of wealth did go some way to erode distinctions of class and to create a more open and tolerant society, but it did not entirely abolish them any more than it abolished poverty itself.[49] However, said one local clergyman in 1964 in response to pleas to move with the times, there was a place for everything, and the place for 'Yeah, Yeah, Yeah' was in the Youth Club and not the church itself. Instead of singing 'the same long drawn-out hymns every Sunday', some teenage correspondents of the *Chronicle and Echo* had asked, was it not possible 'to put the words we sing to modern tunes with a beat'? 'Of course they are right! We do need a few changes', admitted one Methodist minister, 'Revolutionary changes are being suggested — Latin into English, tambourines to guitars . . . [but] the Church isn't here to be popular, but to do a job . . . I cannot minister in a church tied to the Top Ten, up and down like a yo-yo . . .'.[50]

Youth clubs included, the churches remained a focus of many social activities, but formal observance continued to decline, and the de-population of the central areas of the town led to the merger of some parishes or congregations: Castle Hill with Commercial Street, Queen's Road Methodist Chapel with Kettering Road, and St Sepulchre with St Andrew. St Katherine's church was demolished in 1950, its place taken by Memorial Gardens which in 1952 came to house 'Northampton's most pilloried work of art', the statue 'Woman with Fish' by the sculptor Frank Dobson. The Fish, 'a creature of improbably gargantuan proportions', was the main object of criticism, but in 1965 the Woman herself was beheaded by vandals. However, some new churches and chapels were opened on suburban estates, among them St Augustine's at King's Heath and a Congregationalist chapel at Headlands. Temporarily much enlarged during the war by evacuees and Italian and German prisoners of war, the Roman Catholic population of Northampton had been steadily increasing, and along with an extension to the Cathedral in the 1950s, new Catholic churches were also built at Duston, Dallington and Kingsthorpe.

The question of Sunday games continued to rumble on for some time after the war. 'The average Northamptonian is bewildered', wrote the *Independent* of the Council's decision in 1950 to allow them in summer but not in winter.[51] Where was the logic in this? Fears of the 'Continental Sunday', of the growing practice of treating the Sabbath like any other day, were cited in explanation. Following a public vote in favour, the cinemas were now permitted to open on Sundays, and this seasonal limitation of Sunday games was in the way of a 'not too much too soon' concession to the general trend. In any event, the Council itself was hardly any less bewildered than the public by the legalities of Sunday games. There was, the Town Clerk pointed out in 1948, no statute or bye-law which directly prohibited the playing of football in the municipal parks on Sundays, and 'provided that they do not erect posts and flags and provided that they do not obstruct, disturb or annoy other persons using the park', and provided they played on a properly marked-out pitch, the Council had no powers to prevent it. On the other hand, it had no powers either to override the provisions of the Sunday Observance Act of 1625. The Act prohibited people from meeting outside their own parishes on Sundays 'for any sports and pastimes whatsoever' and while it 'has not been invoked for a very long time, it remains on the statute book and could be used if anyone felt disposed to do so.'[52]

Offenders were liable to a fine of 3s. 4d., roughly half the cost of hiring a football pitch in the park, and considerably less than the cost of prosecuting them. The Council did not feel disposed to invoke it, and in due course gave its blessing to winter games on Sundays too. Sports apart, the parks continued to host Sunday band concerts, weekday evening dances and a whole variety of regular or occasional entertainments. In the 1940s and '50s, 'Holiday at Home' programmes were arranged for the summer industrial holiday, including Punch and Judy shows, sports competitions and, in 1948, an open-air Shakespearean performance by the Northampton Drama Club in the courtyard of Abington House.[53] Along with an Industries and Trades Exhibition staged by the Chamber of Commerce, Festival of Britain Week in 1951 was celebrated with bands and displays, and the coronation of Her Majesty Queen Elizabeth II in 1953 with a procession of illuminated boats and searchlight and firework displays in Becket's Park, the former Cow Meadow re-named thus in 1935. In 1946 the Council also purchased Delapre Abbey and 586 acres of land from the Bouverie estate. The latter too became a municipal park, while the Abbey itself was leased to a succession of different bodies before it came to house the Northamptonshire Record Office in 1957.

Some 40% of the land within the borough in 1958 was still devoted to parks, woodland and allotments, and as one visitor noted in that year, Northampton still retained the role and much of the atmosphere of a country market town. One of 'the few cities of 100,000 inhabitants in Britain where a rise and fall in the price of cattle or grain or pigs can set a lot of tongues chattering excitedly in the town pubs', he wrote, 'where a crowded city skyline can be seen over the backs of prize cattle; where a five minute walk from the Town Hall can bring you to the edge of miles of almost unbroken countryside'. Over 200,000 animals passed through the Cattle Market each year and 10,000 sheep were bought and sold at the September Ram Fair alone. Moreover, the Council had its own municipal farm — 'and makes a profit from the venture' — and the annual agricultural show, one of the largest in the country, was sponsored by one of the giants of local industry, British Timken. Northampton's rural aspects, as the author concluded, 'have not only survived. They play a notable part in the appearance and activities of the town'.[54]

Nevertheless, its commercial and industrial functions consumed more space with every passing year. Almost half the 1,200 acres of agricultural land within the borough were scheduled for other purposes under the 1951 Development Plan. An obligatory requirement of the Town and Country Planning Act of 1947, this was a 20-year scheme for reconstruction and improvement which would be, as its architects rightly anticipated, much subject to 'changing economic circumstances, both local and national'. Housing and central road improvements were among the priorities identified by its authors, along with the need to attract new industries to the town, for unless the local footwear industry could increase its share of national output, unless there was a large increase in domestic consumption or demand for exports, it would continue to shed its labour — and 'none of these possibilities is likely'.[55]

Footwear rationing ended in 1948, but by the 1950s domestic consumers had a wider range of other goods on which to spend their disposable income. Moreover, in 1951 Northampton and the county were already producing 80% of all British footwear, and both were facing fierce all-round competition from foreign manufacturers. In the meantime, new machinery and productive methods continued to increase productivity and reduce the need for labour. In the post-war period these included conveyor belts for moving work within the factory, 'slip-lasting' — a process by which the sole was cemented onto a soft sock stitched to the upper — and the use of adhesive soles and vulcanised soles and heels, the latter moulded onto leather uppers. Time- as well as labour-saving, vulcanisation was said to reduce the number of processes involved in attaching soles to uppers from 39 to seven, and total production time from four days to one.

Such innovations demanded greater technical and scientific expertise on the part of manufacturers and managers, but they often added to the already monotonous nature of the shoemakers' work. 'His job becomes more and more automatic, uninteresting and exacting', wrote N.U.B.S.O. General Secretary George Chester of this trend in the 1930s: 'There is no creative joy; no sense of satisfaction in the expression of craft; no anticipation of a satisfactory completed product . . . An industry without a sense of joy in production becomes soulless'.[56] 'I used to say . . . .', recalled one local shoemaker, '"Why do these people run when they leave the factory?" and me mother used to say, "Well, you'll find out when you work in one!" and the fact was that they worked so hard, so repetitiously, that when they put the tools down they couldn't stop them . . .'.[57] However, changes in productive processes also continued to erode earlier differences of income and status between shoe workers. As one delegate put it to the N.U.B.S.O. annual conference in 1953: 'We are all one happy family now'.

Most of the labour displaced by new machinery or methods was in fact male, and the already high proportion of female shoe workers continued to grow. Over the industry as a whole women accounted for 35% of the labour force in 1924, 42% in 1935, and 46% in 1951. This increase was also linked to public demand for more intricate styles of footwear and a higher demand for closers in turn. This was particularly true of women's fashion footwear, which in 1951 accounted for 30% of Northampton's total output against 20% in 1945. Between 1951-75, however, the numbers employed in the Northampton trade declined from 15,437 to 5,548, in the associated leather trades from 1,777 to 803. The number of footwear manufacturers in the town also fell from 55 in 1952 to 37 in 1964. Small and large concerns — those with under 200 or over 500 employees — generally survived better than those of medium size. The former were often old established family firms catering for localised markets, less vulnerable to competitive pressures than to the death of a proprietor and the absence of an heir able or willing to continue the business. The latter were better equipped to meet new demands for capital or specialist knowledge, and often had risk-spreading interests in other areas of manufacture, not uncommonly in engineering.

The same trend is evident in other centres of footwear manufacture during this period, as is the tendency towards amalgamations and takeovers. Only seven new firms were founded in the East Midlands between 1957-80, but in the former year 37% of the labour force were employed in companies later taken over by others. Several were absorbed by the British Shoe Corporation, the creation of the property millionaire Charles Clore, who took over the Sears True-Form company in 1953. Founded in 1891 by J. G. Sears, it was headed between 1916-49 by W. T. Sears, a long-serving County Councillor and J.P. who also had a stud farm at Weston Favell. In due course B.S.C. also embraced Manfield's along with such other household names as Dolcis, Saxone and Freeman Hardy and Willis, while in 1964 Barratt's became a part of the Leeds-based Stylo group of the Ziff family. The main target of these new entrepreneurs was the extensive retailing outlets of established firms, outlets for cheap footwear imported from the Far East and Eastern Europe.

Production itself was 'rationalised' by closing some premises and concentrating manufacture in others. More labour was shed in the process, but many manufacturers were no happier than their workers about the direction the industry was now taking. The single-minded pursuit of profits which characterised B.S.C. affronted a deep sense of pride in their product, a firmly-held belief that — for all the automation applied to its making, the lack of 'creative joy' felt by the makers themselves — a shoe was still a work of art and not simply a means of making money. 'They are stuck on making shoes as their fathers and mothers did', said one so-called 'money man' of these 'shoe men': 'They will never go forward . . . they always want something else to change to accommodate them'.[58] This was as much of an exaggeration as some of the statements which issued from the other side, but love could sometimes be blinkered if not blind. It was 'a great relief to me', said one 'shoe man' when his Chairman's plans to diversify into the clothing trade fell through, for 'I couldn't see what this had to do with shoes'. Nor was shoemaking ever entirely carried on 'for the glory of making shoes and not for the economic necessity of making a profit', but the very extremes of language on both sides testifies to the mental gulf between them: between those who made 'good shoes which they could be proud of', and those who were, in their own words, 'going to make money instead of shoes'.[59]

'We may soon have a problem of "surplus men"', wrote the *Independent* in 1947: 'from a man's point of view the scales are becoming increasingly weighted in favour of women'.[60] There was in fact little long-term unemployment among adult males in Northampton, or indeed in Britain as a whole, during the 1940s and '50s. The average unemployment rate rarely rose above 3%, by contrast with the 10% or more of the pre-war years, and such were the shortages in some areas and industries that female labour was in ever-increasing demand. One consequence of this, in the words of the *Independent*, was an 'upsurge of feminine assertion'. 'Northampton Women Demand New Status' it reported in May 1947: 'No More "Sink and Washtub" wives . . . it is nothing less than an all-round demand by women for an entirely new place and status in the affairs of the nation'.[61] Some thought they had already earnt it through their wartime contribution. Indeed, 'most of them are tired of hearing of their efficiency, their steadiness of hand and nerve, their readiness for sacrifice . . . it has all happened before. One has only to look through old newspaper files to find that statesmen and leaders of industry were giving the same somewhat astonished praise to women twenty-five years ago'.[62]

Most were quickly replaced by men once the war was over. Female employees in the Council's Transport Department were declared 'redundant' in March 1946 and discharged with a letter of thanks and a social event organised by the Transport Manager Mr. Cameron, for 'in view of the arduous nature of the work performed by the women during the war period, some little additional recognition of their service was fitting'.[63] However, the British loss of life from the Second World War was much less severe than the First, and there were now potential husbands enough for those women who wanted one. Those offered nothing more attractive than 'a lifetime spent between the sink and the washtub' could negotiate better terms or find a more enlightened suitor, or they could take one of the 'still more alternatives to marriage' offered by the post-war economy. There were no 'surplus women' now; but as the 'average' females consulted by the *Independent* pointed out, until women were paid the same wages as men for the same work, until they were 'taught with the idea that they will be doing "a job of work"', the scales would still be weighted against them.

Some 60% of all women of working age in Northampton were in paid employment in 1966,[64] but 'the greater the variety . . . the more remote is the possibility that all or a major part of the area's industries will hit the skids at the same time', and the post-war Council was as anxious as its predecessors to promote a more diverse economic structure. This was coupled with a policy of encouraging manufacturers to move production beyond the central areas of the town. The number of footwear factories in inner areas did in fact decline alongside the fortunes of the industry itself, and while some were taken over by other manufacturing concerns, others were in due course demolished or converted into warehouses or offices. However, the Council's policy was also linked to plans to redevelop the town centre, raising the spectre of Compulsory Purchase Orders and stimulating an advance outward movement. Few such Orders were necessary, but others were more directly persuaded to move by the refusal of planning permission for expansion on central sites. They were, on the other hand, offered somewhere else to go. The Council and private developers between them provided several specialist industrial estates, separated from residential and commercial developments, at Kings Heath and St James's, on the Thornton Estate at Kingsthorpe, and on the Bedford and Weedon Roads.[65]

These estates were intended not only for local firms, but for the new industries which the Council hoped to attract to Northampton. By 1970 many of their occupants were in fact newcomers to the town, but once again the Council's efforts were hindered by central policies to encourage growth in economically-depressed areas. Industrial Development Certificates were a main tool of this policy. Generously dispensed to companies wishing to locate in economically depressed areas, they were difficult to obtain in those of relative prosperity, Northampton included. Despite the continuing decline of the footwear industry, the local unemployment rate was consistently below the national average, and it was by this rather than the unbalanced nature of local industry that its needs were judged by government. The most the Council could do in the circumstances was provide for industrial growth as and when it occurred — by, for instance, acquiring new land for industrial development through an extension of the borough boundaries. First proposed in 1948 and again in 1959, when it encountered a vigorous 'Hands Off Duston' campaign led by the local parish council, this mainly west- and north-wards expansion was finally effected in 1965.

All this said, however, Northampton's economic structure did become rather more diverse in the post-war period. The service sector continued to expand, reducing the relative weight of manufacturing industry in the local economy. In 1965 it accounted for 54% of the total employed against 47% in 1951, a significant part of the increase attributable to local government, retailing and distributive services. It was well situated for the latter, and all the more so once the Northampton section of the M1 motorway was opened in 1959. Beyond the service sector, the trend towards consolidation in the brewing industry continued. Phipps and Co. merged with the Northampton Brewery Co. in 1957 to form the Phipps Northampton Brewery Co. Taken over in turn by Watney Mann in 1960, the latter was itself absorbed by Grand Metropolitan twelve years later. Brewing was a capital- rather than labour-intensive industry, but the printing and clothing trades continued to expand alongside smaller new or established industries, among them chemicals and toy-making.

However, the main area of growth was in engineering, and perverse as it may seem, by the mid-1960s this was a source of almost as much anxiety as the corollary decline of the footwear trade. A major employer of female as well as male labour, engineering accounted for some 8% of the occupied workforce in 1951. By 1958, though 'only by a negligible percentage' it had overtaken footwear as the main employer of manufacturing labour. In 1965, however, it employed some 17% of all occupied workers in the town, a higher proportion than the footwear and clothing industries combined. The diversity of its own products, from miniature models to motor and aeroplane components and electrical instruments, gave it some inbuilt protection; but exchanging heavy dependence on one industry for equally heavy dependence on another was not the objective at all, and in the Council's view prevention was far preferable to the cure which might be needed if local engineering firms began to 'hit the skids'.

It was a view supported in 1965 by the government-sponsored *Northampton, Bedford and North Bucks. Study*, which pointed to a clear need to 'broaden the base of overall employment

45. Map showing the extension of the Borough boundaries, published to mark the *Independent*'s 60th anniversary in 1965. The 1905 boundary shown here is in fact that of the 1901 extension, which embraced Kingsthorpe, St James's and Far Cotton.

and increase the range of possibilities'.[66] Otherwise known as the 'Sub-City Regional Plan', this was one of several studies into means of relieving population congestion in south-eastern England, where some 17 million people were now concentrated in an area of around 10,000 square miles. The method envisaged here was the expansion of a 'necklace' of existing towns to counter the 'pull' of London, but it had yet to be published when, in February 1965 and along with Peterborough and Ipswich, Northampton learnt that it had been selected for development as a 'New Town'. The Borough Council had no prior notice of this announcement, made to the Commons by Minister of Housing Richard Crossman, but the decision was not entirely unexpected. Three years earlier the Town and Country Planning Association had suggested that Northampton could be expanded to take some of the 'overspill' from London, although one contemporary journal strongly disagreed. In its own opinion, Northampton was 'already big enough . . . mainly free from the pervasive influence of London and Birmingham, and the pace seems to remain civilised'.[67]

There was no need, it argued, for Northampton to encroach any further on the surrounding countryside, nor any point in risking the loss of its 'personality'. In the *South East Study* of 1964, however, Northampton was named as one of six towns 'which might provide scope for expansion on a considerable scale — of the order of 50,000 to 100,000 over and above the natural growth of each area'.[68] The order of expansion envisaged in 1965 was 70,000 incomers from the south-east region by 1981. Allowing for natural growth, this would bring its total population from 130,000 to 230,000 over the same period of time, and to around 260,000 by 1991. This was a massive rate of expansion, as unprecedented in the history of New Town developments as the machinery eventually devised to accomplish it. The broad basis of this was stated in the Minister's statement in February 1965. A New Town development corporation would be set up to work with the Borough Council — but the terms were still negotiable, the physical boundaries of Greater Northampton had yet to be drawn, and the objections had yet to be heard.

Notes

 1. *N.I.*, 6 May 1949.
 2. Ibid.
 3. Ibid.
 4. Ibid.
 5. Northampton Labour Party, *Labour's First Budget* (1946).
 6. Four versions of the customary law of Northampton survive. See Lee, F., *Archives Leges Ville Norht: the Laws of the Town of Northampton* (1951).
 7. *Labour's First Budget*, op.cit.
 8. Ibid.
 9. National Assistance Act, 1 (1948).
10. Quoted in Fraser, D., *The Evolution of the British Welfare State* (1980 edn.), p.221.
11. *N.I.*, 30 Jan. 1948.
12. N.C.B.C., Health Report (1947).
13. Ibid. (1946).
14. Ibid. (1930).
15. N.C.B.C., Minutes of Special Committee re the Blind Persons Act 1920.
16. Ibid., Health Report (1948).
17. *Castle: Journal of Northampton N.A.L.G.O.*, 10 (Nov. 1953).
18. N.C.B.C., Minutes of Childrens' Committee, 7 Dec. 1960.
19. Ibid., Minutes of Secondary Education Sub-Committee, 2 June 1947.
20. *N.I.*, 8 July 1955.
21. Ibid.
22. *C.&E.*, cutting Dec. 1966, otherwise undated.
23. *N.I.*, 8 July 1955.

24. Ministry of Education Circular 94/46 (1946).
25. Quoted in Walmsley, D., *An Ever-Rolling Stream* (1989), p.111.
26. Report of Local Government Manpower Commission (1951).
27. N.C.B.C., Health Report (1947).
28. *C.&E.*, 1 June 1962.
29. *N.I.*, 6 May 1949.
30. N.C.B.C., Health Reports (1944; 1940).
31. *N.I.*, 21 May 1948.
32. N.C.B.C. Minutes, 7 Oct. 1946.
33. *N.I.*, 6 May 1949.
34. N.C.B.C., Town Clerk's Letter Book, 9 Nov. 1950.
35. Ministry of Health Circular 108/48 (1948).
36. N.C.B.C., Minutes of Housing Committee, 15 Nov. 1954.
37. Ibid., Report of Borough Treasurer on Suggested Capital Programme, 21 Oct. 1957.
38. N.C.B.C., Housing Exhibition leaflet, May 1947.
39. A total of 160 steel or concrete pre-fabricated houses (B.I.S.F., Orlit and D.S.I.R.) were built between 1945-60.
40. N.C.B.C., Housing Exhibition leaflet, op.cit.
41. *Municipal Journal* (4 July 1952). See also 'Kings Heath: a new community at Northampton', *The Builder* (30 Oct. 1951).
42. *The Builder* (23 Feb. 1951).
43. *N.I.*, 17 April 1909.
44. N.C.B.C., Minutes of Housing Committee, Housing Manager's Report, 3 Sept. 1959.
45. Ibid., Borough Treasurer's Report on Housing Subsidies Bill, 21 Nov. 1955; Borough Treasurer's Report on Housing Accounts, March 1957.
46. Ibid., Housing Manager's Report, 3 Sept. 1959.
47. Ibid., 15 Dec. 1952.
48. Ibid., Housing Manager's Reports, 19 Dec. 1955; 3 June 1957.
49. See, for instance, Coates, K., & Silburn, R., *Poverty: the Forgotten Englishmen* (1970).
50. *C.&E.*, 31 Jan. 1964.
51. *N.I.*, 3 Nov. 1950.
52. N.C.B.C. Minutes, 5 Jan. 1948.
53. Ibid., 5 April 1948.
54. Joseph, S. G., 'Northampton: the town-country relationship', *Official Architecture and Planning*, 21, 3 (March 1958).
55. N.C.B.C., Development Plan (1951).
56. Quoted in Fox, A., *History of the National Union of Boot and Shoe Operatives, 1874-1957* (1958).
57. N.B.C. Community Programme, *Northampton Remembers Boot and Shoe* (1988), p.46.
58. Mounfield, P. R., Unwin, D. J., & Guy, K., *Processes of Change in the East Midlands Footwear Industry* (1982), Ch.13.
59. Ibid.
60. *N.I.*, 23 May 1947.
61. Ibid.
62. Leutkens, C., *Women and a New Society* (1946), p.9.
63. N.C.B.C. Minutes, 13 March 1946.
64. *C.&E.*, 1 July 1966.
65. Roberts, J. M., 'Diversification and Decentralisation of Industry in Northampton', *East Midlands Geographer*, 7, 3 (June 1979).
66. Ministry of Housing, *Northampton, Bedford and North Bucks. Study* (1965).
67. 'Re-planning Northampton', *Architects' Journal* (3 Jan. 1962).
68. Ministry of Housing, *South East Study* (1964).

Chapter Eight

Full and Equal Partnership: 'New Town' Northampton

Whatever we do, we do in the face of 130,000 people — not 15 cows. The people are there — and they are real . . .

Dr. John Weston, first Chairman of the Northampton Development Corporation, quoted in
Northampton Chronicle and Echo, 2 December 1971

The government, the town council, the developers and even the people of the town have all conspired to make sure the eventual Northampton, for better or for worse, is quite different from what seemed a good idea in 1969 . . .

Northampton Chronicle and Echo: Building a Future, 15 May 1984

'If you wait for the authorities to build new towns', said the founder of the Garden Cities Association, Ebenezer Howard, 'you will be older than Methuselah before they start. The only way to get anything done is to do it yourself'.[1] The new town of Letchworth, founded in 1902, was the first fruit of this philosophy, followed soon after the First World War by Welwyn Garden City. Spaciously laid out amid green fields, free from the factory smoke of the towns and the functional ugliness of many of their buildings, Letchworth was intended to be a self-supporting community of some 30,000 people. Like similar ventures elsewhere, it was the product of a wider late 19th-century reaction against urban industrial society and all its alleged physical and social 'evils', one which manifested itself not only in a growing body of critical historical literature and poetical epitaphs on a lost 'civilisation', but in the birds and flowers of William Morris wallpapers and the 'rustic' design of Garden City dwellings themselves.

The 'do-it-yourself' approach to new towns had its limitations, however. The public were none too eager to invest in such novel ventures, the Letchworth shareholders had to wait 20 years for their first dividend, and the Welwyn project was only kept afloat by a loan from central government. It was finally completed by the Government itself after the Second World War to cater for some of the London 'overspill'. By then, however, as part of a national policy to regulate land use and urban growth and to secure a more even distribution of population, Government was committed to building new towns of its own. Directed by a new Ministry of Town and Country Planning, this strategy rested on three separate but related pieces of legislation. The National Parks and Access to the Countryside Act of 1949 was designed to preserve areas of open countryside as the 'lungs' of the cities; the Town and Country Planning Act of 1947 was mainly concerned with controlling the environment of existing towns; and the New Towns Act of the previous year with relieving the pressure on large centres of population and stimulating growth in other areas.

London was most in need of relief, and the first new towns to be designated under the Act — Stevenage, Crawley, Hemel Hempstead and Harlow, in that order — were all within 30 miles of the capital. The last of these 'Mark I' new towns was Corby, designated in 1950 and 80 miles distant. Here the main aim was to encourage a greater diversity of industry alongside the dangerously dominant steelworks, but in due course it too was intended to draw population from London. A second clutch followed in the early 1960s, among them Skelmersdale, to take the Merseyside overspill, and Cumbernauld and Livingston to cater for that of Glasgow. Along with Peterborough and Ipswich, Northampton was one of the 'Mark III' towns planned for later in the decade as attention turned back to the still congested south-east. 'Another kind of new town', as Richard Crossman described them, they were to be developed alongside one of a more traditional nature, albeit on the 'city' scale of an anticipated quarter of a million inhabitants.

Milton Keynes, that is; but although it would embrace Bletchley and two other existing small towns, it was still much in the 'green field' tradition of most previous New Town development. Such sites had the advantage of cheaper land and a relatively blank sheet when it came to planning them, but there were obvious advantages in expanding existing towns to take additional population. If on a lesser scale than that envisaged in Northampton and its fellow 'famous boroughs', it had been done before. Corby, Hemel Hempstead and the Essex town of Basildon had populations of 15-25,000 before their own New Town designation. They also had roads, shops, schools, sewerage and water services and other necessary facilities, and it took less time to build on an existing infrastructure than to start from scratch. It was less true perhaps of Corby, no more than a small village until the steelworks were built in the 1930s, but established communities also had, in the planners' phrase, 'depth in time' — that intangible compound of history and tradition which gave them the 'atmosphere' often lacking in entirely new developments.

'Character, ethos and culture', as it was said of Northampton, but it had much more to offer than this. Good communications, for instance, in the form of the two miles distant M1 motorway, and although it remained on a loop line — 'a legacy from a Victorian landowner's keep-out attitude', wrote the *Architects' Journal*, doing its bit to perpetuate the old myth[2] — it was little more than an hour by rail from London. The local unemployment rate in the early 1960s was well below the national average, and there were persistent shortages of labour in some sectors of the economy. Unexpanded Northampton was already capable of supporting a higher level of population. With the planned expansion, it had the potential to absorb an unprecedented number of newcomers within a time-scale which was, by previous standards of New Town development, very short indeed.

This form of development, it will be seen, posed particular challenges of its own; but no matter their type or where they were built, New Towns would certainly make more inroads into the countryside. An 'enormous land grab', cried a leading article in the journal of the Northamptonshire branch of the National Farmers' Union: 'The farmer will be the one to suffer most. He immediately loses his raw material, the land. This would be bad enough if he were to be paid very generous compensation . . . But under present compensation arrangements, he gets a mere pittance, and is presumably supposed to console himself with the knowledge that he is doing good to 70,000 or more Londoners . . .'. Then there was 'all the sentimental nonsense produced by planners about the need for access to the countryside for the teeming masses. So those who have not had their land taken away will have it trampled on by the 70,000 Londoners dumped into Northampton and encouraged to get out of it again into the remaining vestiges of the countryside. What a crazy world!'.[3]

The area finally designated for expansion was progressively reduced from the 23,750 acres originally anticipated to 21,280 following objections from the County Council, and to 19,952 after a Public Enquiry in October 1967. It included the recently-extended County Borough itself, which accounted for roughly half of it, with the greater part of the remainder lying to the south and east. In some cases, however, the proposed boundaries cut right through existing farms, threatening to leave their occupants with too little land to return a living. Separating a farmer from his Dutch barn and his corn dryer, one complained, was without 'rhyme or reason . . . With a farm, you should take the lot or leave it alone'.[4] Powers of compulsory purchase within a designated area had a limited timespan and would not inevitably be used, but the mere prospect was enough to deter new investment. It was 'utterly useless', said another, 'to spend money . . . on buildings that may not last 10 years'.[5] And what of the agricultural labourers displaced not only from their jobs but from the homes still often 'tied' to them? In Northamptonshire as a whole their numbers had fallen by some 50% since 1950, but farming was still 'a way of life to many of them, and they are not just waiting to go into other industries'.[6]

Both the N.F.U. and the National Union of Agricultural Workers claimed that the quality of much land had been underestimated. This was a complex issue, but in Ipswich, where no less than seven alternative plans were considered before the Draft Designation Order was issued, expansion was scheduled on land classified by the Government's own consultants as of high agricultural value. Here, largely by impaling it on its undertaking to safeguard such land, the N.F.U. claimed a 'total victory', and the whole project was eventually abandoned.[7] There was still no denying that some agricultural land would have to be sacrificed to national housing needs, and as the N.F.U. acknowledged, victory in one area could ultimately be won only at the cost of another. The same argument could be applied to the rural villages embraced by Northampton's draft designated area, among them Wootton, Collingtree and Great and Little Billing. Opposition to expansion here was focused on the threat to their 'community spirit' and the possibility of industrial development. The Inspector conducting the 1967 Public Enquiry was 'particularly impressed . . . by the evidence of social activities, associations and organisations' which they presented, but while he thought every effort should be made to safeguard and encourage these, they remained within the area recommended and subsequently approved for expansion.[8]

What of the reaction from Northampton itself? 'Northampton as a large city fills me with dismay', wrote one resident of the preliminary planning proposals in 1966: 'Town planning and overspill populations may be a necessity, but there will be heartache for those who have lived in Northampton all their lives and love their home town . . . And for whom will there be prosperity? What difference will the new Northampton make to the average person?'.[9] Quite a lot, said the planners, in terms of new jobs, new trade and new community facilities. 'On paper', wrote another resident,

> the scheme for the expansion of Northampton paints the usual planners' rosy picture of a civic paradise flowing with milk and honey, while thousands of happy human beings, emancipated at last from their former restricted urban misery, dance endlessly round the magnificent maypole of Greater Northampton. The reality, unfortunately, will be a very different matter. Seventy thousand Londoners, all pushing and shoving to get the best positions for themselves, will be let loose on this unhappy area, out-manouvring the native population and ultimately submerging them as certainly as the Normans submerged the Saxons . . . Who owns this town anyway, the ratepayers of Northampton or a team of external planners and bureaucrats . . . ?[10]

This was mild by comparison with the reception accorded to the post-war Minister of Town and Country Planning, Lewis Silkin, by the inhabitants of Stevenage when presented with plans for a similar number of incomers. Greeted at a public meeting with cries of 'Dictator!' and 'Gestapo!', he emerged to find his car with four flat tyres and sand in the petrol tank.[11] However, Stevenage had a population of only 7,000 at the time, while Northampton's 130,000 was already close to double that of the anticipated number of newcomers. The 'Saxons' would not be easily submerged, and they already included innumerable immigrants from various areas of Britain and over 12 nationalities from beyond its own shores, among them West Indians, Greek and Turkish Cypriots, Poles and Italians.[12] Even so, this fear of a new unrecognisable Northampton, geared to the needs of the incomers rather than the established population, was perfectly natural and understandable, and something only time could really dispel.

It has been said, however, that the reaction of the majority of Northamptonians was no discernible reaction at all. 'After the first announcement that the town was destined for expansion', wrote the *Mercury and Herald*, 'enthusiasm on the part of some and opposition by others were noticeable, but gradually the dead hand of apathy settled on Northampton'.[13]

The general attitude towards this monumental and potentially revolutionary plan, wrote the local author Jeremy Seabrook, was one of 'benign indifference'. No doubt there were some among the 'silent thousands' who felt that the faceless 'THEY' had already made up their minds, and that any protest was a waste of breath and ink. This was not in fact the case, but so slowly did matters proceed that for long periods at a stretch there was no visible sign of them proceeding at all — and until there was something tangible to approve of or object to, it was really quite difficult to become emotional about it.

'A year of plans', wrote the *Chronicle and Echo* of 1966: plans to reorganise the educational system, plans for a southern relief road — 'better known as the Bridge-street crossing problem' — and the preliminary expansion plan itself. And 'little action', it added tartly.[14] The designation of a New Town always involved a lengthy process of consultation and enquiry, plan and counter-plan, reconsideration and revision, but at times even the Borough Council itself had no clear idea of what, if anything, was in motion. 'Around the summer of 1966', recalled the then Deputy Town Clerk Alan Parkhouse, 'a deadly stillness fell upon Whitehall. No longer were we urged to use the motorway. On the contrary, a slow train via Aberdeen would have been equally effective . . . Had the money run out? Was Northampton to be spared the trials and tribulations of acting as welcoming host to 70,000 newcomers from the metropolis?'.[15] No answers were forthcoming. The public spending cuts of that year, a change of Minister and some general re-thinking by the Labour government on the wisdom of 'Mark III' new towns were responsible for much of this deafening silence, but it was infinitely frustrating from the Council's own point of view. The work already in progress on the redevelopment of the town centre, including the southern relief road, had to be suspended pending a final decision on expansion, and 'with or without a further 70,000 people, Northampton's centre was crying out for redevelopment'.[16]

The Northampton New Town (Designation) Order was finally issued in February 1968, three years after Richard Crossman's first announcement to the Commons. In December that year the public was invited to view more detailed planning proposals at an exhibition at the Guildhall. Like the *Northampton, Bedford and North Bucks. Study* and the preliminary plans of 1966, these were the work of Hugh Wilson, ex-Chief Architect and Planning Officer to the Scottish new town of Cumbernauld, and J. Lewis Womersley, former Borough Architect of Northampton itself and more recently Architect to the Sheffield City Council. As the *Chronicle and Echo* pointed out, even these proposals had yet to be set in any kind of concrete. They were not 'THE PLAN', they were merely the planners' vision of how an expanded Northampton might look. Even the 1969 *Northampton Master Plan* itself was still open to adjustment and objection, although it roused little of the latter. However, wrote the *Chronicle and Echo* after viewing these earlier proposals, 'the building of the Greater Northampton now envisaged conjures up a task of such size, complexity and cost that the ordinary citizen must be forgiven if he wonders whether it can ever be accomplished'.[17]

If there was any typical reaction at all, it was this, not doubt so much as sheer 'it will never get off the drawing board' disbelief. The 'Bridge-street crossing problem' itself was regularly invoked in support of this view. Identified as a matter of urgency in the 1925 Development Plan, it remained unrelieved and as much 'a source of grievous irritation' as it was over 40 years earlier. What real chance then of building over 30,000 new houses, innumerable factories, warehouses and offices, two high-speed roads, a major sports centre, shopping centres and community centres, and of creating tens of thousands of new jobs within 13 years, at an estimated total cost of £327 million? A sample survey conducted in 1966 by the Institute of Community Studies suggested that, far from being apathetic or indifferent, many Northamptonians were positively in favour of the expansion plans. Almost 60% of those consulted approved or strongly approved, and only 11% held a definite contrary opinion — but few of them believed it could actually be done.

'I believe that the time-table is optimistic', said the Conservative councillor and shoe manufacturer J. T. Lewis in 1966, 'but I am informed that, provided finance is made available, it is physically possible to implement this programme'.[18] Money was critical, of course. The vexatious Bridge Street level crossing was largely a legacy of inter-war economies and post-war 'squeeze and freeze', and there was really a world of difference between a local authority doing what it could with limited finances and a government agency charged with getting something done. The question of who would pay for what was among those to be settled in the future, but the expectation of greater capital resources was one reason for the Council's own acceptance of the expansion plans. 'This is great news', said the Labour councillor Ron Dilleigh of the initial announcement in 1965, for it 'will enable us to do things we could not possibly afford otherwise'.[19]

Not all councillors were quite so enthusiastic, but few of them believed there was any real choice. If Northampton refused to co-operate, the planned expansion would almost certainly take place somewhere else within the same sub-region: Wellingborough, perhaps, or another green field Milton Keynes, still close enough to Northampton to have very damaging effects on its economy. The town did need the new industries, the new sources of non-manufacturing employment which would come with its own development, and if 'these proposals are rejected, we are accepting the status quo, restriction and ultimate stagnation. Others more enlightened will seize the glittering opportunities presented to us'.[20] The question was never put to a vote of the full Council, but in May 1965 it approved it in principle by setting up a Town Expansion Committee and giving it delegated powers to deal with matters arising from the proposals. Its eight members were equally divided between Conservatives and Labour and appointed for a three year term.[21]

The Council was almost as finely balanced in the early 1960s. One third of its members were still subject to annual re-election, and neither party enjoyed any security of tenure. So tight was the contest that in the 1964 municipal elections control came to rest on one single ballot paper in St George's ward. It bore two crosses, one for the Labour candidate and the other, partially crossed out, for the Liberal. The paper was not admitted, and the result was settled by placing the names of the Labour and Tory candidates in the Town Clerk's pocket in separate pepper-pots. That drawn out by the Returning Officer held the Conservative name, giving them the seat and a 25-23 majority in the Council, but this was reversed later in the year when an election court judged that the seat should go to Labour.[22] The re-drawing of the ward boundaries after the 1965 extension of the borough became the source of a protracted dispute, for the manner of their drawing could clearly influence the outcome of future elections. That year's elections were in fact delayed from May to November by an official enquiry, which confirmed an earlier decision by the Labour Home Secretary Frank Soskice to accept an alternative scheme put forward by Conservative councillors. The latter won the majority, but if town expansion was to be effectively carried out, then it could not become an arena for party political conflict. As the document setting out the bases of their relationship put it, both the Council and the body with which it was to work to accomplish the expansion must be of a 'single mind'.

Under the New Towns Acts of 1946 and 1965, this would normally be undertaken by a development corporation, a body very different in many ways from a local authority. Created by order of the relevant Minister — the Minister for Housing and Local Government at this time — its members were not elected but appointed by him. While required to 'have regard to the desirability of securing the services of one or more persons resident in or having special knowledge of the locality', and to consult first with the relevant local authorities, he was not legally obliged to appoint the one or take the advice of the other. The corporations had powers to make legal contracts, to purchase land compulsorily, and to build houses and roads. In effect, they were a statutory form of development company, responsible for the whole development within a designated area, but with the benefit of access to loans from central government. For that reason, they were also accountable to the public — not directly to the local community where their work was done, but by way of the Minister to Parliament itself. In practice, they enjoyed a high degree of independence in conducting their affairs, but unlike a local authority, they had a limited lifespan and 'one single objective'. Their task was to bring the new town into being, and then to hand it on to another authority.

The Minister of Housing himself, Richard Crossman, did not much care for them. They were 'autocratic', he said, and 'town development is essentially a local government affair . . . I like it better because it is responsible to elected bodies'.[23] Local authorities remained responsible for the normal statutory services in a New Town area, but like it or not, they really had too much else to do to undertake such large-scale development or expansion themselves. This was generally accepted, but the relationship between the elected local governors and the corporations themselves was central to the success or otherwise of the operation. Very often in the history of such developments it was one of rivalry, suspicion and resentment at the 'imposition' of a powerful body of 'outsiders'. By one development corporation, said Crossman, he was taken to see '*their* housing, and shown how much better it was than the Urban District Council housing', while elsewhere 'there is a tremendous row between the corporation and the U.D.C. because the master plan just published shows that the whole present town centre is due for demolition and will be replaced by a new one a mile away . . . The U.D.C. felt the usual hate and suspicion of the corporation with their brand new offices, their big salaries and their air of being the feudal masters'.[24]

Such extreme high-handedness was really quite rare, but local authorities themselves could be uncooperative or downright obstructive, if for no other reason than to demonstrate to the electorate that they still exercised some power over events. Local self-respect and a sense of identity both reposed to some extent in the local governing body, and if it surrendered its place too lightly, they would not suffer it to be re-elected. This could be true even of a small rural district council with a relatively brief history, but in an ancient borough like Northampton with a centuries-old tradition of local self-government there was infinitely more room for potentially destructive conflict. The machinery of the New Towns Act 1965 would have to be employed in expanding the town. There was no real alternative to this, but there was no question in the minds of the Council that it would have to be modified. The imposition of an unelected development corporation with the powers usual to such bodies in Northampton would quite simply be politically unacceptable.

Any such course, as the Ministry itself was well aware, would also be attended by very real practical difficulties and dangers. A 'new' town could not simply be tacked onto an established community. Their services had to be integrated, and new development had to proceed alongside redevelopment and improvement in existing areas. There had to be a comprehensive view of the whole, and a co-ordinated approach to creating it. The type of industries attracted to an expanded town, for instance, could change its whole character. The new population also had to be integrated with the old. As the *Northampton Master Plan* put it in 1969, 'the introduction of new population on a large scale must not result in two competing towns', but unless the local authority and the development corporation itself worked closely and co-operatively together, this was quite likely to be the undesirable outcome.

These and other points were put by Cllr. Ron Dilleigh, Chairman of the Finance Committee, at a meeting in March 1965 between Borough councillors and officers and a team from the Ministry of Housing, headed by its Permanent Secretary, Dame Evelyn Sharp. The Council, he said, would have no objection to a development corporation if its powers were limited to to the compulsory purchase of land. This could then be released to the Council and private developers, but it would otherwise prefer to undertake the expansion itself, with the aid of loans and a direct grant from the government itself. 'What you fear', replied Dame Evelyn, 'is that because a development corporation is the Ministry's child then in the event of a dispute the Minister might be tempted to arbitrate in favour of its own child'. This was true enough : but 'our objection to your proposal is that it involves money from us which we wouldn't get back'.[25] She doubted too that the Council could do the work at the necessary pace. Houses would have to be built at the rate of 3,000 a year, for instance, more than double the rate of past new town developments.

Nevertheless, there was clearly a need for a different kind of approach in Northampton, a new kind of arrangement to ensure, in Richard Crossman's words, that 'the relationship between corporation and authority should be one not of domination, but full and equal partnership'.[26] The terms of this relationship were set out in an 'Agreed Memorandum' in May 1965. It had no legal force and was very much a statement of what was 'hoped', and what the bodies involved 'might like' to do — but the 'object all through should be to get a common approach', and it 'will be clear that the Corporation and the County Borough Council will have to work in closest harmony'. The whole existing borough would be included in the designated area. Development corporations were able to purchase land within such an area more cheaply than on the open market, and it 'could be very helpful to the County Borough Council if the Corporation could exercise this power on their behalf in the old town'.

The Corporation, however, 'would not exercise their acquisition or development powers in the existing town except at the request of, or in agreement with, the County Borough Council'. The unelected, in other words, would not touch the 'old' town without the sanction of the elected. This was a point of some political importance. The public would not look kindly on any other arrangement; but if the Council itself wished to build in the new area, 'no difficulty should arise over that'. In due course it would reap new rate income from expansion, but in practice services would have to be provided in advance of the increase in rateable value, placing additional burdens on existing ratepayers. To avoid this, the Corporation 'would be prepared' to contribute to the cost of the local authority services required for the expansion, but both would eventually bear an broadly equal part of the final costs of expansion. And so far as the members of this still non-existent body were concerned, 'the Minister would think it appropriate that the personnel of the Corporation should be agreed between himself and the County Borough Council . . . the County Borough Council has particularly asked for four representatives'.[27]

The Northampton Development Corporation was established in September 1968 under the chairmanship of Sir William Hart C.M.G., recently retired Director-General of the Greater London Council. Four of its eight remaining members — two Conservatives, two Labour — were in fact members of the original Town Expansion Committee: Councillors Ron Dilleigh and J. T. Lewis, ex-Councillor Carol Trusler, and Alderman J. B. Corrin, Chairman of the Anglia Society, the successor by way of the Town and County Benefit Building Society to the 19th-century Freehold Land Society. Among its other members were the County Councillor Humphrey Cripps, and Roland Freeman, a member of the Greater London Council. As Sir William pointed out, they were there not as representatives of other interested bodies, but as 'the best people to undertake the task of expanding Northampton'. 'Partnership' was the word which governed their relations with the Council itself, but as Richard Crossman observed, this required 'more than a platitudinous declaration of intent. It requires a clear understanding between the parties as to their roles and functions, and a close day-to-day working together of officers at all levels'.[28]

Development corporations normally appointed a full range of professional, technical and administrative staff to undertake their work, directed overall by a General Manager.

The first General Manager of the Northampton Development Corporation was Dr. John Weston, formerly Director of the Building Research Station, who was appointed early in 1969. Other senior staff were appointed soon afterwards: Gordon Redfern as Chief Architect, a post he had formerly held with the Cwmbran Development Corporation; Basil Bean, a one-time assistant borough treasurer, as Chief Finance Officer; and Leslie Austin-Crowe, nine years with the Harlow Development Corporation and seven at Basingstoke, as Chief Estates Officer. Engineering, legal and housing management departments would normally have been established as well, but in a town the size of Northampton much of the requisite experience and expertise were already available through the Borough Council. There was little point in duplicating them, and much to be gained in terms of 'close and effective relations', by a sharing of staff and responsibilities between the two bodies.

It was thus agreed that the Corporation's engineering work, both planning and construction itself, would be carried out on a fee basis by the Borough Engineer's Department. Similarly, the Town Clerk's Department would handle its legal business, charging the normal private practice fee for all work undertaken, and the Housing Department would manage its housing, collecting the rents and maintaining the properties. The Borough Treasurer's Department provided facilities for its accounting staff, but its own Chief Financial Officer advised it on financial matters. When the Corporation came to be wound up and its assets transferred, there would be a negotiated settlement with the Council, and in the circumstances it was inappropriate for the Borough Treasurer himself to advise it. By 1972 the full-time equivalent of around 100 Council staff were engaged on work for the Corporation, but it was the Corporation's Chief Estates Officer who took on the crucial task of attracting new industry and other employment to Northampton. More will be said of this later, but it was clearly sensible to have one officer dealing with the disposal of sites for industrial and commercial development, whether in the Council's preserve of the 'old' town or beyond it. An incoming employer 'does not necessarily come in saying "I want to establish an office in the town centre or the expansion area". He says "I want an office in Northampton"', and shuffling him between two different agencies could well persuade him to take his jobs elsewhere.[29]

It was not without its tensions, but in Northampton 'partnership' did work. 'I emphasise the living spirit rather than the dead mechanics of the relationship', said Sir William Hart, 'In any partnership personal confidence and the ability to get on together are vital requirements. Fortunately we have them in Northampton. Of course we have had, and no doubt shall have in the future, our differences, but we are able frankly to discuss them and so far to resolve them. It is possible to co-ordinate the activities of an independent development corporation and a powerful democratically elected council given the will to succeed and the right personalities'.[30] There were 'close and cordial relations at all levels', noted the Corporation's Annual Report in 1970, but it took a little longer to dispel the public's own lingering suspicion of it, as it did to remove their doubt that anything would ever get off the drawing board and onto the ground.

In April 1970, however, work began on the first of the Corporation's housing estates, on Lumbertubs Lane in what was now known as the Eastern District. The area to the south of the town would constitute a second later phase of development. The Eastern District was intended to accommodate some 45,000 people and four Employment Areas — with commercial as well as industrial premises — and was scheduled for completion in 1977. The detailed plan was not approved until 1972, but the first Lumbertubs houses were occupied early in 1971. Designed by the Midlands Housing Consortium, they were built on a prefabricated timber frame, with a brick lower storey topped by timber cladding. They were faster to build than traditional brick dwellings, and of the same type used by the Council on its own most recent estate at Briar Hill, but the Lumbertubs Residents

46. Borough Council and (*below*) Development Corporation houses on the Briar Hill and Southfields Estates.

Association for one did not like them at all. 'We are not snobs, but we are wondering what class of people we are going to get on our doorstep . . . better class citizens won't live here', while in another view, they stood out 'like a sore thumb . . . I cannot believe that it is beyond the wit of man to find an alternative that blends more harmoniously in these beautiful surroundings'.[31]

In their as yet isolated rural splendour they were rather conspicuous, but they would 'blend' in time, and as the Corporation's own architects got to work, such 'off the peg' designs would soon give way to more imaginative and varied developments. The majority of newcomers were expected to be in the younger age group, many of them with children. Three-bed dwellings and two-bed 'starter' homes thus formed the majority of new developments, but one-bed homes were also provided for the elderly and single adults. The aim was a mix of age groups on each estate, but in this and other respects the Corporation had to work within the limited construction costs laid down by the Government's Housing Cost Yardstick. 'If you don't conform to it, you don't get their money', but the relatively high density building and fixed price contracts which conformity demanded posed a succession of problems. One- and two-bed dwellings, for instance, were relatively expensive to build, and the corporation was unable to provide as many as it would have wished. Moreover, it complained on several occasions, the Yardstick could also lead to a lowering of the quality of materials, a reduction in the rate at which new dwellings could be completed, and a shrinking pool of contractors willing to build them.

'[We] find difficulty in ensuring designs of high quality within the constraints imposed by the cost yardstick', it wrote in 1972, 'This is particularly troublesome towards the end of the year when prices have soared'.[32] The yardstick always lagged behind increases in the costs of materials and labour. Within their fixed price limits contractors were often obliged to cut back on both, and in the longer term they became increasingly reluctant to tender for new contracts. 'The financial constraints', the Corporation continued in 1973, 'are undoubtedly a major contributory cause to the difficulties in achieving so far the steady progress in the housing field which is essential'.[33] It was 'far too slow', said Sir William Hart in the previous year, but it was never intended that the Corporation should build all the projected 3,000 new homes a year itself. It was government policy to encourage private housing development in New Towns, and part of the Corporation's own task to make land available for the purpose.

In Northampton these included not only private firms and individuals but a number of housing associations. The latter were able to provide low-rental housing with the aid of funds from the government-sponsored Housing Corporation. A young people's hostel at Weston Favell and flats for the elderly on the Lings development were among their own particular projects, but the Corporation also sold a limited number of plots for luxury housing. Demand outstripped what it was prepared to supply, but private developers provided an average of 500 new dwellings a year between 1968-78. Over and above those re-housed from London, the expanding Northampton was expected to attract new population from other areas, requiring a wide range of housing to cater for different incomes and tastes. Around a quarter of those interviewed in a survey of potential incomers in 1966 had a gross income of £25 per week, the minimum necessary at that time to buy a house in Northampton, but many rented first and hoped to buy later. This was not an option open to the majority, but the Corporation's Shared Ownership scheme was designed to ease their path to owner-occupation. Tenants paid rent on a proportion of their house, and a mortgage on the remainder. The latter could be increased as circumstances allowed, enabling at least some of the 400 who took up the offer to become full home-owners.

Northampton already had a wide range of housing before expansion, 53% of it owner-occupied against a national average of 44%. More than 1,500 new Council dwellings were built between 1964-72, bringing their total to over 10,000, around a quarter of the total housing in the unexpanded town. A high proportion were one-bed flats and bungalows for the elderly, many of them re-housed from too-large dwellings or from some of the 17,000 judged sub-standard by the M.O.H. in 1964. The vast majority were capable of improvement at a moderate cost, but 'much relief of hardship will stem from these rehousings', as the Housing Manager noted in 1972, 'and many indirect benefits will accrue'. Under-occupied council houses would be released for larger families, more private housing for the 'younger, more affluent and able' families who would raise it to a higher standard, and 'a whole host of social, financial and health aspects will be served'.[34] Similar processes were expected to aid the integration of the existing population and the newcomers, producing a gradual two-way movement between old and new areas as tenants sought to become owner-occupiers, or existing owners looked to new surroundings or a more modern house.

Not all newcomers to the town moved into its newly developed areas, of course. Many came independently of the official 'overspill' programme, and rented or bought an older property, and as a further aid to integration the Corporation and the Council agreed to house a certain number of each other's applicants. Around 70% of those moving into Northampton in the early 1970s were Londoners, and no matter what others might think of them, those accommodated on the Corporation's housing estates were generally very happy with their new homes. Poor housing was paramount among their reasons for leaving London. Over half of those interviewed in an Institute of Community Studies survey in 1966 shared their homes with at least one other family. Half the households of three or more had only one bedroom, while two fifths of their houses had no bath.[35] After a fire in the same year, one six-room London house was found to be occupied by 29 people.[36] 'Damp running down the walls and mice and no hot water and only an outside toilet . . . anywhere had to be better than that', said one young woman in a different survey, but isolation with two young children on the 16th floor of a tower block was not really so very much better.[37]

Even the decently housed often faced a long and expensive journey to work, and complained of the general 'hustle and bustle' of life in the capital. 'Just getting out of London' was her aim, said one young schoolteacher: 'The financial side didn't worry me . . . my one concern was to get out'.[38] Many newcomers did find themselves financially stretched, however. The Corporation's rents were often higher than those they were paying in London, while wage rates in Northampton were generally lower — although this was offset in part by the lower local cost of living, and they also had access to rent and rate rebates. Those judged incapable of paying even with this aid had their applications turned down, but others found themselves better housed at a much lower cost. In London, said one, 'the cheapest decent place I could get for the family was 15 guineas a week. Here for much less we have a nice house on the Thorplands Estate and our only complaints are that there is no chemist shop and the bus service is poor . . . Northampton people are nice and friendly . . . As for that football team I've been to see them once, and if I go again it will only be to ask for a refund'.[39]

The Cobblers' meteoric rise from the Fourth to the First Division between 1961-5, it is no doubt well known, was followed by an equally meteoric descent. By 1969 they were back where they started from, but if the quality of the football left something to be desired, Northampton itself was highly rated by many of its new inhabitants. 'We loved the place on sight', said one young couple of their home on the Thorplands development, which won its architect Gordon Redfern a national housing award. Here 'everything is so clean and new . . . You can hear the birds sing in the morning and a few minutes walk away there are green fields and lovely villages . . . we've got our own garden . . . [and] down in the town everybody is so friendly, it's quite amazing'. 'I have found the house, the town and the people marvellous', said another couple, 'The people here are so friendly . . .'.[40] There were some tensions between the two, of course. 'We keep getting blamed for everything that goes wrong', complained one incomer, but 'its not just us, you know'.[41] Nor was it. There was an increase in recorded crime in Northampton during the 1970s, and in crimes of violence in particular. The town centre was colourfully described as a 'muggatorium', but the same trend was in evidence all over Britain at this time, and while many of those brought before the local courts were recent immigrants, just as many were not.

In general, however, the new Northamptonians did receive a friendly reception from the old. It helped, of course, that they arrived gradually and in quite small numbers at first; that far from 'regaling us . . . with the wonders of their city and their reluctance to leave it', they complimented the citizens on their own; and that low local rates of unemployment dispelled much of the suspicion that 'they'll take our jobs'. New jobs had to be created, of course, but while much effort had been invested in informing and consulting and reassuring the townspeople about the expansion plans, potential newcomers had also been given 'a realistic view of what is in store'. This was primarily the task of the Corporation's Arrivals Officers, who visited each family considering a move. As well as providing them with factual information, and encouraging them to look at Northampton firsthand, they pointed to the potential drawbacks: not only the possible financial pressures, but the separation from family and friends, and the fact that a new environment would not automatically solve every problem.

However nice the house, however friendly the people, many did find it difficult to settle at first. They felt lonely and isolated, and some families cracked under the strain of new pressures added to old tensions. 'They think a change of scenery will improve the situation', as one welfare organisation put it, but 'being in a strange and sometimes lonely place only brings the situation to a head more quickly'.[42] Once in Northampton, however, the Arrivals Officers maintained their contact, providing introductions to local organisations, helping new residents to establish their own, and passing on their comments and complaints to the planners. Residents' Councils were also formed in due course and — though often with a time-lag which was itself a source of complaint — the new estates were equipped with shops, community centres, schools, health centres and pubs. The latter were allotted at the ratio of one for every 4,500 people, hardly generous when compared with the one per 164 of 1901 — but now of course there were more varied forms of entertainment available.

At the Weston Favell Centre, some three miles from the town centre, facilities were grouped together on a grand scale. Alongside parking spaces for 1,200 cars, there was the Lings Forum Leisure Centre, with swimming pool, sports hall, tennis courts, playing fields and restaurant; a major shopping centre which housed, amongst others, the largest Tesco store in Europe; two schools, a library, day nursery and health centre; and Emmanuel Church, an interdenominational church built by a non-profit making body of local Anglicans, Methodists and Baptists, Shared Churches (Northampton) Ltd. New shopping facilities and other amenities were also provided in the town centre as part of the Borough Council's redevelopment scheme. Traffic congestion and a lack of adequate parking facilities were among the pressing problems evident even in 1965, and as part of the preliminary expansion study the Council commissioned Messrs. Wilson and Womersley to draw up planning proposals which could be used as a basis for central redevelopment whether expansion went ahead or not.

The town centre, they concluded, consisted largely of late 19th-century buildings 'coming to the end of their useful life'. In the view of some, these few words were loaded with sinister significance. 'This is the kind of comment we are coming to expect from so many modern town planning offices', cried one resident', 'So often things which do not bend before their wholesale reconstruction programmes are described either as "nearing the end of their useful life", or a very favourite card, "unsafe"'.[43] 'Outworn properties', was the phrase used in the 1951 Development Plan, but it chose its words with care where the Guildhall was concerned. There 'is much division of opinion', it noted, 'as to whether Edward Godwin's Guildhall, despite its magnificent pseudo-Gothic facade and internal carving, should be pulled down on the grounds that it is unsuited internally to present-day working conditions'.[44]

This was putting it mildly. Its internal arrangements, it is true, were inconvenient for employees and public alike. An information desk, suggested the *Chronicle and Echo* in 1959, might be an improvement — preferably staffed by an 'attractive (and well-informed) young woman'[45] — but it was undeniably too small. Different municipal departments were already scattered around various parts of the town, and there was much to be said in favour of concentrating them in a new civic centre. The post-war Labour Council had planned to do exactly that, but lacked sufficient funds. The Guildhall had been admitted to the Ministry of Housing's list of buildings of architectural merit after the 1951 argument over its fate, but that gave it only limited protection. Would it now be declared an 'unsightly relic' and swept away — like the old *Peacock Inn* on Market Square — by the tide of modernistic 'improvement'? Certainly not, was the answer; but Wilson and Womersley's plans did include a new civic centre, along with a pedestrian shopping precinct, new bus station, additional hotels, a covered market, and parking for 24,000 cars. Something would have to go, but unless Northampton wished to live in a permanent snarl of traffic and otherwise suffer eternal inconvenience in the name of conservation, something would have to be done.

In 1969 the Council appointed the private Grosvenor and Eaton Estates Development Company, which had undertaken similar projects in Chester, to work with Wilson and Womersley to prepare detailed plans.[46] In the following year, however, 'serious differences of opinion . . . over matters which we sincerely feel to be of fundamental importance' led the latter to part company with the Council.[47] The manner in which pedestrians were to be separated from traffic was at the root of these differences, and 'we could see no meeting point at all'. The Ministry of Transport itself rejected the proposed 'Busway' on the grounds of cost. This was basically a road encircling the town centre with a separate bus-lane, leading to and from a new bus station, but otherwise excluding public transport from the central areas. However, the Council went ahead with Wilson and Womersley's plan for a high speed dual-carriageway linking St James's to the west, by way of inner areas of the town, with Cliftonville to the east. This £13 million 'Expressway', as it was called, caused a positive public uproar when the details were published in 1971.

Lying in its route were some 1,000 houses, the Clare Street Drill Hall, at this time the largest public hall available in the town, and several churches, schools and pubs. An Expressway Action Group was duly formed, and the Conservative-controlled Council was mercilessly criticised for contemplating such wanton destruction. There was a genuine need for some sort of central relief road, but in 1973 the Labour party promised to scrap the scheme if they won the next election, and when they won it, they did — putting a permanent end to the project with new housing developments along its route. In the meantime work had begun on the new Grosvenor Shopping Centre to the north of Market Square. The Welsh House was among the buildings scheduled for demolition here. Built in 1595, it was one of only two domestic buildings in Northampton dating from before the Great Fire of 1675. It had been much altered during the 19th century, and although it had been given listed building status in 1951, the only original features remaining were the first floor windows, an interior staircase, and the scroll bearing the Welsh motto from which it took its name: 'Heb dyw, heb dym, Dwya digon', translated as 'Without God, without everything, with God, enough'.

However, following protests from the Northamptonshire Record Society and a petition organised by the *Mercury and Herald*, the Welsh House was not only retained but rebuilt in

47. The Welsh House in Market Square, built in 1595 and restored to its original 16th-century style in the 1970s. To the left is part of the Grosvenor Shopping Centre, which was opened in 1975.

its original 16th-century style. There was also a 'strong feeling' in the town in favour of retaining the existing market, which had been on the same site since 1235. Plans for a new covered market were in due course dropped, and those for the civic centre postponed, but the 371,000 sq. ft. Grosvenor Centre itself was opened in 1975. It was linked to a 1,000-place car park and to the new Greyfriars Bus Station, which took its name from the mediaeval friary once on the same site. The adjacent Northampton House was one of several new office developments intended to make up existing deficiencies and expand the range of commercial and administrative employment. Among the others were the Marefair offices into which Barclays Bank moved its national Barclaycard headquarters, sited in North-ampton since 1966. Through the offices of Leslie Austin-Crowe, Chief Estates Officer of the Development Corporation, the Council also leased a large central site to Saxon Inns Ltd. for development as a major new hotel, the *Saxon Inn*, which is now the *Northampton Moat House Hotel*.

Beyond the centre itself, at Delapre Park, the Council built a Golf Complex with practice greens, floodlit driving ranges and shop and restaurant in addition to nine and 18-hole courses, while in 1983 the Royal Theatre and Opera House — 'worth preserving at all costs', said the Northampton Civic Society — was supplemented by a new multi-purpose entertainment centre on the redundant site of the United Counties bus station in Derngate. Along with £650,000 from its amenities fund, which had also been used to subsidise the Royal Theatre itself, the land was given to the Council by the Development Corporation, which had earlier purchased it for £600,000. It was equipped internally with a unique 'air-bed' system which allowed the auditorium seating to be re-arranged in line with the

48.   The Derngate Centre, a £10 million multi-purpose entertainment centre opened by the Borough. Council in 1983 on the site of the old United Counties bus station in Derngate.

demands of different productions, which ranged from theatre and opera to all-in wrestling and dancing. The £10 million costs of building it were the source of many complaints from the ratepayers, who were subsidising it in 1984 to the tune of £6.58 per head; but, said one councillor, 'if the hall were not built now when the land is available . . . then it would never be built'. Derngate, said another, 'will be a credit to Northampton for the next one hundred years'.[48]

Not everyone was happy with what was being done in the town centre or in the expansion area itself, but there were some approving comments from outside. 'Expectations of new town development are tempered by experience', wrote the *Architects' Journal* in 1972: 'We have learnt not to expect too much, and it comes as a pleasant surprise to find that

Northampton . . . promises to lift itself above the commonplace'.[49] Among the projects cited over the years as evidence of 'a certain flair' were the Carlsberg Brewery, opened on the site of the old Phipps Brewery in 1972; the Express Lifts testing tower, a 127-metre-high reinforced concrete structure known locally as the 'lighthouse'; and the new club house of the Working Man's Fancy, a pigeon fanciers' club formed at the turn of the century. Strikingly adorned with fawn brown and chrome yellow cladding, this was commonly referred to as the 'spaceship' or the 'bumble bee'.[50] By the mid-1970s, however, the expansion plans were themselves being tempered by economic recession, slower than anticipated population growth, and the fear that the New Towns were 'beggaring' the large cities they were intended to serve.

The introduction of a three-day working week early in 1974 in the train of the miners' strike led some firms to abandon or postpone their proposed moves to Northampton. The Corporation was 'hopeful that the difficulties are of a temporary nature, and that a return to the rapid commercial and industrial growth of the town will soon follow the restoration of the full working week'.[51] The economic crisis continued, however. Development corporations had to take their share of cuts in public expenditure, but money was not the only factor. Between 1961-74 the population of Greater London fell by some 800,000 to just over seven million. Between 1971-4 it was shedding people at an average rate of over 80,000 a year against the 53,000 of the previous decade. On the surface this was a cause for some satisfaction. The New Towns were after all designed to relieve this and other large centres of their 'overspill', but when this consisted largely of the 'relatively fortunate' members of society, accompanied by a large proportion of their manufacturing industry, then as the Department of Environment acknowledged in 1975, they 'would be likely to increase rather than diminish the social problems of these cities'.[52]

The majority of those who moved out were young people — average age 33 — and most were already in paid employment. They left behind the 'least fortunate' unemployed, elderly and other low income groups, whose proportionately greater need for social services had to be borne by a shrinking financial base. In the eight years to 1974 a total of 809 firms moved out of London to new or expanding towns within the sub-region. Half came from inner areas of the city, and some 70% of the total were engaged in manufacturing industry. Over a matter of 12 years or so the capital lost almost half a million manufacturing jobs. By 1975 not only the age structure of its population but its whole economy was in danger of becoming seriously unbalanced; and 'any extension of such schemes', wrote the Greater London Council early in 1976, 'would be likely to be detrimental to dealing with urgent social and employment problems in London and to tackling pressing needs of urban renewal . . . the New Town development corporations should look elsewhere'.[53]

In 1977 revised and reduced plans were announced for the development of Northampton's Southern District. The 36,000 people it was originally intended to take were cut to 20,000, while Northampton's overall population target for 1991 was revised from 230,000 to 180,000. However, there would be no abrupt ending of the new town programmes. As the Environment Secretary Peter Shore noted when announcing a slowing of the pace, he must 'take account of the infrastructure already provided . . . and the need for them to develop into balanced and viable communities. The third-generation New Towns are one of the outstanding successes of post-war Britain and nothing I am doing should reduce their ability to continue building on the foundations already laid'.[54] The announcement that the Northampton Development Corporation would be wound up within three or four years did not come until February 1981. In the meantime, however, its 'partnership' with the Borough Council had been extended to reflect the new responsibilities laid on the County Council by the local government reform of 1974.

Based broadly on the recommendations of the Redcliffe-Maud report of 1969, the Local

Government Act of 1972 abolished existing county borough and urban and rural district councils, and substituted a two-tier system of county and district councils. In the large conurbations these consisted of metropolitan counties and districts, with a rather different distribution of responsibilities from those in non-metropolitan areas. In the latter, some services formerly administered at borough or district level were transferred to the county councils, among them education, social services, fire services, libraries and trading standards. At the same time, responsibility for water and sewerage, and personal health services, was also transferred to other new — and unelected — local bodies. These reforms were underpinned by the same 'big is more efficient' philosophy which led to the amalgamation of police forces in 1966, but the removal of such key services from their traditional sphere of influence was much resented in many former county boroughs. Co-ordination and integration of services over a larger area could result in a more efficient and cost-effective delivery, but big could also be remote and cumbersome, and the arguments provoked by the reform continue yet. Albeit on a temporary basis, the county boroughs also lost their often ancient borough status, and with it their right to elect a mayor. In Northampton an early application was made for its restoration, duly granted in the form of a new charter in 1974. On a more permanent basis, however, the Act also abolished the office of alderman — thus belatedly fulfilling the Council's own pleas that 'all members . . . should be elected direct' when it petitioned for county borough status in 1888.[55]

The borough boundaries were also extended in 1974 to embrace the whole expansion area, but in view of its new responsibilities within it, the County Council was invited to join the 'partnership'. Its relevant chief officers worked with the planning team, and its representatives sat on the Corporation's Board. There was a degree of overlap between its Borough and County Council members — the borough now had its own seats on the County Council itself — but by the later 1970s there had also been several changes of personnel. Sir William Hart was succeeded as Chairman in 1976 by Mr. A. R. Davis. Like Mr. T. J. Nardecchia, who took over as Chairman on the death of Mr. Davis in 1984, they were existing members of the Board. Both Jack Corrin and Ron Dilleigh resigned in 1979 on surrendering their seats in the Council, the former on retiring after some 30 years of public service, the most recent of them as leader of the Conservative group. His place on the Board was taken by the new Conservative leader Cyril Benton, and that of Ron Dilleigh by the Labour councillor Tony Berry. Dilleigh, a councillor for 23 years, contested his St Crispin's seat as an Independent following a dispute with the local Labour party, failing to gain election by a mere nine votes.

In the same elections, which gave the Conservatives an overall majority of thirteen, Cllr. Stanley Liburd became Northampton's first black representative when he took a seat for Labour in the St Alban ward. A native of the West Indian island of Nevis, he was one of the many who answered the Macmillan appeal for labour in the 1950s and had been resident in Northampton for some 20 years. Among the candidates contesting these elections were a handful of Liberals and a rather larger complement of women than in the past, but there were still relatively few working class councillors. Councillors should really not be judged by their jobs alone, as one candidate pointed out a few years later, but the attendance allowances now paid to them were often insufficient to cover lost earnings, and the demands of time grew ever heavier as Council business grew ever more complex. The latter, in the opinion of one working man, demanded knowledge and expertise which he for one did not possess, and 'to put me in charge of running a multi-million pound business which, in effect, is what Northampton Borough Council is, would be disastrous . . . we do not want unqualified and incompetent people running our town'.[56]

Rather than 'amateurs trying to cope with their own jobs and a mound of council work as well', would it not be better to pay councillors to devote their whole time to the job, asked the *Chronicle and Echo*? It thought not, and on the whole, so did the councillors themselves. Professional councillors, one suggested, were the only real way of ensuring that 'it was they who made the real decisions . . . rather than the full time officials'. They were already in being in several continental countries; but 'I do not think anybody should make money out of being a councillor', said another. Moreover, for all its faults, the present system allowed the Council to draw on 'expertise from a wide variety of walks of life', and professional councillors, it was thought, could easily become remote from the electorate itself. Under the 1972 Local Government Act Northampton had dispensed with the annual one-third elections, but the risk of being 'kicked out' after four years would still deter many from giving up their existing jobs. 'It would become even more important for them to win re-election every four years', the newspaper itself concluded, 'and I cannot see how this would aid the cause of open government'.[57]

The County Council, however, found itself much in need of financial aid in fulfilling its responsibilities in the expansion areas. It too would have to provide services in advance of new rate income, and along with Northampton itself it also had Corby and the 'expanding towns' of Wellingborough and Daventry within its administrative area. The latter were being developed on a lesser scale under different legislative machinery, but in the case of Northampton at least, it received revenue and capital aid totalling some £40 million from the Development Corporation itself. Much of the latter went on building or improving roads, but when it came to providing health facilities for the expanding population, the Corporation's ability to help was much more limited. In 1966 the Borough M.O.H. had pointed to the expansion plans themselves as an opportunity to integrate local health services. A Health Services Advisory Committee was set up to work with the Council and the Corporation, and a temporary health centre providing a full range of services was established in two converted houses in the Eastern District. The 'medical and health care services for the Expansion Area', the M.O.H. concluded in 1972, 'are more favourably placed for meeting the needs of the newcomers than seemed possible only a short time ago'.[58]

In 1974, however, following a reform of the National Health Service, the Council's own responsibilities in this respect were transferred to the new Northamptonshire Area Health Authority, which came under the umbrella of the Oxford Regional Health Authority. The better integration of services was the aim, but while welcoming it in principle the M.O.H. thought it 'unfortunate' that 'reorganisation . . . while overcoming some of the existing administrative difficulties, should create new ones, not least the need to introduce cumbersome consultative machinery to ensure that local government and the health services do plan together for the clearly identified needs of their area . . .'.[59] These were rather prophetic words. Vowing to put a stop to further expansion 'by all means at its disposal', in 1977 the Northampton Community Health Council mounted a 'Don't come to Northampton' campaign warning newcomers of the inadequacies of the health services in the area. But 'Don't blame us', replied the Development Corporation. He was 'sorry', said Basil Bean, that the Community Council 'seems to be opposing the Development Corporation in its aim to promote the growth and prosperity of the town . . . its target should really be the Oxford Regional Health Authority'.[60]

Rightly or wrongly, health care provision was not an area for which development corporations were allocated responsibility or funds. According to one book on the subject, health 'is not considered to be plannable', but in the words of one local physician, both the Oxford and Northamptonshire Health Authorities were themselves in a 'ludicrous dilemma'. The latter covered not only Northampton, Corby, Wellingborough and Daventry but also Milton Keynes. The delayed provision of hospital facilities there put still more strain on the General Hospital in Northampton, but these five expanding areas added up to a rate of population increase in Northamptonshire which was the highest in the country. Overall, said the British Medical Association, in 1977 it had facilities 'for 20,000 less people than are there already'. It was a 'monstrous case', but the Northamptonshire Authority's allocation of funds was based on calculations two years in arrears, it was well on target for a £2 million overspend — and 'Don't blame us, blame the Government'.[61]

In the event some £2.5 million was diverted by the Treasury from the Corporation's house-building programme into improving health facilities in Northampton. Attracting new jobs to the town, however, was the Corporation's responsibility, and one it took very seriously. The service sector, it has been said elsewhere, had already gone some way to reduce the weight of manufacturing industry in the local economy. In 1965 it accounted for 52% of the total labour force against 47% in 1956 — but this was still below the national average of 57%, and there was clearly some room for growth here. The same was true in the manufacturing sector itself, boosted in advance of expansion by the arrival of the American-based Avon Cosmetics company, which established its European manufacturing headquarters on an £18 million site at Nunn Mills. The unemployment rate in Northampton in the later 1960s was less than one per cent, and established firms competing for already scarce labour would not welcome an early influx of new employers. The initial aim, therefore, was to encourage an expansion of existing areas of employment, introducing new commercial or industrial ventures later to make good any deficiences and achieve a healthy overall balance.

British Timken, for instance, which already employed around 3,000 people, was experiencing difficulty in recruiting skilled engineering workers, while Northampton Transport had similar problems in recruiting sufficient drivers. Such vacancies were advertised within the Greater London area, and applicants were put in touch with the Development Corporation for advice on housing prospects and other facilities. Local firms in need of larger premises or in the path of clearance schemes were offered a unit on one of several Employment Areas. Carefully segregated from residential building, but with easy access to major roads and the M1 motorway, much attention was also paid to creating an attractive as well as an efficient working environment. The 300-acre Moulton Park Employment Area, for instance, was situated on elevated ground and visible from a distance in several directions.

Here landscaping and the screening of open storage areas contributed to producing a 'harmonious entity', while on another site overlooked from the surrounding hill slopes, 'roofscale detailing is equally as important as elevational treatment. . . . . It is important that existing trees be retained and supplemented by generous new planting . . . Developments in excess of two storeys in height will generally not be permitted'.[62] Provided they conformed to these and general planning regulations, those firms who wished to do so could have their factory or warehouse or offices built on the Corporation's estates to their own specifications. The first 18 units completed on Moulton Park in 1971 were 'off the peg' designs of varying sizes, and all were let to Northampton firms. In due course the Anglia Building Society also moved its headquarters here from its Abington Street premises. In the longer term however there was a need to attract new employers from elsewhere, and on its own and the Council's behalf the Corporation launched a vigorous campaign to do exactly that.

It included national press advertisements, 'Come to Northampton' exhibitions, and a wide range of publications targeted on the industrial and business community. Contacts were also made with the professional agencies to which they might turn for advice — estate agents, merchant banks, financial consultants and the like — not only in Britain but also in Europe and North America. Northampton was advertised too by less conventional and often pioneering means, by the Corporation's sponsorship of the 'World Masters' Squash Racquets tournament at Wembley, for instance, or the 'Affordable Home' competition operated in conjunction with *Woman* magazine. Architects and builders between them were invited to submit a design for a low-cost housing development, and to agree to build it if they were successful. It was won by a Rushden combination, which built 41 houses at Hunsbury Green on land sold to by the Corporation at a discount. Conditional on an undertaking to live in it for at least two years, one of them was awarded in turn to the winners of the 'Most Wanted Features' competition in which readers were invited to put housing design features in an order of priority.[63]

Two years earlier the Corporation had also issued a record comprising an expanded version of a thirty second advertising jingle broadcast on the commercial London Broadcasting Company radio station. 'Sixty miles by road or rail; Factories for rent, houses for sale' now became:

> Sixty miles by road or rail,
> Is the love in my fairy tale.
> Sixty miles to reach my guy in Northampton
> It's a feeling I can't explain.
> I just can't wait to be in Northampton —
> Northampton, Northampton, Northampton,
> Middle England.[64]

Various slighting comments have been passed on these lyrics, but the sheer novelty of the venture was enough to ensure it the desired exposure. The 500 unsolicited requests for copies of the record, and the royalties received from its subsequent commercial issue by E.M.I., were unexpected bonuses; but the simplest messages are often the most effective, and Northampton was not the only place to which a re-locating employer might choose to move.

As a 1977 survey of firms on the Corporation's Employment Areas suggests, the initial decision to move was often based on 'push' factors. Lack of space for expansion and otherwise inadequate premises were much the most common factors cited, followed by high rents or rates, an insufficient supply of labour, and the threat of compulsory purchase. In deciding *where* to move, however, 'pull' factors were of the greatest importance. Top of the companies' list of Northampton's positive attractions was its geographical position in relation to the motorway network, linking it directly to London, and by way of the M45 to Birmingham and beyond. Much value was also placed on the appeal of the area to key workers, on an ample supply of all kinds of labour, and on Northampton's good industrial relations record. Favourable leasing terms, and the availability of suitable premises had also weighed significantly in their final decision,[65] but none of these advantages was necessarily obvious to a prospective new employer, nor to the workforce which he might want to bring with him.

Particularly for a large enterprise, the choice of a new site was never lightly made. As with the Black and Decker company, which has recently built a new £8 million automated warehouse in Northampton, 'many options' would be considered before a final decision was reached. Thus, initial interest had to be followed up with detailed information, by visits and the sort of presentations to an employer's workforce which were a part of the work of the Arrivals Officers. There also had to be a flexible approach to an employer's needs and preferences regarding sites and premises, accompanied by the services which would make an eventual move as smooth as possible for all concerned. Northampton had to be 'sold' from start to finish, and while the Council itself had sold it to the Avon and Carlsberg Brewery companies before the Corporation moved in, it was the latter's task to do so on the larger scale which successful 'New Town' expansion now required.

Over 200 major companies were in fact persuaded to move to Northampton between 1970-85, many from London and other areas of Britain, but many others from the United States and Western Europe. They included Henry Telfer Ltd., one of the largest with around

49. Aerial view of Moulton Park Employment Area, the first of four major employment areas to be promoted by the Development Corporation.

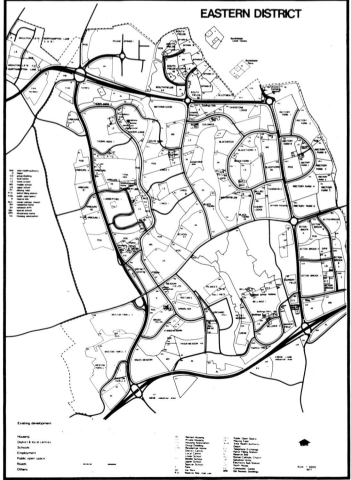

50. Map of the Eastern District, the first of the two expansion areas created by the Northampton Development Corporation.

2,000 employees and one of several in the food and drink trades; the furniture chain M.F.I., employing over 300 people at its national distribution centre; Levi Strauss with its British headquarters at Moulton Park; the after-sales base of Saab G.B.; and the express freight company T.N.T. I.P.E.C.. From its own depot on the Round Spinney Employment Area it could deliver to most of its European customers within 48 hours, aided by the Northampton Inland Clearance Depot which it also owned. This was an inland customs depot where goods could be cleared for import and export without the often lengthy delays at seaports, and it was a facility which served to attract other companies to Northampton in its own turn.

Blackwood Hodge, the world's largest distributors of earth-moving equipment, moved its own base to premises at Hunsbury Hill. Founded in 1941 by Bernard Sunley, in 1980 it contributed £1.7 million from the Bernard Sunley Charitable Foundation towards the establishment of the Blackwood Hodge Management Centre at Nene College, now known as the Sunley Management Centre and funded jointly by industry and government to provide managerial training at all levels. The National Leathersellers Centre, one of the few remaining bases for advanced leather technology in the world, also moved to the Nene College Campus in 1978, thus retaining Northampton's traditional links with the industry. Not that the leather and footwear industries had ceased to be significant. In 1968 there were still 28 shoe manufacturers in the town, among them such old-established firms as Crockett and Jones, Church and Co., G. T. Hawkins and Manfield's, and there are a similar number still. Nor was it only large companies who contributed to the greater diversity of employment which Northampton achieved during the expansion period. Equally important in terms of balance, as well as the numbers they employed in total, were the many smaller firms who moved into Northampton or expanded their existing operations in the town, many of them engaged in light manufacturing or in service industries.

Over 18,000 new jobs had been created by 30 June 1985 when the Development Corporation was finally dissolved, and despite the addition of 35,000 people and the economic recession which pushed up unemployment rates in the early 1980s, that of Northampton was 3% below the national average. The final tally from the expansion years also included 42 miles of new roads, 20,000 new houses — 8,124 built by the Corporation, around 4,000 by the Borough Council, and the rest by private developers or housing associations — plus 10 million square feet of new office or factory space, 10 community centres, 10 local shopping centres and over 20 schools, at a capital cost of some £200 million. Some of the Corporation's assets, including industrial premises and the Weston Favell Shopping Centre, were sold in advance of the wind-up, raising some complaints that the town was being sold off 'over our heads. Industrial estates are being sold in blocks too large and expensive for firms to buy', and they 'should not have to be subject to the whims of landlords who have no intention of living in the town'.[66]

By way of rents and property sales and other returns on investments, new towns were in due course expected to repay the capital costs of building them, but in view of its shorter than anticipated lifespan the Corporation was under some pressure to speed up the process. Vacant industrial land was transferred on its dissolution to the Commission for the New Towns, the body normally responsible for managing the assets of new towns. In Northampton's case, however, many were transferred directly to the Borough Council under a negotiated agreement. They included the Corporation's housing stock, with its 'healthy' revenue account, and a package of 'Community Related Assets' consisting of some 300 acres of open space, seven community centres, and Upton Hall, complete with 30 acres of land and £300,000 towards the costs of repairs and refurbishment. Several local shopping centres and pubs, and some land for housing development were included to defray the future running costs of community facilities. The Corporation also contributed £250,000 towards an extension to the Central Museum and Art Gallery, intended in part to house the fruits of its Archaeological Unit, whose work in advance of development has shed much new and valuable light on Northampton's more distant past.[67]

'I liked my Northampton as it was', was one verdict on the final 'New Town' results. The speaker was not alone — but what sort of town would an unexpanded Northampton have been in 1985? 'Very depressed' in one view, and this too was shared by many others. 'Over 13 years of spending a Government investment of more than £200 million' wrote the journal *Business in Northamptonshire* in 1983, 'the Development Corporation has converted a town dependent on traditional industries in serious decline to a thriving, expanding and commercially highly desirable area at the hub of as much national economic activity as deep recession allows . . .'.[68] This may be going a little too far. Neither the footwear nor the engineering industries were in 'serious decline' when the expansion proposals were first announced in 1965. The former was holding its high-quality own, and the latter was in some ways too healthy for the overall good of the town. There was a need for more balance, but Northampton's economic structure had become rather more diverse in recent years, and an official five-year sample census in 1966 suggested that its population was already increasing spontaneously and at quite a rapid rate. The anticipated newcomers did not begin to arrive in any significant numbers until the early 1970s, but by 1971 the population had grown to 133,000 from 105,000 ten years earlier.

Northampton was already a relatively prosperous and thriving town when the Development Corporation moved in, and it might have remained so even without its help. No one will ever know; but the Borough Council was willing to take the aid and the newcomers rather than the risk, and when it moved out again, the Corporation left a town not only a good deal larger but better equipped to face the challenges of the future. 'The sound economic base provided by new industry and commerce, first rate housing and the leisure and social facilities', concluded the Corporation itself, 'have all played their part in ensuring the town's continued progress and prosperity. The impetus remains to continue Northampton's record of growth and achievement throughout years to come'.[69] But as the *Chronicle and Echo* warned, 'it would be far too easy for everyone in Northampton to sit back and fondly imagine that business investments will just keep rolling in. It is a temptation that will have to be avoided . . . in these days when money is tight, and dozens of places around the country are trying to attract companies on the move, it is increasingly important that Northampton should hold its own'.[70] 'Our challenge today', as the Chamber of Commerce put it, 'is not how to create, but how to sustain, this growth and momentum'.[71]

Without the Corporation's publicity trumpets at its disposal, Northampton has continued to blow its own, and over the past five years the momentum has been well maintained. The development of the Southern District has continued under a £75 million scheme including 2,000 new homes, two schools and the Danes Camp Leisure Centre, opened in 1987 and equipped with leisure pool, sports hall and health and fitness centre. The target of 16,550 new homes between 1983 and 2001 is expected to be 'substantially exceeded', and at present rates of growth the population will reach the 200,000 mark by the latter year. Among the companies who have recently established national distribution centres in Northampton are Coca-Cola and Schweppes Beverages Ltd., which has now received planning permission for a new 54-acre site for a canning factory and manufacturing site, and Baxters Healthcare, major suppliers to the National Health Service. New land for industrial development is now in very short supply, but major new office developments along with a £20 million riverside business and leisure park are among the many projects under way or in the planning.[72] Having recently celebrated the 800th anniversary of the town's first charter in November 1989, the Borough Council itself has entered the era of competitive tendering and that long-elusive alternative to the rates — the community charge, commonly known as the 'poll tax'. In this respect as in others, future historians of Northampton will surely find no lack of interesting material. As for what the future will hold — in the immortal words of Herbert Asquith, who cast such stern Prime Ministerial eyes on the Northampton suffragettes, we will have to wait and see.

Notes

1. Quoted in Schaffer, F., *The New Town Story* (1970), p.5.
2. 'Northampton: moving towards expansion', *Architects' Journal* (14 Dec. 1966).
3. *C.&E.*, 22 Oct. 1966.
4. Ibid., 7 Oct. 1967.
5. Ibid.
6. Ibid.
7. Schaffer, op. cit., pp.32-3.
8. Report of the Inquiry into the Northampton New Town Draft Designation Order (Dec. 1967).
9. *C.&E.*, 5 May 1966.
10. Ibid., 15 Aug. 1966.
11. Schaffer, op. cit., p.28.
12. N.C.B.C., Census of Immigrant Children in Schools (Nov. 1967).
13. Barty-King, H., *Expanding Northampton* (1985), p.58.
14. *C.&E.*, cutting Dec. 1966, otherwise undated.
15. Barty-King, op.cit., p.50.
16. Ibid.
17. *C.&E.*, 5 Dec. 1968.
18. Ibid., 22 Oct. 1966.
19. Quoted in *C.&E.*, *Building a Future* (1984).
20. Cllr. J. T. Lewis, quoted in *C.&E.*, 22 Oct. 1966.
21. N.C.B.C., Minutes of Finance & General Purposes Committee, 26 April 1965.
22. *C.&E.*, 22 Nov. 1965.
23. Crossman, R., *Diaries of a Cabinet Minister*, Vol.1, p.307.
24. Ibid., pp.355 & 460.
25. Barty-King, op.cit., p.37.
26. Ministry of Housing & Local Government (hereafter M.H.L.G.), Press Release No. 200, 20 Aug. 1965.
27. M.H.L.G., Agreed Memorandum, 10 May 1965.
28. Crossman, op.cit., p.309.
29. Barty-King, op. cit., p.79.
30. Ibid., p.80.
31. Ibid., p.96.
32. Northampton Development Corporation (hereafter N.D.C.), Annual Report (1972).
33. Ibid. (1973).
34. N.C.B.C., Housing Report (1971-2).
35. Barty-King, op. cit., p.59.
36. *C.&E.*, 22 Oct. 1966.
37. See Parker, A., *The People of Providence* (1983), for a study of life on an inner London housing estate.
38. Salt, J., & Flowerdew, R., 'Labour Migration from London', *London Journal*, 6, 1 (1980).
39. Barty-King, op.cit., p.124.
40. Ibid., pp.102-3.
41. Quoted in 'Shoe Town, New Town' exhibition, Northampton Central Museum.
42. Annual Report of the Diocesan Welfare Committee (1977).
43. *C.&E.*, 15 Aug. 1966.
44. N.C.B.C., Development Plan (1951).
45. *C.&E.*, 21 Aug. 1959.
46. N.C.B.C., Minutes of Town Expansion Committee, 22 Oct. 1969.
47. Ibid., 18 March 1970.
48. Barty-King, op.cit., p.165.

49. 'Northampton: a progress report', *Architects' Journal* (15 Nov. 1972).
50. *Architects' Journal* (3 Nov. 1982; 22 Feb. 1978).
51. N.D.C. Annual Report (1974).
52. Greater London Council, *Planned Growth Outside London* (1975).
53. Greater London Council, quoted in Barty-King, op.cit, p.145.
54. Statement to House of Commons, 5 April 1977.
55. Petition re Local Government Act 1888 (April 1888).
56. *C.&E.*, 16 May 1983.
57. Ibid., 9 April 1981.
58. N.C.B.C. Health Report (1972).
59. Ibid.
60. *C.&E.*, 26 Oct. 1977.
61. Ibid., 31 Oct. 1977.
62. Quoted in Barty-King, op.cit., p.121.
63. Ibid., p.152.
64. Ibid., p.153.
65. Roberts, J., 'Diversification and Decentralisation of Industry in Northampton', *East Midlands Geographer*, 7, 3 (June 1979).
66. *C.&E.*, 'Building a Future' (1984).
67. See Williams, J., *Saxon and Mediaeval Northampton* (1982).
68. *Business in Northamptonshire* (March 1983).
69. N.D.C. Annual Report (1984).
70. Barty-King, op. cit., p.182.
71. Ibid., p.183.
72. *C.&E.*, 24 April 1989.

Population and Houses, 1831-1981

	Population	Occupied Dwellings	Average of Persons per Occupied Dwelling
1831	15,351	3,091	5.0
1841	21,242	4,138	5.1
1851	26,657	4,886	5.4
1861	32,813	6,150	5.3
1871	41,168	7,804	5.4
1881	51,881	9,658	5.4
1891	61,012	11,488	5.3
1901	87,021	17,602	4.9
1911	90,064	18,950	4.7
1921	90,895	19,893	4.5
1931	92,341	23,141	4.0
1941	No Census		
1951	104,432	30,677	3.4
1961	105,421	35,045	3.0
1971	133,800	45,885	2.9
1981	157,217	61,083	2.6

Sources: Official Census Returns; Northampton Borough Council Annual Report, 1982

Note: the borough boundaries were extended in 1901, 1931, 1965 and 1974.

Appendix 2

Deaths in Northampton per 1,000 of the population, 1876-1973

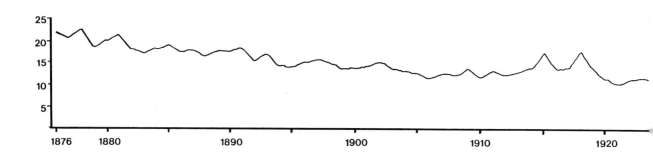

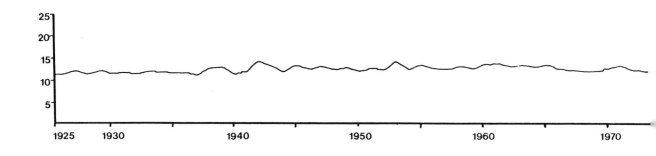

Source: N.C.B.C./N.C.B. Health Reports.

Infant deaths in Northampton per 1,000 live births, 1878-1973

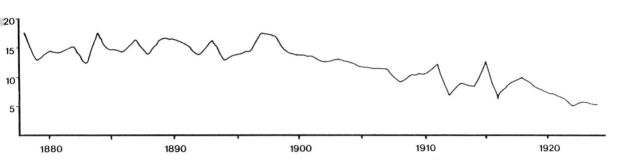

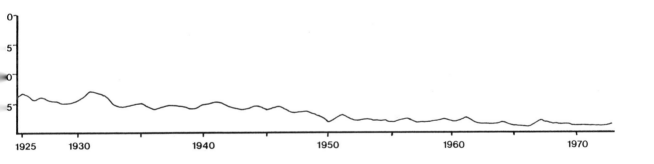

Source: N.C.B.C./N.B.C. Health Reports.

Appendix 4

Birth rate in Northampton per 1,000 of the population, 1881-1973

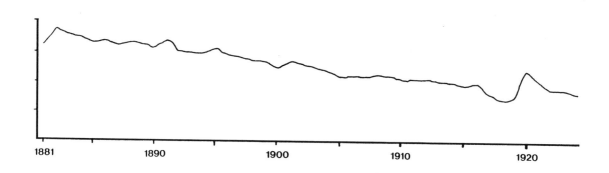

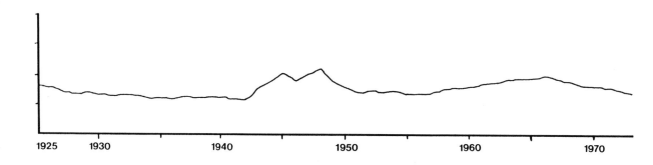

Source: N.C.B.C./N.C.B. Health Reports.

Mayors of the Borough of Northampton, 1835-1990

1835	Charles Freeman	1878	William Dennis	1919	Fred Kilby
1836	George Peach	1879	Joseph Gurney	1920	William Harvey
1837	George Peach	1880	Robert Derby		Reeves O.B.E.
1838	Thomas Hagger	1881	William John Pierce	1921	George Smith Whiting
1839	Thomas Sharp	1882	William Coulson	1922	Charles Earl
1840	William Williams	1883	Moses Philip Manfield	1923	Thomas Davies Lewis
1841	William Turner	1884	Thomas Adams	1924	Horace Walter Dover
1842	Edward Harrison Barwell	1885	Thomas Adams	1925	John George Cowling
		1886	Richard Cleaver	1926	James Peach
1843	Edward Harrison Barwell	1887	Frederick Covington	1927	Joseph Rogers
		1888	James Barry	1928	Arthur E. Ray
1844	Edward Harrison Barwell	1889	William Mills	1929	Ralph Austin Smith
		1890	George Norman	1930	Ernest Ingman
1845	John Groom	1891	Edwin Bridgewater	1931	Charles John Scott
1846	Thomas Sharp	1892	Henry Martin	1932	Percy F. Hanafy
1847	Joseph Wykes	1893	Henry Edward Randall		Helen E. Hanafy
1848	Joseph Wykes			1933	Edward Allitt
1849	Francis Parker	1894	William Tomes	1934	Albert Burrows
1850	Francis Parker	1895	Frederick Ellen	1935	Sidney Perkins
1851	Thomas Hagger	1896	Henry Edward Randall	1936	George Wilson Beattie
1852	Philadelphus Jeyes			1937	John Veasey Collier
1853	William Williams	1897	William P. Hannen	1938	William Howes Percival
1854	William Dennis	1898	Francis Tonsley		
1855	Christopher Markham	1899	Joseph Jeffery		Arthur William Lyne O.B.E.
1856	William Thomas Higgins	1900	Frederick George Adnitt	1939	Herbert A. Glenn
1857	William Hensman	1901	Frederick George Adnitt	1941	James E. Bugby
1858	William Roberts			1942	William Lees
1859	Edmund Francis Law	1902	Thomas Purser	1943	Alfred Weston
1860	Pickering Phipps	1903	Edward Lewis	1944	Sydney Strickland
1861	Henry Philip Markham	1904	Albert Ernest Marlow	1945	Frederick A. Watts
1862	John Phipps	1905	James Manfield	1946	Percival C. Williams
1863	Mark Dorman	1906	Edward Lawrence Poulton		(to Sept. 1947)
1864	Thomas Osborne				Sydney Strickland
1865	James Barry	1907	Thomas L. Wright	1947	Harriett May Nicholls
1866	Pickering Phipps	1908	John Brown	1948	Harriett May Nicholls
1867	J. Berridge Norman	1909	Henry Butterfield	1949	Leonard Smith
1868	J. Middleton Vernon	1910	Samuel Yarde	1950	Cyril A. Chown
1869	William Adkins	1911	Lee Fyson Cogan	1951	Frank Lee
1870	Pickering Phipps Perry	1912	William H. Reeves	1952	Percy W. Adams
1871	Henry Marshall	1913	George Wilson Beattie	1953	William A. Pickering
1872	William Jones	1914	Frederick Charles Parker	1954	John Veasey Collier O.B.E.
1873	Richard Turner				
1874	William Adkins	1915	Joseph Elias Pearse	1955	Walter Lewis
1875	Joseph Gurney	1916	John Woods	1956	Thomas H. Cockerill
1876	George Turner	1917	Abraham John Chown	1957	Frederick P. Saunders
1877	Thomas Tebbutt	1918	John James Martin	1958	Victor J. H. Harris

1959	George Nutt	1969	John Poole	1980	Mary Finch
1960	Charles Maurice	1970	Philip Gibson	1981	Alexander H. W.
	Newton M.B.E.	1971	Charles E. Stopford		Prouse
	Elsie E. Wilkinson	1972	Kenneth R. Pearson	1982	Reginald W. Harris
1961	Kathleen M. Gibbs	1973	Evelyn E. Fitzhugh[1]	1983	Roger M. Winter
1962	Ernest F. Tompkins	1974	Evelyn E. Fitzhugh[2]	1984	Stanley T. James
1963	George James Hackett		John L. Rawlings	1985	Ronald E. Lindsell
1964	John Bowes Corrin	1975	John L. Gardner	1986	Cyril R. Benton
	O.B.E.	1976	John T. Barnes	1987	Trevor R. Bailey
1965	Donald Wilson	1977	Mark O. Aldridge	1988	Ronald G. Liddington
1966	Grace Brown	1978	David A. Walmsley	1989	Malcolm F. Lloyd
1967	Thomas H. Dockrell	1979	Fred Desborough	1990	Geoffrey P. Howes
1968	Ruth G. Perkins				

Notes

1. The Local Government Act 1972 resulted in the loss of County Borough status, and consequently of the office of Mayor. Between 1973-4, the Council had the status of a District Council, with an elected Chairman.

2. Borough status was re-granted under a new charter in 1974, and the Council now became Northampton Borough Council. Mrs. Fitzhugh served as Mayor from April to early May 1974.

Town Clerks/Chief Executives and Town Clerks of Northampton, 1835-1990

Town Clerks:

1835   Theophilus Jeyes (appointed 1800)
1837   John Hensman
1857   John Jeffery
1868   William Shoosmith
1902   Herbert Hankinson
1928   William Rupert Kew
1945   Charles Edwin Vivian Rowe
1969   Alan Charles Parkhouse (to 1974)[1]

Chief Executives and Town Clerks[2]:

1974   Alan Charles Parkhouse
1986   Roger John Bowring Morris

Notes:

1. Including period of appointment as Chief Executive to Northampton District Council in 1973.
2. Title after formation of new Northampton Borough Council in 1974.

Chief Constables of the Northampton Borough Police

1836   Joseph Ball (Superintendent, appointed 1829)
1851   Henry Keenan
1887   Frederick H. Mardlin
1924   John Williamson C.B.E.
1955   Dennis Roy Baker (to amalgamation 1 April 1966)

Borough Medical Officers of Health, 1876-1974

1876   Lee Fyson Cogan L.R.C.P., L.M., M.R.C.S. Eng.
1903   James Beatty M.A., M.D., D.P.H.
1907   J. Doig McCrindle M.B., Ch.B., D.P.H.
1926   Stephen Rowland M.D., D.P.H.
1946   J. Carrick Payton M.D., Ch.B., D.P.H.
1964   William Edgar M.B., Ch.B., D.P.H., D.C.H. (to local government health reform 1974).

Northampton Council Education Authority

a. Chairmen of the Education Committee:

1903   Ald. Edward L. Poulton
1907   Ald. Rowland Hill
1920   Ald. Ernest W. Sykes
1930   Cllr. James Peach
1934   Cllr. William H. Percival
1952   Ald. Arthur L. Chown
1955   Ald. Frederick Tollit
1958   Ald. Arthur L. Chown
1963   Ald. Frederick Tollit
1965   Ald. Arthur L. Chown
1967   Cllr. David A. Walmsley (to local government reform 1974)

b. Secretaries of Education/Chief Education officers:

1903   S. Beattie
1919   H. C. Perrin
1921   A. C. Boyde
1931   H. C. Perrin
1950   H. A. Skerrett
1968   M. J. Henley (to local government reform 1974)

Appendix 10

The Freemen of the Borough of Northampton

Until the Municipal Corporations Act of 1835 the freemen of a municipal borough formed a constituent part of the Borough Corporation, enjoying certain rights and privileges which varied from place to place. In Northampton they included exemption from tolls within the town, the benefit of certain charities, the right to pasture six head of cattle on the town's common lands, and the right to vote in parliamentary elections in the borough. Most of these rights were retained after the municipal reform of 1835, but the freemen ceased to form a part of the Corporation as such.

Under the Act of 1778 enclosing Northampton's open fields, the Racecourse was vested in a body of Trustees for the use of the freemen. They also claimed rights of pasture and other rights in common land elsewhere in town, including Cow Meadow, Midsummer Meadow, Calves Holme, Baumsholme, and the 'new commons' in the parish of St Giles. Like the Racecourse itself these were much used for general recreation, and in 1882, after a series of disputes over access, and 'in order that some of the lands specified could be utilised as public parks and recreation grounds', the freemen agreed to surrender their rights in the commons to the Corporation in exchange for a perpetual annuity of £800. This arrangement was confirmed under the Northampton Corporation Act of 1882. The annuity was administered by 12 Freemen's Trustees elected from among the freemen themselves, and payments made in turn to a certain number of freemen and widows of freemen each year. The perpetual annuity was itself extinguished in exchange for a lump sum payment of £10,000 under the Northampton Act 1988.

The freedom of the Borough was formerly acquired in one of five ways:

1. **By birth**: all sons of freemen born within the borough were entitled to admission to the Freemen's Roll on coming of age, on payment of a fee of £1 2s.
2. **By apprenticeship**: after a seven year apprenticeship to a freeman within the Borough, on payment of a fee of £1 15s. 6d.
3. **By marriage**: to the daughter of a freeman, born after her father's admission to the Roll, on payment of a fee of £9 4s. At certain times before 1835 it was the custom to admit the widows or daughters of late freemen as freewomen.This conferred the right to participate in certain municipal charities, but not the parliamentary vote.
4. **By purchase**: persons resident in the Borough could be admitted on payment of a sum fixed by the Corporation.
5. **By gift**: before 1835 the freedom was occasionally conferred as an honour, or in recognition of services rendered to the Borough. This is not to be confused with the granting of the Honorary Freedom of the Borough, which carries no financial advantages of any kind.

It may now be acquired only by birth, apprenticeship or marriage, or under the discretionary procedure of Section 4(2) of the Northampton Act 1988.

Sources: Cox, J. C. (ed.), *Records of the Borough of Northampton*, Vol. 2 (1898); *Report of the Royal Commission on Municipal Corporations*, PPXXV (1835); N.C.B.C., Memorandum as to the Freemen's Annuity (1909).

Roll of Honorary Freemen of Northampton and Marching Honorary Freedoms of the Borough to 1990

1. Honorary Freedoms:

Ex-Alderman Sir Moses Philip Manfield	3 July 1899
Councillor James Barry	6 May 1901
General Sir Henry Sinclair Horne K.C.B., K.G.M.B.	26 September 1919
Alderman Samuel Smith Campion J.P.	24 October 1923
Councillor Frederick Ellen J.P.	24 October 1923
Colonel Sir John Brown K.C.B., C.B.E.	29 May 1934
William Rupert Kew	13 October 1945
Alderman Arthur William Lyne O.B.E., J.P.	22 April 1958
Ex-Alderman Harriett May Nicholls	26 January 1965
Ex-Alderman William Lees	26 January 1965
Alderman John Bowes Corrin O.B.E., F.C.A.	20 March 1972
Reginald Thomas Paget Q.C., M.P.	20 March 1972
(Lord Paget of Northampton)	
Alan Charles Parkhouse M.A. (Oxon)	6 June 1986
(Town Clerk from 1969; Chief Executive and Town Clerk, 1974-86)	
Ex-Mayor David Arthur Walmsley LL.B. (London)	14 May 1988
(Chairman of the Education Committee, 1967-74; Mayor 1978-9)	
Her Royal Highness the Princess of Wales	8 June 1989
Dr. Malcolm H. Arnold C.B.E.	20 November 1989

2. Marching Honorary Freedoms of the Borough:

Northamptonshire Regiment	8 June 1946
118 Recovery Co. Royal Electrical and Mechanical Engineers (Volunteers)	23 April 1983
Royal Pioneer Corps	29 March 1984
Northampton Members of the Northampton & Wellingborough Branch of the National Union of Footwear, Leather & Allied Trades	6 December 1984
Northamptonshire Police	25 April 1990

Appendix 12

Sample Balance Sheets

a. Northampton Corporation 1855

Receipts:	(£s)
Rates	4,312
Rents	1,133
Sales of Property	648
Administration of Justice	2,930
Interest	84
Miscellaneous (including sale of stray sheep)	58
	£9,165

Expenditure:	(£s)
Salaries & allowances	479
Administration of Justice	5,455
Rents, rates, taxes	330
Extra-parochial relief	100
Care of lunatics	13
Interest	466
Municipal election expenses	52
Printing, advertising	80
Capital repayment	500
Miscellaneous (including repairs & maintenance, & upkeep of Old Commons)	1,386
	£9,165

b. Northampton Borough Council 1985

Receipts:		(£000s)
Rates		
Domestic	2,681	
Commercial	1,979	
Industrial	972	
Other non-domestic	903	
		6,535
Rents from Council dwellings		4,842
Bus fares		3,116
Fees & charges		8,875
Government grants		15,679
Agency reimbursements		4,918
Property maintenance funds		301
Interest — gross		746
Reduction of balances		53
		£45,065 million

Expenditure: (£000s)
Housing
    Council   12,244
    Private   2,738   14,982
Refuse collection   1,531
Environmental health   1,343
Leisure   2,782
Transport
    Buses   4,091
    Other   2,190   6,281
Town development   1,906
Trading services (incl. Derngate)   3,551
Museums & cemeteries   481
Agency services   4,958
Miscellaneous services   6,520
Rate collection   629
Contributions to other funds   101
                                                                   ─────────────
                                                                   £45,065 million
                                                                   ─────────────

Sources: Northampton Corporation, Abstract of Borough Fund Account, 1855; Northampton Borough Council, Statement of Accounts 1984-5

Northampton Development Corporation, 1968-85

Chairmen of the Board:

1968 Sir William Hart C.M.G.
1976 A. R. Davis C.B.E., J.P., D.L.
1984 T. J. Nardecchia O.B.E., B.Sc., F.R.I.C.S.

Members of the Board:

J. B. Corrin O.B.E., F.C.A.	1968-79
C. H. Cripps M.A., F.R.S.C., D.S.C., L.L.D.	1968-85
R. P. Dilleigh	1968-79
R. Freeman B.Sc. (Econ), F.C.C.S.	1968-70
D. A. E. Harwin F.R.I.C.S.	1968-74
Lord Hirshfield F.C.A.	1968-76
J. T. Lewis T.D., D.L.	1968-73
Miss C. M. Trusler	1968-85
G. Chase Gardener	1970-74
Mrs. M. Jenkin	1974-78
A. R. Davis C.B.E., D.L., J.P.	1975-76
T. J. Nardecchia O.B.E., B.Sc., F.R.I.C.S.	1977-84
Sir Gordon Roberts C.B.E., J.P., D.L.	1977-85
D. A. Walmsley L.L.B.	1977-85
G. W. Tremlett O.B.E.	1979-83
J Lowther C.B.E.	1979-85
C. R. Benton	1980-85
A. J. R. Berry B.Sc.	1980-85
J. G. Kane	1982-85

General Managers:

1969 Dr. John C. Weston, Ph.D., F.I.O.B.
1977 Basil Bean C.B.E., I.P.F.A.
1980 Leslie Austin-Crowe B.Sc., F.R.I.C.S. (to 1985)

Select Chronology

1834 Poor Law Amendment Act: relief to be given only through the workhouse. Elected Boards of Guardians: eligibility for franchise and office based on property qualifications — women not otherwise excluded.

1835 Municipal Corporations Act: places Borough Corporation on an elective basis. Franchise and office confined to male ratepayers fulfilling property and residential qualifications.

1842 Chadwick Sanitary Report.

1843 Northampton Improvement Act extending public health role of Improvement Commissioners.

1845 Opening of Blisworth-Peterborough railway line via Northampton.

1848 Public Health Act: mainly permissive local powers to undertake sanitary reforms. Reform of Borough Police Force. Foundation of Northampton Freehold Land Society.

1855 Formation in Northampton of radical New Reform Association.

1856 County and Borough Police Act: central grants contingent on annual certificate of efficiency.

1859 Footwear trade dispute re closing machines.

1864 New Guildhall opened.

1866 Formation of Northampton branch of National Reform League.

1867 Parliamentary Reform Act extending franchise to male urban householders.

1868 Charles Bradlaugh first contests Northampton parliamentary seat.

1869 Municipal Franchise Act widening the range of eligible ratepayers. Women not excluded if otherwise qualified.

1870 Forster's Education Act: local School Boards to supplement voluntary educational provision — women eligible for election.

1871 Northampton Improvement Act extending powers of Improvement Commission.

1872 Public Health Act: national network of Sanitary Authorities with obligatory duties. Ballot Act: secret ballot in parliamentary and borough council elections.

1873 New Cattle Market opened on Cow Meadow.

1874 Conservative capture of both Borough seats in general election (Feb.) and by-election (Oct.); Liberal/Radical agreement to share parliamentary and municipal nominations.

1875 Dissolution of Northampton Improvement Commission — responsibilities taken over by Borough Council.

1876 Divisions among Northampton Liberals lead to formation of rival Old and New Liberal Associations.

1880 Bradlaugh elected as M.P. for Northampton, but barred from taking seat in Parliament. Formation of Northampton Liberal and Radical Union.

1881 Formation of Northampton Street Tramways Company.

1882 Abolition of property qualifications for municipal office. Northampton Corporation Act extinguishing freemen's rights in common land.

1884 Municipal takeover of Waterworks Company under Northampton Corporation Waterworks Act.

1886 Formation of Northampton Social Democratic Federation. Bradlaugh permitted to take seat in Parliament following constitutional reform.

1887 Footwear trade dispute re wage rates.

1888 Local Government Act: boroughs with populations of over 50,000, including Northampton, became county boroughs with the same powers and responsibilities as newly-created county councils. Some central grants to local authorities replaced by Assigned Revenues. Northampton Volunteer Fire Brigade taken over by Borough Police.

1892 Guildhall extension opened.

1894 Abolition of property qualification for election to Poor Law Boards.

1895 'Great Lockout' in footwear trade.

1901 Extension of borough boundaries. Municipal takeover of Tramways Company. System extended and electrified 1904.

1902 Balfour's Education Act. Abolition of Northampton School Board and transfer of responsibilities to Education Committee of Borough Council 1903.

1907 County and Borough Councils (Qualification) Act: women eligible for election to municipal corporations.

1910 New Public Library opened in Abington Street.

1912 Borough Council approves plan for first municipal housing in Northampton.

1918 Representation of the People Act: extends parliamentary franchise and establishes standard franchise for election of borough councils and Poor Law Boards. Women of 30 years of age and over eligible to vote. Abolition of disenfranchisement of paupers for all local government purposes.

1919 Addison's Housing Act: central subsidies for municipal housing. Cut by 'Geddes Axe' in 1921 but reintroduced on reduced scale 1923 & 1924.

1925 Rating and Valuation Act: introduces unified local rate and uniform property assessments.

1928 Representation of the People (Equal Franchise) Act: franchise extended to men and women aged 21 or over.

1929 Local Government Act: Assigned Revenues replaced by General Exchequer Contributions. Repeal of Poor Laws: responsibilities of Poor Law Board taken over by Public Assistance Committee of Borough Council.

1931 Extension of borough boundaries.

1932 Opening of new Northampton Technical College.

1941 Completion of Mounts complex, comprising new indoor baths, fire and police stations.

1944 Butler Education Act providing for major reform of educational system.

1945 Election of first Labour Council in Northampton.

1948 National Assistance Act: transfer of responsibility for poor relief from local to central government. Introduction of National Health Service: control of local authority and most voluntary hospitals passes to Regional Hospital Boards; personal and preventative health services provided by Borough Council. Local Government Act: abolition of ratepaying qualification for municpal franchise; reimbursement of councillors for loss of earnings; General Exchequer Contributions replaced by Exchequer Equalisation Grants.

1958 Exchequer Equalisation Grants replaced by Rate Deficiency Grants.

1965 Commons announcement of 'New Town' development of Northampton. Extension of borough boundaries.

1966 Amalgamation of Borough and County police forces to form Northamptonshire Police.

1969 Publication of *Northampton Master Plan*, approved 1970. Representation of the People Act: reduction of voting age to 18.

1970 Work begins on first Development Corporation housing estate at Lumbertubs.

1971 Publication of detailed plans for Eastern District expansion.

1972 Local Government Act: provides for abolition of county borough councils, which now become district councils, and transfer of education, social services, fire and certain other services to reorganised county councils. Responsibility for water and sewerage and personal health services to be transferred to appointed local Boards.

1973 Publication of plans for Southern District expansion

1974 Northampton's borough status re-granted under new charter: Council becomes Northampton Borough Council. Extension of borough boundaries to include 'designated area' of New Town development.

1977 Commons announcement of cut-backs in 'New Town' development.

1981 Government announcement of dissolution of Northampton Development Corporation within the next three or four years.

1985 Dissolution of Northampton Development Corporation.

Bibliography

Official Publications
Royal Commission on the Poor Laws (1834)
Royal Commission on Municipal Corporations (1835)
Report on the Sanitary Condition of the Labouring Population (1842)
Royal Commission on the Employment of Children (1864)
Royal Commission on Employment (1892)
Royal Commission on Rating and Valuation (1901)
Royal Commission on the Distribution of Land (1940)
Social Insurance and Allied Services (1942)
South East Study (1964)
Northampton, Bedford and North Bucks. Study (1965)

N.B. detailed references are given in the footnotes

Principal Local Government Sources
(i)   Northampton Board of Improvement Commissioners:
      Minutes of Meetings
      Minutes of Committee Meetings
(ii) Northampton Corporation
(iii) Northampton County Borough Council
(iv) Northampton Borough Council:
      Annual Abstracts of Accounts
      Annual Estimates
      Annual Reports (1980-85)
      Borough Surveyor's Reports
      Chief Constable's Reports
      Council Yearbooks
      Health Reports
      Minutes of Committee Meetings
      Minutes of Council Meetings
      School Medical Service Reports
      Town Clerk's Letter Books
(v)   Northampton Development Corporation:
      Annual Reports (1970-84)
(vi) Northampton Poor Law Union Board of Guardians:
      Admission and Discharge Books
      Annual Accounts
      Declarations of Acceptance of Office
      Guardians' Motion Book
      Minutes of Meetings
      Outdoor Relief Lists
      Visiting Committee Minute Books

Newspapers and periodicals
Architects Journal
Boot and Shoe Record
British Shoe Trades Journal
Footwear

Local Government Review
Local Government Studies
Municipal Journal
Northampton Chronicle and Echo
Northampton Herald
Northampton Independent
Northampton Mercury
Northampton Pioneer
Northampton Socialist
Northamptonshire County Magazine
Northamptonshire Nonconformist
Northamptonshire Notes and Queries
Northamptonshire Past and Present
Shoe and Leather Record
The Ratepayer
Town and Country Planning

Primary Sources

Appeal from the Northampton Society of Operative Cordwainers to the Boot and Shoe Manufacturers of
    Northampton (1838)
Amendments of Rules of Court, United Brothers, No.2932, Ancient Order of Foresters (1864)
Buchanan, G., Report on the Sanitary State of Northampton (1870)
College Street Cycling Club Annual Programme (1890)
Friendly Society held at the Shakespeare, Rules and Orders (1819)
Manuscript Diary of Municipal Politics (1935-97)
Northampton Artisans' and Labourers' Friend Society, Annual Reports
Northampton Bills of Mortality
Northampton British School, Report of the Committee (1851)
Northampton 'Friend in Deed' Friendly Society of Tradesmen, Rules and Orders (1828)
Northampton Friendly Society, Rules (1888)
Northampton Friendly Society of Tradesmen, Rules and Orders (1843)
Northampton General Cemetery Company, Prospectus (1846)
Northampton General Infirmary Annual Reports
Northampton Golf Club, Rules (1907)
Northampton Good Samaritan Society Annual Reports
Northampton Homeopathic Dispensary, Annual Report (1865-6)
Northampton Society for Clothing the Poor, Rules (1821)
Northampton Victoria Cycling Club, Annual Programme (1888)
Northampton Workers Educational Association, Rules (1907)
Northamptonshire Boot and Shoemakers' Mutual Protection Society, Rules (1858)
Northamptonshire Cycling Club, Rules (s.d.)

Books and Pamphlets

General

Arnstein, W. L., *The Bradlaugh Case* (1966)
Bellamy, C., *Managing Local-Central Relations, 1871-1919: the Local Government Board in its Fiscal and Cultural
    Context* (1988)
Brand, J., *Local Government Reform in England, 1888-1974* (1974)
Cobden Club, *Local Government and Taxation in the United Kingdom* (1882)
Curtis, J., et al., *Background to New Towns* (1974)
Dunleavy, P., *The Politics of Mass Housing in Britain, 1945-75* (1976)
Fox, A., *History of the National Union of Boot and Shoe Operatives, 1874-1957* (1958)
Fraser, D., *Urban Politics in Victorian Britain* (1976)

Fraser, D., *The Evolution of the British Welfare State* (1980 edn.)
Greater London Council, *Planned Growth Outside London* (1975)
Grose, C., *Bibliography of British Municipal History* (1915)
Hepworth, N. P., *The Finance of Local Government* (1980)
Hollis, P., *Ladies Elect: Women in English Local Government, 1865-1914* (1987)
Howard, E., *Tomorrow, a Peaceful Path to Real Reform* (1989)
Keith-Lucas, B., *English Local Government in the Nineteenth and Twentieth Centuries* (1977)
Keith-Lucas, B., *The English Local Government Franchise* (1952)
Laski, H., Jennings, I., & Robson, W., *A Century of Municipal Progress* (1935)
Leleux, R., *Regional History of Railways: The East Midlands* (1976)
Loughlin, M., Gelfand, M. D., & Young, G. K., *Half a Century of Municipal Decline* (1985)
Mounfield, P. R., Unwin, D. J., & Guy, G., *Processes of Change in the Footwear Industry of the East Midlands* (1982)
Osborn, F. J., & Whittick, A., *New Towns: Their Origins, Achievements and Progress* (1977)
Pearce, C., *The Machinery of Change in Local Government* (1975)
Redcliffe-Maud, Lord, & Wood, B., *English Local Government Reformed* (1974)
Royle, E., *The Infidel Tradition* (1976)
Schaffer, F., *The New Town Story* (1970)
Shaw, G. B., *The Commonsense of Municipal Trading* (1904)
Simon, E., *A City Council from Within* (1926)
Smith, J. T., *Local Self-Government and Centralisation* (1851)
Thornhill, W.(ed.), *Growth and Reform of English Local Government* (1971)

Local
Centenary History of Commercial Street Congregationalist Church (1929)
History of the Northampton Mercury, 1720-1901 (1902)
Northampton Past and Present: a Handy Guide Book (1896)
State of Northampton from the Beginning of the Fire (1675)
Where to Buy at Northampton (c.1891)

Ancient Order of Foresters, *Guide to Northampton* (1908)
Archer, J., *Castle Hill Sunday School* (1910)
Archer, J., *Northamptonshire Congregationalism* (1936)
Arnold, W., *Recollections of William Arnold: a Northamptonshire Shoe Manufacturer's Autobiography* (1915)
Ball, M., *The Lancasterian School in Northampton* (s.d.)
Barthorp, M., *The Northamptonshire Regiment* (1974)
Barty-King, H., *Expanding Northampton* (1985)
Battiscombe, D., *The Spencers of Althorp* (1984)
Bowley, A. L., & Burnett-Hurst, A. R., *Livlihood and Poverty* (1915)
Bowley, A. L., & Hogg, M. H., *Has Poverty Diminished?* (1925)
Bradbury, J., *Government and County: A History of Northamptonshire County Council, 1889-1989* (1989)
Brooks, D., *Mechanics Institutes in and around Northampton* (1970)
Brown, R. W., *Nunn Mills* (1926)
Burman, A., *Northampton in the Making, Part 1: The Changing Scene* (1988)
Burman, A., *Northampton in the Making, Part 2: Going Places* (1989)
Burman, A., *Northampton in the Making, Part 3: Great Occasions* (1989)
Burrow, F., *History of Northampton Conservative Club* (1985)
Campion, S. S., *Northampton Guide* (1912)
Cater, F. I., *Northamptonshire Nonconformity 250 Years Ago* (1912)
Coldham, J. D., *Northamptonshire Cricket* (1959)
Coleman, R., & Rajczonek, *Steaming into Northamptonshire* (1988)
Cowley, R., *Policing Northamptonshire* (1986)
Deacon, M., *Philip Doddridge of Northampton* (1980)
Dorman, T. P., *History of the Pomfret Lodge of Freemasons, Northampton* (1910)
Eason, A. V., *Remember Now Thy Creator: History of the Northampton Boys' Brigade* (1982)

Emrys Williams, Sir W., *The Arts in Northampton* (1966)
Foss, A., & Trick, K., *St Andrew's Hospital: the First 150 Years* (1989)
Fuller, R., *The Bassett-Lowke Story* (1984)
Garnett, R., *Phipps-Faire: A History* (1988)
Gibson, M. L., *History of Aviation in Northamptonshire* (1987)
Glazebrook, C., *History of Northampton's Town Halls* (1970)
Godfrey, B., *Castle Hill Meeting* (1947)
Godfrey, B., *Story of Primrose Hill Chapel, 1865-1945* (1945)
Gordon, W. J., *Midland Sketches* (1898)
Grande, F., *The Cobblers: Northampton Town F.C.* (1985)
Greenall, R. L., *History of Northamptonshire and the Soke of Peterborough* (1979)
Greenall, R. L. (ed.), *Philip Doddridge, Nonconformity and Northampton* (1981)
Hatley, V. A., *The St Giles Shoe School* (1966)
Hatley, V. A., *Phoenix in the Drapery: the Story of Percival's Bank, Northampton* (1966)
Holloway, B. G. (ed.), *The Northamptonshire Home Guard, 1940-45* (1949)
Holloway, W. H., *Northamptonshire and the Great War* (1924)
Lees, T., *Short History of Northampton Grammar School, 1541-1941* (1947)
McFarlane, T., *History of the Northamptonshire Ambulance Service* (1985)
Manfield and Sons, *The Story of a British Industry* (1908)
Markham, C., & Fox, J. C. (ed.), *Records of the Borough of Northampton* (2 vols.) (1898)
Northampton Arts Development, *In Living Memory: Life in the 'Boroughs'* (1987)
Northampton Borough Council, *The Parks of Northampton* (1984)
Northampton Borough Council, *Northampton Remembers: Boot and Shoe* (1988)
Northampton Borough Council, *Northampton Remembers: The Guildhall*
Northampton Borough Council, *Northampton: 800 Years, 1189-1989* (1989)
Northampton Borough Council, *Souvenir of Annual Meeting, 25 May 1989* (1989)
Northampton Borough Council, *Short History of Northampton Borough Police Force* (1990)
Northampton Chamber of Commerce, *The Future of Northampton* (1964)
Northampton County Borough Council, *Proposals for the Development and Reconstruction of Northampton* (1925)
Northampton County Borough Council, *Northampton Development Plan* (1951)
Northampton County Borough Council, *Christianity in Northampton* (1966)
Northampton Football Club, *Centenary History, 1881-1981* (1981)
Northampton Museums, *Shoe and Leather Bibliography* (1966)
Northampton Museums, *Abington Museum: A Short History* (1966)
Northampton Salvation Army, *One Hundred Years of Service: Story of Northampton Central Corps, Salvation Army* (1980)
Northampton Salvation Army, *They Shall Come from the East: Northampton No.2 Corps, Salvation Army* (1981)
Northampton Town and County Building Society, *A Century of Service* (1948)
Northamptonshire Libraries, *Old Northampton* (1973)
Northamptonshire Libraries, *Life in Old Northampton* (1975)
Northamptonshire Libraries, *The Boot and Shoe Industry in Northampton* (1976)
Northamptonshire Libraries, *Northamptonshire at War, 1939-45* (1978)
Northamptonshire Police, *One Hundred and Fifty Years of Policing in Northamptonshire, 1840-1990* (1990)
Page, W. (ed.), *Victoria County History of Northamptonshire, vol.3* (1930)
Parker, W., *Eighty Years of Athleticism, 1863-1943* (1946)
Pretty, E., *Wetton's Guidebook to Northampton and its Vicinity* (1849)
Reynolds, E., *Northampton Repertory Theatre, 1927-77* (1978)
Rhodes, J., *The Nene Valley Railway* (1983)
Sergeantson, R. M., *The Castle of Northampton* (1908)
Sibley, G., *Northampton Club Cricket: a Centenary History* (1986)
Smith, A. J. E., *Northampton Corporation Transport Department* (s.d.)
Speed, P. F., *Learning and Teaching in Victorian Times: Campbell Street School* (1964)
Tomalin, W., & Mawby, J. C., *History of Adnitt Road Baptist Chapel, 1899-1949* (1949)
Waddy, F. F., *History of Northampton General Hospital, 1743-1948* (1974)
Wake, J., & Pantin, W. A., *Delapre Abbey* (1959)

Walmsley, D. (ed.), *An Ever-Rolling Stream: The On-Going Story of the Development of Higher Education in Northampton and Northamptonshire* (1989)

Warwick, L., & Burman, A., *Northampton in Old Picture Postcards* (1988)

White, A. P., *The Story of Northampton* (1914)

Williams, J. H., *Saxon and Mediaeval Northampton* (1982)

Williamson, J., *History of Northampton Borough Police, 1850-1950* (1950)

Wilson, D. E., *Northampton Fire Station, 1935-85* (1986)

Wilson, H., & Womersley, J. L., *Expansion of Northampton: Planning Proposals* (1968)

Wilson, H., & Womersley, J. L., *Northampton Master Plan* (1969)

Wright, W., *Souvenir Commemorating 75 Years of Co-operative Effort in Northampton* (1945)

Articles

'A. E. Marlow and the St James's Works', *Footwear* (Feb. 1909)

'Cambridge University and Northampton', *Northamptonshire County Magazine*, 6 (1933)

'Kings Heath: a new community at Northampton', *The Builder* (30 Oct. 1951)

'Low-cost Housing Competition', *The Builder* (23 February 1951)

'Northampton: a progress report', *Architects' Journal*, 176 (3 Nov. 1972)

'Northampton: a special report', *The Times* (15 Mch. 1972)

'Northampton: a special report', *The Guardian* (3 Nov. 1978)

'Northampton: a special report', *The Times* (18 Sept. 1981)

'Northampton's tramways', *Municipal Journal*, 13 (29 July 1904)

'Some Broken Mayoralties', *Northamptonshire County Magazine*, 2 (1929)

Allsobrook, D. I., 'The work of the Northamptonshire Educational Society, 1854-74', *History of Education*, 2, 1 (Jan. 1973)

Ashplant, T. G., 'Northamptonshire's Working Men's Clubs, 1880-1914', *N.P. & P.*, 8, 1 (1989-90)

Bailey, B. A., 'Monks Park, Northampton: the story of a town property', *N.P. & P.*, 6 (1981-2)

Barrie, E. A., 'The development of Northampton', *Municipal Journal* (4 July 1952)

Brooker, K., 'The Northampton shoemakers' reaction to industrialisation: some thoughts', *N.P. & P.*, 6 (1980)

Brooker, K., 'James Gribble and the Raunds strike of 1905', *N.P. & P.*, 6 (1981-2)

Brundage, A., 'The landed interest and the new Poor Law', *English Historical Review* (Jan. 1972)

Brunner, E., 'The Origins of Industrial Peace: the case of the British boot and shoe industry', *Oxford Economic Papers*, Nos. 1 & 2 (June 1949)

Childs, D. R., & Whittle, J., 'Re-planning Northampton', *Architects' Journal* (3 Jan. 1962)

Dickie, M., ' Liberals, Radicals and Socialists in Northampton before the Great War, *N.P. & P.*, 7 (1983-4)

Dickie, M., 'Northampton's working class home owners: myth or reality', *N.P. & P.*, 8 (1989-90)

Dumsday, J., 'When the trumpets cease to blow', *Town and Country Planning*, 53 (Nov. 1984)

Dyer, A., 'Northampton in 1524', *N.P. & P.*, 6 (1978-83)

Gordon, P., 'A County Parliament: the first Northamptonshire County Council', *N.P. & P.*, 7 (1985-6)

Graham, S., 'Northampton', *The Guardian* (7 July 1975)

Hart, W. O., 'Northampton makes a start', *Town and County Planning* (Jan.-Feb. 1969)

Hatley, V. A., 'Northampton re-vindicated: more light on why the main line missed the town', *N.P.&P.*, 2 (1959)

Hatley, V. A., 'Some aspects of Northampton's history, 1815-51', *N.P. & P.*, 3 (1965-6)

Hatley, V. A., 'Battle for the Mace', *N.P.&P.*, 4 (1966-71)

Hatley, V. A., 'Monsters in Campbell Square: the early history of two industrial premises in Northampton', *N.P. & P.*, 4 (1966-7)

Hatley, V. A., 'Literacy at Northampton, 1761-1900: third interim report', *N.P. & P.*, 5 (1976)

Hatley, V. A., 'Lords, locks and coal: a study in 18th-century Northampton history', *N.P. & P.*, 6 (1980-81)

Hatley, V. A., 'Northampton hoodwinked? How a main line of railway missed the town a second time', *Journal of Transport History*, 3, 3 (May 1966)

Hatley, W. W., 'Northamptonshire memories', *N.P. & P.*, 2 (1956) .

Hatley, W. W., 'Northamptonshire memories II', *N.P. & P.*, 2 (1956)

Hatley, W. W., 'Bradlaugh and Labouchere: an episode in constitutional history', *N.P. & P.*, 2 (1959)

Hobsbawm, E. J., & Scott, J. W., 'Political shoemakers', *Past and Present*, 89 (1980)

Hold, T., 'The Royal Agricultural Show at Northampton in the year 1847', *N.P. & P.*, 7 (1988-9)

Howarth, J., 'The Liberal revival in Northamptonshire', *Historical Journal* (1969)

Howarth, J., 'Politics and society in late Victorian Northamptonshire', *N.P. & P.*, 4 (1970-1)

Joseph, S. G., 'Northampton : the town-country relationship', *Official Architecture and Planning*, 21, 3 (March 1958)

Kennett, D. H., 'The geography of coaching in early 19th century Northamptonshire', *N.P. & P.*, 5 (1974)

Lawes, J., 'Voluntary schools and basic education in Northampton, 1800-71', *N.P. & P.*, 5 (1976)

Morris, R. J. B., 'Northampton's local legislation, 1430-1988', *N.P. & P.*, 8 (1989-90)

Mounfield, P. R., 'The footwear industry of the East Midlands: locational pattern and problems of origin', *East Midlands Geographer*, 3 (1964)

Mounfield, P. R., 'The footwear industry of the East Midlands: Northamptonshire to 1700', *East Midlands Geographer*, 3 (1965)

Mounfield, P. R., 'The footwear industry of the East Midlands: Northamptonshire 1700-1911', *East Midlands Geographer*, 3 (1965)

Mounfield, P. R., 'The footwear industry of the East Midlands: Northamptonshire and Leicestershire since 1911', *East Midlands Geographer*, 4 (1967)

Nuttall, G. F., 'Philip Doddridge and Northamptonshire', *N.P. & P.*, 6 (1980)

Nuttall, G. F., 'Northamptonshire and the modern question: a turning point in 18th century Dissent', *Journal of Theological Studies*, 16 (1965)

Porter, J. H., 'The Northampton Arbitration Board and the shoe industry dispute of 1887', *N.P. & P.*, 4 (1968-9)

Porter, J. H., 'The Northampton Boot and Shoe Arbitration Board before 1914', *N.P. & P.*, 6 ((1981-2)

Powell, D., 'William Cowper and the Northampton Bills of Mortality', *N.P. & P.*, 5 (1973)

Rake, D. J., 'Spatial changes in industrial activity in the East Midlands since 1945, 3: Footwear', *East Midlands Geographer*, 6 (1975)

Richards, G., 'Power in the past: the Northampton Electric Light and Power Co., 1890-1920', *Electricity News* (Jan. 1973)

Roberts, J. M., 'Diversification and decentralisation of industry in Northampton', *East Midlands Geographer*, 7, 3 (June 1979)

Royle, E., 'Charles Bradlaugh, Freethought and Northampton', *N.P. & P.*, 6 (1980)

Salt, J., & Flowerdew, R., 'Labour migration from London', *London Journal*, 6, 1 (1980)

Sargent, C. P., 'Physical factors affecting the localisation of the boot and shoe trade in England', *Geography*, 23 (Dec. 1938)

Shorthouse, R. W., 'J.P.s in Northamptonshire, 1830-45', *N.P. & P.*, 5 (1969-70)

Swann, J. M., 'A sequel to the shoe industry dispute of 1887', *N.P. & P.*, 4 (1969-70)

Tilley, M., & Carter J., 'Carlsberg Brewery', *Architects Journal*, 160 (13 Nov. 1974)

Trimble, N., 'Industry in the new towns of Britain', *Town and County Planning*, 41 (1973)

Wake, H., 'Short account of the founding of St Andrew's Hospital, Northampton', *N.P. & P.*, 7 (1984-5)

Williams, J., 'The forty men of Northampton's first customal and the development of borough government in late 12th-century Northampton', *N.P. & P.*, 7 (1986-7)

Williams, J., 'Northampton's Mediaeval Guildhalls', *N.P. & P.*, 7 (1983-4)

Unpublished Theses

Berry, A. J., 'Northampton: a study of town expansion, political structures and processes' (Ph.D., University of Leicester, 1987)

Brooker, K., 'Transformation of the small master economy in the boot and shoe industry, 1887-1914', (Ph.D., University of Hull, 1986)

Brundage, A. L., 'The landed interest and the establishment of the new Poor Law in Northamptonshire', (Ph.D., University of California and Los Angeles, 1970)

Collins, M. F., 'Changes in land use in the borough of Northampton during the past one hundred years', (B.Lit., University of Oxford, 1970)

Coupe, R. T., 'The intra-urban residential process: a case study of Northampton', (University of London, King's, 1981)

D'Arcy, F. A., 'Charles Bradlaugh and the world of popular radicalism', (Ph.D., University of Hull, 1978)

Dickie, M., 'The ideology of the Northampton Labour Party in the inter-war years', (M.A., University of Warwick, 1982)

Dickie, M., 'Town patriotism and the rise of Labour in Northampton, 1918-39', (Ph.D., University of Warwick, 1987)

Griffin, W. C., 'The Northampton boot and shoe industry and its significance for social change in the borough', (M.A., University of Wales, Cardiff, 1969)

Lawrence, P., 'The origins, planning and marketing of a new town: Northampton', (dissertation, Middlesex Polytechnic, 1983)

Mortimer, A., 'The footwear industry of Leicestershire and Northamptonshire since 1951', (dissertation, University of Leicester, 1975)

Mounfield, P. R., 'The location of footwear manufacture in England and Wales', (Ph.D., University of Nottingham, 1962)

Roberts, F., 'A Board School for St James's', (Dip.Ed,, University of Leicester, 1967)

Rose, D., 'Home ownership, uneven development and industrial change in late 19th-century Britain', (D.Phil., University of Sussex, 1984)

Index